THE TRIUMPH OF EVIL

THE REALITY OF THE USA'S COLD WAR VICTORY

BY AUSTIN MURPHY

EUROPEAN PRESS ACADEMIC PUBLISHING

2000

ISBN 88-8398-002-6

Via Valle Bantini,4 - Fucecchio (FI) Italy
www.e-p-a-p.com
cover design by Biz Stone
Printed in Italy

TABLE OF CONTENTS

Tables

ACKNOWLEDGEMENTS

I would like to thank the editor of the European Press Academic Publishing, Dr. Roberto Di Quirico, for his extraordinarily useful help in improving the structure of this book. I am also very grateful to my employer, Oakland University, which provided funding for the research needed for one of the chapters (Chapter 5). In addition, I owe my very young children a great debt for showing me that communism, cooperation, and sharing are innate human characteristics, and that capitalism, egoism, and selfishness are unnatural traits that capitalist societies force people to learn very early in their lives (and that communist countries can only slowly remove from human culture).

Dedicated to the knowledge that anyone who aids the USA in its international terrorism is committing a crime against humanity.

PREFACE

The *Triumph of Evil* represents a wake-up call to the world. Barraged by the most effective propaganda machine in history, I myself long believed at least partially in the make-believe world reported by the mainstream press and the USA establishment. However, having experienced the opening of the Berlin Wall first hand, I began to learn (as explained in the prelude to this book) that the stories told in the Western media often greatly distort the true reality of events. Having subsequently further researched the facts, I now feel an obligation to cite them for those who also wish to wake up to *The Reality of the USA's Cold War Victory.*

To begin, using a very objective measure of analysis, the Introduction to this book documents the fact that the USA is the most evil nation in history. In particular, the USA has deliberately killed more unarmed innocent civilians than any other country in the world (including even more than Nazi Germany). This conclusion is consistent with the main body of the book, which clearly shows that the "bad guys" won the Cold War.

Chapter 1 conclusively demonstrates the fact that the USA propaganda about the evils of communism is largely either greatly exaggerated or pure myth. In fact, communism represents a very good alternative to the very horrible USA capitalist system, as communist countries are not only more benevolent but also economically more efficient. Communist countries were poor relative to the leading capitalist countries only because they were relatively much poorer before they became communist, and, despite exhibiting faster economic growth than capitalist countries, they had not caught up by 1990.

Chapter 2 uses the case of the divided Germany to more exactly detail the relative advantages and disadvantages of communism and capitalism in practice. East and West Germany are ideal for a comparison because the people and culture were very similar before the division into separate communist and capitalist countries after World War II. The findings show that communism is a superior system in virtually all respects. However, West Germany began with far greater income and wealth than East Germany, and faster economic growth in East Germany had reduced this income disparity by the time of its demise in 1990 but had not eliminated it. The higher incomes of West Germany represented an extremely important attraction by itself in making people prefer to live in West Germany. In addition, the relative poverty of East Germany also forced additional disadvantages on East Germans in terms of the government repression needed to prevent the richer and much more powerful West Germany from using capitalist economic warfare, propaganda, outright sabotage, and other activities to undermine the East German communist system.

Chapter 3 describes more details of the East German system that help clarify exactly how and why the communist system (despite its superiority) was overthrown in 1989-90. Contrary to popular belief, East Germans were not seeking to rid themselves of an undesirable system but, instead, were revolting against their relative poverty.

Continuing with the German case, Chapter 4 provides a detailed comparison of the economic efficiency of the communist and capitalist financial systems. While there are similarities, the communist financial system is shown to be more effective overall. Despite its superior efficiency, East Germany was poorer than West Germany because it had had to pay an enormous amount of reparations to the Soviet Union after World War II. These reparations payments, which represented partial compensation for all the damages inflicted on the Soviet Union by Nazi Germany as a whole, had a value equal to several times East Germany's annual output. West Germany, on the other hand, was not only spared from having to make such payments, but it also received substantial financial aid from the richer USA (which had been untouched by World War II). While the greater financial and economic efficiency of the East German system allowed it to partially catch up for the huge difference in incomes that existed in the two countries at their founding in 1949, it was not able to fully overtake West Germany by 1989.

Chapter 5 details an economic plan for how East Germany could have survived and prospered, even with the opening of the Berlin Wall, even with forced economic integration, and even with the East Germans' natural desire for Western income levels. While the plan (which I created in 1989 and presented to various leaders shortly after the opening of the Berlin Wall) has never been used in practice, economic analysis indicates that it provides a viable means for countries to prosperously survive in a capitalist world (and actually offers a very positive alternative to traditional forms of both capitalism and communism).

Chapter 6 explains how the USA's Cold War victory has resulted in the world turning more and more toward free-market systems (i.e., global capitalism). The defeat of the communist Soviet Union has not only created a very powerful propaganda tool for the USA and its capitalist system, but it has also removed the one world power that used to be able to challenge USA domination and counter USA threats. The USA's successful push toward a world market economy (via persuasion and extortion) is shown to have led to widespread poverty and economic catastrophes, especially related to currency crises, and especially in the newly capitalist countries of the former Soviet Union and Eastern Europe. In addition, the economic disaster of the German unification itself is explained to have contributed to a chain of events that has further contributed to the worldwide economic crises.

Chapter 7 concludes the book with a political analysis of USA world domination after the Cold War. As indicated there, the atrocities of the USA and the cruelty of the USA's capitalist system continue unabated.

The Triumph of Evil: the Reality of the USA's Cold War Victory is a factual book that leads to one implication for action: overthrow the evil capitalist system by voting it out of power. In the hands of the people, the facts will ensure that the Cold War victory for the USA and capitalism was only a temporary one, and that justice will eventually prevail via the ballot box.

PRELUDE

"BETTER RICH AND HEALTHY..."

Previous to experiencing the revolutionary events surrounding the opening of the Berlin Wall in 1989-90, I must also admit to having largely believed in the great USA propaganda story about how wonderful capitalism is compared to communist societies. However, one of the first things I learned in my visits to East Germany was that it was different from the roboticized, repressed, cold, and stoical stereotyping of communist East Germany which I had been led to believe by Western media to be the truth.

An early clue to the actual facts of the East German people and culture occurred during my first visit there on May 1, 1988. In particular, on that festive holiday in East Berlin, I found a kiosk which sold an assortment of interesting items, including stickers with the printed statement "Lieber reich und gesund als arm und krank," which translated to "Better rich and healthy than poor and sick." Astounded at such a sign that seemed to advocate striving for riches in the relatively poor (compared to the West) and reputedly repressive communist country, I asked the kiosk saleswoman if such statements were permitted in East Germany. After some discussion with her colleagues, she explained that the sticker had been designed as a counter to the Western slogan that one had to choose between being either rich and sick, or poor and healthy. After all, why not have the best of all possible worlds, which was what East Germany was trying to develop. Little did I realize at the time that East Germans would soon be achieving access to Western riches far faster than they had ever believed possible, albeit at the price of having to endure the sickness of Western capitalism.

To further illustrate my naivety at the time, I relate another episode from Berlin that occurred about one year later in July 1989, just before the revolution in East Germany broke out. The event is very trivial, but it does provide an indication of the biases that USA propaganda had put into my mind, as well as something about the actual situation in East Germany during the Cold War.

As part of my attempt to experience various aspects of East German culture (and meet new and exciting people) in the early summer of 1989, I visited a local group of the Free German Youth in East Berlin that had advertised its disco party in an East German tour guide book. About 75% of all East German youth were members of the Free German Youth, but only those with some interest in or support of communist politics tended to be active in the events or disco parties of this East German government organization. After conversing with several East German teenagers at the disco for some time (during which they repeatedly emphasized that they didn't want war, although I had never brought up the subject), one teenager asked if I wanted to hear some good jokes. After I answered positively, I was asked if I knew the difference between neutron bombs and East German coffee. When I said I didn't know, he answered that he didn't know either, since both mercilessly kill people without damaging coffee cups or other objects. When I, being unaware of the poor quality of East German powder coffee, didn't laugh, the East German asked me another question. He wanted to know what the difference was between the East German government leaders and terrorists. When I said I didn't know, he answered that terrorists have supporters. Shocked by the anti-government overtone (in what I had been led by USA propaganda to believe was a police state), I didn't laugh because I again wasn't even sure if I understood the joke. When he explained that the East German leaders were not too popular, I asked whether it was permitted to make such jokes in East Germany. He laughingly said that everybody did it. Then he asked me of what crime an East German was convicted of for calling the East German leader an idiot. When I indicated that I didn't know, he told me it was for the crime of revealing a state secret. After he told me several more anti-government jokes but still failed to generate even a smile from me, he said I didn't have any sense of humor. When I asked where he had learned the jokes, he told me that he had heard it from friends and that everybody knew the jokes. When I asked whether it was East or West German friends, he said that he had heard it from East Germans, but that some of the jokes had probably been invented by the West Germans and been exported to East Germany. When I continued to express shock at people being allowed to tell such jokes in East Germany, he assured me it was OK to say what one wanted in East Germany, as long as one wasn't trying to overthrow the government.

Being on a research assignment in Berlin for the entire period from the summer of 1989 to the summer of 1990, I experienced first-hand (and participated in) what I believe to be one of the most incredible revolutions in history. During that time, I learned much about the Cold War, the USA, East Germany, communism, and capitalism from direct observations, discussions, and actions (my actions also apparently led the East German secret police to create a file on me in their counterintelligence department, which investigated foreigners suspected of engaging in espionage and subversion in East Germany).

Although my initial interest and knowledge in the subject matter of this book grew out of first-hand experience, I have verified all information herein with published sources (and so I cite the relevant authors and publication year in parenthesis in the text or footnotes of this book). I have also investigated contrary published allegations, but I have refuted the distorted opinions with facts. My experiences in 1989-90, combined with subsequent events and research, have slowly woken me up to face the fact that my country (the USA) is the most evil one on the face of the earth and in the history of mankind.

INTRODUCTION

AN OBJECTIVE ANALYSIS OF RELATIVE POSITION IN THE HISTORY OF DELIBERATE EXTERMINATIONS OF HUMAN BEINGS

> *"I spent 33 years and 4 months in active military service as part of this country's most agile military force, the Marine Corps. I served in all commissioned ranks from Second Lieutenant to Major General. And during that period I spent most of my time being a high-class muscleman for Big Business, for Wall Street, for the bankers. In short, I was a racketeer, a gangster for capitalism. I helped make Mexico, especially Tampico, safe for American oil interests in 1914. I helped make Haiti and Cuba a decent place for the National City bank boys to collect revenues in. I helped in the raping of half a dozen Central America republics for the benefit of Wall Street. The record of racketeering is long. I helped purify Nicaragua for the international banking house of Brown Brothers in 1909-1912. I brought light to the Dominican Republic for American sugar interests in 1916. In China I helped to see that Standard Oil went its way unmolested. During those years I had, as the boys in the back room would say, a swell racket. Looking back on it, I feel I could have given Al Capone a few hints. The best he could do was to operate his racket in three districts. We Marines operated on three continents."*
>
> --Maj. Gen. Smedley Butler, USMC (ret.), November 1935.

Most Americans learn in school, through the mainstream media, and from Hollywood that they are and have always been the "good guys" fighting evil villains (Schulz, 1982), as symbolized by John Wayne, or the recently deceased Roy Rogers in his old western movies (Rickey, 1998). Most Americans are made to believe that their system stands for democracy, freedom, human rights, and honest hard work in the pursuit of happiness within a capitalist framework, and they are led to see anyone who opposes their model system, especially communists, as the "bad guys" (Zinn, 1995). This attitude has resulted in the USA being internationally perceived by some to be the "capital of global arrogance" (Azad, 1998).

Americans' attitudes (arrogant or otherwise) are heavily shaped by a press that has become increasingly concentrated under the control of just a few USA companies (Foerstel, 2000). Jensen (2000) has reported that six media firms now "control most of the world's information: Time Warner, Viacom/CBS, Disney, Bertelsmann, General Electric, and the News Corp." Even these few companies work together closely with each other in many joint ventures (McChesney, 2000). As stated by Phillips (2000), "Media is no longer a competitive industry but rather an oligopolic collective of like-minded rich, white, upper-class elites with shared agendas seeking to expand their power and influence globally. This concentrated media can easily manipulate (and censor) the information provided to the public to help it achieve its capitalist goals. For instance, in response to a question regarding the media's silence on a particular issue that would have portrayed corporate America in a negative light, one television station manager bluntly stated, "We paid $3 billion for these stations, and we have the right to make the news. The news is what we say it is" (Clark, 2000).

"The six largest U.S. firms accounted for more than 90 percent of U.S. theatre revenue," and "half a dozen major chains" rule "the roost" in the newspaper industry (McChesney, 2000). "More and more places are becoming 'one-paper' towns," and "radio is now dominated by a few mega-companies, each of which own hundreds of stations" (Jackson, 2000), while "U.S. book publishing is now dominated by seven firms, the music industry by five, cable TV by six," and "nearly all of these are now parts of vast media conglomerates" (McChesney, 2000). "The ownership and control of news media by an increasingly small and select group of business owners is bound to restrict the kinds of stories that get widely reported" (Lewis, 2000). One journalist put it more subtly, "If you know that they really don't want certain stories at the top, you're not going to do those kinds of stories" (Andersen, 2000).

While there are small and alternative media organizations (Foerstel, 2000), their credibility is often marginalized, such as by comparing them with fantasy magazines like the *National Enquirer* if their views vary substantially from those of the mainstream giants, which thereby set the standards. Some of the big media/entertainment conglomerates have a significant amount of non-media commercial holdings (including in the armaments industry), and, in the interest of their own corporate profit maximization (as well as that of their rich corporate advertising clients), they have a natural pro-USA-capitalism (and even pro-war) bias (Foerstel, 2000). Also contributing to the media's pro-USA-capitalism prejudice is the fact that "the media corporations and the sponsoring corporations [i.e., the large corporate advertisers which effectively use their advertising expenditures to buy the media] are themselves tightly interlocked" (Jackson, 2000).

The media's pro-USA bias is further reinforced by the heavy reliance of the press on USA government sources of information for their gathering and analysis of news, which can lead to extreme distortions in reporting to the public (Herman and Chomsky, 1988). In particular, with respect to international events, the mainstream media often just regurgitates stories created by the CIA for propaganda purposes (Goff, 2000). Saadawi (2000) concludes, "Never before in history has there been such domination of people's minds by the mass media....How can we be free to choose if the media injects us day and night with false information?"

While "tabloid" or "yellow journalism" has long existed in the capitalist media to incite people to war and for other ends (such as to mobilize support for launching the War of 1898 against Spain), a form of capitalist journalism has developed in the USA and in Western countries that even more blatantly admits to being particularly biased and one-sided (Pirocanac, 2000). This new "journalism of attachment" is designed to provide a type of psychological "therapy" reporting which attempts to make the journalists and their readers feel good about themselves and their country regardless of the facts (Independent Commission of Inquiry, 1999). It represents the philosophy of "giving the people what they want" irrespective of factual information, or lack thereof (Schlechter, 2000). Since the advertisers who pay for television and other media are looking for audiences with money to spend, the "people" the press feel obligated to satisfy are those with more money, whose very wealth naturally makes them right-wing anticommunists, and whom the media do not want to turn off with overly "liberal" reporting (Foerstel, 2000). There is thus no "market" for anti-USA and anti-capitalist facts and reports, and so capitalism naturally censors such information (Johnstone, 2000).

Although the USA media often report some evil actions of the USA and its politicians, most of the attention is focused on relatively minor issues, such as sex scandals, which are said to represent exceptions that can be corrected with better human morals (Zinn, 1995). The worst excesses are either ignored or distorted as a great triumph for the USA (Foerstel, 2000). However, as a result of the criticism on minor issues, the USA press is widely perceived as being objective and perhaps even overly critical (Herman and Chomsky, 1988). In fact, the USA media covers politicians' personal lives and sexual behavior so extensively that attention is deflected from the terrible atrocities American political leaders have allowed the USA to commit (Foerstel, 2000).

The possibility exists that even the USA leaders have been brainwashed by the media propaganda, which itself is so powerful that it often convinces even the propagandists themselves (Smith, 2000). The result is a classic case of denial, whereby people do not want to hear, investigate, or believe facts contrary to the "good" image created. For instance, within the context of comments about a "rediscovery of our values," the very popular President Ronald Reagan stated in January 1989 (a few years before he himself was afflicted with Alzheimer's related memory loss), "If we forget what we did, we won't know who we are" (Greene, 1999). This statement was either incredibly naive (demonstrating extraordinary ignorance of how terrible we Americans really have been as a people), extremely cynical (in terms of deliberately attempting to help dupe us Americans into a false sense of pride in the terrorism committed by the USA), or subconsciously factual (that we won't even realize that we represent a mass murdering nation of zombies, unless we wake up to the historical facts and cure our nation's sickness).

Even those who recognize that the USA has committed many crimes against humanity typically try to justify the USA's atrocities by asserting that the USA has not been as terrible as other countries. For instance, the USA media is often so successful in vilifying the USA's enemies (like the Serbs) that even many left-wing critics of the USA and its policies are fooled into supporting some atrocities such as the USA's deliberate bombings of civilian targets in Yugoslavia in 1999 (Foerstel,

2000). Despite the propaganda barrage against the enemies of the USA, an investigation of the facts indicates that it is the USA which has been acting imperialistically and immorally, engaging in actions that are little different from the very evil policies employed by Adolf Hitler who also vilified and slaughtered masses of innocent people (Johnstone, 2000).

In fact, a careful analysis of history and current affairs indicates that the USA has committed the worst atrocities in world history. A mere listing of the crimes committed by the USA in its history provides educational perspective on this issue, but an objective measure of atrocities is required in order to establish unbiased evidence on the subject.

For this purpose, the estimated body count of unarmed innocent civilians deliberately killed by a country can be used to keep score. According to that numeric measure, the USA is indeed number 1, although it may be only slightly ahead of Nazi Germany and Spain. Other countries in the top ten are listed to provide perspective, as are a few other countries with a reputation for infamous atrocities.

Evidence on USA Atrocities

The USA has killed over 11 million unarmed civilians in a long continuous history of engaging in massive extermination campaigns, terrorism, imperialism, and other atrocities. This history ranges from the genocide of native American Indians (and stealing of their land) to the enslavement of African blacks; from the imperialist invasion of Mexico in the first half of the 1800s (enabling the USA to seize more land from the Indians) to the War of 1898 that was launched to permit the USA to seize Spain's colonies; from the Monroe Doctrine (which effectively solidified the USA policy of controlling or colonizing the Western Hemisphere) to the frequent invasions of Latin American countries that have continued throughout the 1900s to ensure governments there remain largely under the control of the USA; from the terrorist aerial bombings of civilian targets that have killed millions of unarmed innocent civilians over the last 50+ years in places like Korea, Vietnam, Laos, Cambodia, Iraq, etc. (and maimed millions more) to the murder of millions of unarmed civilians by CIA-imposed dictators such as in Indonesia, Guatemala, El Salvador, Chile, etc. (Zinn, 1995). A more exact breakdown of the body count follows:

TABLE 1:
TALLY OF UNARMED CIVILIANS DELIBERATELY KILLED BY THE USA

Unarmed Civilians	Number Killed	Years	Primary Source
Indians	5,000,000+	pre-1910	Churchill (1994)
Filipinos	1,000,000	1899-1906	Schirmer and Shalom (1987)
Ger., Jap.	500,000	1942-45	Markusen and Kopf (1995)
Koreans	1,000,000+	1945-53	Ho, Hui, and Ho (1993)
Indonesians	500,000+	1965-66	Griswold (1979)
Vietnamese	1,000,000+	1965-73	Herman (1970)
Cambodians	500,000+	1969-73	Herman & Chomsky (1988)
Iraqis	1,000,000+	1991-98	IAC (1998b)
Miscellaneous	500,000+	1946-98	Blum (1995)
Others	Unknown	History of USA	
Total	11,000,000+	History of USA	

Although each of the foregoing extermination campaigns is fairly well documented in the listed references, the breadth and depth of the USA atrocities merit providing more details and perspective.

The USA's Beginning Genocide

To begin the analysis with the USA's first, longest, and largest mass murder, it is first necessary to estimate how many Indians were in what is now the USA before the arrival of the white invaders. This task is especially important because USA propaganda would have people believe that the USA was largely a vast unsettled wilderness (occupied by only a few "non peoples called savages") before the invasion of the whites (Jennings, 1975).

Henige (1998) has provided an abundance of facts indicating overestimation of the original Indian populations in Central and South America, but the Indian population existing within the USA before the arrival of the Europeans has been widely underestimated by a very large amount for much of the nineteenth and twentieth centuries (Churchill, 1994). While the USA was originally estimated by many early observers to be populated with millions of Indians (Thornton, 1987), even these guesses may have been far too low (at least partially because they were lacking in documented analysis). Nevertheless, many successive researchers have discounted (instead of more appropriately raised) such prior estimates, resulting in a compounded reduction in the already low numbers that lack scientific justification and that are unquestionably far below the actual original level of the native American population (Churchill, 1994).

There is a very important political purpose and personal nationalistic bias in reporting very low numbers. In particular, underestimating the original Indian population makes the USA seem almost vacant originally before white occupation, thereby creating the impression that the conquest of the territory was a "settlement" as opposed to an invasion and mass killing (Johansson, 1982). There was also an important legal reason for the extremely low bias in early Indian population estimates, as British colonial law only allowed settlers to seize vacant territory and did not permit the taking of land by force or fraud (Jaimes, 1992).

Jennings (1975) has indicated that many of the low estimates of the original Indian population are based on "official" USA government sources, such as a Smithsonian Institute book listing numbers estimated "without specific documentation" by Mooney (1928).[1] The meaninglessness of such government estimates is easily illustrated by Mooney's count of only 25,000 Indians in all of New England in the early 1600s, when one tribe living in a small 800 square mile area of New England alone numbered over 30,000 at that time, and when there is documentation of other densely settled territories of New England (numbering as many as 100 Indians per square mile) as well (Jennings, 1975). Similarly, whereas Mooney (1928) estimated scarcely a million Indians for the entire USA, archaeological evidence indicates millions of Indians lived in the eastern end of the Ohio Valley alone (Jennings, 1975). Nevertheless, modern authors, even those sympathetic to the Indians like Brown (1970), often recite ridiculously low numbers based on the "official" USA count. Mooney's "official" (1928) book actually implies less than one Indian per square mile on the 3+ million square miles of the USA. Such a low estimate is obviously ludicrous when one considers that there was a well-documented one Indian on average per square mile in "one of the world's areas least hospitable to human habitation" in a Western Hemisphere desert (Dobyns, 1966). Even numbers below ten million Indians in the USA appear somewhat absurd in light of researchers estimating 8 million or more Indians on a single island (Hispaniola) in the Caribbean. (Thomson, 1998).

A much more plausible estimate of the original North American Indian population is provided by Domenech (1860), an unbiased European, who traveled extensively among the native Americans, studied many reports of other travelers and researchers, provided an analysis of many of the hundreds of Indian tribes in the USA, and stated the number of Indians north of Mexico to have been 16-17 million in the mid-seventeenth century. A similar estimate based on other data is provided by Sale (1991), who estimated 15 million Indians north of Mexico. Churchill (1994) has stated the number of Indians living north of Mexico was most likely between 12.5 million and 18.5 million before the invasion by the whites. Because Canada was very sparsely settled by Indians (Thompson, 1966), originally with "four or five or more times" as many Indians in the USA as in Canada due to the existence of "four or five times" as much land suitable for agriculture (Jaffe, 1992), most of the 12.5-18.5 million Indians north of Mexico lived in what is now the USA at the time of the white invasion. However, thousands fled subsequently to Canada (Brown, 1970), which developed a relatively benevolent relationship with the Indians (Daunton and Halper, 1999), to escape the USA's attacks (Jennings, 1993).

Churchill's (1994) range of estimates is partially derived from the typically observed 90-99% "disappearance" rates for native populations in various areas of the Western Hemisphere cited by Dobyns (1966), who suggested assuming no more than a 98% elimination rate. With the low point for the number of Indians north of Mexico being 370,000 (of which 250,000 were in the USA) at the end of the nineteenth century (Thornton, 1987), a division by one minus the maximum recommended disappearance rate of .98 (i.e., a division by .02) indicates 18.5 million Indians. Using the 250,000 figure for the continuous 48 USA states alone in the calculation implies 12.5 million Indians there. However, it is virtually certain that far more than 12.5 million of the 18.5 million Indians were originally in the USA territory, since a large number of the modern Indians in Canada were descendants of refugees from the USA's imperialist policies (Jennings, 1993), and since the USA's genocidal policies (Churchill, 1994) surely made the survival rate for Indians in the USA much lower than in Canada.

In any event, such population estimates based on average disappearance rates in various places observed in the Americas are very likely on the low side. In particular, there is substantial evidence (some of which is reported subsequently in this Introduction) that the USA had a deliberate extermination strategy that was far more effective and continuous than the Indian policies used by the other white invaders (Churchill, 1994). As a result, it is probable that the USA had a much higher elimination rate than the rest of the occupiers of Indian land (thus indicating an extermination rate over 98%, and therefore implying an Indian population in excess of 18.5 million north of Mexico).

Thompson (1966) has recommended an alternative method of estimating the original Indian population as the number that could exist on the land given the technology and resources (assuming the population would stabilize at that level). While Dobyns (1966) has indicated that only 2 million square miles in the USA were "fit for Indian habitation, Kroeber (1939) has estimated over 150 Indians per square mile on various large tracks of hospitable inland and coastal USA territory. Extrapolating those figures implies that the USA could have potentially supported over {150x2 million}=300 million Indians if it were everywhere as densely settled as in the most populated areas.

However, although about half of the 2 million square miles of hospitable USA territory were fertile river valleys (Dobyns, 1983), not all hospitable areas of the USA could have supported 150 Indians per square mile. For instance, Thomas (1976) provides widespread evidence of typical crop yields for Indians in the USA that were high enough to maintain populations as dense as 90 people per square mile on typically hospitable land, even after allowing for sizable fields left uncultivated for decades to permit soil rejuvenation (and some hunting). The latter, more realistic figure implies that the USA could have supported as many as 180 million Indians.

A more conservative estimate is implied by Dobyns (1983), who has cited a study indicating that fifteenth century North American Indian farming methods could have supported between 10 and 25 Indians per square kilometer of average hospitable territory (or over 20-50 per square mile). One reason for using Dobyns's lower figures is that many Indians also engaged in a significant amount of hunting and fishing, in addition to farming, and those activities tended to use up more territory than pure farming (Thomas, 1976).

Dobyns (1976) has cited one estimate of 5 purely hunter-gatherers per square mile of mountainous territory in the USA and 10 per square mile for hunter-gatherer-fishers, but he also cites another estimate (from a nineteenth century researcher) of 50 Indian hunter-gatherers-fishers per square mile over a large 25,000 square mile stretch of California territory. Using the more conservative former numbers, Thompson's (1966) methodology would imply only 10-20 million Indians on the 2 million square miles of hospitable territory in the USA if no Indians were farmers. Because most Indians were engaged in agriculture as well as hunting and fishing (Dobyns, 1983), the number of Indians per square mile would actually be between 5 and 90. Thus, the estimate of 20-50 Indians per square mile is very feasible, implying 40-100 million Indians on the two million hospitable square miles of the USA.

While even these lower figures may seem high compared to the ridiculously low estimates put out by the USA government, an Indian population density of 20-50 per square mile is comparable to that of less populated areas of Europe in the same era. In particular, the number of people per square mile (of combined hospitable or inhospitable land) in Europe ranged between 10 and 100 in different countries in the late fourteenth century (well before Columbus "discovered" America), even though the bubonic plague had just wiped out 1/3 of the European population at that time (Hobhouse, 1989). Given that less efficient crops were planted in Europe than what the Indians historically planted in what is now the USA (Thomas, 1976), given that Europe had less fertile soil and a more inhospitable climate in many places than the hospitable areas of the USA (Hobhouse, 1989), and given that people also engaged in an extensive amount of hunting in Europe (Sale, 1991), there is no reason to believe that Indian population densities should be substantially lower than the range of European ones. In fact, detailed empirical research provides widespread evidence that Indians in the USA could indeed subsist on similar acreage (and therefore with similar population density) as Europeans, and they could do so with less ground preparation and mechanization because of their heavy use of efficient crops like corn (Thomas, 1976).[2] In addition, since Indian lifespans in many parts of the USA have been found to be similar to those in Europe at the time (Thornton, 1987), it is very likely that they could have grown to a similar population density. Moreover, it should also be mentioned that a population density of 20-50 Indians per square mile is far less than the 125 Indians per square mile estimated to have originally existed in the 200,000 square miles of Central Mexico where farming technology was no more advanced than that used at the time by Indians in what is now the USA (Borah and Cook, 1969). An estimate of 20-50 Indians per square mile for the USA is also substantially lower than estimated for many other parts of Central and South America (Denevan, 1976).

It should be emphasized that the estimate of 40-100 million Indians on the hospitable territory of the USA ignores the Indians on the 1,000,000 square miles of desert in the 48 mainland USA states (MacLeod, 1928), as well as those native Americans in Alaska and Hawaii. Given that there were some Indians who lived in even the extremely arid USA deserts (Domenech, 1860), and given that Hawaii was home to hundreds of thousands aborigines (Larsen, 1994), 90% of whom were also exterminated by the USA invaders (Jennings, 1975), the latter numbers may not be trivial.

Another estimate of the original Indian population in the USA can be obtained from actual sightings of Indians by settlers. For instance, after the Europeans had unsuccessfully tried to colonize Virginia in the sixteenth century (Dobyns, 1976b), a second white invasion of the territory led a Virginia colony secretary to make notes in 1612 indicating 0.7 Indian warriors observed per square mile on hospitable land (MacLeod, 1928). However, Dobyns (1966) mentions that many potential warriors (or young adult males) may never have been seen because they died from disease or retreated further inland before being sighted in battle formation. In addition, since many Indian warriors may have engaged in guerrilla warfare instead of deliberately forming into mass countable groups that could be decimated by the white invaders' superior firepower (Jennings, 1975), many more warriors may not have been counted. The number of unobserved young adult Indian males could have been especially large in Virginia, since Indians in the southeastern states of the USA were less likely to be organized into tribes that would send warriors out to face settlers and soldiers (Hobhouse, 1989). Even the large organized tribes of Virginia "avoided out-in-the-open battles," and retreat was often their only option for escaping from the deadly settlers (Sale, 1991). Moreover, even for Indian tribes that did fight, military service itself was voluntary, and so not all young Indian males were warriors (Novack, 1972). Assuming that 50-90% of the young

Indian males may have died or retreated inland before being observed in massed battle formation, there would be between 1.4 to 7 young adult males per square mile. Assuming 4 Indians per young adult male as in some overly conservative prior research (Denevan, 1976), that implies 5.6 to 28 Indians per square. Given two million square miles of hospitable land in the USA (Dobyns, 1966), there would be between 11.2 million and 56 million Indians in what is now the USA. Since there is evidence that there were actually five (Dobyns, 1983) or six (Denevan, 1996) Indians per young adult male (as opposed to the four assumed in the calculations), and sometimes as many as twelve (Domenech, 1860), these figures could rationally be increased by 25-50% or more (to at least 15-70 million Indians in the continental USA).

Dobyns (1983) has provided more detailed data indicating there were actually 11.2-12.5 Indians per warrior, as not all young males were available to fight on the front lines, and because there were numerous older and younger male Indians as well as females. Such a higher multiplier seems especially plausible if the multiplier itself is to incorporate the information provided in the previous paragraph about not all warriors being observed. Using the lower end of the 11.2-12.5 range, the Virginia sightings of 0.7 warriors per square mile therefore imply 7.8 Indians per square mile, or 15.6 million Indians extrapolated to all 2 million hospitable square miles of the continental USA. This figure should be increased somewhat to allow for the Indians on inhospitable lands in the continental USA, as well as on land in Hawaii and Alaska. Moreover, given that Virginia (the basis for the extrapolated estimates) was probably less densely settled than other areas like New England (Hobhouse, 1989), it is certainly possible that the number of Indians in what is now the USA originally far exceeded 16 million.

Dobyns (1983) actually cites estimates of over 10 Indians per square mile in Virginia and over 30 Indians per square mile in New England. These figures imply 20-60 million Indians in the USA if the other of the 2 million square miles of hospitable land in the USA were equally densely settled. While MacLeod (1928) has estimated that only 1.5 million square miles of the USA were originally inhabited by the Indians, largely because of an assumption that the mountains and vast Midwestern prairie lands were not cultivated by them, this hypothesis appears to be in error. In particular, some of the mountains of the USA may have been occupied with as many as 5 Indians per square mile (Dobyns, 1976a), and archaeological evidence indicates that there were originally a large number of actual Indian towns on the Midwestern prairies (*Mississippi Valley Historical Review,* 1925) and that the Indians on those prairies were originally farmers who existed on diets heavy in corn (Larsen, 1994). Regardless, even making the false assumption that the prairies and mountains were totally vacant, the numbers still indicate at least 15-45 million Indians in the USA. Thus, it is pretty clear that there were originally far more than 10 million Indians in what is now the continental USA, as recent scholarly estimates indicate (White, 1995).

By the mid-nineteenth century, Domenech (1860), an unbiased French observer (whose own travels as well as his study of other Indian voyageurs led him to believe that the USA government estimates for the Indian population to be only ¼ of the true total at the time), estimated the number of Indians in the USA to have fallen to between one and two million (as he reported that the "greater part" of the hundreds of Indian tribes had disappeared or were "almost extinct" by 1860). By the time most Indians had been rounded up and sentenced to desert reservations in 1890 (or forced to flee into Mexico or Canada), their number in the continental USA had dropped further to only 250,000 (Thornton, 1987). Even after having well over 95% of their population eliminated by the turn of the century, the Indians still had to endure several more decades in their desert concentration camps. In the meantime, most of the remaining Indian children were separated from their parents so that American Christianity could be taught to them without "pagan" parent influence, and only afterwards were they finally granted USA citizenship and allowed to leave their reservations (Churchill, 1994). Even after citizenship had been granted, the Indians remained poor, since the few resources on their desert reservations were often given to the "non-Indians" (who alone had sufficient capital to exploit them), and since, outside the reservations, "those few [Indians] who do obtain employment paying a decent wage or salary are often expected to act like whites if they expect to be promoted or retained" (Meister, 1976).

The disappearance of the native Americans in the USA cannot be attributable to assimilation into white society, as marriage and association with Indians was generally frowned upon religiously and socially until the twentieth century (Jennings, 1993) and was even illegal in some areas of the USA (Waters, 1977). However, many of the remaining 250,000 Indians of the USA at the end of the nineteenth century were of mixed race (Dobyns, 1983), as temporary sexual relationships had frequently developed out of contacts with white traders (McCracken, 1959). While granting Indians citizenship in the twentieth century has increased their assimilation into the overall USA society to the point where the number of people with some partial Indian ancestry has risen to about 10 million (or less than 5% of the USA population), the number of people in the USA with some partial Indian ancestry outside the reservations was only a few hundred thousand in 1900 (Johansson, 1982). The latter figure represents about 1% of the overall combined 76 million Indians and non-Indians living in the USA in 1900 (*World Almanac,* 1998), and represents substantially less than 10% of the original Indian population before the invasion of the whites. These numbers stand in sharp contrast with those of neighboring Mexico, which immediately granted citizenship to Indians upon its founding (Jennings, 1993), and which today has a population that is 90% at least part-Indian (compared to only 4% of the USA population having any Indian heritage) and that includes about 30 million pure Indians (U.S. News & World Report, 1993).

While a significant portion of the Indians in the USA may have died out because of diseases spread by the invading whites, researchers such as Meister (1976) have documented the fact that it wasn't the contact with the whites but the brutal practices of the white invaders (such as removing Indians from their land, food, and water sources) that led to the high Indian death rate from disease (and that led to the virtual extermination of the Indians in the USA). Domenech (1860) has explained that Indians actually increased their population over time when allowed to live stationarily in peace in a fertile area, but that migrations forced upon them by the USA destroyed their morale, frequently drove them to alcohol, and weakened their ability to resist disease. Regardless, while a severe epidemic or widespread outbreak of disease might temporarily drop a population level by a third under normal conditions (Hobhouse, 1989), it took an invasion and outright genocidal policies to virtually exterminate the Indians (Thornton, 1997). In addition, although many Indians may have died in intertribal battles (Thornton, 1987), such fighting had been fairly minimal until the whites employed military force to push Indians tribes ever farther westward into other Indian tribes' territories (Jennings, 1975, 1993).

Assuming at a minimum the lower end of the range of Churchill's (1994) possibly very low estimates (i.e., 12.5 million) for the number of Indians originally being in what is now the USA, assuming one half of the Indians in the USA were killed by or intermarried with the Spanish and others who had occupied parts of what is now the USA for a time (such as in Florida and the Southwest), assuming an extremely high estimate of 500,000 Indian warriors were killed while engaged in battle with armed forces (Thornton, 1987), assuming a half million Indians in the USA fled to Canada or Mexico, and assuming normal population growth of 0% (due to the disease, hunger, and dislocation caused by the white invasion potentially reducing the Indian birth rate to the level of the normal death rate), one arrives at an extremely conservative estimate of 5 million Indian noncombatants killed by the USA. However, given that there were likely far more than 12.5 million Indians originally living in what is now the USA, given that the rate at which the Spanish and others killed or married Indians was only a small fraction of the USA extermination rate (Cook, 1943), and given that the Spanish and others occupied only a portion of the USA and only for a time, it is likely that the number of Indians killed by the USA far exceeds 5 million (and is probably greater than 10 million, although only the absolute minimum figures are included in the conservative Table 1 count).

The European "settlers" in the USA had been involved in the slaughtering of Indians at least since their invasions at Roanoake in 1607 and Plymouth in 1620 (Churchill, 1994). Although Britain advised the settlers to pay for the land they seized, such a requirement was virtually impossible to enforce (Chalk and Jonassohn, 1990), especially since the colony states had been made fairly autonomous (Osgood, 1957). Even when local British military forces formally forbade settlers from invading Indian territories (in an attempt to keep the peace with the Indians), enforcement was very difficult without more troops and more formal British laws (Downes, 1940). As a result, until 1763, the settlers were able to freely steal from the Indians and kill any of them who got in the way, and, even in instances of actual settler purchases of land from the native Americans, fraud was normally involved (Chalk and Jonassohn, 1990).[3] Within such an environment, fighting naturally broke out frequently (Utley and Washburn, 1985). In an attempt to help protect both themselves and their land from the invading American settlers, many Indians allied themselves with the French in various wars, as well as politically with Britain in some of the continuous disputes over settlers stealing Indian property (Chalk and Jonassohn, 1990).

Finally, Britain, which sought to exploit the Indians via trade as opposed to land theft (Jaimes, 1992), established in 1763 a blanket proclamation that formally forbade American settlers from stealing more land from the Indians, setting a boundary at the Allegheny mountains (Smith, 2000). While frontiersmen like George Washington saw the proclamation as a "temporary expedient to quiet the minds of the Indians," and while there were numerous attempted breaches of this law (including an outright military invasion of Indian territory by Virginia militia in 1774), the Indians (with some British encouragement in the complex political environment) had some success in enforcing the proclamation (Downes, 1940). In fact, the 1763 legal infringement on settlers' "right" to steal Indian lands was one of the primary motivating factors in the American settlers' revolution from British rule 12 years later (Novack, 1972), although important tax and trade issues were also involved in the conflict (Smith, 2000). Most Indians quite naturally sided with the British against the USA in the American Revolutionary War (which lasted until at least 1782 west of the Allegheny mountains), as, despite some French political assistance later in the war, USA attempts to win Indian neutrality with treaties promising to steal no more Indian land and to engage in friendly trade (through which the Indians hoped to obtain the weapons needed to defend against settler encroachments on their land) were foiled by continued USA settler invasions of Indian territory and by the USA's failure to pay for goods traded with the Indians (Downes, 1940).

After the USA victory over Britain, the white American settlers were "freed" from British legislation prohibiting the theft of more land from the native Americans. As a result, it became possible for more USA territories and states to be created out of further areas stolen from the Indians. The USA initially claimed all Indian territory as its own, arrogantly announced that the Indians as a whole had no rights whatsoever to their own land, and offered the Indian nations the choice of various small reservations under USA dominion or the "destruction" of their "women and children" (Downes, 1940). However, USA military invasions of Indian territory were initially defeated in the early 1790s, and so the USA resorted thereafter to using local military superiority to force individual Indian tribes/nations to enter into treaties to give up a portion of their land in return for the USA agreeing to stop its attacks (Jennings, 1993). Such treaties were similar to those entered into by the USA in the 1775-1782 war (Downes, 1940), although this pacification strategy was not completely successful in holding all Indian military forces at bay in the American Revolutionary war or in subsequent conflicts such as in the War of 1812 (Utley and Washburn, 1985).

The USA pacification treaties with the Indians were substantially different from those typically entered into earlier by the European colonial powers. In particular, the European colonists had generally engaged in treaties with Indians merely in order to form alliances with them to promote trade, although it is true that allied Indians were often encouraged to fight other tribes who were cooperating with competing European powers (Jennings, 1975). In contrast, the USA's strategy was to use each successive treaty to "keep the natives quiet" on the frontier until the newest conquered possessions could be fully absorbed and "resources could be mustered and organized" to allow armed settlers and soldiers to invade other Indian territories that the USA had guaranteed by treaty not to seize (Jennings, 1993). Grinde (1975) provides an illustrative case study whereby settlers in the 1800s invaded Cherokee land guaranteed by federal treaty and engaged in widespread killing of Indians there, but Federal officials generally allowed such behavior, legally asserting in the Cherokee case that the Federal treaties were overridden by local government rights (such as that of the state of Georgia here) which invariably sided with the settlers and left the Indians with no rights.

USA purchases of land from European powers, as well as the USA's seizure of territory from Mexico in an imperialist war that the USA launched in the middle of the nineteenth century (Zinn, 1995), enabled the USA to carry on its strategy of engaging in pacification/extermination of ever more Indians. Frequently, after settlers had invaded the Indian territories guaranteed by prior treaties (and had begun taking or destroying Indian food sources on the Indian lands), the Indians were paid a nominal amount for the lands they were forced to give up (under threat of more violent expulsion) in a new treaty that would also be broken by the USA at some point thereafter (Domenech, 1860). The USA eventually signed over 350 treaties with various Indian tribes or nations, and it broke each and every one of them (UAINE, 1998). Only thereby was the USA able to expand westward.

While the American Revolutionary War had freed the USA from the all-important British infringement on the country's "right" to steal more land, the original 13 USA states generally maintained most of the same laws that they had created when they were autonomous states under British colonial rule. These laws included providing rewards for the extermination of Indians. In particular, the state governments set up by the settlers had begun in 1641 to establish legislation that offered rewards for the killing of any and all Indians (including men, women, and children, although special rewards were offered for Indian boy scalps), with such legislation continuing in effect into the late nineteenth century (Waters, 1977). Note that these laws and killings could scarcely be blamed on European countries, since the colony states had had full autonomy in setting such laws. In particular, the American settlers had locally elected their own legislatures and many other government officials (generally exhibiting even more democracy than existed in England itself), and "the common people probably had a stronger voice in their government in the English colonies than they did in any other part of the world at that time" (Chitwood, 1948).

Having seen the prior "success" of the extermination laws in the eastern states, many of the new territories seized by the USA also adopted legislation paying for the killing of any and all Indians. Over ten territories and states with such extermination laws, including California, Colorado, Connecticut, Georgia, Indiana, Kentucky, Massachusetts, New York, North Dakota, Oregon, Pennsylvania, South Dakota, Texas, and Virginia, are listed just as examples by Waters (1977) and Churchill (1994).

Although the individual states and territories were allowed to set up their own decentralized reward system for killing Indians, the genocide campaign was national in scope. The country's first president, George Washington, told his fellow Americans that Indians were to be "hunted like beasts," and the USA hero Thomas Jefferson said that the USA should "pursue [the Indians] into extermination" (Churchill, 1994). As a result, Indians were hunted like animals, and their springs were deliberately poisoned (Waters, 1977). Their villages were burned, their crops were destroyed, and successful efforts were undertaken to keep them from obtaining fish for food (Craven, 1968). In addition, diseases were deliberately spread among the Indians, and force was frequently used to drive the Indians from their hunting and crop lands (Thornton, 1987). Cook (1943) wrote that, to USA citizens, "all Indians were vermin, to be treated as such.... Since the quickest and easiest way to get rid of his troublesome presence was to kill him off, this procedure was adopted as standard for some years. Thus was carried on the policy which had wiped out *en masse* tribe after tribe across the continent." Stannard (1992) reported, "In 1784 a British visitor to America observed that 'white Americans have the most rancorous antipathy to the whole race of Indians; nothing is more common than to hear them talk of extirpating them totally from the face of the earth, men, women, and children." This attitude eventually resulted in the "American aphorism 'The only good Indian is a dead Indian'" (Brown, 1970).

Besides being offered cash rewards for killing Indians, USA citizens were also given a strong incentive to kill (or disperse or otherwise dispose of) the native American Indians in order to be able to seize their land that the USA government claimed and "sold" very cheaply (Strobel and Peterson, 1999). Miller (1975) has documented one case where a few USA settlers shot thousands of unarmed Indians (possibly over 10,000, including many on a reservation designated by the whites) from one peaceful tribe alone (the Yuki) over a short period of a few years in the mid-nineteenth century, and, despite the successful slaughter of virtually the entire tribe with almost no settler casualties, the murderers actually protested formally to their state governor when soldiers refused to help with the massacre. While the speed of the genocidal actions of this case (with over 90% of the tribe being directly murdered in less than a decade) may have exceeded the norm, the latter settler protest provides evidence that such genocidal acts were not only normally sanctioned but also expected.

However, not all 5+ million Indians were shot. In true capitalist fashion, the USA succeeded in its genocide at a minimum cost in terms of resources expended, as those Indians who fled the livable land seized by the USA with its guns often died of starvation and disease

(Jaimes, 1992). To further expedite the extermination process at minimal expense, dogs were often used to hunt down the Indians (to save on the labor costs of hunting them), and, once caught, Indian children were sometimes killed by bashing their heads against trees to save gunpowder costs (Waters, 1977). Few Indians put up a fight, since 70% of the Indian tribes were outright pacifists (Sale, 1991), and since most of the rest also realized that they could not win against the superior firepower of the white killers (Merriam, 1905). In this extermination campaign, stationary Indian farmers had little chance of survival, and so some Indians attempted to escape from the USA's New Order by becoming strictly mobile hunters of buffalo and other game (Hobhouse, 1989), giving up their extensive agricultural pursuits even on the breadbasket of the Midwest (Larsen, 1994). Although this non-stationary form of life was contrary to most Indians' nature (Domenech, 1860), a number of Indians were able to successfully adapt to this environment, with one tribe (the Navajo which had historically been composed of nomadic hunters) even being able to prosper under these conditions, more than doubling its population between 1600 and 1860 (Meister, 1976). Nonetheless, in the end, few were able to escape from the genocidal policies of the USA, which reacted to the Indian hunting strategy by deliberately killing tens of millions of their buffalo food (and other game) in a deliberate attempt to starve the remaining Indians into extinction (Thornton, 1987).

Nevertheless, because even these efficient extermination procedures were not fast enough for some white invaders, the USA frequently resorted to deliberately spreading diseases, such as by having items (like blankets) known to be infected with deadly germs put in or near Indian settlements (Stannard, 1992). Jennings (1988) documents allegations that offering Indians "gifts" infected with smallpox was a "widespread" practice on the western frontier in the 1800s as well as earlier (Jennings, 1988). There were also very serious Indian accusations of the USA infecting Indian prisoners with smallpox prior to releasing them back into their tribes to cause epidemics (*Mississippi Valley Historical Review,* 1925). Evidence exists that the deliberate spreading of disease by USA settlers began in the 1600s (Jaimes, 1992) and continued into the late 1800s (Stearn and Stearn, 1945). Although "such things ... were not likely to be advertised to the world by the perpetrators" (*Mississippi*

Valley Historical Review, 1925), concrete evidence has been uncovered for at least some of the terrible deeds (Jennings, 1988). In just one such campaign alone in the mid-nineteenth century, the USA may have killed several hundred thousand Indians by giving them blankets known to be infected with smallpox (Jaimes, 1992). Perhaps, partly as a result, there were Indian religious movements that preached a refusal to accept any gifts, tradable goods, or other items that had been in contact with the white settlers (Downes, 1940).

Although other European invaders, especially the Spanish, also deliberately slaughtered many Indians (Stannard, 1992), the USA was by far the most atrocious. Just for instance, according to Cook (1943), the Indian population in California fell by only 33% between 1770 and 1848 during Spanish and Mexican rule, but it fell by over 80% from this lower level during the first 32 years of USA rule from 1848-1880.[4] In addition, in contrast to the fact that a significant portion of the drop in Indian population under Spanish and Mexican rule was due to Christian conversions and interracial marriages assimilating a number of the Indians into the "civilized" society, virtually all of the decline in Indian population under USA rule was caused by extermination policies that did not allow interracial marriages and assimilation until much later. In the USA, not just the military but virtually all who came into contact with the Indians were involved in the genocide, as the various local governments themselves had not only legalized the slaughter, but they also paid rewards for the killings (Waters, 1977).

While the exact number of Indians slaughtered by the USA is not known, the evidence is too overwhelming to seriously question the deliberate and extensive nature of the genocide. The evidence also provides substantial support for a hypothesis that the number of unarmed innocent Indians deliberately killed by the USA far exceeds the very conservative 5 million estimated here.

Subsequent USA Killings of Innocent Unarmed Civilians

Scarcely had the USA's virtual extermination of the Indians been accomplished, and the USA sought out more lands to steal and more people to slaughter. After attacking and defeating Spain in the War of 1898, the USA proceeded to seize some of Spain's former colonies such as the Philippines (Copeland, 2000). Although the people in many of the new lands now claimed by the USA did not conduct any major rebellion against their new rulers, a large Filipino resistance army had seized almost the entire Philippines from the Spanish before USA troops arrived, and the USA invaders had to wage an outright war against the Filipino people until 1902 (and fight off sporadic Filipino resistance until 1915) in order to subdue the native population (Agoncillo, 1969). In retaliation for the resistance to the USA's colonial conquest, the USA directly massacred hundreds of thousands of Filipino civilians, while hundreds of thousands more died of starvation and disease trying to escape the massacre-- over 600,000 were killed on the Luzon island alone by early 1901 according to the commanding USA general there (Franklin Bell), and that was before numerous subsequent massacres, in one of which over 100,000 more Filipinos on Luzon were killed according to statistics compiled by USA government officials (Schirmer and Shalom, 1987). A USA Congressman who observed the "pacification" of the Philippines stated that the USA army "simply swept the country and wherever and whenever they could get hold of a Filipino they killed him" (Karnow, 1989).

The USA first began its newest form of terrorism through aerial bombardments of civilian targets in a war against enemies almost as atrocious: Nazi Germany and fascist Japan. Although the Germans and Japanese also committed terrible extermination campaigns in World War II, there is little moral difference between the German and Japanese killings of unarmed civilians perceived to be enemies and the USA's slaughter of unarmed innocent German and Japanese civilians in its deliberate terrorist bombardments of civilian targets, especially given the many USA aerial attacks that were deliberately aimed at civilian living quarters (Markusen and Kopf, 1995). It should also be mentioned that Churchill (1994) has uncovered documents indicating the Nazis were merely following the USA's role model with respect to exterminating unwanted people. While figures provided by Markusen and Kopf (1995) indicate only 500,000 civilians killed by USA bombings in World War II, *Webster's* (1992) reports well over 1,000,000 German and Japanese civilian deaths in World War II. Since the USA dominated the aerial terror bombing campaign (with the only other major player, Britain, engaging in much smaller operations), most of those civilians must have been killed by the USA (Markusen and Kopf, 1995).

As for more modern atrocities through USA aerial terrorist bombings, the slaughter of over 250,000 unarmed Laotian civilians during the period 1965-73 and of over 500,000 innocent unarmed Cambodian civilians during the 1969-73 interval (as estimated by the Finnish Inquiry Commission) is indicative (Herman and Chomsky, 1988). These exterminations occurred at a time when there were no Cambodians or Laotians fighting Americans in any form. Given the fanatical anticommunism of many brainwashed Americans who do not perceive communists as people worthy of life, it should also be mentioned that few if any of the Cambodians and Laotians were even communists initially.

Although in Vietnam there were indeed armed communist guerrillas fighting Americans, they were actually only struggling for the right to the free elections that the French had promised upon their departure from the colony (Blum, 1995). Slaughtering possibly as many as ten innocent civilians with terrorist aerial bombings for every one "enemy" soldier killed (successfully exterminating an estimated 1,000,000 civilians by 1970) seems to represent deliberate murder, especially if these actions are considered in the light of the various extermination statements made by American leaders at the time (Herman, 1970). To try and justify such actions as being part of normal warfare is tantamount to trying to justify Hitler's mass murder of the Jews because a small fraction might have taken up arms against him (Markusen and Kopf, 1995).

Thayer (1985) cites estimates of *only* 200,000-400,000 civilians having died in Vietnam, but his figures are based on the number of civilians being admitted to South Vietnamese hospitals, and these numbers ignore the massive number of civilians killed in remote or communist-controlled areas where USA air attacks were concentrated. While an exact figure for the number of Vietnamese civilians murdered by the USA is not known, McNamara (1999) has cited Vietnamese government evidence of over one million Vietnamese civilian and military casualties per year, implying that millions of civilians were killed during the period of the heaviest USA involvement between 1965 and 1973, since estimates of military deaths (which may be more accurately measured) are only a million or so for the whole war (Burns and Leitenberg, 1984). Vietnam officially reports 2 million civilian dead (CNN, 2000b), which would imply far more than 1 million maliciously murdered by the USA, given that Thayer's (1985) data imply collateral civilian casualties from actual military battles between opposing ground forces numbered far less than 400,000, and given that the communists themselves deliberately killed only about 40,000 civilians (Lewy, 1978). Herman and Chomsky (1988) report the total number of Vietnamese killed in the USA's war against Vietnam to be about 3 million, but all these figures may underestimate the true total, especially if one considers not only the direct murdering of civilians via USA aerial bombings and via traditional executions (by USA and puppet South Vietnamese ground forces) but also those killed indirectly as a result of the USA's deliberate attempts to murder millions by starvation through the destruction of food supplies (Zinn, 1995).

Even in Iraq, where the USA might have seemed justified in fighting the Iraqis who had seized Kuwait in an almost bloodless invasion, it should be mentioned that Kuwait was an artificially created monarchy (Salinger and Laurent, 1991), which continues to maintain a repressive rule of that area of the world even after its "liberation" from Iraqi rule (Associated Press, 2000b). In particular, Kuwait was carved out of a larger Iraq shortly after World War I by the British (and made formally "independent" in 1961), so that the vast oil resources there could continue to be controlled by capitalist companies subsequent to Britain giving up its Middle Eastern colonies (Blum, 1995). There is also some evidence that the USA plotted to encourage/provoke Iraq into its invasion in 1990 to retake the territory (Salinger and Laurent, 1991). Regardless, for purpose of the body count, the USA's terrorist aerial bombardments on Iraq attacked mostly civilian targets (including civilian air raid shelters deliberately), directly resulting in the death of approximately 50,000 Iraqi civilians (Clark, 1992) and almost completely destroying the civilian economy (Laffin, 1994). Moreover, the USA bombings deliberately and systematically destroyed vital civilian targets (such as irrigation systems, power plants, and sewage disposal systems), and this destruction combined with the continuing embargo against Iraq have resulted in extremely poor sanitary conditions, inadequate medical services, hunger, and related disease that has killed over one million Iraqi civilians, a very large number of whom are children according to a United Nations (UN) study (Flounders, 1998b). In addition, the USA's use of depleted uranium weapons in the 1991 war continue to cause tens of thousands of cases of terminal illnesses (such as leukemia and cancer) for those who live near to where such weapons were used (IAC, 1998b).

Although the USA was able to use the UN as a cover for its military attacks on Iraq in 1991, the USA alone was responsible for its massive bombing of civilian targets, and although the embargo of Iraq was originally agreed to by the UN in 1990 after Iraq occupied Kuwait, it has been the USA vetoes (with British support) of UN proposals to lift the trade sanctions that have perpetuated the embargo long after the Iraqi withdrawal (Flounders, 1998b). While the USA has agreed to loosen the trade sanctions in recent years to allow the import of some nutritional items (including alcohol) and luxury goods (like cars), many necessities (like parts to rebuild Iraq's power and transportation infrastructure, agricultural and medical equipment or components, and even medicines) are still held up by the USA, as the USA continues to try to terrorize the Iraqi people into overthrowing their leader, whom the USA government leaders just happen not to like (King, 2000). Even a USA congressional representative has recently called the USA-led (and USA-enforced) embargo against Iraq "a horrendous policy—it's infanticide" (CNN, 2000a). USA Secretary of State Madeleine Albright's statement that the mass killing of civilians in Iraq is "worth it" as a means to achieve the desired political goal of removing Saddam Hussein from power verifies the deliberate nature of the USA's extermination of innocent Iraqi civilians (IAC, 1998b).

As for the crimes of the CIA and its controlled leaders, Indonesia is a good example. There in 1965, the CIA had one of its allied Indonesian military leaders (Suharto) overthrow the elected government in a coup and then proceed to murder close to one million unarmed communists and other civilians, who had been part of, or identified with, a previously elected coalition government (Griswold, 1979). While the CIA gave the Indonesian government a great deal of latitude in slaughtering virtually any people with left-wing opinions, the CIA also provided lists of thousands of specific Indonesians to be exterminated (Blum, 1995). The communists here, like the Jews under Hitler, offered virtually no resistance as they were killed by combinations of army troops, police, and gangs or paramilitary forces that were specifically armed by the CIA for the task (Levene and Roberts, 1999). In addition, the same CIA ally (Suharto) slaughtered hundreds of thousands of innocent people in one of his annexed provinces (East Timor) in the 1970s and 1980s (Blum, 1995). While some of the estimates of the number killed exceed a million in the 1965-66 blood bath alone (Levene and Roberts, 1999), Amnesty International estimates between 500,000 and 1,000,000 were murdered in the 1965-66 extermination campaign, while a further 200,000 have been killed in East Timor (Blum, 1995). Although some might not blame the USA in cases like this indirect mass murder, to exonerate the USA here would be equivalent to excusing Hitler for most of his murders, because he had foreign followers and "protectorate" governments in Croatia, Ukraine, Lithuania, Poland, Romania, Austria, and other countries carry out much of his slaughter, and because most of his victims (including most Jews) were foreigners in terms of never having resided in Germany (Markusen and Kopf, 1995).

The largest extermination campaign not yet mentioned occurred in Korea. In particular, the South Korean military dictatorship that was put into power by the USA after World War II was busy killing unarmed civilians with left-wing opinions in South Korea even before the Korean War broke out in 1950. Ho, Hui, and Ho (1993) estimate that about 100,000 unarmed South Korean civilians were executed by the South Korean government before 1950, while Scheffer (1999) cites a South Korean army veteran's estimate of several hundred thousand. The Korean war itself (provoked by frequent South Korean military invasions of North Korea) gave the South Korean government the ability to greatly increase the number of executions without attracting too much international notice (Blum, 1995). In addition, early in the war, the U.S. military officially ordered all civilian refugees to be shot (*Workers World,* 2000b). Ho, Hui, and Ho (1993) estimate that one million South Korean civilians were murdered by USA and South Korean forces during the 1950-53 war, while several hundred thousand North Korean civilians were slaughtered during the short time of occupation by USA and South Korean forces (often via gruesome procedures such as by burying masses of people alive, burning large groups of civilians alive in locked buildings, and even pouring gasoline down the throats of babies screaming for milk). Until recently, any South Korean who talked about these crimes (including victims or relatives of victims) faced a prison sentence in their country (Griswold, 2000).

Halliday (1981) indicates the extent of such USA atrocities in Korea to be "probably true," and he reports specific evidence such as a USA diplomat admitting to the killing of over 100,000 South Korean civilians after the USA reoccupation of South Korea, and the sending of thugs and dispossessed landlords to North Korea during the temporary USA occupation of that country in 1950. Besides these mass murders, the USA slaughtered many more North Korean civilians in its terror bombings of North Korea that destroyed virtually all civilian buildings there during the Korean War (Smith et al., 1996). As a result, demographics indicate that the North Korean male (female) population fell from 4,782,000 in 1949 to 3,982,000 in 1953, while the female population fell from 4,840,000 to 4,509,000 over the same time interval (Halliday, 1981). These numbers, which are consistent with those estimated by McCormack and Selden (1978), indicate over a million North Koreans lost even assuming the birth rate actually fell to the normal peacetime death rate during this stressful period (the 331,000 drop in the North Korean female population imply that a large portion of those killed were indeed innocent civilians). A plausible estimate is that 12-15% of the North Korean people (or 1.2 to 1.4 million people) alone were killed during the Korean War (Smith et al., 1996), not to mention the million or so South Korean civilians killed by the USA and its puppets, for a total of about 2 million civilians (Ayling, 2000).

A general source of details on the crimes of the USA since World War II is Blum (1995). The list of mass murders committed by USA bombings or CIA puppets includes dozens of additional countries, among the most infamous of which were the slaughtering of over 150,000 Guatemalans in what Amnesty International has called a "program of political murder" (Harbury, 1994), at least 75,000 El Salvadorian civilians (Blum, 1995), at least 40,000 Colombians (McInerney, 1998), and at least 10,000 Chileans (Sandford, 1976),[5] not to mention the thousands of civilians who have been killed by USA actions in many other countries such as Iran, Nicaragua, and Angola (Blum, 1995).[6]

The body count in Table 1 does not incorporate any USA crimes which may have been committed but for which there is currently little or no evidence. For instance, Keeler (1989) reports that the CIA had an Operation Pique that was designed to affect the mental attitudes and behavior of employees at nuclear power plants in communist Eastern Europe, implying some intent to cause a nuclear meltdown/holocaust.

Given the very bizarre and otherwise virtually inexplicable behavior of the employees who caused the nuclear disaster at Chernobyl in the Soviet Union in 1986 (Medvedev, 1991), it is possible that the USA's Operation Pique may have had something to do with it (and therefore may be responsible for the thousands of deaths which resulted but which are not counted here).

In addition, because the focus is on the deliberate murder of unarmed civilians, Table 1 does not count the many unarmed Japanese POWs who were slaughtered by the USA (Dower, 1986). Nor are all the people killed by USA embargoes counted in Table 1, as only the million Iraqi civilians clearly and deliberately killed by the USA through a combination of blockade and terror bombing of civilian targets are included in the 11+ million figure.[7] Nor does this analysis count the effect of the USA's use of modern US biological weapons, some of which may have been deliberately launched against countries like Cuba (Franklin, 1992) and North Korea (Ho, Hui, and Ho, 1993), and others may have just "escaped" the laboratory (Horowitz, 1997).

This analysis also does not incorporate some of the other atrocities deliberately committed by the USA, in which there may have been a substantial amount of harm and torture inflicted but few dead bodies. For instance, there is some evidence that the CIA/NSA does engage in mind control torture (often through cults and other front organizations), and even estimates as high as 10 million victims (many of whom may, as a result, have their lives wasted in mental asylums or be lost through suicide and other unnatural deaths) have been cited in a 1995 Texas conference on the subject (sponsored by the Freedom of Thought Foundation) in the video "The Rosetta Stone to the Unconscious." Note here that the NSA stands for the National Security Agency, about which most Americans knew nothing for decades, although it was the largest "intelligence" organization in the USA (Bamford, 1983), thereby providing an indication of the enormous potential for secret undisclosed crimes of the USA secret police (since most Americans had never even heard of the NSA much less knew of its covert actions). Some interesting sources on the CIA/NSA crimes committed in the USA are Bowart (1978), Stich (1994), and Constantine (1995), who also document some of the cooperation between the USA "intelligence" agencies and organized crime, including joint efforts to sell narcotics. The latter activities may not really be so surprising given that the drug trade was actually instrumental in the spreading of British capitalism and colonial rule (Tho'Mas, 1997). While some of the reports on the activities described in this paragraph (but not countable in the aggregate documented body count reported in Table 1) may be exaggerated (or distorted in some way, as would be expected in mind torture activities), they merit mention because of the paucity of mainstream media coverage of the evidence on these issues and because of the lack of evidence refuting the claims.

The foregoing measurement of the USA's mass murders also does not include its part in one of the worst atrocities in history: the enslavement of millions of Africans. Tens of millions of Africans died (mostly on land) while being forcefully transported to their new "homes" in America (Stannard, 1992). Capitalist countries spread a belief that Africans were "half-animal" in order to "justify" their cruel enslavement (Chin, 2000), at the same time that they spread the gospel that free trade (including in people) would benefit all. However, the facts indicate that "there can be no doubt that the level of culture among the masses of Negroes in West Africa in the fifteenth century was higher than that of northern Europe, by any standard of measurement—homes, clothes, artistic creation and appreciation, political organization and religious consistency" (DuBois, 1965). Africans were also way ahead of the whites in many areas of technology, astronomy, and navigation at the time, possibly even having "discovered" America a century before Columbus bungled into it (Chin, 2000).

However, despite the cultural superiority of African culture, the European colonialists had superior weaponry through which they were able to win control of Africa by application of direct military force and by paying and arming African "allies" (Davidson, 1961). The African puppets of the whites were manipulated (through intrigues, bribes, and threats) into serving the will of their European masters to have the human "goods" delivered (in return for more weapons and luxury items) into the middle of the nineteenth century (Isaacman and Isaacman, 1983). The slave trade itself robbed Africa of its prime workers and created a chaotic society that focused on obtaining slaves for export instead of on domestic production of real goods (DuBois, 1965). In particular, the African economic and social system was destroyed by Europeans' profitable use of exploitative trade strategies, which involved selling mass produced luxury goods to the African rich (especially to the slave trading puppets themselves) in return for slaves and other commodities, thereby reducing the demand for traditional African production for the black masses and thus bankrupting local African producers. This system is actually very similar to the methods utilized by the USA today to destroy foreign economies and to economically enslave much of the world, as will be explained later in Chapters 6 and 7.

Although the USA was not the only country involved in committing atrocities against slaves, the USA treatment of Africans was in many respects worse than the other major players such as the Spanish. In particular, there were less slaves brought to the USA than to the Spanish colonies (at least partially because the USA had less people and money than the Spanish colonies initially), and so the USA was not able to murder, rape, and torture as many as the Spanish. However, the USA slavery laws were much more atrocious insofar as they made the blacks and their descendants slaves forever, whereas the Spanish did not enslave the offspring and even allowed most of their existing slaves to earn or buy their freedom eventually (Teepen, 1998). For instance, in contrast to the early nineteenth century USA where blacks were almost always slaves, the proportion of the African population that was free had risen in 1808 (after only 100 years of slavery) to over 75% in one Spanish colony of the Western Hemisphere (Sharp, 1976).

In addition, many think slavery ended in the USA in the 1860s, after the northern USA states executed a plan to free the slaves in the southern states (formally announced in 1863) as part of a successful military/political effort to win (by 1865) a very bloody civil war, which began (in 1861) when the northern states tried to impose a protectionist tariff system on the country as a whole, and the southern states (which wanted "free trade" in both goods and people) seceded from the union in protest (Copeland, 2000). However, after the southern whites lost the civil war, they created a form of neo-slavery by forcing blacks to sign work contracts that essentially sold their freedom and lives to white owners in return for being allowed to live (Lewis, 1998). Because the blacks had no money, no food, and no land, they had no other choice (Zinn, 1995). This "efficient" system (which provided capitalists not only with the advantage of cheap black labor and lowered the cost of agricultural raw materials for industry but also drove down the cost of competing white labor and thereby made USA industry even more competitive) lasted into the 1900s (Finkin, 1997).

As documented by Patterson (1970), such explicit forms of slavery have been replaced with more subtle forms of racism and wage slavery in the twentieth century that are similar to those used by Nazi Germany against the Jews before their extermination in World War II, and data indicate that this system has resulted in the early death of over 30,000 blacks per year in the USA (cumulating to millions of deaths over time). The significantly higher death rates for USA blacks have continued into the twenty-first century, with USA blacks still having a life expectancy over five years less than for USA whites (mostly because of poverty), and with blacks therefore continuing to have to pay higher life insurance premiums (Paltrow, 2000) that (among many other biases) further impoverish them (and therefore actually contribute to the higher death rates themselves in a typically circular capitalist process of making the poor ever poorer). Perhaps fittingly, the USA continues to honor explicit slaveowners on almost all of its paper money (including George Washington, Thomas Jefferson, Andrew Jackson, Ulysses Grant, and Benjamin Franklin), with even the exception of Abraham Lincoln (on the $5 bill) having once said, "I do not stand pledged for the prohibition of the slave trade between the states. I, as much as any man, am in favor of having the superior position assigned to the White race" (Cosby, 1998). With many of these slaveowners (such as Andrew Jackson and George Washington) also having been mass murderers of Indians (Churchill, 1994), it seems appropriate to honor them on the very money and wealth which was derived in large part from the policies of black slavery and Indian genocide.

The Table 1 count also does not include the many millions of other people who died in the USA in the past as a result of the capitalist economic system. Besides slavery, this system caused harsh working conditions (as exemplified by many male and female children as young as 6 years old having to work 100 hours per week just to survive), unemployment, poor living conditions, and general poverty (Zinn, 1995). The resulting deaths do not appear to be deliberate, even though the only crime for which these millions were killed was that they were born poor in a capitalist society.

Nor does this analysis of USA mass murders incorporate any of the repressive aspects of the formal police state that exists in the USA itself. In particular, the USA is a leader in the number of police per capita and in the percent of the population locked up in prison, with 5 times as many prisoners per capita as the rest of the world (Butterfield, 2000). The per capita prison population in the USA in the 1980s (and today) was actually more than twice as high as that in what the USA used to refer to as the Eastern European communist "police states" (UN, 1994). In addition, the total number of uniformed, undercover, private, secret police, and related administrative personnel in the USA is about 1% of the population (Reynolds, 1994) and even exceeds the per capita numbers of 1988 East Germany, which was reputed to be among the most notorious of the "police states" of Eastern Europe (Diedrich, Ehlert, and Wenzke, 1998).

Other Countries Ranked in the Top Ten in Exterminations of People

While other countries have also committed mass murder on a grand scale, their atrocities rank lower than the USA in all cases. Only two other countries even come close to the USA in terms of the magnitude of their extermination campaigns.

Germany ranks number 2 in mass murders largely because Nazi Germany under Hitler's capitalist rule in the 1933-45 interval deliberately killed over 10 million civilians (most during the war years of 1941-45), including over 5 million non-Jewish Soviet civilians, 5 million Jews, and hundreds of thousands of others (Markusen and Kopf, 1995). Many were executed directly, but millions of others were deliberately slaughtered more indirectly through hunger and disease in concentration camps or in scorched-earth occupied territories (Elliot, 1972). The Nazis actually used the USA as a role model in some of their racial policies and extermination campaigns (Churchill, 1994) that so greatly enhanced the profits (and stock prices) of the German corporations, which had been instrumental in financing Hitler's democratic election to power (Feinberg, 1999). For instance, a December 2, 1941 German Economic Armament Staff report stated the objective of the scorched-earth policies in the occupied territories as "the elimination of the surplus eaters (Jews and the population of the Ukrainian cities such as

Kiev, which receive no food rations at all)," indicating deliberate mass murder (Wytwycky, 1982). Slightly less than half the Soviets and only about half the Jews were killed with poison gas or executions (Elliot, 1972). The number of civilians (especially the number of Soviet and Polish civilians) killed by Nazi Germany would be even larger if all those who died of exploitation (i.e., overwork and undernourishment) were included, as Elliot (1972) and Wytwycky (1982) have indicated.

The Nazi holocaust was not the first mass murder committed by Germany. In particular, German troops had previously used a practice of violently forcing "undesirable" natives in their South West African colony in the late nineteenth century into an unlivable desert (and firing at any Africans trying to return to their own land), thereby exterminating tens of thousands of the Herero people there (Levene and Roberts, 1999). Eventually, some of the remaining natives were allowed into concentration camps, where harsh conditions killed thousands more. There are certainly similarities here to the USA's genocide of the native Americans, although it is clearly on a far smaller scale and did not employ all the gruesome tactics used by the USA (e.g., the Germans did not offer rewards for the killing of any and all natives, did not deliberately spread disease, and did not deliberately destroy native food and water resources—moreover, the Germans always allowed the live capture of female natives and spoke of the "annihilation" of the Herero nation as opposed to the extermination of the people themselves, providing for some possibility of an "enslavement" alternative). Regardless, Germany's killings of the Soviets, Jews, Herero, and others are not sufficiently large to put the country into first place, especially since the eleven million estimated killed by the USA represents an extremely low estimate (as previously explained) and may greatly understate the true number of victims (which may very well exceed 20 million).

Spain ranks number 3 in terms of mass murders because it committed genocide of Indians in its conquest of Central and South America in the middle of this millenium, with many Indian noncombatants being slaughtered with a combination of weapons and dogs, and many more dying indirectly through starvation and disease as they fled the massacres (Stannard, 1992). While some have estimated a "disappearance" of tens of millions of Indians from Spanish colonies in the Western Hemisphere (Stannard, 1992), estimates of initial Indian populations in Central and South America may have been way too high, as explained in Denevan (1976) and Henige (1998). In addition, of the millions of Indians who did once live in Spanish America, many were killed in battle and from related causes (such as from starvation and disease on the front lines of military sieges of fortified cities defended by armed combatants), and many more died as a result of the harsh living and working conditions they had to endure as Spanish slaves (Chalk and Jonassohn, 1990) or as overtaxed serfs (Borah and Cook, 1969).

A large portion of the Indians in Spanish America died of disease, which spread rapidly in the environment of Spanish conquest (Stannard, 1992), but Spain's official policy was one of forcing the conversion of the Indians to Christianity and subservience as opposed to outright genocide (Jaimes, 1992). As a result, except for the deaths resulting from some of the initial genocidal policies followed by the Spanish Conquistadors, who may have engaged in willful extermination policies that contributed to the spreading of disease (Larsen, 1994), most of the Indian deaths are not counted as deliberate murders. In particular, the Spanish generally sought via slavery (and extracting raw materials like gold from their land) to economically exploit the Indians (and not kill them), and, in contrast to the USA policy of offering rewards for the killing of natives, Spain even punished "heroes" like Columbus just for excessively exploiting the Indians (Chalk and Jonassohn, 1990). In addition, a significant portion of the decline in the Indian population of Central and South America can be attributable to the Spanish policy of separating the Indian male slaves from the females for substantial periods of time and by working them so hard even when they were allowed to meet that they had "little inclination for marital communication; in this fashion they ceased procreation" (Cook, 1998). Moreover, a large part of the reduction in the pure Indian population in the Spanish colonies was due to interracial mating, as many Indians were assimilated into society via Christian conversions, and most Spanish freely married with the Indians (Driver, 1961). Although Spain has also committed atrocities against non-Indian peoples, such as during the Inquisition (which mostly involved the Christian murder of non-Christians), it has not been involved in any material atrocities in the last few decades. An exact number of noncombatants deliberately killed by the Spanish is not known, but it may exceed 5 million (Stannard, 1992).

The remaining countries in the top ten killed far less people. For instance, number 4 Pakistan murdered as many as three million Bengalis in 1971 (Chalk and Jonassohn, 1990), number 5 Japan slaughtered over a million Chinese civilians in its invasion of China in the 1930s and 1940s as well as conducted several lesser atrocities (Markusen and Kopf, 1995), number 6 Turkey exterminated over a million unarmed Armenian civilians between 1915 and 1922, as well as thousands of people in the Balkans in prior years (Levene and Roberts, 1999) and thousands of Kurds in subsequent years (Andreopoulos, 1994), number 7 czarist Russia slaughtered over a million people in a purge of Circassians from its Caucasus provinces (Levene and Roberts, 1999), number 8 Nigeria killed over a million of its ethnic Ibo civilians (via flagrant mass murder, blatant aerial bombings of civilians, and deliberate efforts to prevent Red Cross and other relief supplies from reaching a starving civilian population) in a war against its secessionist Biafra province (Forsyth, 1969), number 9 France massacred over 500,000 in its colonies (Smith, 2000), and number 10 Britain legalized the killing of hundreds of thousands of people, including over 200,000 aborigines in Australia after ruling the country to be "uninhabited" in 1788 (Reynolds, 1995), and over 300,000 Irish in the seventeenth century (Levene and Roberts, 1999) in a parliament-approved campaign that "treated all sections of Irish as if they were, not humans but beasts," and that imposed the death penalty for Irish found repeatedly communicating with Catholic priests or failing to leave land seized by British soldiers (MacManus, 1973).[8] It is interesting to observe that, with the exception of Japan, all of the countries in the top ten are religiously Christian or Moslem.

In addition, all of the countries in the top ten just happen to be capitalist ones, even though no "credit" is being given here for the millions who have died of starvation and disease as a result of colonialism and other methods of capitalist economic exploitation, as those people (like the millions who perished in the slave trade) died as a result of the cruelty of the capitalist economic system as opposed to being deliberately killed (Marx and Engels, 1988b). The criteria used in this study to measure the magnitude of human exterminations ignores all such deaths which are not clearly deliberate. For instance, the deaths of millions of slaves who died in transit from Africa were not caused by deliberate extermination policies, but instead by poor living conditions that can be attributed to the capitalist system which put a positive value on the slaves' lives but not high enough to provide them with adequate food, water, quarters, medicine, and sanitary conditions (Miller, 1988). To provide perspective here, it should be mentioned that there is some evidence that the death rate of the "free" white crew members who transported the slaves was about as high as that of the slaves (Curtin, 1969), providing an indication of the relative value (and the kill rate) of workers in general under capitalism (but not implying a general intent to kill them).[9]

From a legal perspective, the primary reason for not including deaths related to pure economic exploitation in the atrocity count is the fact that deliberately killing workers (even one's own slaves), was generally against the law, even though such murder was only a misdemeanor in the USA when the victim was a slave (Nicholson, 1994). Thus, under this legal framework, the massive deaths resulting from capitalist economic exploitation are not considered intentional killings. However, the executions of runaway slaves are (although the numbers are too small relative to the other USA mass murders to be listed separately in Table 1 and are instead essentially incorporated into the "Other" account), just as the mass slaughter of civilians of specific countries with bombings and embargoes is counted as deliberate murder because it was not only allowed but even ordered by the USA (and killing Indians in any fashion was obviously even more deliberate insofar as it was not only legal but also encouraged by the USA with rewards of money and land).

Caveats on the Reputation of Communist Atrocities

Given the distorted reputation of communist countries in the capitalist press (Herman and Chomsky, 1988), some may find it surprising that no communist countries made the top ten, especially since even many skeptics of the mainstream media (and left-wing critics of the USA) often recite the anticommunist propaganda they hear in the mainstream press, such as by referring to the Union of Soviet Socialist Republics (USSR) as "one of the twentieth century's most bloody dictatorships" (Strobel and Peterson, 2000). However, the widespread belief that communist governments have killed millions is largely a myth that is spread by the capitalist press, which is heavily influenced by the CIA and its fanatical anticommunist allies (Blum, 1995).[10]

For example, many blame Pol Pot for the deaths of millions of his own people during his rule of Cambodia between 1975 and 1979, with some being executed for collaborating in the USA's murder of a half million Cambodian civilians through aerial bombardments, and with many more being killed for attempting a coup against him in reaction to his military attacks on Vietnam revolving around a border dispute (Kiernan, 1996). However, the neutral Finnish Inquiry Commission investigated and found that the number executed by Pol Pot was *only* between 75,000 and 150,000 (Herman and Chomsky, 1988).

While it is true that hundreds of thousands of Cambodians died of starvation and disease under Pol Pot's regime, these deaths do not appear to be any more deliberate than the poor who die of similar causes under capitalism. In fact, many of these deaths were the result of the USA bombings themselves, which had destroyed Cambodian agriculture (via the destruction of 75% of its draft animals and substantial amounts of rural housing, as well as the depopulation of the countryside that resulted from millions fleeing to the cities to escape the USA bombings). Despite a forecast by sources close to the USA government that a million people would die in 1975 if Cambodia were deprived of USA aid (which had been partially feeding the starving, refugee-swollen cities before Pol Pot seized power), the USA not only stopped aid after Pol Pot became ruler but also imposed an embargo against the country it had so terribly bombed (Herman and Chomsky, 1988). Some imports of food from communist China and Pol Pot's forcing of the city dwellers to the farms shortly after his takeover in 1975 prevented the disaster from being any worse (Kiernan, 1996).

It should also be mentioned that, subsequent to Pol Pot's removal from power (which occurred after the Vietnamese army counterattacked and occupied Cambodia in 1979), the USA supported Pol Pot in his guerrilla war against the occupying Vietnamese troops (Blum, 1995). In addition, given the USA history of using diplomacy, bribes, and extortion to stir up tensions between communist countries (Griswold, 1972), it is possible that the USA itself had played a part in promoting the deadly rivalry between Cambodia and Vietnam that motivated many of Pol Pot's killings (Klinghoffer, 1998). Regardless, Pol Pot's execution of 75,000-150,000 people is a horrible crime, although it is not enough to make the top ten.[11]

In a similar grotesque exaggeration of the truth, Rummel (1991) and others claim that communist China murdered tens of millions of people, especially during the period 1950-52 (shortly after the communist seizure of power) and during the Cultural Revolution in the 1960s. However, such estimates are largely based on various sources that are either unpublished or published for propaganda purposes by the Anti-Communist League of Nationalist China on the island of Taiwan, which appears to have completely fabricated the numbers (Teiwes, 1997), in an apparent attempt to "justify" its military attacks on communist China that continued long after the communists' seizure of power (Associated Press, 1950). Schuman (1956) even saw and talked with some specific people in communist China after they were alleged to have been executed.

More accurate figures are provided by Chinese government sources. In particular, Grunfeld (1996) has found a substantial amount of evidence indicating that Chinese government reports in such matters (despite being cloaked in ideological verbiage) are fairly reliable, especially in comparison to Western estimates that are often based on limited and biased refugee claims, "wild exaggerations," or even outright fabrications.[12] For instance, in the 1950-52 interval (at a time when China was fighting the USA in Korea in a war that threatened to escalate into China itself), the Chinese government publicly reported (and displayed) its executions, many of which were also publicized in the USA press at the time (Associated Press, 1951).

The local Chinese government announced a total of 28,332 executions for one province (Kwantung) during the 1950-1951 interval, and if that figure were extrapolated proportionally to the rest of the country, it would imply about 400,000 official deaths (Stavis, 1978). However, that province was a coastal one near Hong Kong and may have had an abnormally high number of executions. Other information provided by Chinese government leaders indicates 135,000 executions nationwide based on 800,000 official trials and a reported 16.8% execution rate of "counterrevolutionaries" at the height of the death sentence campaign in 1951 (Meisner, 1999). In addition to the official government death sentences, there were also many executions carried out independently by the local peasants, who may very well have killed tens of thousands of landlords (in retaliation for the prior decades of mass starvation inflicted upon them) and other perceived enemies such as agents or supporters of the former Nationalist Chinese government on the mainland (Teiweis, 1997).

There is one Chinese source estimate of 710,000 victims between 1950 and 1952 (Gong, 1994), but that figure may reflect a speech made by Mao in the 1950s that referred to so many "liquidations" (Stavis, 1978), which the anticommunist propagandist Rummel (1991) himself admits "could simply mean to remove, deactivate, or make ineffective, rather than kill." In addition, since there was still some fighting going on with as many as 400,000 Nationalist Chinese guerrillas or bandits at the time (Gong, 1994), and since the western and southwestern parts of mainland China remained under Nationalist Chinese rule until 1951 (Kwong, 1997), it is possible that some of the 710,000 "liquidations" were related to the killing (or disbursing) of soldiers and armed guerrillas, and some of the actual executions may have been of noncivilian POWs. Moreover, fear of arrest during the 1950-52 strife may have motivated as many as 500,000 people to commit suicide (Teiweis, 1997), and these deaths may have been included in the 710,000 "liquidations." While the suicides were certainly caused by the communist Chinese seizure of power and subsequent campaign of public trials, they could not be considered willful murders (especially given the fairly low rate of death sentences in the trials). As a result, the true number of deliberate killings of unarmed civilians is likely to have been far below 710,000 during the 1950-52 interval.

Gong (1994) cites an official Chinese report of 230,000 people put under public surveillance and 1,270,000 imprisoned by the communist party in the 1950-52 interval. If the officially cited ratio of about 1 execution for every 6 convictions were applied to that data (with the other 5 of 6 convicted people being put under surveillance or imprisoned), it would indicate about 300,000 executions during that period. However, even that number may be an overestimate, as the official rate of sentencing "counterrevolutionaries" to be put under public surveillance (32%) documented by Meisner (1999) was much higher than Gong's (1994) figures indicate. The differences in the imprisonment rates may be due to the fact that the latter figures include many people imprisoned for party/political corruption (Schuman, 1956) as opposed to "counterrevolutionary" activities. Applying to Gong's (1994) data Meisner's (1999) cited ratio of about 1 execution for every 2 people put under observation would imply less than 200,000 executions over the 1950-52 period.

Mao did clearly admit that several of his leaders killed 35,000 people through cruel treatment in prisons during the Cultural Revolution during the 1960s, but it should also be mentioned that he had those leaders responsible tried and executed (MacFarquhar, 1993). While there was some violent fighting during the Cultural Revolution (Dietrich, 1994), and while MacFarquhar (1993) cites some estimates of the number of killed in the hundreds of thousands, he admits such high numbers are based on flimsy evidence that extrapolates potentially exaggerated guesses of killings from refugees fleeing areas with a greater amount of disorder. As Deleyne (1974) indicated, the rhetoric during the Cultural Revolution was very violent, there were a significant number of arrests, and two hundred thousand people were thrown out of the Communist Party, but there was very little actual violence, and the number of people actually killed in the 1960s probably approximates the Chinese government estimate of 35,000. The total number of people killed by communist China is therefore probably low enough to keep the country out of the top ten in mass murders, although more evidence on the issue is certainly needed to be sure of the exact number.[13]

Rummel (1991) and MacFarquhar (1993) have also blamed Mao for tens of millions of Chinese deaths during a famine in 1958-61, but the magnitude of such deaths may be overstated, and they certainly do not represent deliberate killings. In particular, managerial errors (especially with respect to a rapid attempt to attain huge economies of scale without adequately addressing small group incentive and initiative issues), a relatively greater investment focus on industry (for national security reasons related to ongoing USA Cold War threats), and very poor weather caused the catastrophe (Meurs, 1999). In addition, it should also be mentioned that, even if there had been as many as 10 million additional deaths annually (compared to 6 million officially recorded by the Chinese government) during that 3-year disaster (Aston et al., 1984), it would not have even brought the death rate up to the level of the pre-communist era. For instance, Deleyne (1974) states that the annual death rate in China had been 3.4% in normal peaceful (and "prosperous") times in the 1930s under capitalism, whereas the death rate had fallen to 1.1% by the mid-1950s under communism.[14] Applying the difference of 2.3% to a population of 600 million Chinese, yields a figure of over 10 million lives saved per year by Mao's communist policies that both increased incomes in the aggregate and equalized them across the population. Even if a catastrophic extra 10 million deaths did occur annually in the famine of 1958-61, the annual death rate was still below that of pre-communist China during normal times, and so Mao's policies saved few lives even in the years of his worst mistakes and misfortune.

The Soviet Union is also reputed to have murdered tens of millions of people, mostly during the period of Stalin's rule between 1930 and 1953 (Rummel, 1990). In the first chapter of this book, this allegation along with many other myths about Eastern Europe, communism, and its collapse, will be shown to be untrue.[15]

Conclusion

This objective investigation indicates that the USA, which has had the most continuous, widespread history of committing atrocities of any country in the world, is truly number 1 in exterminating innocent unarmed civilians. Although this finding is in contrast to the opinion held by so many Americans that the USA is the "good guy," it is consistent with the perception of parts of the rest of the world that often view the USA and its world policeman policies as hypocritical (Thadani, 1998). The measured discoveries of this research are also consistent with the opinion of some that the USA is "the biggest terrorist in the world" (Moorehead, 1998).

CHAPTER 1

THE DOCUMENTED FACTS ABOUT EASTERN EUROPE AND COMMUNISM: A REFUTATION OF POPULAR MYTHS ABOUT THE TRUE GOOD GUYS

While most have a false impression of USA benevolence or "kindness," many believe that the former governments of Eastern Europe (and other communist states) were (and are) horribly totalitarian, economically inefficient societies that collapsed because they did not serve the people of those countries (Pipes, 1993). This chapter explains the true causes of the disintegration of communism in Eastern Europe, provides facts refuting the popular myths surrounding Eastern Europe and communism, and clarifies why the USA won the Cold War despite having an inferior system.

Economic Phenomena Contributing to the Collapse of Communism in Eastern Europe

The virtually bloodless collapse of communism in Eastern Europe has caused many to conclude that the communist system was removed there largely as a result of its own economic failure to improve the standard of living of the people (Campbell, 1992). While it is true that economics did play a roll in the fall of communism, the communist system itself was actually reasonably effective economically, as is indicated by the higher average real economic growth rates experienced by Eastern Europe under communism (compared to capitalist countries) from 1946-89, as well as before that time interval in the Soviet Union where communism took hold earlier in 1917 (Murphy, 1998). In fact, Eastern

Europe enjoyed higher growth rates than Western Europe even in its final critical years (IMF, 1993), and the fall of communism in Eastern Europe can be more attributed to the economic failure of the system in existence there prior to communism than to the mistakes and problems of communism itself.

In particular, prior to communism, Eastern Europe had had substantially lower economic output per capita than Western Europe and the USA (Mead, 1994). For instance, the gross national product (GNP) per capita of Russia was about 10% of that of the USA during peacetime before communism in 1913 (Gregory, 1982), and GNP per capita was even lower by the time of the communist revolution there in 1917 (Hutchings, 1982). Thereafter, real GNP per capita in the Soviet Union under communism caught up significantly, rising to 31% of USA GNP per capita by 1991 (UN, 1994).[1] That performance occurred despite the very destructive Foreign Interventionist Civil War of 1918-22 (Krivosheev, 1997), which reduced Soviet output by about half (Hutchings, 1982), and despite the almost as destructive Nazi invasion of 1941-44, which reduced Soviet GNP by over 20% (Maddison, 1969).[2] After growing faster than the USA in all peaceful decades up to the political collapse of Eastern Europe in 1990,[3] Russia's economy deteriorated enormously following the capitalist takeover by Yeltsin, with real GNP falling by about 50% between 1991 and 1996 (IMF, 1997a). A comparison of real economic growth rates in the Soviet Union and the USA shortly before and after the collapse of Eastern European communism in 1990 is provided in Table 2:

TABLE 2

ANNUAL REAL ECONOMIC GROWTH RATES IN RUSSIA AND THE USA IN THE YEARS JUST BEFORE AND AFTER THE END OF COMMUNISM

	Communism in Eastern Europe						,	Capitalism
								Annual
Country:	1975-84	1985	1986	1987	1988	1989	1990	1991-98
Soviet Union	4.1%	1.7%	3.6%	2.8%	5.3%	3.0%	-2.3%	
Russia								-7.9%
USA	2.5%	3.2%	2.9%	3.1%	3.9%	2.5%	1.2%	2.5%

Source: IMF (1993, 1998).

Similarly, real economic growth in all of Eastern Europe under communism was estimated to be higher than in Western Europe under capitalism (as well as higher than in the USA) even in communism's final decade (the 1980s), and real economic output fell by over 30% in Eastern Europe as a whole in the 1990s after the reimposition of capitalism (IMF, 1998: 171).

So why was communism overthrown in Eastern Europe, if real economic growth was higher than under capitalism? One answer can be found in the area's historic poverty. Although communism had partially bridged the huge gulf in standard of living differences between Eastern Europe and developed capitalist countries, it had not completely done so, and many people began to incorrectly associate communism with poverty. Increasing contact and communication with richer capitalist countries contributed to this feeling.[4] As a result, many Eastern Europeans (including many of their leaders) began to falsely perceive capitalism to be a get-rich-quick scheme to bring their standard of living up to the level of the developed capitalist countries (Marcy, 1990).

Other Factors Contributing to the Collapse of Communism in Eastern Europe

There were, of course, other factors that reduced people's support for the communist system in Eastern Europe and therefore contributed to its demise. Many of these other factors related back to the economic problems in Eastern Europe. However, the Soviet participation in a civil war in Afghanistan may have played a role independent of economics in reducing support for, and confidence in, the communist system.

General Problems Relating to the Economy

The efficiency of communism may have enabled Eastern Europe to overtake the richest capitalist countries by 1989 (and may have thereby avoided communism's undeserved reputation for economic inefficiency) if it had not suffered so much destruction from war and had not therefore also felt the need to expend enormous resources on defense. In particular, the Soviet Union had been invaded militarily by over a dozen countries in the first 25 years of its existence (including by the very powerful capitalist countries of the USA, Britain, Germany, and Japan). Subsequently, it had been subjected to various threatening Cold War acts by the USA, including a massive number of military flights over

Soviet territory, as well as frequent attempted assassinations and sabotage by USA spies and infiltrators (Smith, 2000). Many of those infiltrators and others seeking to instigate armed revolution in the Soviet Union had earlier collaborated with the Nazi invaders during their temporary occupation of a portion of the USSR in World War II, and some of those terrorists preaching "freedom, democracy, and other humanitarian concerns" had even been members of Nazi extermination squads (Blum, 1995). Although the absolute amount of military spending was lower in the Soviet Union than in the USA, the Soviet leaders felt it necessary to spend a larger portion of their smaller GNP in order to maintain relative military parity as a deterrent to more attacks (Campbell, 1974). Without this higher percentage of GNP allocated to defense spending, a larger amount of resources would have been available for consumption and productive investment, and the Soviet Union no doubt would have come closer to catching up with the USA in terms of satisfying consumer desires by 1989.

In addition, the technological embargo imposed by the richer Western countries against Eastern Europe contributed to the inability of that area to fully meet its consumers' demand for high-tech goods. Just for instance, the cost of producing modern semiconductors was over 20 times higher in Eastern Europe in 1989 than it would have cost to purchase them on the "free" world market (Krakat, 1996). Despite the embargo, Eastern Europe was able to attain a level of technology that was at least on par with that of many capitalist countries with similar GNP per capita, and less than a decade behind that of the USA (Smith, 2000), but the embargo certainly increased the cost of technology and inhibited the ability of Eastern Europe Union to satisfy their consumers' wishes (Parrott, 1985).

The inability to satisfy consumer high-tech demand as well as rich Western countries also contributed to a perception that communist systems were backward and uninnovative because they are government-run (as opposed to systems that theoretically concentrate innovation in the private or corporate sector). Despite this false perception, there is actually some evidence that governments encourage more long-term innovation than rich capitalists or corporate bureaucrats who are more risk-averse and focus more on short-term profits (*Der Spiegel*, 1998), and it was not the innovation of the capitalist countries but their riches that allowed them to be able to afford the investments needed to develop the leading technologies. The greater wealth of capitalist countries not only enabled them to spend a far larger absolute amount of money on research and development, but also generally a larger percent of their much higher income (DeBlasi, 2000). The capitalist riches themselves arose through centuries of colonialism, imperialism, slavery, and other forms of foreign exploitation (which were enforced via strong military forces that were able to increase their relative strength as the relative income disparities between the countries grew), as explained by Bittorf (1992) and Darity (1992). Exploitation in the form of horrible work and living conditions for the domestic masses (that included forcing 6-year-old children to work 100+ hour weeks just to survive) also contributed to the capitalists' accumulation of wealth and technology (Marx and Engels, 1988b). Despite the riches of private capitalist individuals and businesses, it has actually been governments that have originally been responsible for many of the major innovations in the world, such as related to computers, electronics, the internet, space exploration, and atomic energy (Marcy, 1990). Even communist China, despite its very low level of income per capita (that still has far to go to catch up with the West), has managed to become among the world leaders in innovation in many areas, such as in gene research (Leggett and Johnson, 2000) and in the development of important practical agricultural processes or new plant strains (Meurs, 1999).

Although economic misconceptions directly contributed to the collapse of communism, there were certainly other factors involved as well. For instance, a desire for the political freedoms of the developed capitalist countries, not just their riches, played a part in Eastern Europe turning away from communism. However, to some extent, it was the greater wealth of the developed capitalist countries that enabled them to engage in the many threatening actions and wars that motivated communist repression to restrict some political freedoms (Blum, 1995).

Similarly, the Eastern European people's desire for greater travel freedom, especially in East Germany, also motivated them to overthrow communism. However, it was the relative economic poverty of Eastern Europe that heavily contributed to the restrictive travel policies which were implemented to combat the drain of important skilled workers (like doctors and nurses) to the higher incomes of Western Europe (Apel,

1966). East Germany had the most restrictive travel policies because West Germany tried to entice its skilled workers to emigrate not only through much better-paying jobs (easily obtainable because of similar culture and language and, more importantly, because of West Germany's offer of immediate and automatic citizenship to East German immigrants) but also with sizable cash payments and many other benefits (*Der Tagesspiegel,* 1990f).[5] West Germany could afford to be so "generous" to East German immigrants because it had impoverished East Germany after World War II by forcing it alone to pay the entire amount of the enormous reparations to the Soviet Union that was contracted for Germany as a whole by the USA at Potsdam in 1945 (Apel, 1966).

Other forms of economic warfare and extortion (where the far greater wealth of the capitalist countries gave them powerful advantages) also played a part in communist Eastern Europe moving toward capitalist systems. In particular, lucrative trade, loans, and aid were often offered to communist countries if they conducted capitalistic economic "reforms", while "non-reforming" communist countries were typically confronted with trade barriers. Moreover, the threat of an escalation of the arms race, which was especially counterproductive to the poorer communist countries that had to expend a larger percent of national income to defense as a result, also produced motivation to appease Western demands for capitalist reforms (Marcy, 1990).

In addition, ethnic, cultural, and religious differences were a factor in the break-up of the Eastern European communist bloc. In particular, many people in Eastern European countries and in the former Soviet Union had resented being dominated by Russians since the pre-communist days of czarist Russia (Matlock, 1995), especially after Russia killed or exiled millions from the Caucasus in the 1800s (Levene and Roberts, 1999). However, economic subsidies and investments in the non-Russian republics of the Soviet Union (as well as the grant of some political autonomy) had greatly reduced such tensions under communism (Marcy, 1990) and eliminated the need for ethnic-related repression (Getty, Rittersporn and Zemskov, 1993). The ethnic problems reemerged only under Gorbachev's capitalist reforms in the mid-1980s under Perestroika, as those free market policies resanctified the quest for personal or regional gain (at the expense of others), which encouraged ethnic or nationalist movements (Marcy, 1990). For instance, an earlier Soviet policy of investing substantial sums into less developed areas of the Soviet Union (in order to bring their income closer to that of the historically richer Russians) was drastically cut back under Perestroika for reasons of economic efficiency, and those who opposed such reforms under Gorbachev were purged from power, thereby magnifying the resentment of Russian domination and causing a reawakening of the nationalist or independence movements (Marcy, 1990). The Soviet Union's decision to charge its Eastern European allies capitalist market prices for oil in the late 1980s also contributed to the 1989 revolutions among its Eastern European allies, as the resulting slowing of economic growth there increased the people's dissatisfaction with the communist system (and their Russian defenders), especially in East Germany (Ritschl, 1996) where the original revolution broke out. The Joint Economic Committee (1988) of the USA Congress itself was well aware of the fact that the capitalist reforms which the USA was pressuring Eastern Europe to undertake quite naturally increased income inequality, which caused "tensions among the nationality groups."

The War in Afghanistan

Also potentially contributing to unrest among ethnic groups in the Soviet bloc (especially in the Moslem republics of the USSR), and to dissatisfaction amongst the Soviet people in general, was the 1979-89 military participation of the USSR in a civil war in Moslem Afghanistan, which provided some evidence of actual Soviet atrocities that led many people in the Soviet Union to question the legitimacy and morality of their government and leaders (Kuperman, 1999). The conflict started when CIA-financed rebels began terrorist attacks against a communist government (Blum, 1995), which had (completely independent of the Soviet Union or its agents) overthrown a feudal dictatorship earlier in 1978 (Rodman, 1994). This government then invited Soviet military forces into the country to aid in stopping the CIA-sponsored terrorism (Blum, 1995). The rebel terrorists were being led by "ultra-conservative" Moslem religious leaders and landowners, who initially were largely supported by bandits and smugglers (especially on the border with Pakistan), and later by many Afghan males (especially in rural areas) who opposed the communist government acts which decommodified women (i.e., forbid their sale) and which offered education (including literacy) and other rights to Afghan females (Urban, 1990).

However, the Soviet Union refrained from sending more than military advisors to help out until late December 1979 (Zeloga, 1995). The communist Afghan leader who had requested Soviet support was overthrown and murdered by a USA-educated extremist, whom the Soviets believed was a CIA agent attempting to discredit communism (Rodman, 1994). Before significant Soviet military forces arrived, the Afghan extremist (whom the Soviets themselves executed in their "invasion") had ordered the killing of thousands of civilians, and many Afghan soldiers (and entire government military units) had defected to the rebels, exasperating the level of violent conflict (Girardet, 1985). It should be mentioned that violence in Afghanistan did not really start with the communist seizure of power in 1978, as there had been widespread tribal feuding in Afghan rural areas before 1978 that was not related to the communists or Soviets and that had created over a hundred thousand refugees at one point in the mid-1970s (Urban, 1990).

Even after the removal of the extremist Afghan ruler, Amnesty International reported that hundreds more civilians were subsequently executed or tortured to death in prison under the more moderate communist government installed by the Soviets (U.S. Dept. of State, 1988). Nonetheless, it should be emphasized that the communist repression in Afghanistan was motivated by possibly even more horrifying actions conducted by the foreign-supplied rebels, who themselves had long engaged in widespread murderous acts of terrorism against civilians in Afghanistan (Blum, 1995), and who later (beginning in the 1980s) launched numerous terrorist attacks against civilian targets within the Soviet Union itself (Amstutz, 1986). In reaction, the communists made many successful attempts to infiltrate and disrupt rebel forces or peacefully bribe them into defection or cease-fires (Girardet, 1985), but they also conducted military raids and aerial attacks on rebel positions that killed tens of thousands of people, including many civilians (Amstutz, 1986). In addition, although Soviet soldiers were forbidden from even arresting civilians unless there was evidence of them having weapons or breaking laws (and although they even allowed many anticommunist civilians to keep weapons if they were thought to be needed to defend against rebel terrorist attacks), Soviet troops did fire back directly when fired upon, no doubt killing many civilians in the process (Tamarov, 1992).

There is also some evidence that communist troops did deliberately shoot innocent Afghan civilians on numerous different occasions, murdering hundreds of them (U.S. Dept. of State, 1985). While not justifying such murders, it must be mentioned that motivation for some of the Soviet atrocities was related to the killing of Soviet soldiers by civilians (even communist civilians), to whom the CIA-financed rebels paid cash rewards for each Soviet soldier murdered (Tamarov, 1992). Also contributing to some Soviet atrocities was soldiers' frustration with civilians' refusal to provide information on the perpetrators of rebel crimes (Reese, 2000). Regardless, it must be emphasized that Soviet soldiers involved in committing atrocities were "harshly disciplined" (Urban, 1990), and there was never any systematic or premeditated effort to kill civilians. Moreover although there is evidence that some Soviet soldiers engaged in robbing Afghan civilians, Soviet soldiers were also very frequently involved in stealing from their own military (largely to finance the purchase of narcotics that substituted for the normal vodka to which Soviet soldiers had better access in the USSR), and, in any event, any illegal "freelance" actions against civilians was "punished severely," as admitted even by Soviet soldiers who had defected to the USA (Alexiev, 1988). The Soviet army behavior in Afghanistan actually compares favorably to that of the USA army in its most recent major action, the 1991 Persian Gulf War, which is glorified in the USA despite war crimes such as ground troops committing mass murder of defenseless Iraqi POWs and civilians (even though USA troops were hardly ever threatened in the entire war and mostly only by friendly fire and never by civilians or POWs), and which created a promoted hero out of a general who deliberately slaughtered Iraqi troops while they were retreating exactly as they had agreed to do after an armistice had been entered into (Hersh, 2000).

Specific evidence on the extent of civilian killings in Afghanistan is provided by the U.S. Department of State (1987), which reported unidentified sources indicating as many as 15,000 civilians killed during the first 8 months of 1987, during which time it was stated that "civilian casualties were enormous" as a result of Soviet counterinsurgency operations that were launched as reprisals for rebel raids into the Soviet Union itself. If 1987, which was a year of average Soviet military casualties but less accurate aerial bombings due to rebel acquisition of

Stinger missiles (Zaloga, 1995), had been an average year for civilian deaths in the 1979-89 war, the total would be 225,000 civilians killed in the war. Since the USA-reported reported civilian kill rate in 1987 was probably very biased upward (given that it no doubt includes civilian death tolls grossly exaggerated by the rebels for propaganda purposes), and since civilian casualties may have been abnormally high in 1987 due to decreased accuracy of Soviet aerial bombings that year, the number of civilian deaths was unquestionable far less than 225,000, but that figure can be used as an upward bound. Since the rebels did engage in widespread bombings of civilian targets that had destroyed over a thousand schools and hospitals in rural areas covering 90% of the country in the first few years of the war (Bradsher, 1983), since the rebels frequently conducted rocket attacks and bombings on residential areas of heavily populated cities (Blum, 1995), since the rebels assassinated virtually every government official and communist party member they could (as well as most communist supporters and sympathizers, and frequently any unknown or uncooperative people), with one unit of 1200 rebels in one Afghan city assassinating 600 people in a 2-year period alone (Girardet, 1995), since the rebels even murdered Western journalists in order to be able to steal their cameras (Urban, 1990), since the rebels had such heavy weaponry that they could not even be labeled a traditional guerrilla force (Jalali and Grau, 1995), since the rebels had about as many soldiers (approximately 200,000) as the Soviet/Afghan communists (Girardet, 1985), and since the rebels often engaged in inter-group feuding that may have directly led to the deaths tens of thousands of people (Urban, 1990), it is likely that the rebels may have killed at least half of the civilians, leaving the communists with responsibility for less than 115,000 civilian deaths.

Given survey evidence (of Afghan refugees in Pakistan) indicating that aerial bombings of civilian targets caused the deaths of under 50% of the civilians killed by communist fire (U.S. State Dept., 1987), and given that most of the remaining deaths were likely to have been unintentional battlefield casualties (i.e., the result of ground forces actually fighting armed rebels), it is probable that the communists deliberately killed less than half the civilians for whose deaths they were responsible. Because many of the reports of heavy communist bombings of civilian areas in Afghanistan had no truth to them, being clearly fabricated by the rebels for propaganda purposes (Urban, 1990), and because many of the other stories of alleged communist atrocities were also invented by the rebels and their CIA supporters (Blum, 1995), it is likely that the number of civilians deliberately killed by the communists in Afghanistan was only a very small fraction of 115,000 (and definitely far less than 60,000).

Further evidence on this issue is provided by the fact that it wasn't until 1984 that the communist air force utilized any high-level strategic bombers such as TU-16 aircraft (Girardet, 1985), which, like the USA B-52 bombers in Vietnam, result in more indiscriminate killings via saturation bombings. Communist air power in Afghanistan, which consisted largely of about 1000 helicopters, MIG fighters, and SU-25 tactical bombers (McMichael, 1999), was generally used to support ground troops (Girardet, 1985). Even the Soviet strategic bombers were effectively used to assist combined ground/air offensives as opposed to engaging in mass killings/terrorizing of civilians (Urban, 1990). Some Western analysts were astounded that the communists rarely even made pure aerial attacks on supply lines, which were vital to the rebels (Girardet, 1985), or on other targets far in the rear of enemy troops (Kuperman, 1999). The failure of the communists to use air power alone to attack such important targets, which were so important to the Afghan rebels, and which the Soviets did instead block or ambush with air-lifted ground forces at various times (Girardet, 1985), provides evidence of the inhibitions the communists had about potentially attacking innocent civilians. Even in cases where pure aerial attacks were launched against rebel-controlled villages in reprisal for rebel atrocities, there is evidence (from anticommunist sources) that the Soviets had a standard policy of warning the civilians (by loudspeaker) to leave the villages before-hand (Alexiev, 1988).

Similarly, despite allegations of some limited communist use of chemical weapons in the war and despite a Western perception that chemical weapons would have been very effective militarily in the Afghan terrain if widely employed against populated rebel positions, the Soviets apparently believed they created too much risk of "many collateral civilian and friendly casualties" (McMichael, 1991). A leading British expert journalist has called the allegations of any Soviet use of chemical weapons "a complete lie ... a CIA fabrication" (Urban, 1990). All the evidence therefore seems to imply that communist air power was mostly directed against military targets (i.e., areas with armed rebels generally engaged in combat), and that most of the civilians killed by communist aircraft (as well as ground forces) represented true unintentional battlefield casualties. The number of civilians deliberately killed by the communist forces may have therefore amounted to only a few thousand, especially since the total number of civilian killings is probably greatly overestimated (as mentioned previously).[6]

Communist troops in Afghanistan did conduct raids to methodically destroy villages and farms in order to inhibit their use as rebel supply centers (in a scorched-earth policy designed for rebel-controlled rural areas), but there was no actual attempt to kill civilians or commit genocide. In fact, affected residents were welcomed into government-controlled cities (Bradsher, 1983), and displaced people were even offered rewards for settling in government-protected rural areas (Urban, 1990). Hundreds of thousands of people did move to government-controlled cities, although more (millions) preferred to flee into refugee camps in neighboring countries like Pakistan, which were safe from the continuous rebel terrorist attacks on government-protected areas in Afghanistan (Girardet, 1985) and which were also almost never attacked by the communists (Urban, 1990). At least partially contributing to the fact that so many refugees chose resettlement in neighboring countries was the heavy outside humanitarian aid provided to ensure tolerable living conditions in the foreign refugee camps (Amstutz, 1986). Regardless, within this civil war environment, many civilians may have died for health reasons, although there was no mass starvation like there was in peaceful times during the prior rule of the Afghan feudal dictatorship of the early 1970s (when as many as 100,000 Afghans died of hunger in the peaceful 1971-72 period alone before the communists took power), and the biggest health hazard of the 1980s in Afghanistan was induced by an extreme shortage of medical personnel in rebel-controlled areas that was largely caused by Afghan doctors leaving for higher pay in foreign capitalist countries (Girardet, 1985).

Although the actual extent of communist atrocities in Afghanistan was no doubt far less than widely claimed, publicity about them certainly caused some Soviet citizens to question the validity of their country's official policy of benevolence (Kuperman, 1999). This reduced confidence in their government and leaders may have led many to yearn for a change.

Minority of Leaders Dismantle Communism Against Will of Majority of People

While there were numerous factors that contributed to a desire among some to turn away from communism, it is especially important to point out that the majority of the Eastern European people did not want to eliminate their system (although they may have wanted to reform aspects of it). Communism was actually dismantled by various Eastern European leaders who acted against the will of the people.

For instance, the Soviet people (including a majority in the subsequently independent Caucasus and South Asia) had voted overwhelmingly (over 70%) in favor of preserving the system in early 1991 in a free plebiscite on the issue (Becker, 1999a). However, despite this vote, the "free-market" advocate Yeltsin led the dissolution of the Soviet Union later in 1991 in a major power grab (Wayland, 2000a). Somewhat later, in 1996, the dissolution of the Soviet Union was voted to have been unconstitutional by a Russian parliament elected under Yeltsin's new constitution (*Wall Street Journal,* 1996), but it was too late because the continuing, hostile capitalist President Yeltsin had already created dictatorial powers for himself (Wayland, 2000a). Nevertheless, despite heavy marketing and positive media coverage of capitalist politicians in Russia in the 1990s (and virtually no effective marketing by communists there), one survey indicated that 58% of the Russian population believed in 1999 that "it would have been better if the country had stayed as it was before 1985," and only 27% of the Russians disagreed with that opinion (*Economist,* 1999c).

Similarly, the majority of the people in East Germany (the country that had led the 1989-90 revolution in Eastern Europe) wanted to preserve a reformed version of their communist country. In particular, an unbiased survey conducted by East and West Germans in December 1989 (shortly after the opening of the Berlin Wall) indicated that over 71% of East Germans were in favor of keeping their socialist system and 73% were in favor of maintaining a separate country (Bahrmann and Links, 1994). However, as will be explained in Chapters 2-4, various East German leaders gave in to Western pressure to open up their economy and political system, thereby enabling an overwhelming combination of West German bribes, extortion, and marketing to destroy the East German economy and the people's will to preserve their system and independence.

It should also be noted that the people in some Eastern European countries, such as Serbia (*Economist,* 1993) and Bulgaria (*Economist,* 1990), actually voted to maintain rule by reformed versions of their communist parties even after opening up their political system to Western-style elections that permitted manipulation by Western media and economic extortion (IAC, 1998a). Despite the fact that anticommunist capitalists exercise a virtual monopoly over the media in some countries like Russia (Associated Press, 1996a) and threaten to "resist" (implying economic boycotts and even civil war or other "upheavals") if the people vote communism back into power (Associated Press, 1996b), many Eastern Europeans continue to vote for left-wing political parties that are reformed versions of the communist parties which previously ruled Eastern Europe (Murphy, 1995). Such parties have been elected into power in Hungary, Poland, Bulgaria, and Lithuania in the mid-1990s (*Economist,* 1995), as well as in Yugoslavia (*Economist,* 1997) and Mongolia (Associated Press, 2000).

Dispelling Other Common Myths about Communism

Many people have many other misconceptions about communism and the causes of its collapse. These misconceptions are spread by the myths and strong anticommunist bias that exists in the mainstream press which is controlled by concentrated capitalist money and is heavily influenced by the CIA (Herman and Chomsky, 1988). As stated by Ralph "McGehee, a highly decorated CIA veteran, 'Disinformation is a large part of [the CIA's] covert action responsibility, and the American people are the primary target audience of its lies'" (Goff, 2000).

Quality of Life, Freedom and Individuality

Due to the widespread existence of a dominating one-party rule and more leveled income under communism, there is often the perception that normal life was harshly regimented under communism (Pipes, 1993). In fact, communism freed people from unemployment, poverty, crime, major money anxieties, excessive social frictions, and economic inequalities and thereby actually created the opportunity for a higher quality of life (Falck, 1998), as Marx and Engels (1988a) predicted.

Some evidence on the relative value of rights and freedoms under communism is provided by a recent 1999 Russian survey (Whitehouse, 1999). This survey found that 68% of the Russian people felt "the right to free education, medical help, and financial support in old age" to be among the most important human rights, and 53% indicated as important "the right to a well-paid job in one's area of expertise," whereas only 14% and 8% mentioned "freedom of speech" and "the right to elect one's leaders", respectively, as important. In addition, even though only 23% listed "the right to private property" to be important, a separate question found 40% wanting a Western-style capitalist/democratic system, perhaps because they still associated a higher standard of living with such systems (and incorrectly assumed, as so many do, that the capitalist system was the cause of Western wealth). Despite the latter perception among a significant number of Russians that is perpetuated with Russian capitalist political slogans like "Don't you want to live as in Europe?", an even more recent survey indicated that 48% of the Russian people prefer "state planning and distribution" compared to only 35% of Russians favoring "private property and the market" (*Economist,* 1999).

Further evidence on the value of the various benefits of communism is available from a very limited survey that I conducted of Germans who had emigrated from communist East Germany to capitalist West Germany before unification in 1990. The survey found that the emigrants would have been willing to give up 21.04% of their West German income to have the communist advantages of virtual elimination of unemployment, drugs, crime, uncertain prices, and life-sustaining money anxieties. The survey also indicated that these same Germans would have been willing to give up 6.69% of their income to avoid having the East German political system and secret police. A separate and more thorough survey of East Germans in the 1990s indicated that they had felt overall freer from government interference in the 1980s in communist East Germany than they did in the united capitalist Germany in the 1990s (Northoff, 1995). This latter finding is especially important for putting the relative value of communist freedoms and repression in an interesting perspective.

Exaggerations of Political Repression

Much of the USA government and mainstream press propaganda

about political repression and secret police in Eastern Europe was exaggerated (Marcy, 1990). Just for instance, in December 1989, it was reported worldwide in the mainstream press that Romania had killed over 60,000 peaceful demonstrators, when in fact a thorough investigation by the government that overthrew the communists indicated only 142 demonstrators were killed and only after they had violently attacked police forces and indicated their intention to overthrow the government (Ratesh, 1991). Exaggerated claims of communist atrocities (which in the case of Romania led to a brief civil war that did kill hundreds of armed soldiers and police) often result from CIA disinformation, which is spread through press sources in countries allied with the USA against communism, or through private organizations and individuals funded (overtly or covertly) by the CIA (Blum, 1995).

The claim that Stalin and other Soviet leaders killed millions (Conquest, 1990) also appears to be wildly exaggerated. More recent evidence from the Soviet archives opened up by the anticommunist Yeltsin government indicate that the total number of death sentences (including of both existing prisoners and those outside captivity) over the 1921-1953 interval (covering the period of Stalin's partial and complete rule) was between 775,866 and 786,098 (Getty, Rittersporn, and Zemskov, 1993). Given that the archive data originates from anti-Stalin (and even anticommunist) sources, it is extremely unlikely that they underestimate the true number (Thurston, 1996). In addition, the Soviet Union has long admitted to executing at least 12,733 people between 1917 and 1921, mostly during the Foreign Interventionist Civil War of 1918-22, although it is possible that as many as 40,000 more may have been executed unofficially (Andics, 1969). These data would seem to imply about 800,000 executions.

The figure of 800,000 may greatly overestimate the number of actual executions, as it includes many who were sentenced to death but who were not actually caught or who had their sentences reduced (Getty, Rittersporn, and Zemskov, 1993). In fact, Vinton (1993) has provided evidence indicating that the number of executions was significantly below the number of civilian prisoners sentenced to death in the Soviet Union, with only 7305 executions in a sample of 11,000 prisoners authorized to be executed in 1940 (or scarcely 60%).

In addition, most (681,692) of the 780,000 or so death sentences passed under Stalin were issued during the 1937-38 period (Getty, Rittersporn, and Zemskov, 1993), when Soviet paranoia about foreign subversion reached its zenith due to a 1936 alliance between Nazi Germany and fascist Japan that was specifically directed against the Soviet Union (Manning, 1993) and due to a public 1936 resolution by a group of influential anti-Stalin foreigners (the Fourth International which was allied with the popular but exiled Russian dissident Leo Trotsky) advocating the overthrow of the Soviet government by illegal means (Glotzer, 1968). Stalin initially set a cap of 186,500 imprisonments and 72,950 death penalties for a 1937 special operation to combat this threat that was to be carried out by local 3-man tribunals called "troikas" (Getty, Rittersporn, and Zemskov, 1993). As the tribunals passed death sentences before the accused had even been arrested, local authorities requested increases in their own quotas (Knight, 1993), and there was an official request in 1938 for a doubling of the amount of prisoner transport that had been initially requisitioned to carry out the original campaign "quotas" of the tribunals (Getty, Rittersporn, and Zemskov, 1993). However, even if there had been twice as many actual executions as originally planned, the number would still be less than 150,000. Many of those sentenced by the tribunals may have escaped capture, and many more may have had their death sentence refused or revoked by higher authorities before arrest/execution could take place, especially since Stalin later realized that excesses had been committed in the 1937-38 period, had a number of convictions overturned, and had many of the responsible local leaders punished (Thurston, 1996).

Soviet records indicate only about 300,000 actual arrests for anti-Soviet activities or political crimes during this 1937-38 interval (Davies, 1997). With a ratio of 1 execution for every 3 arrests as originally specified by Stalin, that figure would imply about 100,000 executions. Since some of the people sentenced to death may have already been in confinement, and since there is some evidence of a 50,000 increase in the total number of deaths in labor camps over the 1937-38 interval that was probably caused by such executions (Getty, Rittersporn, and Zemskov, 1993), the total number executed by the troika campaign would probably be around 150,000. There were also 30,514 death sentences passed by military courts and 4387 by regular courts during the 1937-38 period, but, even if all these death sentences were carried out, the total number remains under 200,000. Such a "low" number seems especially likely given the fact that aggregate death rates (from all causes) throughout the Soviet Union were actually lower in 1937-38 than in prior years (Wheatcroft, 1993).

Assuming the remaining 100,000 or so death sentences passed in the other years of Stalin's reign (i.e., 1921-36 and 1939-53) resulted in a 60% execution rate, as per the Vinton (1993) sample, the total number executed by Stalin's Soviet Union would be about 250,000. Even with the thousands executed between 1917 and 1921, it is plausible that the number of unarmed civilians killed between 1917-1953 amounted to considerably less than a quarter million given that thousands of these victims may have been Soviet soldiers (Freeze, 1997), given that some may have been armed bandits and guerrillas (Getty, 1985), and given that at least 14,000 of the actual executions were of foreign POWs (Vinton, 1993). A USA former attaché to the Soviet Union, George Kennan, has stated that the number executed was really only in the tens of thousands (Smith, 2000), and so it is very likely that the true number of unarmed civilians killed by the Soviet Union over its entire history (including the thousands killed in Afghanistan more recently) is too small for the country to make the top ten in mass murders.

There were no doubt many innocent victims during the 1937-38 Stalin purge, but it should also be mentioned that there is substantial evidence from the Soviet archives of Soviet citizens advocating treasonable offenses such as the violent overthrow of the Soviet government or foreign invasion of the Soviet Union (Davies, 1997). In addition, the Soviet Union felt itself so threatened by subversion and imminent military invasions by Japan and Germany (which occurred in full force in 1938 and 1941, respectively) that it perceived a need to undertake a nationwide campaign to eliminate potential internal enemies (Manning, 1993). Moreover, these external threats were further fueled by the fact that the Russian nobility and czarists (over a million of whom had emigrated after the communist revolution in 1917) had given financial aid to the German Nazis in the 1930s for the purpose of using them (once they had successfully taken power in Germany) to help them overthrow the Soviet government (Feinberg, 1999).[8] Forged documents and misinformation spread by Nazi Germany to incriminate innocent and patriotic Soviets also contributed to Soviet paranoia (Andrew and Gordievsky,

1990). It must also be remembered that Soviet fear of foreign-sponsored subversion in the 1930s existed within the context of guerrilla warfare fought against the Soviet Union by some of the same groups of people who had fought with the foreign invaders against the Soviet Union in the 1918-22 Foreign Interventionist Civil War (Conquest, 1986).

While the 1937-38 purges were very repressive and tragic by almost any measure, they may have helped prevent the fascists from inciting a successful rebellion or coup in the Soviet Union (Thurston, 1996). Such a threat was a very real one given that the German Nazis did succeed in using political intrigues, threats, economic pressure, and offers of territorial gains to bring other Eastern European countries into their orbit, including Bulgaria, Romania, and Hungary, as well as Yugoslavia for a short period of time (Miller, 1975), given that the Soviet Union had been subjected to a brutal 1918-22 civil war which was launched by rebels who were supported by over a million foreign invading troops from over a dozen capitalist countries (Schulz, 1982), given that there was a large amount of sabotage committed by Soviet citizens in the 1930s (Conquest, 1986), and given that there were a significant number of Soviet dissidents who were in favor of overthrowing the Soviet government even if it required an invasion by Germany or some other foreign power (Davies, 1997). It is also possible that the Germans and Japanese had spread sufficient misinformation to lead many people to believe in the existence of an alliance between the exiled Trotsky and the fascist countries that offered Germany and Japan some Soviet territories in return for helping the Russian dissident take power in the remaining part of Russia (Glotzer, 1968). In addition, many people may have worked independently to sabotage the Soviet Union in the hope that they would thereby contribute to a foreign overthrow of the Soviet Union (Rittersporn, 1992), especially since Nazi Germany did make extensive efforts to incite uprisings, cause subversive actions, and create ethnic conflicts in Eastern Europe and the Soviet Union (Schulz, 1982). Although the Soviet Union may have falsely blamed Trotsky for advocating cooperation with the fascists, even Trotsky admitted that some of the victims of Stalin's repression may have indeed been German or Japanese agents (Glotzer, 1968). Despite the Soviet Union's success in defeating the subsequent invasions by fascist Japan (in 1938) and Germany (1941-44), the danger posed by the Nazi spies and saboteurs in

Eastern Europe is illustrated by the fact that the CIA considered them so effective that it adopted virtually the entire Nazi network into its own system of terrorism in Eastern Europe after World War II (von Schnitzler, 1992). The CIA also extensively used Trotskyites and other anti-Stalin leftists in its very powerful anticommunist propaganda machine (Saunders, 1999).

Evidence from the Soviet archives indicates that the officials responsible for the political repression of the 1930s sincerely felt the victims were guilty of some crime such as sabotage, spying, or treason (Thurston, 1996), and many of the executions of the Great Purge were reported in the local Soviet press at the time (Conquest, 1990). Even when there was proven to be no direct connection between the accused and the fascist foreign powers, there was often a strong belief that the suspects were foreign sympathizers who were working on their own (without formal direction) to contribute to the overthrow of the Soviet Union (Rittersporn, 1992). It should also be noted that much of the 1937-38 repression, often called the Great Purge, was actually directed against the widespread banditry and criminal activity (such as theft, smuggling, misuse of public office for personal gain, and swindles) that was occurring in the Soviet Union at the time (Getty, 1985). In addition to the executions, there were also many imprisoned, and hundreds of thousands of people were expelled from the Communist Party during the Great Purge for being incompetent, corrupt, and/or excessively bureaucratic, with such targeting of inept or dishonest Soviet bureaucrats being fairly popular among the average Soviet citizens (Davies, 1997).

Like the myths of millions of executions, the fairy tales that Stalin had tens of millions of people arrested and permanently thrown into prison or labor camps to die in the 1930-53 interval (Conquest, 1990) appear to be untrue. In particular, the Soviet archives indicate that the number of people in Soviet prisons, gulags, and labor camps in the 1930s, 1940s, and 1950s averaged about 2 million, of whom 20-40% were released each year, (Getty, Rittersporn, and Zemskov, 1993). This average, which includes desperate World War II years, is similar to the number imprisoned in the USA in the 1990s (Catalinotto, 1998a) and is only slightly higher as a percentage of the population.

It should also be noted that the annual death rate for the Soviet interned population was about 4%, which incorporates the effect of prisoner executions (Getty, Rittersporn, and Zemskov, 1993). Excluding the desperate World War II years, the death rate in the Soviet prisons, gulags, and labor camps was only 2.5% (Getty, Rittersporn, and Zemskov, 1993), which is even below that of the average "free" citizen in capitalist Russia under the czar in peacetime in 1913 (Wheatcroft, 1993). This finding is not very surprising, given that about 1/3 of the confined people were not even required to work (Bacon, 1994), and given that the maximum work week was 84 hours in even the harshest Soviet labor camps during the most desperate wartime years (Rummel, 1990). The latter maximum (and unusual) work week actually compares favorably to the 100-hour work weeks that existed even for "free" 6-year old children during peacetime in the capitalist industrial revolution (Marx and Engels, 1988b), although it may seem high compared to the 7-hour day worked by the typical Soviet citizen under Stalin (Davies, 1997).

In addition, it should also be mentioned that most of the arrests under Stalin were motivated by an attempt to stamp out civil crimes such as banditry, theft, misuse of public office for personal gain, smuggling, and swindles, with less than 10% of the arrests during Stalin's rule being for political reasons or secret police matters (Getty, Rittersporn, and Zemskov, 1993). The Soviet archives reveal a great deal more political dissent permitted in Stalin's Soviet Union (including a widespread amount of criticism of individual government policies and local leaders) than is normally perceived in the West (Davies, 1997). Given that the regular police, the political or secret police, prison guards, some national guard troops, and fire fighters (who were in the same ministry as the police) comprised scarcely 0.2% of the Soviet population under Stalin (Thurston, 1996), severe repression would have been impossible even if the Soviet Union had wanted to exercise it. In comparison, the USA today has many times more police as a percentage of the population (about 1%), not to mention prison guards, national guard troops, and fire fighters included in the numbers used to compute the far smaller 0.2% ratio for the Soviet Union.

In any event, it is possible that the communist countries of Eastern Europe would have become politically less repressive and more democratic (especially over time), if there hadn't been overt and covert efforts by capitalist powers to overthrow their governments (Blum, 1995), including subversion conducted in the USSR as late as the 1980s that the USA government admitted to in the 1990s (Chossudovsky, 1997). These efforts at violent subversion were initially carried out mostly by the British (before World War II) and then later more so by the USA through the CIA, which did succeed in one case in violently overthrowing a very democratic communist government in Chile in 1973 (Blum, 1995). If the communists had truly been as evil and dictatorial as they are portrayed to be in the capitalist press, the peaceful revolution of 1989 in Eastern Europe (with virtually no related deaths except in Romania) could never have occurred.

Moreover, it is far from clear whether the communist countries acted more repressively against people with capitalist views than capitalist countries have acted against communists (Schulz, 1982). Most who are not communists are probably not aware of the harassment, economic penalties (such as loss of a job for political reasons), torture, imprisonment, and murder that even goes on in developed capitalist countries, not to mention the atrocities that occur in less developed capitalist countries like Greece, Zaire, post-1973 Chile, etc. (Blum, 1995). Just as "ordinary Germans" in Hitler's Nazi Germany (i.e., those who weren't communists or other people that Hitler hated) "had little to fear from the Nazis" (Associated Press, 2000h), those who don't have communist views are often not affected by capitalist government repression, and so most don't feel threatened by it in any way. Nonetheless, despite the fact that political repression by modern capitalist states does not directly affect the majority of the population (just as Hitler's capitalist German government directly repressed only a minority of the German population), political repression by capitalist governments has claimed millions of victims, such as close to a million unarmed civilians with left-wing political views killed by a dictator put into power in Indonesia by the CIA in 1965-66 (Griswold, 1979), as previously mentioned in the Introduction.

In stark contrast to capitalism, there is long-term evidence from earlier cultures such as the North American Indians that communist societies can be very natural, free, and democratic (Novack, 1972). Some evidence on the relative attractiveness of these societies can be found from the fact that a large portion of white people taken prisoner by the

Indians in the USA willingly stayed with them and refused offers to return to the white capitalist society (Downes, 1940). Some of the initial Spanish explorers/conquerors of the Western Hemisphere reported that many of the Indians lived in a virtual communist paradise without shortages, money, government, or violence (Sale, 1991). Although some of the communist Indian tribes did engage in some limited fighting, especially when invaded, attacked, or threatened (Churchill, 1994), there were also many earlier communist peoples, such as the aborigines of Australia (Reynolds, 1995) and 70% of Indian tribes (Sale, 1991), who were almost completely pacifists. Even the Indian tribes that occasionally fought other tribes did so much less ferociously than capitalist societies and were "internally more peaceful" with far less crime (Jennings, 1993).

Ancient communal societies show that violence, crime, and wars are not innate to human nature but are instead the product of egotistical ideologies and systems such as capitalism (Marcy, 1990). For instance, capitalism in the USA promotes an unnatural self-centeredness that has resulted in a long history of engaging in extermination campaigns and other atrocities, as documented in the Introduction. In contrast, evidence of a modern communist country that remains somewhat democratic (despite the USA's enormous efforts to use virtually all possible means to overthrow it) is provided by the Cuban political system. Cuba not only allows free voting, but also has a procedure to allow for the recall of elected officials (that is often used effectively in practice against unpopular politicians), has the Cuban people themselves make political nominations (instead of political parties or the CIA), and prohibits candidates (or the CIA) from spending money on electoral campaigns (Scheffer, 1998).

Some evidence that capitalist countries are also far more imperialistic, militaristic, intolerant, and evil than modern communist countries has been discussed in the Introduction. A general analysis of these issues, especially with respect to the political repression of the capitalist superpower, the USA, is also provided by Schulz (1982), who documents some of the terrorism carried out by the nearly one million CIA agents worldwide that engage in scores of covert action each year to ensure the widespread existence of capitalist governments friendly to the USA. Further evidence is provided by Blum (1995), who describes the events around dozens of the over 400 military invasions and bombings conducted by the USA just since World War II (Wilson, 1999a) that have often led to severe political repression. That these imperialist actions are nothing new is documented by the *World Almanac* (1998) itself, which lists 23 separate USA military actions or "interventions" (mostly periodic Latin American invasions) that occurred in the 1900s before World War II (and that excludes the World War I related actions). Even before 1900, the USA had engaged in over 100 invasions to ensure USA control of (or influence over) many countries (Zinn, 1995).

In contrast to the widespread imperialism of the capitalist USA alone, there have been a mere 10 communist invasions of other countries. In addition, the USA's imperialist actions themselves at least partially justify four of the invasions by communist countries, with the only exceptions being Cambodia's invasion of Vietnam in the late 1970s (which was described earlier in the Introduction),[7] and the Soviet Union's invasion of 5 Baltic countries in the 1939-40 period as part of a deal with capitalist Germany for the USSR to reclaim land (and a defensive perimeter) lost in the 1918-22 Foreign Interventionist Civil War (Bullock, 1992). For instance, the Soviet invasions of Hungary in 1956 and Czechoslovakia in 1968 were motivated by paranoia surrounding the CIA's attempts to instigate revolts in those countries (Blum, 1995), while North Korea's invasion of South Korea in 1950 represented merely an escalation of the open border warfare that had been initiated by the South Korean dictatorship created by the USA (Ho Hui, and Ho, 1993). In addition, as previously mentioned, the Soviet invasion of Afghanistan in 1979 was conducted only after a terrorist war was launched against the established communist government by CIA-financed rebels, who were bought by the USA with billions of dollars in cash, additional drug trading profits, and a promise of a return to a fanatically religious feudal tyranny in order to deliberately provoke Soviet intervention (Feinberg, 1998). Longer-term evidence that capitalism in general has been causing an ever-increasing number of people to die in wars, even as a percent of the population, is provided by Urlanis (1971).

Myths About Communist Economic Inefficiency and Resource Misallocation

Besides falsely believing that communist countries violently kill far more people than capitalist countries, a large number of people (including many academics) also believe that communism has caused poverty and resource misallocation which are responsible for massive numbers of deaths relating to starvation and disease (MacFarquhar, 1993). In fact, the reverse is far closer to the truth. In particular, communism has saved hundreds of millions of lives through not only faster real income growth but also greater income equality. For example, not only did communist Eastern Europe grow more rapidly than capitalist countries (at the same time it had less income inequalities than capitalist countries),[9] but communist China has grown faster economically than any country in the world for some time. In particular, the average annual rate of growth in China was 12.1% for the period 1992-1996 and 7.3% for 1975-91, compared with an average of about 3% for capitalist countries (IMF, 1997b).[10] In addition, despite real income per capita still being only 1/7 that of the USA in 1991, less than 10% of the Chinese population lives in poverty (UN, 1994) compared to about 20% of the population in the much richer USA according to the UN (Associated Press, 1997). As a result of such successes, the annual death rate in China actually fell to about 1% of the population shortly after the communist revolution in China in 1949, which was far less than the 3% annual death rate that had previously existed in peaceful and famine-free times under capitalism (Deleyne, 1974). As documented in the Introduction, communism therefore actually resulted in the saving of over ten million lives per year in China, and the only exception was the interval 1958-61 when, due to horrible weather that caused a terrible famine, the death rate temporarily rose back close to the same level as it had previously been in normal times before communism. It should be mentioned that Chinese death rates during the 1958-61 catastrophe remained far below those reported by Ho (1959) for China during capitalist famines. Although inadequate storage and some mistakes made during the Great Leap Forward contributed to the human disaster in 1958-61, it is interesting that so many authors such as MacFarquhar (1993) blame communism for these deaths but ignore the fact that the death rate in these worst years under communism was comparable to the level in normal years under capitalism in China. Such biased authors also tend to ignore the fact that 35 million people die of hunger each year in the current capitalist world order (Flounders, 1998b).

Similar to the case of communist China, many falsely blame Stalin's

Soviet Union for over ten million famine-related deaths in the Soviet Union in the 1930s (Conquest, 1986), although the facts indicate Stalin and the Soviet Union actually saved the lives of millions of people. The 1930s in the Soviet Union represented a time of severe civil strife, widespread banditry, and even guerrilla warfare (Getty, 1985), which started when rich Russian farmers and rural merchants (called kulaks), who controlled most of the agricultural machinery and capital in the 1920s, and who often charged peasants interest rates of 100% or more for use of the needed equipment, sought to increase their profits by refusing to supply food to the cities at prices set by the government (Meurs, 1999). Stalin countered this attempt to extort higher prices with a collectivization of the farms that many farmers resisted.[11] The rich farmers and rural merchants themselves were initially allowed to join the collectives, but their resistance to the process later caused the government to assign most of these millions of people to jobs elsewhere (Conquest, 1986). Many were sent to other provinces, or to work camps, such as in Siberia, especially if there was evidence they been involved in the widespread activity of destroying food or committing sabotage in protest against collectivization (Campbell, 1974). Farmers indeed committed about 10,000 separate acts of terrorism (about half being violence against people and the other half being destruction of property) in each of the years 1929 and 1930 alone (Meurs, 1999).

Meanwhile, because of the frequent practice of farmers refusing to work and even destroying food, and because of bad weather, many farmers did not have enough food to make the mandatory sales of grain to the state at a fixed price (Conquest, 1986), with such sales representing a sort of land tax except that consumer goods were provided in return for the tax payment. Although the government procured less food than it had in the late 1920s to keep the city dwellers fed (Meurs, 1999), there was insufficient grain left for some farmers, and hunger and related disease existed in this environment, especially in the Ukraine in the early 1930s (Koenker and Bachman, 1997). Nevertheless, Tottle (1987) has documented an enormous body of evidence indicating that much of the information on the famine-related deaths are completely fraudulent or wildly exaggerated, with the sources of the false propaganda being Nazi Germany in the 1930s, rich anticommunist Americans, and various Ukrainians who fled to the West after collaborating with the

Nazis during Hitler's occupation in the early 1940s. For instance, many pictures alleged to have been taken of victims of the 1932-33 famine were actually from the famine that resulted from the 1918-22 civil war, and many of the stories were made up by people who had never even visited areas they claimed to have witnessed.

Despite these facts, Conquest (1986) claims that Stalin is responsible for about 15 million deaths in the 1930s. He bases his numbers on his citation that the Soviet population grew from 158 million to about 169 million between early 1930 and early 1939, whereas a population of 184 million would have been expected with a more "normal" population growth based on the growth rates of the late 1920s.[12] However, this computation ignores the fact that birth rates tend to be lower during periods of rapid industrialization (Schmid, 1998), such as during the 1930s in the Soviet Union. The erroneous population growth extrapolation also does not fully take into account the lower birth rate that can be expected to occur during periods of civil strife, famine, hunger, disease, and massive displacement of people, it fails to take into consideration the deaths stemming from armed conflict which included widespread guerrilla warfare and even an invasion by Japan in 1938 that had to be defeated by the Soviet Union (Conquest, 1986), and it ignores the fact that many left the Soviet Union as refugees from this situation (Nove, 1993). Wheatcroft (1993) provides concrete information on newborns in the Soviet Union, indicating that birth rates were about 1.5% lower in the 1932-36 interval than in the 1920s and were about 0.5% lower during the other years of the 1930s. These lower birth rates alone explain all of the lower growth in the population during the 1930s.[13]

With the exception of 1933, documented death rates in the Soviet Union averaged less than 2% per year in the 1930s and were even lower than the approximate 2% average death rate reported for the late 1920s (which was a time of relative tranquility), and the death rate of 3.7% reported for the catastrophic year of 1933 was very close to the annual death rate (also over 3%) in Russia under capitalism in 1913 (Wheatcroft, 1993), which had been a year of peace and an abnormally abundant harvest there.[14] Thus, it appears that, despite the tragic executions and famine, Stalin and communism actually saved millions of lives.

Myths About Specific Aspects of Communist Efficiency

Besides the widespread false impressions that exist about the general efficiency of communist countries like China and the Soviet Union, there seems to be a popular misconception about specific aspects of the economic efficiency of communism.[15] In particular, many people mistakenly believe that the communist economies must be inefficient based on an assumption that they do not allow for decentralized decision making and result in long waiting lines and shortages. Waiting lines, shortages, and waste did often exist in communist countries because the government purposely set the prices of many goods too low to clear (and also because richer capitalist countries placed embargoes on the export of the high technology goods to communist countries). However, the low fixed prices (and the right to a job with income) did ensure that everyone in communist countries had the right to essentials like food, housing, medicine, and clothes (aus erster Hand, 1987), unlike in capitalist countries where a large portion of the population do not have access to such essentials (Chossudovsky, 1997) even in far richer capitalist countries such as the USA (Strobel and Peterson, 1999). Also, the centralized fixing of prices greatly reduced the amount of time spent on wasteful tasks performed in capitalist countries of price shopping, price negotiation, and attempts to avoid marketing manipulation and fraud (Furlough and Strikwerda, 1999). The relative efficiency of centralized government administration can be seen by comparing government and private systems in the USA itself. For instance, in the insurance industry, expenses (administrative, marketing and other costs) as a percent of collected insurance premiums are only 1% for centralized government social security, whereas they amount to 50% for private insurance companies (Smith, 1994). The fact that private capitalist systems are actually outright counterproductive is easily illustrated with examples like chemical/pharmaceutical firms making money on treatments for cancers they themselves cause by failing to remove carcinogens from their chemical products (Phillips, 2000). Note that these inefficiencies and counterproductive activities enhance the reported income levels of the capitalist countries (since the extra insurance costs, sale of carcinogens, and cancer treatments all go into GDP income statistics), just as do the costs of the higher crime rates in capitalist countries that amount to about 10% of GDP in the USA (*US News & World Report*, 1994).

The overall relative inefficiency of capitalism was especially well demonstrated by Gorbachev's own capitalist reforms of the Soviet Union in the late 1980s under his Perestroika policies, which resulted in an increase in the number of administrators, greater white collar crime (as well as greater crime in general),[16] and lower economic growth (Marcy, 1990). The planning and administrative advantages of communism, combined with full employment and some economies of scale and scope, represent some of the reasons why communist countries did grow faster in real terms than capitalist countries, despite all the wars and other obstacles put in their way by the external environment. More specific analysis of these issues are provided later in Chapter 4 in a direct comparison of communist and capitalist financial systems in Germany.

IMPLICATIONS OF THE EMPIRICAL EXPERIENCES OF EASTERN EUROPE AND COMMUNISM

Overall, the facts indicate that communist systems serve their people far better than most give them credit. Despite their accomplishments, the communists lost the Cold War essentially because they started out so much poorer than their rich capitalist adversaries, and a few people took power who effectively surrendered.

Although there are only a few communist countries left in the world, the empirical experiences of Eastern Europe and other communist countries can be useful for providing some perspective on what might happen if a communist government were elected in a rich country such as the USA. In particular, given the prior accomplishments under communism, one might expect higher real income growth and less poverty. In addition, over 95% of the people would be better off if the transitory form of communism that existed in communist Eastern Europe were applied. For instance, in the USA, dividing 1999 Gross Domestic Product (GDP) by the number of people employed, the average income would be about $70,000 per worker.

In addition, under communism, taxes would probably be much lower, because there would be no need for the huge military spending now used to maintain USA world domination (Blum, 1995),[17] and because communist governments tend to be more efficient than their bureaucratic capitalist counterparts.[18] As in communist Eastern Europe, higher pay would be available to the most productive and skilled (implying over $150,000 in annual income being available to the most skilled in the USA), and so only the millionaires and billionaires would be economically worse off. The advantages of communism to an extremely large portion of the population becomes even more apparent when one considers the fact that it is substantially more likely for a middle class American to fall into poverty than to rise into the upper class (Strobel and Peterson, 1999), thus implying that communism may be desirable not only because it increases incomes for almost all Americans but also because it greatly reduces the undesirable downward component of income variation.[19]

Communism was theoretically and ideally designed to eventually eliminate the need for government, as capitalistic egoism was supposed to be slowly delearned after potentially hundreds of years of transitory communism or socialism, at which time all could share equally in consumption/income according to their need (Hahn, Kosing, and Rupprecht, 1983). If such a purer form of communism were applied that distributed GNP equally among all USA residents (not just the employed), each person would be entitled to about $35,000 per year, or about $140,000 annually for a family of four. Note that this latter calculation incorporates social security and similar transfer payments to retirees and others not working, and so an even smaller percentage of this latter income would be taken away in taxes. In addition, the latter figure might easily be 10-20% higher because cheap child care facilities and the availability of jobs for all under communism would increase employment and GDP. Some might assert that output might actually decline under pure communism without material incentives for harder work and productivity, largely because capitalist economists tend to view work as "irksome, involving 'disutility' that must be overcome by wages to secure the labor needed for production," but, in contrast, anthropologists (recognizing past cultures such as the aborigines and Indians to have thrived without such incentives) perceive work as "the fundamental condition of human existence ... through which the individual is able to define himself as a full and valued member of society" (Strobel and Peterson, 1999). One can observe from youth engaged in sport activities how natural it is to exhibit extreme exertion and enthusiasm without monetary rewards, so that it is certainly possible that several hundred years of communist society in transition would allow us adults to learn what is natural to youth (and past societies).

Regardless, through a great reduction in unemployment, poverty, crime, money anxieties, and social frictions, communism can permit a higher quality of life, more freedom, and greater individuality, just as it did in earlier communist societies (Zinn, 1995). A detailed, documented analysis of the advantages of communism (in transition) in the modern world (and a comparison with capitalism) is provided in the next chapter using the German case as an empirical example.

CHAPTER 2

AN POST-MORTEM COMPARISON OF COMMUNIST AND CAPITALIST SOCIETIES USING THE GERMAN CASE AS AN ILLUSTRATION

Many believe the collapse of East Germany represented evidence that the country's communist society was inferior to the West German capitalist one, insofar as the East German people did vote to replace their own system with the West German one in 1990. However, the voting was heavily biased by the greater riches offered by West Germany, and, contrary to popular myth (Christ, 1991) and related propaganda (Summer, 1994), these superior riches were not derived from the capitalist system itself but from the postwar treatment of Germany. This chapter uses the most recent data and information to show that, despite its very serious disadvantage of starting with much less wealth, the communist East German society was superior in many respects.

Dominating Influence of Mandatory East German Reparations Payments

Real income per capita started at a far lower level in East Germany because of reparations payments it had to make shortly after World War II, and, despite faster real economic growth in East Germany, it had not yet caught up with West German levels by 1989. In particular, in the 15 years after World War II, the Soviet Union extracted over 50 billion Marks in reparations from East Germany than West Germany paid (Apel, 1966). More recent West German government estimates of total East German reparations and other payments to the Soviet Union indicate a figure over 100 billion Marks (Merkel and Wahl, 1991), which represented several times tiny East Germany's National Income or annual output at the time of the payments (most of which occurred between 1945 and 1953). While West Germany also made some postwar payments related to Nazi Germany's atrocities and war defeat (including compensation to war victims), they were largely offset by Marshall Plan aid given to West Germany by the USA shortly after World War II (Apel, 1966). If East Germany had instead been able to invest the 100 billion Marks in reparations (starting in 1953 and reinvesting all capital and earnings each year) at its average 18% rate of return on investments (Naumann and Truempler, 1990), it would have compounded to give East Germans income per capita equal to about 15 times the level in West Germany in 1989.[1]

Instead, however, the enormous reparations caused East German income per capita to be only about 2/5 that of West Germany in the 1950s (Merkel and Wahl, 1991), although it had risen to 2/3 of the West German level by 1989 (Gregory and Stuart, 1995). It was the discrepancy in personal income arising from differences in reparations that had caused East Germany to build the Berlin Wall in 1961 in order to prevent its skilled workers (such as essential doctors and nurses) from being "bought" by the richer West Germany (Apel, 1966). In fact, before the Berlin Wall was erected, several million East Germans (especially skilled workers like doctors and engineers) moved to West Germany for the higher incomes available there, and this migration resulted in a large loss to the East German economy (Apel, 1966). Besides the large net migrations of people, black market activities and outright sabotage by both the CIA and West Germany also helped motivate the building of the Wall (Blum, 1995).

Given that East German income would have been higher than in West Germany without the reparations payments, it can be deduced that it would not have been necessary for East Germany to have the Berlin Wall if West Germany had made its share of the reparations payments for Nazi Germany's war crimes. In particular, the burden to East Germany would have thereby been enormously reduced and would have allowed its income to be substantially higher. At the same time, West Germany's income would have been reduced by it making its share of the payments. In this situation, it probably would not have been necessary for East Germany to have slightly longer work weeks (since it would not have been necessary to catch up with the West), nor to have such severe shortages (that could have been alleviated with greater wealth), nor to spend so little on pollution control (that reflected East Germany's relative poverty), nor to restrict political freedoms (that East Germany did not want the richer West Germany to take advantage of), nor to have such an obnoxious secret police (whose primary purpose was to keep East Germans from leaving the country for the greater riches of West Germany). All the relative disadvantages of communism in East Germany may therefore derive, at least partially, from its post-war reparations (and not from communism). Thus, it is possible to conclude that communism in East Germany was superior to capitalism in West Germany in all respects (except of course for the super rich, who would become less wealthy and powerful under communism).

A list of the relative advantages of each system is provided in Table 3, followed by a more general discussion.

TABLE 3

A LISTING OF THE RELATIVE ADVANTAGES OF COMMUNISM AND CAPITALISM IN GERMANY

Advantages of Communist Society	Western Advantages[a]
1. No unemployment	1. Shorter work hours[a]
2. No inflation	2. Fewer shortages[a]
3. No life-sustaining anxieties	3. Lower pollution[a]
4. More rights for women and children	4. Political freedom façade[a]
5. Equal educational opportunities	5. More travel freedom[a]
6. Socially more just	6. Less transparent police[a]
7. More natural	7. Greater wealth, i.e., escaped reparations[a]
8. Much less crime	
9. Less overall police control	
10. Not harassed by Western secret police	
11. Not as manipulated by the Western press	
12. Not manipulated by Western marketing	
13. No need to shop around for the best price	
14. Simpler tax system	
15. Faster economic growth	

a. Note that all of the advantages of capitalism in Germany stem at least in part from (or were made possible by) the greater beginning wealth of West Germany.

Advantage of East German Communism

1. No unemployment. The right to work at a job of one's own choice was guaranteed by the East German constitution (Aus erster Hand, 1987). While there were some (mostly alcoholics) who continuously refused to show up for jobs offered by the state, their numbers represented only about 0.2% of the entire East German work force, and only 0.1% of the scheduled work hours of the rest of the labor force was lost due to unexcused absences (Krakat, 1996). These findings are especially noteworthy, given that people were generally protected from being fired (or otherwise penalized) for failing to show up for work or for not working productively (Thuet, 1985). The importance of the communist characteristic of full employment to workers is reflected in a 1999 survey of eastern Germans that indicated about 70% of them felt they had meaningfully less job security in the unified capitalist country in the 1990s than they did in communist East Germany (Kramm, 1999)

2. No inflation. While there was a slight average annual inflation rate of 0.5% in the aggregate economy between 1960 and 1989, consumer prices were held constant over the 1960-1989 interval (Statistisches Amt, 1990). Even the inflation rate in the aggregate economy was 0% in East Germany's final decade, as admitted by the final East German government (Statistisches Amt, 1990),[2] which was both strongly anticommunist and formally allied/unified with the West German government (having been "elected" under heavy economic and political pressure from the West German government). While West German propagandists like Schwarzer (1999) admit that East German aggregate accounts were as accurate as West German ones, they often try to fabricate inflation in East Germany by citing the depreciation of the East German currency in the 1980s on the black markets (or in the context of a very narrowly traded basked of goods). Basing an aggregate inflation rate on such prices of a limited amount of goods in a very narrow market is not only absurd, it is also totally inconsistent with data on East German aggregate purchasing power, as reported by the West German government and various West German banks (Welfens, 1992), which indicate East German inflation figures to be accurate (as will be explained in more detail in Chapter 4).[3]

3. No life-sustaining anxieties. Food, apartments, children's clothing, day care, and mass transportation were heavily subsidized and therefore very cheap regardless of income (Collier, 1985). Work with income was guaranteed by the state as were living quarters (Aus erster Hand, 1987), and a person could not be thrown out of an apartment even if the person didn't pay the very trivial rent (Filmer and Schwan, 1985). All also had the right to free medical care, disability income, and retirement income (Aus erster Hand, 1987), and so it was not necessary for those needing round-the-clock care to burden relatives as 80% in West Germany do (Meyer and Schulze, 1998). A survey of eastern Germans indicated that 58% of the people felt social security is significantly worse in the united capitalist Germany than it had been in communist East Germany (Kramm, 1999).

4. More rights for women and children. Women had initial access to jobs at least as good as those of men in East Germany, although family considerations and other factors may have resulted in them not advancing as far as males later on in life (Voelker and Flap, 1999). Regardless, female employees were about 3 times more likely to hold skilled or white-collar jobs than working women in West Germany (Meyer and Schulze, 1998).

There existed extremely cheap day care in East Germany (open up to 12 hours a day), with 80% of East German children under 3 years of age, 95% of all 3-6 year-olds, and 80% of 6-10 year-olds (when not in regular school) being in nursery schools, kindergartens, or child care groups (Meyer and Schulze, 1998). Although it was not necessary for women to work (and a significant minority did not), the availability of reasonable child care made it much more feasible, with most mothers doing so in order to generate extra spending income for the family (Filmer and Schwan, 1985). Also contributing to more East German women working was the fact that mothers were given one work day a month off to do housework, and women were allowed unlimited work leave to take care of sick children (Meyer and Schulze, 1998). Moreover, a paid maternity leave of 6 months was available after the birth of the first child and up to one year for the second child (Falck, 1998). The maternity leave increased to 18 months for the third and all subsequent children (Schwarzer, 1999). In addition, the work week was shortened while vacation time was lengthened for mothers with more children (Falck, 1998). Also, the state bank offered cheaper credit to families with three or more children, with an interest rate of between 0% and 3%

depending on the number of children (instead of 4% to 6% otherwise), along with a standard 0.2% fee to cover defaults (i.e., a form of credit insurance), although 2% was added to the interest rate for late payments (Autorenkollektiv, 1988).

For older children, there were many sports, cultural, and study activities organized by East German government-sponsored groups like the young pioneers and the Free German Youth. In addition, special holiday facilities existed for children. After unification, these organizations, activities, and facilities were closed down (as such unprofitable things do not exist in the united capitalist Germany), and "children are often left on their own in the afternoons and during the holiday periods" (Meyer and Schulze, 1998).

5. Equal educational opportunities for all. There was no tuition for college, and a living allowance was provided by the state to students without any future debt obligations (Aus erster Hand, 1987). While a small minority of East Germans feel that the educational system is better in the unified Germany, far more eastern Germans (more than double) believe the educational system under communist rule was superior (Kramm, 1999).

6. Socially more just. The difference between high and low wealth levels was much lower than in capitalist countries (thus resulting in no major differences in social class based on wealth), at least partially because of state regulation of wages, which along with all the foregoing social security benefits ensured no true poverty in East Germany (Dietz, 1983). In addition, it was generally almost impossible to become extremely wealthy in East Germany because of 90% tax rates on high levels of profits and because of restrictions on the size of private firms (Buero des Ministerrates, 1970). Such restrictions might represent a disadvantage for a small minority of super rich, but it would not be relevant to the vast majority of people.[4]

7. More natural. The communist system resulted in more natural human relationships. This greater naturalness was reflected in the results of a survey of eastern Germans, who indicated that most felt more comfortable under the old communist system there than under capitalist unification (Kramm, 1999). In particular, the communist East German society was not so plagued by the capitalistic characteristic of personal greed above everything (Aus erster Hand, 1987).

However, relationships were sometimes artificially used for material gain to obtain goods and services in short supply in East Germany, as noted by Voelker and Flap (1997), who conducted a survey that touched on this issue. Their survey indicated that both relatives and "co-workers" actually provided more such material access than "friends." If friendship had truly been based on such material advantages, then the result would have been the opposite (as more friends would have been deliberately chosen that provided such material advantages). This finding is consistent with the hypothesis that any material advantages of true friendship in East Germany may have been the byproduct of the friendship as opposed to the cause. The survey also indicated that people considered to be mere superficial "acquaintances" or "neighbors" played a much smaller role in assisting with access to goods and services in short supply, as would be consistent with a hypothesis that East Germans did not cultivate superficial relationships to gain material advantages.

It should be mentioned that the primary purpose of Voelker and Flap (1997)'s survey was apparently to support a biased opinion/hypothesis that East Germans were unfriendly to their neighbors. However, the two Western researchers were only able to provide supporting evidence for their ridiculous hypothesis by effectively having any neighbors considered to be friends removed from the sample of neighbors (as they themselves admitted in a footnote).

"Friendliness" was generally not a commodity that was "sold" in East Germany, and so East German cashiers, waiters, waitresses, and salespeople in general were actually considered to be rude by foreigners (Filmer and Schwan, 1985), at least partially because of their honest naturalness and lack of superficiality. Perhaps in reflection of this fact, a survey asking East Germans which of 16 different characteristics that they find most important in a partner (such as "loving father/mother," "loyalty," and "has intellectual interests," all three of which ranked highly) indicated the attribute of "has a highly paid job" ranked the absolute lowest in importance, while "has an attractive appearance" ranked fourth from the bottom (Edwards, 1985).

Moreover, Falck (1998) reports in a well-documented book that the greater equality of treatment of men and women in East Germany, and a more natural set of official morals with respect to sex resulted in less conflict between men and women, virtually no prostitution, far less incidence of sexual perversion, and women who were considered by many foreigners to be both more pleasant and more intelligent than in capitalist countries. Also contributing here was the lack of stress with respect to job security, fewer financial worries, and no life-sustaining money anxieties, which also resulted in the well-documented fact that East Germans engaged in sex much more frequently (and with more sexual partners on average) than West Germans (dpa, 1990b). Another study indicated that East German women typically enjoyed sex much more (with a 70% orgasm rate), at least partially because communism allowed East German women to feel equal, far more independent, and far less oppressed (Kleinschmid, 1985).

8. Much less crime. Narcotics were almost nonexistent in East Germany, although there were some illegal homemade drug concoctions, such as combining legal alcoholic beverages with legal tranquilizers and even mixing a detergent with cola (Leopold, 1985). Regardless, murder and violence were rare, and theft was much less prevalent than in the capitalist countries (Diedrich, Ehlert, and Wenzke, 1998). For instance, in 1988, there were 7 criminal acts per thousand residents in East Germany compared to 71 per thousand residents in West Germany (Northoff, 1995). As a result, a 1999 survey of eastern Germans indicated that 81% felt less secure from crime in the unified capitalist Germany than in communist East Germany (Kramm, 1999). An American woman visiting East Germany in the 1980s was astounded that she could actually walk the streets alone at night without any fear (Filmer, 1985a).

9. Less overall police control. For instance, the amount spent per capita on police, secret police, and public security was less in East Germany than in West Germany. In particular, such spending by East Germany was $225 per East German citizen in 1989 (Diedrich, Ehlert, and Wenzke, 1998), using the official exchange rates which approximated purchasing power exchange rates (Collier, 1985), while spending by West Germany on internal security was about $264 per citizen in the same year (Statistisches Bundesamt, 1996).[5]

It should be mentioned that about 1/5 of the total police, secret police, and public security personnel in East Germany were actually heavily-armed military troops (primarily trained to fight armed enemy infiltrators, paratroopers, and saboteurs), whereas all West German military formations are paid for out of defense spending as opposed to public security spending (Diedrich, Ehlert, and Wenzke, 1998). In addition, the East German figures include foreign espionage spending, which is included in West Germany as a separate (and secret) budgeted amount estimated to be about $8 per capita (Schmidt-Eenboom, 1995). Thus, per capita spending figures for East Germany that would be more comparable might be $225x{1-.20}=$180, or about 2/3 that of West Germany's $264+$8=$272. Given that East German income per capita was about 2/3 that of West Germany's in 1989 (Gregory and Stuart, 1995), it can be concluded that East Germany spent about the same percentage of National Income as West Germany.

It should be mentioned that over half of East German spending on internal security was for secret police (Diedrich, Ehlert, and Wenzke, 1998), which was perceived to be needed to defend against the stated intent of the much larger and richer West Germany to take over East Germany (von Schnitzler, 1992). As a result, there were more secret police than other police in East Germany (Diedrich, Ehlert, and Wenzke, 1998). In particular, in 1987, there were 91,015 secret police compared to 15,646 regular police, 6226 police liaisons with neighborhood watch groups, 8294 criminal police, and 6212 traffic cops (with all these figures including supporting administrative personnel). Also included in the East German internal security figures were 31,555 full-time national guard troops (consisting of 11,000 members of a Stasi "Wachregiment" already included in the 91,015 secret police population, 14,115 "Bereitschaftpolizei," and 6400 "Transportpolizei"). There was a total of 8526 prison guards and 3377 immigration officers (as well as almost 10,000 more of the 91,015 secret police who were directly involved in emigration/immigration tasks) also in East German internal security. There were 15,129 security guards (and supporting administrative personnel) in East Germany whose costs are not included in the internal security spending (just as amounts for security guards in West Germany are separately budgeted, there as private business expenditures). Overall, actual secret and other police, prison guards, security guards, and supporting administrative personnel represented about 0.8% of the East German population (with national guard troops and immigration officers representing a further 0.3% of the population).

10. Not harassed by the Western secret police. The all-powerful West German secret police (which inherited Hitler's organization, people, and laws) harassed many people (especially West Germans) with left-wing political opinions, using tactics like entrapment, spreading false rumors, and causing people to lose their jobs (Schulz, 1982), but the East German secret police severely restricted these illegal, harassing activities against East Germans in East Germany. However, the West German and allied secret police were able to tap some phones and open some mail in East Germany (Staadt, 1998), and the East German secret police itself did harass many of its own citizens, especially if they applied to emigrate to West Germany (Henke and Engelmann, 1995).[6] In addition, for a large number of the annual 15 million visits of East Germans to West Germany in the late 1980s (Murphy, 1992b), a secret police security check was required (Diedrich, Ehlert, and Wenzke, 1998). Nonetheless, it must be emphasized that the tactics of the East German secret police generally consisted of openly attempting to persuade people not to take actions that damaged the State (Riecker, Schwarz, and Schneider, 1990), and that tactic was in stark contrast to the West German secret police strategy of doing everything possible to penalize people for any anti-government opinions (Schultz, 1982).

11. Not as manipulated by the Western press. The Western press is heavily influenced throughout the world by the CIA and rich capitalists (Blum, 1995), but there is an especially strong manipulation by the CIA in West Germany (Agee and Wolf, 1975). In addition, the German media is strongly tied to the big-business-oriented Christian Democratic Party (*Der Spiegel*, 1994). While the East German press was strongly ideological and controlled by the government (and thus had its own manipulative bias), that press provided an alternative to the propaganda of West German television, which could be watched by most East Germans, except soldiers and about 15% of East Germans who were out of the West German television range (Filmer and Schwan, 1985).

12. Not manipulated by Western marketing. Prices were determined in East Germany by administrators largely based on cost, although unmanipulated demand and need factors were also considered for many products (Steudtner, Hempel, and Ulrich, 1988). As a result, there were more rational and objective prices, since the people were not manipulated by the advertisements and marketing gimmicks of capitalism.

In comparison capitalist value and price, are determined by how much someone can be convinced to pay for something. For instance, if someone persuades another person to pay $1000 for something totally worthless like a handful of pebbles, the value of this worthless item in capitalism is $1000 regardless of whether the buyer later figures out the stones are worthless. Although capitalist swindles are common, a much more subtle form of distorting value occurs even more frequently (and almost continuously) in capitalism (Furlough and Strikwerda, 1999). In particular, through advertising, sales people, and marketing, it is possible to get consumers to pay much more for the same product, or even buy an inferior (or worthless) product for a higher price. One classic illustration of this phenomenon that is glorified as a genius of capitalist marketing (and even taught in marketing classes at USA universities) is the case of Gary Dahl selling 1.3 million worthless pebbles for $4 a piece as "pet rocks" (Scripps Howard News Service, 1999). Another example is with breakfast cereal. The major brandname cereals usually cost far more than for a generic breakfast cereal of approximately the same type, and these high-priced brandname cereals have about 90% of the market share (Gibson and Ono, 1996). So the market "value" of a good in capitalism can be greatly increased by advertising and other psychological manipulation (Green, 1999), with such marketing strategies being so effective that over 90% of the people are willing to pay the higher "value".

As a result of such potential to exploit consumers and confiscate their money through excess charges (Furlough and Strikwerda, 1999), an enormous amount of resources is spent in capitalism for marketing that manipulates people and distorts reality, with marketing (including retailing) expenses making up half of the cost of the average consumer good (Pride and Ferell, 1997). While marketing can provide valuable information, entertainment, and even positive psychological feelings, it is often difficult, time-consuming, annoying, and mentally disturbing to try to differentiate the manipulative and reality-distorting aspects of marketing from its positive characteristics. Thus, it is unclear whether capitalist marketing creates any net positive value much less covers its enormous cost. Nonetheless, this cost is incorporated into the price of goods and is therefore effectively paid for by consumers whether they like it or not (unless they are willing to expend the enormous amount of time and energy required to sift through the distortions, find and investigate alternatives, and take risks with unfamiliar products/companies).

Some evidence of the net negative effect created by capitalist marketing is provided by the great effort and cost so many people incur to avoid advertising, telephone sales pitches, and general marketing manipulation (Kaufman, 2000). A more subtle (and potentially more damaging) negative effect of capitalist marketing is the "pushing" of products with actual negative long-term value, as exemplified by the unhealthy obesity which is rapidly growing in the current capitalist marketing environment that "encourages us to eat food high in calories and fat" (Winslow, 1999). The fact that capitalist marketing also has the negative effect of keeping good products out of the market is illustrated by the statement made by manager Mark Greenberg, "You can have a good product, but if you don't have good marketing and a good brand name, your're toast" (Kiplinger's, 2000).

13. No need to shop around for the best price. The prices of goods or services of the same type and quality were the same everywhere in East Germany. Although it was often necessary in East Germany to shop around for available goods (Filmer and Schwan, 1985), although used goods were sometimes the only ones that could be found, and although lines to buy goods at East German stores were typically longer than the check-out lines at West German stores, many of the new goods in short supply were readily available without waiting at the very expensive East German exquisite shops (Falck, 1998). Whenever East Germans had the choice of paying higher prices or waiting in line, the latter choice was usually considered superior, especially since it was possible to read or socialize while waiting in line (whereas it is more difficult to engage in other activities simultaneously when engaging in the price/quality shopping necessary in capitalism that requires greater concentration and effort).

14. Simpler tax system for individuals. The state withheld about 15% from wages (up to a maximum of 25% for higher wage-earners) without the need for filing a tax form (*Buero des Ministerrates,* 1966). On the other hand, for private companies, which could exist with 10 or fewer employees, taxes on profits were levied at a steeply progressive rate that reached 90% for income over 250,000 Marks (Buero des Ministerrates, 1970), which was about $150,000 at official exchange rates.

15. Faster real economic growth rate. East Germany's national income grew in real terms about 2% faster annually than the West German economy between 1961 and 1989, as documented in Chapter 4 of this book.[7] However, because the very large reparation payments made by East Germany to the Soviet Union after World War II had caused it to start at a much lower level, it had not yet caught up by the 1980s, being only about 2/3 that of West Germany's at that time (Gregory and Stuart, 1995).

ADVANTAGES OF WEST GERMAN CAPITALISM

1. Shorter work hours. The West German work week was 2 hours shorter, and the West Germans had slightly more paid vacation days and holidays per year (Osmond, 1992). However, it should be mentioned that the East German workers actually had more free time than the average worker in the far richer USA (largely because Americans generally have fewer paid vacation days). In addition, even the apparent relative advantage for capitalist West Germany here may in fact be only on paper, as a 1999 survey indicated that, despite the high level of unemployment in the unified country, more eastern Germans felt they had a greater amount of free time under the old communist system than they do in the unified capitalist Germany (Kramm, 1999). This conflicting survey result may stem from "voluntary" overtime, work brought or conducted at home, and other activities (including work planning and worrying, as well as very stressful job searching) that is not counted in the official work week.

2. Fewer shortages. Waiting lines at West German stores tend to be shorter than those that existed in East Germany. However, one needs to have more money to buy the goods in West Germany, and often it is necessary to do a lot of time-consuming price shopping in order to keep the price from being even higher (Statistisches Bundesamt, 1996). Similarly, in East Germany, there were exquisite shops where goods in short supply elsewhere were easily obtainable at very high prices (Falck, 1998).

Some evidence on the relative time costs of shopping for the best price and availability does exist. For instance, the unified German government has estimated that, under the capitalist system, shopping alone takes up about 15 minutes per day of the average German's time (Statistisches Bundesamt, 1997), which comes to almost 100 hours per year. This figure approximately equals the average number of hours that was spent per capita waiting in line in the communist Soviet Union (Freeze, 1997). It should also be mentioned that the highly centralized and regulated German capitalist system has less competitive pricing practices than more decentralized capitalist systems like in the USA (and so shopping probably takes less time in capitalist Germany than in other capitalist countries), while the Soviet Union probably had longer waiting lines than more efficient and more prosperous communist systems like in East Germany (and so shopping in the communist Soviet Union probably took more time than in other communist countries like East Germany). Thus, it is far from clear that shopping takes more time under the average capitalist system than under the average communist system (without even considering the advantages of communist marketing systems in avoiding the manipulation and fraud that exists in capitalist systems).

Some evidence on this issue directly comparing communist East Germany with capitalist West Germany is provided by Meyer and Schulze (1998). These researchers found that East German families spent less time on housework (including normal shopping but excluding child care upon which East Germans spent substantially less time) than West Germans, despite the fact that East Germans tended to have less access to some household automation (like microwave ovens) and personal transportation (although they did have greater access to inexpensive meals at work which reduced household tasks related to preparing meals). One of the primary time-consuming activities avoided in East Germany was the need to "hunt for bargains and compare prices, quality, and quantity."

A much more important difference existed with respect to the shortage of specific goods and services in East Germany. In particular, there was at least a 10-year waiting time between ordering and receiving a new car (Filmer and Schwan, 1985), and there was a similar wait with respect to a telephone connection in East Germany (Schwarzer, 1999). The system was not actually as incredibly inconvenient as it seems, as it was always possible to buy a used car in East Germany, and there were also ways to obtain a new car in a timely fashion by ordering it 10 years before one had the money available (or having relatives or friends do so 10 years before a child was of driving age). Given that a 25% subsidy from the state significantly reduced the cost of new cars (ADN, 1990), and given that East Germans had about half as many cars as West Germans (Mueller, 1996), the shortage of cars was not nearly as terrible as it may have seemed, especially since East Germany had an extremely cheap but effective mass transportation system (Welfens, 1992). Although the telephone shortage created a more difficult problem, East Germans were able to use inexpensive public pay telephones somewhat effectively, and the cost of telephone service (when finally obtained) was reasonably cheap in comparison to the capital costs of supplying it (Schwarzer, 1999).

It should also be mentioned that many services like repairs had to be requested weeks in advance in East Germany (Filmer and Schwan, 1985). The latter situation motivated many to learn to perform their own services and repairs (just as the high cost of services and repairs in West Germany motivated many to do their own work in those areas).

3. Lower levels of pollution. Because of its relative poverty, East Germany spent less on pollution control than in the richer West Germany (Gregory and Leptin, 1977), as is typical of poorer countries (such as Mexico and Hong Kong) whose people normally value higher consumption of goods over a cleaner environment (Robitaille, 2000). Just for example, one study indicated that the workers of the most polluted city of eastern Germany (Bitterfeld) were ready "to accept environmental pollution" as a price for maintaining their jobs, and the unified capitalist German government itself placed very low priority on pollution problems in eastern Germany, as illustrated by it budgeting only 671 million Marks on pollution control in eastern Germany in the first year after unification, compared to East Germany spending over 2 billion Marks on pollution control in its final year (Welfens, 1992).[8] In fact, despite the closing of so much of East German industry shortly after unification in 1990, the pollutant most dangerous to local human health (sulfur oxide) actually rose in eastern Germany in 1991 from the level in 1989 even though some higher spending by East Germany in its final year had significantly reduced the emissions in 1990 from the 1989 level (Buck, 1996).[9] It should also be mentioned that there is little evidence that the pollution in East Germany had a deadly impact, given that the death rates in the most polluted areas of the country were lower than in the less polluted areas (*Der Tagesspiegel,* 1990m).

4. Political freedom façade. The West German system created the façade of democracy by publicly allowing the formation of different political parties, and that appeared to compare favorably with East Germany, where one needed to obtain permission from the government to start a new political party. However, the West German government can and has outlawed some peaceful political parties and organizations that are not perceived to be consistent with the capitalist order, such as numerous pacifist groups and a fairly popular West German communist party in the 1950s (Angenfort, 1996). Thus, despite the façade of greater political freedom in West Germany, there is a trivial difference in practice between East Germany's requirement to obtain permission to form a political party and West Germany's right to disallow any political parties or organizations it chooses (except that the West German system creates more risks to founder activists with respect to expending the time/money in starting up an organization that is only later ruled to be "verboten").

For instance, in anticipation of unification, the former communist party of East Germany (relabeled the Party of Democratic Socialism from the Socialist Unity Party) revised its platform to meet the constitutional requirements of the united Germany that were the same as in West Germany, which merely annexed East Germany in 1990 (von Schnitzler, 1992). Despite the changes made by the party to be in favor of a market-oriented economic system, to respect private property, and to endorse capitalist-style elections, many German anticommunists believe the party should be outlawed (*Economist,* 1996). The primary reason appears to be because a fraction of the members of the Party of Democratic Socialism (PDS) are openly communists (Autorenkollektiv, 1995), and because financial and other harassment has failed to eliminate the party's popularity (*Economist,* 1995).

Similarly, West Germany also appears freer with respect to making or writing statements about the government, but there are actually laws in West Germany that prohibit slandering government rulers, just as such laws existed in East Germany but were rarely enforced. In addition, although demonstrations are widely thought of as being tolerated in West Germany, there is substantial evidence of police and social repression of demonstrations in West Germany (*Hamburger Abendb-*

latt, 1992). On the other hand, the massive peaceful demonstrations in East Germany in the fall of 1989 (as will be described in Chapter 3) indicate substantially less repression there than is normally assumed, and dissent on particular issues was freely allowed in East Germany insofar as petitions could be (and often were) collected and sent to the East German government for action (Philipsen, 1993).[10] It should also be emphasized that, in capitalist West Germany, only the rich have sufficient money to make their statements or writings sufficiently publicized to have a widespread effect on others' opinions, and it has been well-established that West German elections are controlled by marketing, money, and personalities (Schumacher, 1998).

Moreover, communists are not legally allowed to have jobs in the West German government bureaucracy (von Schnitzler, 1992), and West German businesses (being invariably owned by rich anticommunists) often follow the government's example, thereby virtually prohibiting working people from publicly stating communist opinions in capitalist West Germany (unless there were a few tolerant rich business owners with job openings).[11] A more general form of extortion also exists insofar as rich capitalists often threaten to eliminate jobs (by taking capital out of the country) if a socialist government is elected, and this threat of unemployment is made very clear to the working masses in capitalist societies (Copeland, 2000).

Despite these facts, and despite the fact that the established, ruling West German political parties are widely perceived to be "clubs for a political class that makes its own rules" (Rohwedder, 2000), West German elections are generally held to be more democratic than East German ones. Nevertheless, it should be mentioned that East Germany also had multiple political parties, although they voluntarily formed into a united National Front shortly after World War II to create a coalition bloc designed to prevent a reelection of the capitalist Nazis (Weber, 1988). East Germany also permitted voters to cast secret ballots and always had more then one candidate for each government position (Honecker, 1994). Although election results typically resulted in over 99% of all votes being for candidates or parties that did not favor revolutionary changes in the East German system (just as West German election results generally resulted in over 99% of the people voting for non-revolutionary West German capitalist parties),[12] it was always possible to change the East German system from within the established political parties (including the communist party), as those parties were open to all and encouraged participation in the political process (Filmer and Schwan, 1985). The ability to change the East German system from within is best illustrated by the East German leader who opened up the Berlin Wall and initiated many political reforms in his less than two months in power (Krenz, 1990).

The East German political system was actually more democratic than the West German one in at least two respects. In particular, only East Germany allowed voters to cast votes against the system, and thousands did so at each election (Weber, 1988). Moreover, only East Germany had a free referendum approving its constitution (von Schnitzler, 1992). In addition, the East German political system may have actually resulted in less corruption, since, despite a great deal of West German propaganda to the contrary, the opened East German records indicate far less evidence of bribery and use of a position for personal gain than exists in West Germany (Honecker, 1994).[13]

Nevertheless, after being bombarded with capitalist propaganda (and welfare) for almost a decade, only 20% of East Germans believe the old communist political system was superior, although over 30% believe they are about the same, and less than a majority believe the "democracy" of unified Germany is better than the communist system (Kramm, 1999). Overall, there is actually some question as to whether there is more honest freedom from repression in capitalist Germany, especially given a 1993 survey which indicated that more East Germans felt safer from state infringements in their lives in 1988 under the communist East German government than they did in the 1990s under the united capitalist rule (Northoff, 1995).

5. More travel freedom. West Germans had greater freedom to travel to more countries, at least for those West Germans with sufficient money to be able to afford to travel. However, East Germans had a substantial amount of travel freedom within the vast expanse of Eastern Europe, where travel costs were subsidized by the East German government, especially for youth (Aus erster Hand, 1987), and where vacation travel within East Germany was very heavily subsidized for workers (Filmer and Schwan, 1985). It should also be mentioned that most East Germans were allowed to travel to the West after a long application process and security check (Diedrich, Ehlert, and Wenzke, 1998). In addition, the delay and security check for such travel did not exist for retirees (over 65), who were allowed 30 days of unrestricted stay in the West annually (Filmer and Schwan, 1985). Nevertheless, over 90% of East Germans feel they have greater freedom of travel in the unified Germany than under communist rule (Kramm, 1999), with this clear increase in freedom stemming not only from the opening of the Wall but also from the higher level of income (derived via the huge transfer payments from western Germany) that makes travel more feasible financially.

6. Less transparent police. Although the West German secret police is scarcely noticeable to those with conservative or no political opinions, the West German secret police can be at least as harassing as the East German one for people with the "wrong" left-wing opinions, often inflicting serious damage such as causing a person the loss of a precious job (Schulz, 1982). It should also be mentioned that the regular West German police had such a close relationship with the main branch of the West German secret police (the Verfassungsschutz or "Constitutional Protection") that one West German police insider stated, "One never sees the borders between the Constitutional Protection and the regular police" (*Der Spiegel,* 1992b).

It should also be mentioned that stories related by victims indicate that the repression of the East German secret police was not nearly as terrible as its reputation and generally only occurred in cases of clear law violations or repeated attempts to undermine the East German government (Furian, 1991). Most of the East German secret police's activities were related to security checks involving applications to visit West Germany (Diedrich, Ehlert, and Wenzke, 1998). In fact, of the arrests made by the East German secret police between 1985 and 1988, about 50% were for illegally attempting to emigrate to West Germany, about 20% were for threatening East Germany and its employees (mostly for delaying or refusing an application to emigrate), and about 20% were for working with West German organizations (often to publicly embarrass or otherwise pressure East Germany into allowing them to emigrate), while only about 5% were for treasonous offenses (such as committing sabotage or spying for West Germany), and only 11 (about 0.1% of arrests) were for making public slanderous statements against East

Germany or its leaders (Henke and Engelmann, 1995).

Some East Germans actually felt they had more freedom of speech under communism because, unlike in capitalist West Germany, they felt they could say whatever they wanted without fear of losing their job (Eckart, 1984). However, a majority of East Germans believe they have greater freedom of speech in the unified Germany than they did in communist East Germany (Kramm, 1999). The latter survey results were probably at least partially related to the deliberate transparency of the East German secret police methods which made more people aware of the restrictions on freedom of speech (and possibly also related to the fact that many people in eastern Germany don't have a job and don't realize the job-related penalties which can occur when one says the "wrong" thing).

7. Higher income and wealth (i.e., escaped reparations). As previously mentioned at the beginning of this chapter, West Germany was richer than East Germany. This advantage (like the others indirectly) derived directly from the relative post-war treatment of the two Germanies and not from the type of economic system. In particular, West Germany escaped from having to pay reparations for the crimes committed by capitalist Nazi Germany as a whole against the Soviet Union.

The dominating importance of this factor can be seen from the fact that the flow of people from eastern to western Germany continued unabated even after West Germany annexed East Germany in 1990 (Statistisches Bundesamt, 1996), even after the two areas became virtually identical except in terms of relative income, and even after the massive welfare payments made to the eastern Germans narrowed the income differential. Because capitalist unification in 1990 had destroyed the East German economy, reducing gross national product (GNP) by over 40% (Osmond, 1992), and putting over half the population there out of work, western Germany had to make enormous transfer payments to the eastern part to keep incomes above the levels under communism (Rohwedder, 1996). As mentioned in the introduction to this chapter, the communist system could have grown to being vastly richer than the West German capitalist one if it had not had to make the enormous reparations payments to the Soviet Union, and it certainly could have created far more wealth and income with the large transfer payments of the 1990s than has been the case under capitalist transformation of East Germany (as will be documented in Chapters 4 and 5).

CONCLUSION

Given that virtually all the advantages of West Germany stem from the external postwar treatment of Germany (and given that some of the West German advantages are mere façades), communism dominates capitalism in virtually all respects. This hypothesis is consistent with a survey finding 10 years after the Berlin Wall opening indicating that only 45% of eastern Germans in 1999 feel that capitalist "democracy" is better than the old communist system (Associated Press, 1999c), despite the massive transfer payments (or bribes) to eastern Germans and despite the fact that the capitalist German propaganda machine has continuously blamed communism for East Germany's relative poverty while largely ignoring the true cause (i.e., the massive post-war reparations forced on East Germany alone).[14]

Nevertheless, it is possible that the average East German is at least intuitively aware of the long-term superiority of their system. For instance, a 1999 survey indicated that 67% of East Germans feel the future perspective for the coming generations was better under communism than it was under the unified capitalist Germany (Kramm, 1999), even though 70% of East Germans believe the advantages of unification currently outweigh the disadvantages, mostly because of the improved living standards brought on by the merger with (and welfare payments from) the richer western Germany (Associated Press, 1999c).

Further evidence on this issue is provided by the unbiased survey conducted in mid-December 1989 after the East Germans had been well exposed to the riches of the West without having the reparations reason for their relative poverty explained to them. At that time, the vast majority (over 70%) of the East Germans were in favor of maintaining a socialist system and of maintaining a separate East German country (Bahrmann and Links, 1994). Only after the East German economy and morale were destroyed by a 3:1 exchange rate (that was artificially created on January 1, 1990 and that was ridiculous in comparison to the greater purchasing power of the East German currency) and only after the West German currency and riches were promised immediately to the East Germans in return for a unification vote, did the majority of

East Germans favor unification and capitalism. A detailed analysis of the events of 1989-90 that led to German unification is provided in the next chapter.

CHAPTER 3

A DETAILED AUTOPSY OF THE COLLAPSE OF THE SUPERIOR SYSTEM IN THE DIVIDED GERMANY

Before describing the incredible events of 1989-90 that resulted in the collapse of East Germany and the defeat of communism in the Cold War, it is first necessary to provide some historical background on the situation. Germany had been split into two parts since World War II, and this division was to continue until the revolution of 1989.

Historical Background on the Most Incredible Revolution of our Time

In World War II, Nazi Germany fought a two-front war against the communist Soviet Union on the eastern front and against the capitalist USA and its allies on the western front. Fighting between the capitalist USA and the capitalist Nazis was fairly limited until very late in the war, and Nazi Germany committed 80% of its military strength on the Eastern Front (Becker, 1997a) where over 3 million of its own soldiers died (well over 80% of its total losses in the war) along with approximately 1 million soldiers of its satellite allies (Krivosheev, 1997). While the war never even touched any formal state of the USA, and while the number of Americans who died in that war was counted in the hundreds of thousands, approximately 20 million Soviets lost their lives in the fight against Germany, and their country was badly destroyed by the Nazi invasion.[1]

By the time the war had ended in 1945, Soviet troops had occupied the eastern part of Germany, while the Americans and their capitalist allies (primarily the British and the French) had occupied the western portion of Germany. Because of differences in the ideologies of the USA and the Soviet Union, the two major occupying powers were unable to agree on a peace treaty that would unite Germany back into one country (Autorenkollektiv, 1966). Instead, the eastern portion of Germany developed into a country with its own communist government, while the western portion of Germany developed into a country with its own capitalist government. The eastern German country was called the German Democratic Republic (GDR), or East Germany for short. The western German country was called the Federal Republic of Germany (FRG), or West Germany for short.

West Germany was several times the size of East Germany in terms of land and population. In its constitution (which was created under USA supervision and never approved by German voters), West Germany claimed that it was the sole legitimate government of the German people, which included people in both East and West Germany (von Schnitzler, 1992). According to the West German constitution, East Germany did not exist as a real country, but instead was merely an area of their country that was temporarily under Soviet occupation (Apel, 1966).

Although East Germany was labeled communist, the country would probably be more accurately called a socialist nation in transition toward communism. According to the philosophy of Karl Marx, communism represents a system where wealth is distributed according to need, and such a system can be achieved only after a long period of socialism where the central government controls all wealth but distributes it to people based on work performance (Hahn, Kosing, and Rupprecht, 1983). There were numerous political parties represented in the East German parliament, but the leadership role of the East German Socialist Unity Party was grounded in the East German constitution which had been approved by East German voters (Dietz, 1983).

Despite East German offers to create a united neutral confederation between the two German states in the 1950s (such as on the same basis as had been successfully implemented for the united neutral Austria), West Germany refused to compromise on its goal for outright annexation of East Germany (Hoffman, 1990). As a result, the two Germanies remained separate for over 40 years. Their separation was a product of the Cold War between the capitalist Western countries (led by the United States) and the communist Eastern countries (led by the Soviet Union). In fact, Germany served as a main battlefront for the Cold War, which was waged with economic and political weapons as opposed to military means.[2] Both sides in the Cold War used every available political and economic tool to improve their own situation and reputation, but the capitalist Western countries had (and employed) far greater resources to damage the economy and political position of the other side.[3]

Secret Police and Political Repression

The Cold War resulted in the use of various nonlethal weapons such as spreading propaganda, inciting people to riot, sabotage, and spying, with the USA being overwhelmingly the most aggressive (Blum, 1995).[4] As a result of these activities, both sides in the Cold War developed strong secret police forces, whose job it was to prevent the other side from overthrowing their government although the USA also utilized its secret agents to engage in much more offensive and violent operations (Schulz, 1982).

In East Germany, the secret police force was known as the State Security, or Stasi, which cooperated with Soviet intelligence liaisons or advisors but which was pretty much left on its own to maintain internal security (Henke and Engelmann, 1995). In East Germany's final year, this organization had 91,015 official members and support staff (about 0.5% of the 16.5 million population of East Germany), who were given the task of protecting government leaders and buildings, administering important sports programs, providing national guard services, uncovering plots to overthrow the government, collecting information, conducting statistical analysis, performing passport and emigration control services, and spying in the West (Diedrich, Ehlert, and Wenzke, 1998). One of the largest functions of the Stasi was to conduct security checks on those who applied for permission to visit or emigrate to West Germany (Henke and Engelmann, 1995), as West Germany's constitutionally stated intention to annex East Germany automatically made it an enemy of the East German state (von Schnitzler, 1992). Given that there were over 200 million letters, over 20 million phone calls, and close to 10 million visitors from West Germany each year in the 1980s (Edwards, 1985), the Stasi actually had the resources to monitor only a very small portion of these contacts with the "enemy."

The 91,015 Stasi roster included many purely administrative personnel, including cooks, medical personnel, and others who provided support services to the Stasi that were not directly related in any fashion to the aforementioned tasks. In addition, over 10,000 of the 91,015 represented heavily armed military formations largely trained to fight enemy infiltrators and paratroopers, and almost 10,000 others were uniformed officials directly controlling border crossings (Diedrich, Ehlert, and Wenzke, 1998). Of the total 91,015, only 1418 were undercover agents domestically active in early 1989 (and many of these were used to observe foreign diplomats and tourists), although a further 2232 held full-time civilian positions, such as high-level offices in industry, government, or defense (Wiedmann, 1996).

There were 1380 full-time agents (including some undercover agents) and office personnel involved in observing and controlling religious, cultural, and unusual political activities in East Germany, with some of these Stasi members involved in censorship (Wiedmann, 1996). Besides the several hundred organizations recognized by the East German state (Rein, 1989), there were also over 100 unofficial East German "cultural" groups or organizations with their own "underground" printed periodicals or press, and there also existed a total of 160 underground political groups, with about 2500 active participants, of which only about 60 people were considered by the Stasi to be pure enemies of socialism (Henke and Engelmann, 1995).

Stasi members were, on average, paid about 10% more than the average East German at about 22,000 Marks annually, although generals made two to three times that amount (Gauck, 1991). However, Stasi agents were also required to work long hours and were prohibited from having capitalist friends, except for the purpose of gathering information (Riecker, Schwarz, and Schneider, 1990). The entire budget for the Stasi (including wage and other costs) was slightly over 1% of National Income in 1989 at 3.5 billion Marks, which included only 34 million in West German Marks (Diedrich, Ehlert, and Wenzke, 1998).

For many of their information-gathering activities, the Stasi used informants. The number of people who had knowingly provided information to the Stasi at some time during the history of East Germany was about 600,000 (which is equivalent to about 4% of the East German population), although only 174,000 were listed as informants in 1989 (Mueller-Enbergs, 1996). The 174,000 figure includes a significant number of the over 2 million communist party members, who had merely agreed to cooperate with the Stasi if needed (and often only in special circumstances that might be restricted to providing some overall opinions on worker morale, etc.), but who were rarely if ever contacted (Henke and Engelmann, 1995). Some of the informants hadn't even formally agreed to work for the Stasi but were contacted for information at some point, and many of the informants who were contacted only provided very general information on events, the economic situation, and the overall political climate or mood of the people (Mueller-Enbergs, 1996). Much of the information on individuals was collected with respect to a security clearance check, such as for someone who wished to visit the ideological enemy West Germany. Investigations of those with official business dealings with West Germany were especially strict and thorough to reduce the possibility of taking bribes or other corruption.

About 80% of the informants were listed as gathering general information of the type often provided publicly in West Germany by journalists and their contact sources (such as surveys and reports on businesses/activities not covered in the government-controlled press), 18% of the informants merely offered facilities (such as their apartments) for the meetings between informants and the 13,000 full-time Stasi members who coordinated their activities, and only 2% (or under 4000 people) were involved in observing people suspected of engaging in spying, subversion, illegal political activities, sabotage, attempts to overthrow the government, or other treasonous activities (Henke and Englelmann, 1995). Over 90% of the informants were male, and 99% were adults (Mueller-Enbergs, 1996).

Detailed research on the motivation of Stasi informants has been conducted by Mueller-Enbergs (1996). Most informants were not paid but instead acted out of patriotism, a sense of duty and cooperation with the authorities, the expectations of their position at work (or in the communist party), and social pressure. Some, however, provided information in return for a specific reward, such as very small amounts of additional income, the hope of better career opportunities, and, in much less frequent cases, a reduced jail sentence after having committed a crime like theft. The Stasi considered informants acting out of self-interest as opposed to political conviction to be unreliable and preferred not to have to rely on such people. About a third of those asked to serve as informants refused, and there was generally not any attempt to penalize those who did not cooperate with the Stasi, other than the withdrawal of any rewards offered or hoped for.

The Stasi used telephone taps and room bugs when sufficient information existed for a formal report of suspected criminal activity to be approved (Riecker, Schwarz, and Schneider, 1990). While random bugging was not allowed, technological capacity existed to listen in on up to 20,000 phones in East Berlin alone (Diedrich, Ehlert, and Wenzke, 1998). Only 430 personnel were involved in telephone or room buggings, however, and many of these were spying on foreign embassies and missions.

A total of 530 agents had tasks related to opening mail (Wiedmann, 1996). Although subjective opening of correspondence based on the personal interest of a Stasi agent was prohibited, random opening of mail from West Germany was allowed (Riecker, Schwarz, and Schneider, 1990). Many of those involved in postal interception were merely controlling international mail for smuggling activities related to attempts to avoid import duties and attempts to bring in illegal goods like weapons, narcotics, and right-wing propaganda, and only about 1% of the 30 million packages that were mailed into East Germany each year were intercepted in part or in whole by the Stasi (Diedrich, Ehlert, and Wenzke, 1998).

The Stasi conducted over 100,000 security checks of East Germans each year (many related to applications to visit West Germany), and almost 30,000 people were put under close observation by the Stasi annually, about 1/3 of whom for their activities relating to a delay or refusal of an application to visit or emigrate to West Germany (Henke and Engelmann, 1995). About 2500 people per year were arrested by the Stasi, about 95% of these were convicted of some crime, and most of those convicted were sentenced by East German courts to multiple years in prison (Diedrich, Ehlert, and Wenzke, 1998). Although these conviction and imprisonment rates may seem high, they are actually similar to the rates for Federal crimes in the USA, where "Federal defendants were convicted 87% of the time in fiscal 1998 and nearly three out of four of those found guilty ended up in prison, a Justice Department report says" (*Wall Street Journal,* 2000f).

About half of those convicted of Stasi-related crimes in East Germany had actually been completely investigated by the regular East German police without any Stasi participation whatsoever, although they were formally listed as Stasi arrests/convictions because the nature of their crime (such as threatening an East German government official) was listed as being under Stasi jurisdiction (Henke and Engelmann, 1995). With the exception of about one hundred people arrested annually for treasonous crimes (such as committing sabotage or spying for West Germany), most of the Stasi convictions were related to attempts to emigrate to West Germany (including over half for actual illegal attempts to emigrate to West Germany, and including many others for threatening East German officials or working with West German organizations to pressure East Germany into allowing them to emigrate, as documented in Chapter 2). Although about one hundred people were arrested annually for publicly slandering East Germany in the 1970s, there was a total of only 11 people arrested for that crime between 1985 and 1988.

An interview conducted by Opp and Gern (1993) after unification provides an interesting perspective on the extent of the East German people's perception of secret police activity under communism. In particular, the two investigators asked residents of Leipzig (the capital of East German political demonstrations at least since 1982) whether they had had contact with the police or security forces for political reasons in terms of {i} being watched, {ii} being questioned, {iii} being instructed, or {iv} being taken to the police station, with each "yes" answer having a survey value of 1.0 (cumulating to a score ranging between 0.0 and 4.0 per interviewee). The survey yielded an average score of 0.20, implying that many had never experienced any such "repression" (e.g., if people who had had contact with the secret police had experienced all 4 forms of such "repression," the survey would imply that only 0.20/4=5% of the population had experienced any contact whatsoever with the security forces).

While complete information on West German secret police methods are not available, their numbers have been estimated to also be about

100,000, the majority of whom are undercover agents (Schulz, 1982). Undercover agents are paid up to 100,000 West German Marks (about $60,000) annually tax-free (*Der Spiegel,* 1993b) as well as sometimes offered a good job subsequently in the West German government bureaucracy and/or the dropping of criminal charges or deportation proceedings for criminals and foreigners, respectively (Schulz, 1982). These numbers do not even include the massive army of regular police in West Germany, whose numbers per capita far exceed those of East Germany, and which worked very closely with the West German secret police (*Der Spiegel,* 1992b).

According to one estimate, there were an additional one hundred thousand secret police in West Germany controlled by the occupying USA, British, and French allied troops (Schulz, 1982). In addition, the USA had many agents in East Germany who managed to open mail and listen in on private telephone and other conversations of both average East German citizens as well as the top East German leaders (Staadt, 1998).

Although these figures appear to be lower per capita for West Germany given its larger population, it must be remembered that the Stasi rosters included many people in tasks assumed by others in West Germany, such as support, passport and immigration control, providing internal security against armed infiltrators and paratroopers, etc. It is also important to recall that West Germany spent more per citizen than East Germany on overall internal security, as documented in Chapter 2. Moreover, whereas the occupying forces in West Germany (especially the USA) have tens of thousands of people engaged in secret police activities, only several hundred Soviets were involved in such operations in East Germany which was largely trusted to do that work itself (Andrew, 1999).

The number of West German informants is unknown, but given the fact that companies, unions, and police frequently report on (or are reported to) about political activists, the number may be very large (Schulz, 1982). While existing evidence indicates some West German secret police tactics that are similar to those conducted by the East German secret police with respect to the use of informants, buggings, and mail openings, the extent of such activities may be much greater in West Germany, where superior resources and technology exist (Riecker,

Schwarz, and Schneider, 1990), and where there is evidence of millions of pieces of mail being seized in one year alone (Schulz, 1982).

Perhaps the biggest difference between the two countries' secret police forces may lie in philosophy. The East German secret police had a philosophy that attempted to restrict anyone who didn't love the East German people from becoming a Stasi agent. As a result of this philosophy, the Stasi often tried to talk people out of taking future actions against the state, instead of trying to prove them guilty and send them to prison (Riecker, Schwarz, and Schneider, 1990). This philosophy of emphasizing prevention instead of punishment permeated the entire East German police system and was even grounded in the East German constitution (Weber, 1988). The philosophy was also entrenched in the East German method of raising children, insofar as in communist countries (like East Germany and the Soviet Union) both parents and child care centers were encouraged to lead by example, persuasion, love, praise, non-monetary rewards, habit, and social pressure as opposed to verbal or physical punishment (Autorenkollektiv, 1973). One partial byproduct of this system was the existence of crime rates in East Germany that were 1/10 those in West Germany-- also contributing to the far lower crime rates was a general environment of greater social security and equality in East Germany (Northoff, 1995).

On the other hand, West German secret police is more geared toward the goal of punishing, imprisoning, or terminating enemies of the state, as Schulz (1982) documents. For instance, the West German secret police often try to infiltrate radical left organizations and then entice them with drugs in order to disorient and discredit them and to justify arrests. The West German secret police infiltrators have even provided radical left groups with bombs and weapons in an extreme attempt to both win their trust and entrap them, and some of these weapons have been then used to actually kill innocent people (Schmidt-Eenboom, 1995). Attempts are also usually made to disrupt groups through divisive discussions of unimportant topics and personality conflicts, while lies and rumors are often spread to create personal problems that distract (and demoralize) members (Schulz, 1982). The most powerful tactic typically used by the West German secret police, however, is to prevent those with radical left views from obtaining or keeping a job, which they do by indicating to employers that the individuals are dangerous. Just labeling them communists is usually enough, since most employers are fairly affluent, very anticommunist, and averse to having communist workers, especially given the fact that the West German government even made it illegal for those with communist views to work for the government in any way (von Schnitzler, 1992). The number of victims of West German secret police surveillance and harassment is estimated to be in the millions (Schulz, 1982).

The differences in philosophy may have made the East German secret police more transparent, while many people (except those with radical left views) are not even aware of the existence of the West German secret police. In addition, like their USA counterparts (Stich, 1994), the West German secret police actively engages in weapons and narcotics smuggling as well as other illegal activities (Schmidt-Eenboom, 1995), and the supplemental income from these activities combined with higher government spending per capita on security certainly could help the West German secret police to afford the technology needed to engage in their tasks more secretly. Moreover, I have also been in contact with several West Germans who allege that the West German secret police, like the USA secret police, engages in brainwashing and torture through the use of drugs, hypnosis, and electronic equipment, which are ideal methods for secret repression because they are extremely difficult to prove or find evidence of, and the very damage to the victim's mental health inflicted by this form of repression represents a perfect means of discrediting the victims and their stories as well as distorting their own memories (Bowart, 1978).

To assist the secret police forces, various laws were passed in both East and West Germany to permit the imprisonment of anyone perceived to be an enemy of the state (Furian, 1991). These laws as well as other political legislation, were used in varying degrees to maintain establishment control of the system.

For instance, the West German government outlawed numerous organizations that promoted opinions which it did not want the people to have, including various antiwar groups and a popular communist party that had fought against (and had also been prohibited by) Hitler (Angenfort, 1996). West Germany also made membership in (or assistance to) any political organization connected with East Germany to be illegal. The latter prohibition was extended not only to the East German communist party but also to the Free German Youth, which was a cultural organization charged with the goal of ensuring the East German youth's right to "happiness" (among other socially constructive goals), and to which about 75% of all East German youth belonged (Edwards, 1985). Moreover, the candidate lists from which West German voters are actually allowed to choose are undemocratically selected by bureaucrats in the established, rich, and powerful West German political parties (Rohwedder, 2000), and write-in votes, or otherwise voting against the system, have never been permitted in West Germany.[5] In addition, the West German people were never even allowed to vote on their own constitution which was effectively imposed on them by their USA occupiers after World War II (and they still haven't been able to).[6] As if all these things were not enough, West German laws exist that essentially allow the West German secret police to engage in absolutely any activity (no matter how illegal or immoral) without fear of any chance of prosecution, and this power has effectively given the West German secret police the right to control even the "elected" government officials as opposed to vice versus in East Germany (Schulz, 1982).

As documented in Chapter 2, despite being perceived as much more totalitarian than West Germany, East Germany had many democratic characteristics, including some attributes of democracy that West Germany didn't have, such as the legal right to cast a secret ballot against all the different candidates of the established political parties. The rules for doing so were publicly written at all East German polling locations, and thousands did register a recorded vote against the party slate in each East German election (as will be explained in this chapter, this right to vote against the system was not meaningless). In addition, there were two aspects of East German democracy that were to be particularly important in the peaceful revolution of 1989: the right to engage in limited protest (as long as one was not trying to overthrow the government) and the right to make changes to the country from within the established political parties and government.

Cold War Economics

The most important tool used by the USA in the Cold War was to help its allies grow and prosper economically. By making West Germany richer than East Germany, the USA was able to support its position that capitalism was better. Financial aid and capital from the USA was especially important in the economic reconstruction of West Germany in the years following World War II (Apel, 1966).

On the other hand, the much poorer Soviet Union did not have sufficient wealth to offer such noble assistance to East Germany. Instead, with their own country wrecked by World War II, the Soviets required the East Germans to make enormous reparation payments as compensation for all the damage and killing that the unified Germany had committed. In and apart from the differences in damage inflicted by World War II on the Soviet Union and the USA, the Soviets had inherited a desperately poor country in 1917 when they first took power from the previous feudal leaders of Russia (with national income per capita equal to 1/12 that of the USA at that time, as documented in Chapter 1),[7] and they never could have offered the assistance that the USA provided to the West Germans.

As a result of the difference in the post-War foreign economic assistance/reparations, West Germany very quickly became the much wealthier country (Apel, 1966).[8] This situation provided West Germany with an excellent economic weapon with which to strike at East Germany. In particular, the West German government provided working-age East Germans who moved to West Germany with significant amounts of money and other benefits in order to emigrate to West Germany (retirees were not given such incentives). For instance, free loans and other state assistance of up to 160,000 West German Marks (about $100,000) were offered to each East German emigrant worker, along with a scarce apartment and reimbursement for any property that remained behind in East Germany (*Der Tagesspiegel,* 1990f). In addition, East German emigrants to West Germany were also provided with instant West German citizenship, which allowed them to obtain West German jobs. Being much wealthier and much larger (and being supported by their USA occupiers), West Germany could provide such incentives almost without limit. In over a decade's time, the result was a large net exodus of several million people out of East Germany, which, net of the several hundred thousand West Germans who emigrated to East Germany, represented a loss of over 10% of the East German population (Apel, 1966). According to West German propaganda, this population movement provided West Germany with evidence of the "superiority" of their country, their government, and their economic system. In addition, many of the people who left East Germany were highly skilled individuals (like doctors, nurses, and engineers), who were very difficult and costly for East Germany to replace (Diedrich, Ehlert, and Wenzke, 1998). The East German morale and economy suffered as a result (Apel, 1966).

Besides engaging in a deliberate policy to buy up East Germany's skilled work force, the economic war was also fought with other tools. For instance, West Germany was also able to utilize its superior wealth to promote extensive illegal black market currency trading and smuggling operations that also contributed to damaging the East German economy (Murphy, 1992b). Many such operations were conducted by the West German secret police itself (Schmidt-Eenboom, 1993).

THE BERLIN WALL

This situation continued until 1961, at which time the East German government came to the conclusion that the process of damaging their economy and emptying their country of skilled workers could no longer continue.[9] In 1961, East Germany set up rules that forbade their citizens from traveling to West Germany without special permission. In addition, travel restrictions were placed on West Germans going into East Germany in order to prevent a continuation of the black market currency trading and smuggling that were damaging the East German economy, to inhibit spying by Western secret police, and to stop outright sabotage activities committed by Western secret police (Blum, 1995). Because of the economic crisis caused by the emigrations and black market trading, many East Germans supported the government's restrictive policies at the time (Lahann, 1998).

The travel restriction rules were enforced by barbed wire, minefields, walls, and soldiers along the entire border with West Germany. Although many of these barriers had existed since the early 1950s (and about 150 people had been killed in the border area prior to 1961), the final barrier between the two countries was erected in 1961 in Berlin (Diedrich, Ehlert, and Wenzke, 1998). Berlin was a large city of several million people that was partially in West Germany and partially in East Germany. The part in West Germany was called West Berlin, while the part in East Germany was called East Berlin. After 1961, the city was not only divided politically by different ruling governments, it also was split physically in two by a large wall that separated East Berlin from West Berlin. This wall built on August 13, 1961 was called the Berlin Wall.

It was forbidden for East Germans to try to cross the Berlin Wall, just as it was forbidden for East Germans to enter West Germany through any other border point (which was mined in many places). East German soldiers patrolled the border points constantly, and they were given orders to shoot anyone who tried to cross the border until early in 1989. Over the 28 years from 1961 to 1989, 756 East Germans lost their lives trying to "escape" to the higher income in West Germany, including 239 around the Berlin Wall. Many of the 756 martyrs were shot, while others died from mines and drowning (and some committed suicide when caught). Many more were wounded. It should be mentioned that the average number of about 30 killed per year is fairly small in comparison to, for example, the hundreds of Mexicans who die on average *each year* trying to "escape" into the United States (Reifenberg, 1996), which does absorb 300,000 Mexican immigrants annually (Millman, 2000). However, the 756 German deaths do represent a human tragedy nonetheless (it should also be mentioned for comparison purposes that fewer Mexicans have been shot by USA border guards, as most Mexican "refugees" trying to "escape" to the higher pay in the USA have died from drowning, cold, starvation, and other "natural" causes while trying to pass through less well-guarded but inhospitable border areas).

Between 1961 and 1989, about 50,000 East Germans (averaging over one thousand annually) were apprehended alive for attempting to escape and put into East German jails for one or more years. Over 90% of all attempts at illegal border crossings failed (Diedrich, Ehlert, and Wenzke, 1998), with most being discovered by East German security forces while still in the planning stage (Hertle, 1996).

In the first few years of the Wall, only a few thousand East Germans were allowed to legally cross over into West Germany, and most of these people were loyal communist party members on political and business endeavors. After a few more years, the East German government relaxed its restrictions and allowed more frequent entries by West Germans and permitted its own senior citizens to freely cross over if they were over 65 years old (Merritt and Merritt, 1985). Travel freedom was markedly increased after 1972 when West Germany formally recognized the existence of a separate government in the East German zone, although it continued to refuse to recognize the legitimacy of a separate East German state or acknowledge its existence with an embassy (von Schnitzler, 1992). By the 1980s, trips to West Germany were possible for East German citizens who were over 50 years old, or who had relatives in West Germany, and some others were also allowed to visit West Germany after a long bureaucratic wait of several years and a security clearance from the Stasi. In 1987, although 300,000 applications for visits to the West were refused by the East German government, 1,297,399 East Germans under the retirement age were granted the legal right to visit West Germany (Hertle, 1996). In 1988, the number of visits by East Germans into West Germany was over 15 million, over 99.9% of whom returned to East Germany (Murphy, 1992b).

Nevertheless, the Wall remained successful in inhibiting most activities that were damaging to the East German economy. For instance, far less than 1% of those East Germans who visited West Germany chose to stay there (Hertle, 1996), and illegal smuggling operations remained curtailed (Murphy, 1992b). However, to be able to minimize such activities in the face of relaxed travel restrictions (as well as to inhibit the spying and subversion that more contacts between East and West Germans allowed), increased security checks were required, especially on those seeking to visit West Germany, and so the Stasi had doubled its numbers from 1972 to its peak level of 1989 (Diedrich, Ehlert, and Wenzke, 1998). Although East Germany had managed to survive most of the 1950s before the Wall with less than 20,000 Stasi members, it perceived greater Stasi control as a means of allowing more travel freedom while simultaneously preventing the resulting economic damage that occurred in the 1950s.

STATUS SYMBOLS IN EAST GERMANY

Despite increased travel freedom in the 1980s for some, many young East Germans without West German relatives were still forbidden from visiting West Germany, and this situation caused jealousies and discontent. These jealousies were heightened by the fact that the existence of West German relatives (and/or friends) often meant presents and opportunities to receive West German goods (Whetten, 1980).

A few dozen of the top leaders in the East German government and numerous East German business travelers were among those who received Western gifts via their business dealings and/or who could access such goods in Western shops or in a "ghetto" for the East German elite in Wandlitz (Schabowski, 1991). However, most communist party members and Stasi agents were greatly disadvantaged in this respect as they were strongly discouraged from having any West German friends (Keithly, 1992). In fact, many East Germans saw no advantages to being in the communist party and instead only disadvantages, which included having a significant amount of time used up in Party meetings and a percentage of income deducted for Party dues (Eckart, 1984). Although moral pressure was put on East Germans in more responsible positions to join the communist party, a belief in its purpose must also have played a part in over 2 million East Germans (over 10% of the total population) joining the Party (Dietz, 1983), since they thereby gave up time, money, and potentially even access to West German goods.

West German goods were a big status symbol in East Germany, because the East German government severely restricted imports from Western capitalist countries (Murphy, 1992b). Restricting imports from West Germany had helped protect the East German economy from unemployment (as explained in more detail in subsequent chapters) and had allowed the East German economy to grow faster than West Germany in the years since 1961 (as documented in Chapter 4 of this book). However, because the East German economy had not grown fast enough to make up for the pre-1961 difference in economic prosperity and was still only 2/3 the size of West Germany's per capita by 1989 (Gregory and Stuart, 1995), many of the goods in East Germany were of lower quality, being on the same level as inexpensive West German goods. For example, the most prevalent East German car (the Trabant) was similar to the VW Beetle with respect to reliability, durability, easy repairs, inexpensive cost, good gas mileage, small size, low maximum speed, some safety problems (in a crash), and old design (Woodruff, 1997). Besides generally having less luxurious and less modern goods, there was an especially serious scarcity of high technology goods like computers in East Germany because of the Western technology embargo against communist countries (Hertle, 1996). The higher standard of living in West Germany combined with a reputation for high quality and high technology made possession of West German products a very prestigious belonging.

As a result, some categorized East Germans into two classes. The upper class had West German relatives with consequent opportunities to travel to the West and obtain Western goods (Keithly, 1992), whereas the lower class, which comprised about 50% of the East German population (Filmer, 1985a), had no West German relatives.

The jealousy, frustration, and discontent caused by this "two class" system were magnified by other problems in East Germany. In particular, there was a shortage of some consumer goods like cars (Filmer and Schwan, 1985) and telephones (Schwarzer, 1999) that resulted in a wait of over 10 years after ordering. In addition, some goods (such as fresh tropical fruit like bananas and pineapples) were rarely available (like only around Christmas) and/or obtainable only after physically waiting in line for hours, and many services (like repairs) had to be requested weeks in advance and/or required payment of a negotiable tip (Filmer and Schwan, 1985).

Some of the negative effects of the shortages could be reduced or eliminated in various ways, as previously mentioned in Chapter 2. For instance, it was always possible to buy second-hand goods. The latter opportunity was especially useful for obtaining a car without an extensive wait, although many East Germans also greatly reduced the inconvenience of the normal 10-year wait for a new car by having relatives order a new car 10 years before a child was of driving age at the same time that they begin saving for the purchase to ensure timely payment for delivery. Nevertheless, although there were 225 cars per 1000 residents of East Germany in 1988 (Mueller, 1996), that still compared somewhat unfavorably with about 1 car per 2 citizens in West Germany (Kusch et al., 1991), and the overall consumption situation made East Germans feel their own economy and system to be that much more inferior to the West German system (Filmer and Schwann, 1985).

ESCAPING FROM EAST GERMANY

As a result, many East Germans had a desire not only to visit West Germany but also to live there. West Germany offered higher wages and other monetary benefits as well as the opportunity to purchase consumer goods that were not available in East Germany. A 1988 survey of East Germans who wanted to leave their country indicated that 42% desired to emigrate because of the shortage of consumption goods in their country, while 27% stated that they wanted to leave primarily to attain greater freedom to travel (Falck, 1998).

Details and statistics on emigration attempts are provided by Eisenfeld (1996). Thousands of East Germans applied to their government for permission to emigrate each year, with the numbers rising to tens of thousands by the late 1980s. Only a fraction of the applications were granted, and there was generally a fairly long waiting period (of several months to years) even for the emigration visas eventually obtained. For instance, there were 284,700 new applications for emigration between 1980 and June 1989, but only 158,800 were allowed to leave, while 87,100 withdrew their applications "voluntarily" during this time. On June 30, 1989, there were a total of 125,400 unfilled applications (up from 113,500 on December 31, 1988).

Applicants for emigration visas were generally subjected to considerable pressure to cancel their requests to leave the country. While gentler means of persuasion were often used, the applicants were also subjected to a thorough Stasi investigation that sometimes proved to be harassing. Several hundred of the applicants each year were arrested and found guilty of various crimes as a result of such investigations, and thousands more were subjected to warnings. In addition, the applicants were generally informed of the risk of possibly never being allowed to reenter East Germany and the resulting difficulties of seeing their friends and family again. Many responded negatively to this pressure (with tens of thousands complaining each year to the head of the East German government about their treatment), thousands quit their jobs, and some even began voicing vocal opposition to East Germany in an attempt to pressure the government into seeing their continued stay as not only useless but even counterproductive for the country. Those actually allowed to leave were subsequently denounced publicly as agents of foreign powers and even traitors, and although East Germany made some modest (and somewhat inconsistent) efforts to encourage the emigrants to return, only a few hundred decided to do so each year.

To avoid this uncertain and often undesirable application procedure for emigration (or to circumvent it when months or years passed without the application being granted), some chose to try to emigrate illegally. However, because of the Wall and other barriers between the two Germanies, only a few people succeeded each year. There were hundreds of illegal plans or attempts at "escape" each year, but most were foiled by the Stasi even before the border area had been reached.

Besides trying to break through the armed border, there were other ways to emigrate illegally. For instance, a handful of those who visited West Germany each year (less than six thousand in 1988) decided to stay there and not return to East Germany. More might have done so, except such emigration without permission was a violation of East German law and meant not being able to visit East Germany again. In addition, the East German authorities made it clear prior to each visit that it would be unlikely that the friends or families of an illegal emigrant would ever be allowed to visit West Germany. As a result, an emigration made it difficult to be able to see one's East German relatives and friends again (Hertle, 1996). Although meetings between emigrants to West Germany and their East German families and friends often occurred while on vacation in other communist Eastern European countries such as Hungary, the Stasi sometimes used their own network of informants to disrupt such contacts (Eisenfeld, 1996). These tactics helped successfully inhibit well over 99% of East German visitors from staying in West Germany, although the percentage remaining in West Germany had been trending upward at 0.22% in 1987, 0.35% in 1988, and 0.61% in the first half of 1989 (and reaching the 1% mark in August 1989), with most of those staying being vital skilled workers like doctors (Krenz, 1990).

Another way of illegally emigrating was to seek refuge in the West German consulate office in East Berlin. West Germany did not have an actual embassy because it did not officially recognize the legal existence of a separate East Germany), or to seek political asylum in the USA embassy there (Keithly, 1992). Once inside, diplomatic immunity laws prevented the East German police from entry, and papers were generally negotiated for the refugees to emigrate legally (to avoid adverse publicity and other hassles). The problem here was that East German police stood outside the West German consulate office (as well as outside the various foreign embassies) and normally did not allow anyone without permission to enter. Only an unexpected rush by a large group of East Germans had ever succeeded in emigrating this way.

Another way to illegally emigrate to West Germany also existed. In particular, although East Germans could not visit West Germany without permission, they could travel almost without restriction (and fairly cheaply) throughout the expanse of Eastern Europe, including into Czechoslovakia, Hungary, Poland, Romania, Bulgaria, Russia, and other communist countries (*aus erster Hand*, 1987). While these allied countries also had strict border controls with Western countries (and would not allow East Germans into Western countries without visas from the East German government), it was possible to seek refuge in the West German embassies in those countries. Although East Germany had made some arrangements with its allies to try to control entry to the West German embassies in those countries more strictly in an attempt to stop the several dozen East Germans who successfully emigrated in this manner each year (Eisenfeld, 1995), police control of these embassies was not as strong as in East Germany.

Prelude to the Revolution

In the mid-1980s, Michael Gorbachev became the new leader of Soviet Union, and he initiated many capitalist reforms under his Perestroika policies and also announced an official program of greater freedom of speech in a policy called Glasnost (Marcy, 1990). Although some of the other Eastern European countries (like Poland and Hungary) followed the Soviet lead, East Germany and others (like Romania) continued their hard line against capitalist propaganda and reforms (Mittag, 1991).

This situation led to internal inconsistencies within Eastern Europe. For instance, in 1988, one Soviet publication, *Sputnik*, began making such open statements about reforms in communist countries that it was no longer imported into East Germany (Arnold, 1990). Subsequently in early 1989, an ex-spy chief from East Germany published a book that raised some questions about the history of the Soviet Union in the 1930s when it was under the leadership of Joseph Stalin. Printing of this book was discontinued in East Germany after only a few copies had been sold (Wolf, 1991).

As an expression of discontent against the continued hard-line policies in East Germany, a significant number of East Germans voted against the communist party slate in an election there in May of 1989.

Although the East German government reported the party slate to have won over 95% of the votes (just as it had in all previous elections over the prior 40 years), a number of East Germans claimed election fraud (Krenz, 1990). In particular, some East Germans counted the number of their friends who claimed to have voted against the party slate, and that number exceeded the official number of "no" votes reported in some of the local districts, such as in the East German city of Dresden. In actual fact, many of the votes against the party slate were not counted because the list of party candidates had been crossed out with an "X", and East German election rules required each candidate's name to be crossed out with a line for a "no" vote to be registered.[10]

The new freedoms opening up in the communist world had also hit Red China. There, thousands of students demonstrated openly against the government for several months in 1989, with the protests being concentrated on demands for higher pay for intellectuals, lower inflation, and less corruption, although there were also more minor demands for greater political freedom that were advanced for propaganda purposes (Keidel, 1991). However, after the demonstrators called for the overthrow of the government and attacked government security forces, the Chinese army was sent in to restore order, and several hundred demonstrators were killed in June 1989 in what was called the Tiananmen Square massacre (MacFarquhar, 1993). Despite worldwide outrage at the incident, the East German government stated its support for the Chinese government's actions, and many began to fear a similar incident in East Germany (Krenz, 1990).

Meanwhile, on May 2, 1989, a potentially even more revolutionary event had occurred in Hungary, one of East Germany's communist allies in Eastern Europe. On that day, Hungary had eliminated some barbed wire on its western border with neutral Austria to symbolize the toning down of the Cold War (Krenz, 1990). Hungarians (who were not offered the immediate Western citizenship, money, and jobs that emigrating East Germans were) had long been able to travel into Western countries, and so it was largely a symbolic event for them. It also did not change the fact that East Germans still could not cross the Austrian border (397 of 607 East Germans trying to do so in 1988 were caught by the Hungarian border troops and returned to East Germany for prosecution), but the symbolic border opening was widely publicized on West

German TV stations that East Germans were able to watch (Hertle, 1996). Hungary had always been a favorite summer vacation spot for many East Germans (Krenz, 1990), with 800,000 East Germans visiting the country each year, and with several hundred thousand more travelling through the country on the way to other Eastern European destinations (Hertle, 1996). An especially large number typically did so after school ended in East Germany in early July (Krenz, 1990), and there were about 200,000 East Germans in Hungary in the summer of 1989 (Keithly, 1992).

Hungary in the Summer of 1989

The explosive effects of the events in Hungary in the summer of 1989 are documented by Hertle (1996). A small number of East German tourists in Hungary had already taken advantage of the more open border there to have themselves smuggled out in the trunks of the cars of Austrian or West German tourists in May and June of 1989, but nothing earthshattering happened in those two months. However, in mid-July 1989, a few dozen East German tourists in Hungary attempted to drive their own cars openly through the border gate into Austria, having suddenly heard rumors that the border was now "open." Although they were turned away by Hungarian border guards without prosecution, some feared penalties when they returned to East Germany because their passports were stamped as having permission to visit Austria denied. As a result, over 50 East Germans sought refuge in the West German embassy in Hungary.

The existence of refugees at the West German embassy brought international press coverage. Increased press coverage resulted in many personal offers to individual East German tourists by West German and Austrian tourists who promised to smuggle them out. In addition, West German and Austrian tourists freely provided advice on how to seek refuge at the West German embassy in Hungary, which was finally closed on August 14 with 171 East German refugees. Many more East Germans seeking to emigrate camped out in the yard and on the side of the street nearby. To relieve the problem, the Hungarian government built some refugee camps where the East Germans could stay until the problem was resolved. Although Hungary had a treaty with East Germany to repatriate anyone trying to illegally cross over into the West, the Hungarians wanted to maintain good economic relations with the

West Germans in order to continue to be able to access West German credit, capital, and high technology goods.

As the number of refugees grew, so did the press coverage. More press coverage brought more smuggling offers and more advice from tourists to go to the refugee camps, and the whole process started to feed on itself. Some Austrian and West German tourists even began spreading written leaflets to East German tourists in Hungary informing them how to emigrate.

On August 19, 1989, one rich Austrian aristocrat (a descendant of the old Austrian Emperor's family) even held a large party on the Hungarian border and conspired with a non-communist member of the Hungarian government to allow 600 invited East Germans in Hungary to use the opportunity to flee through the Austrian border in mass. Three days later, spurred on by this event, and realizing that the few border guards could not have stopped a large number of people except by shooting them, 240 more East Germans crossed the border into Austria. The fleeing East Germans gambled correctly that the Hungarians did not want to risk such an international incident for an East German problem. However, subsequent attempts in August were stopped by strengthened border troops, who wounded several East Germans attempting to emigrate illegally.

Finally, after thousands of East German refugees had filled the area around the West German embassy and other living quarters provided to them by the Hungarian government, after numerous incidents, and after many East Germans had already been smuggled through the borders, the Hungarian government negotiated a deal with West Germany to let the refugees enter West Germany via the Austrian border in return for a loan of 500 million Deutsche Marks (about $300 million) and some political support. On September 11, Hungary announced that it was breaking its treaty with East Germany on repatriating refugees, and over 12,000 East Germans were allowed to emigrate immediately from Hungary into West Germany, while more East Germans still on vacation there chose to emigrate through the open border later in the month.

As a result, the East German government terminated unrestricted travel to Hungary. Thereafter, travel to Hungary by East Germans would only be allowed with special permission.

The international publicity had made it known to all East Germans that there were reasonably safe ways to emigrate to West Germany. East Germans could watch both East and West German television channels, and so news of the emigrations through Hungary could be seen from both points of view. Those who had been most interested in emigrating now saw a favorable chance, and, although most had initially sought refuge in Hungary, dozens of other refugees had meanwhile also broken their way into the West German embassy of Czechoslovakia and into the West German consular office in East Berlin itself.

The Train Through Dresden

After trips to Hungary were no longer freely allowed in September 1989, East Germans seeking to emigrate began concentrating on the other West German embassy targets. For instance, by the end of September, hundreds of East Germans had taken refuge in the West German embassy in Poland, and many more were breaking into the West German embassy in Czechoslovakia again.

Czechoslovakia was the most popular travel destination for East Germans (9 million East Germans visited Czechoslovakia in 1988) because it was nearby and no special visa was required (Bahrmann and Links, 1994). For those seeking emigration from East Germany, Czechoslovakia was also now an attractive destination because they could not only enter the West German embassy there, but they could also conceivably travel through the lightly guarded Czech border with Hungary, from which they could freely emigrate via the open Hungarian border with Austria. By the end of September, the number of East Germans who had emigrated via Hungary over the prior few months exceeded 20,000, and the West German embassy in Czechoslovakia was soon filled up with thousands of East Germans (Goertemaker, 1994). The East German government then negotiated a similar solution as was imposed on it in the Hungarian case. It "temporarily" terminated unrestricted travel to Czechoslovakia but decided to formally allow the legal emigration of all East German refugees in the West German embassy in Czechoslovakia (Bahr, 1990). As part of the emigration agreement in the Czechoslovakian case, over ten thousand refugees around the West German embassy in Czechoslovakia were to travel by train through the southern part of East Germany before reaching West Germany (Keithly, 1992).

One set of trains filled with refugees was scheduled to ride through the East German city of Dresden early in the morning of October 5, 1989 at about 1:30 A.M., and details of the events that followed are reported by Bahr (1990). To prevent any East Germans in Dresden from climbing aboard the trains in transit to West Germany, the East German police closed off the train station in Dresden late in the night of October 4, 1989. Notified by West German television of the trains that were to pass through, over five thousand East Germans came to look on and complain, frequently claiming to suddenly want to take a train ride somewhere. As the complaints became heated, violence erupted as normal Dresden people (mostly teenagers and very young adults) tried to break into the train station, and others threw rocks at the train station windows. The police counterattacked. Hundreds of people were clubbed and/or arrested by the police.

THE LAST BIRTHDAY OF EAST GERMANY

Meanwhile, in East Berlin, preparations for the 40th anniversary of the founding of the East German government were being made. The borders to tourist traffic were temporarily closed to reduce the possibility of foreign-instigated disorder (preventing myself from meeting a cute East German woman with whom I had an evening rendezvous!), and known East German dissidents were put under especially close observation, as was usual during such times (Riecker, Schwarz, and Schneider, 1990). Communist leaders and sympathizers all over the world were going to attend the October 7 ceremonies, including the leader of the Soviet Union (Michael Gorbachev), and the East German government did not want any embarrassing riots.

On October 6, on the eve of the celebration, over one hundred thousand members of the East German youth organization (the Free German Youth) marched through the center of East Berlin holding torches in demonstration of their support for their country, just as they had on this day for the last few decades. There was one major difference in their peaceful demonstration this time, however. On October 6, 1989, instead of shouting in support of their own country's leader, the Free German Youth chanted "Gorbi, Gorbi, Gorbi" (Krenz, 1990).

As reported by Bahrmann and Links (1994), the ceremonies on October 7, 1989 went smoothly for most of the day. However, early in the evening, a number of people on a central plaza (Alexanderplatz) in East Berlin indicated their intent to express their support for their communist ally, Gorbachev, and the group started walking toward a building (Palast der Republic) where he was meeting with East German leaders. As the group continued across the rest of the plaza and crossed a central park where people often strolled, the crowd grew. Once in front of the building, the crowd shouted chants in support of Gorbachev and sang communist songs. Police were stationed in front of the building, but they and the building were separated from the crowd by a narrow river (with bridges over it blocked by police). Nothing earthshattering happened until plainclothes police began arresting a few people for making remarks that they perceived to be anti-government. The arrests in plain view of the crowd were not popular, and the secret police was jeered. The crowd had grown to over ten thousand people by this time, and they began to lose their fear of the secret police and to feel power in their numbers and in their complementary opinions.

Somewhat later, the crowd began moving back toward the residential section of East Berlin, and the chanting became more militant, with jeers of "Secret police, get out!" The crowd gathered more strength in the residential section, as the demonstrators called on those watching from balconies to join them by chanting "Onto the street." The demonstrators also soon ran into crowds of people returning home from an official fireworks ceremony (celebrating the 40th anniversary of East Germany), but many of these celebrants merely wanted to go home.

Meanwhile, the secret police chief (Erich Mielke) had ordered the police and security forces to hinder the spread of the demonstration (Schabowlski, 1990). Police barriers were set up, but, with many people (including many fireworks celebrants) needing to get to their homes, the various crowds of people began to force their way through the barriers (Riecker, Schwarz, and Schneider, 1990). The crowds were then surrounded by troops and pushed back in a direction away from their homes (*Schnauze,* 1990). With thousands of people being pushed against one another in an unknown direction, and with many people angry at not being allowed to return to their homes, violence broke out (Riecker, Schwarz, and Schneider, 1990), chaos ensued, and the police clubbed and arrested hundreds of demonstrators as well as innocent bystanders (*Schnauze,* 1990).

There were also numerous other much smaller demonstrations on October 7, including in other cities of East Germany, such as in Leipzig and Potsdam (Bahrmann and Links, 1994). However, there had been prior publicity (including circulating flyers) about these events from well-known and well-observed East German dissident groups such as "Neues Forum." Neues Forum was one of the newest, most popular, and most famous dissident groups in East Germany that had been created as a new forum for promoting political discussion, but it had not been formally authorized by the state because the group openly sought to "break the state's power monopoly" to reform the system instead of going through the 200 different organizations already authorized (and encouraged) by the East German government to express their opinions and initiate reforms (Rein, 1989). As a result of the prior information on these demonstrations sponsored by renowned dissidents, the Stasi had been well-prepared for them and had easily broken them up with a few arrests that included several West German, Polish, and other foreigner demonstrators in Potsdam (Maximytschew and Hertle, 1994).

EAST GERMAN POLICE CONTROL

The police patrols, arrests, and clubbings continued through the night of October 7 and the next day in Berlin as the security forces sought to restore order in a situation they did not understand and for which they were ill-prepared (Riecker, Schwarz, and Schneider, 1990). The East German police and troops had been trained to fight criminals and foreign infiltrators but not innocent demonstrators and their own people (Diedrich, Ehlert, and Wenzke, 1998). The East German secret police had put all the well-known East German dissidents under close observation and had quietly dispersed or kept under control the small demonstrations that they had called (as they had always done in the past). The demonstration in the center of Berlin, however, appeared to be spontaneous and without leaders.

In East Germany, demonstrations were illegal unless they were authorized by the government. However, as previously mentioned, East Germany had laws guaranteeing freedom of expression (Philipsen, 1993), and there was nothing illegal in a group of people wandering somewhere to express support for their government or their communist allies (Riecker, Schwarz, and Schneider, 1990). Only when some people in the group made anti-government statements or slandered government leaders was police action allowed (Rein, 1989). By the time this happened in Berlin, there were already over ten thousand people in the crowd (and they were mixing with another group that was returning from a government fireworks festival).

People arrested for making public statements against the government or for leading unauthorized demonstrations were usually released with a warning for first offenses (Riecker, Schwarz, and Schneider, 1990). However, serious and subsequent offenses could be penalized with several years in prison (Furian, 1991). A statement against the government or its laws was considered serious only if the police perceived the action to be threatening to the government and/or to have been initiated by foreigners or others seeking to overthrow the government (Rein, 1989). For instance, jokes about the government were allowed to be told in bars and private gatherings as long as there was no perceived intent to overthrow the system (Schlechte and Schlechte, 1993). Normally, the police (usually the secret police) attempted to persuade any offending individuals from further public anti-government action (Riecker, Schwarz, and Schneider, 1990). In the October 7-8 events in Berlin, however, there were simply too many to persuade, including many who were arrested or injured without having made any anti-government statements and without having been involved in the unauthorized "gathering" at all (*Schnauze*, 1990).

Although no one died in the actions in Berlin on October 7 and 8, there were quite a few hospitalized (including some police troops). The international press came out strongly for the demonstrators and expressed shock at the police brutality (Schumann, 1990). To provide some perspective here, however, it should be pointed out that the East German laws against publicly slandering the country were similar to some American laws (existing in 48 of the 50 USA states) prohibiting flag-burning (Greene, 2000). In addition with respect to laws on demonstrations, it should be mentioned that even in the "free" USA, demonstrations are only allowed if permits (which are not always granted) have been obtained from the government, and masses of intimidating police are often present even when a demonstration is permitted (IAC, 1998a). Moreover, it should also be noted that demonstrators in the USA are often chased down and clubbed, arrested (for "unlawful assembly and crossing police barricades"), and sprayed with harmful chemicals just for engaging in peaceful protests against the world poverty caused by capitalist globalization (Associated Press, 2000g). Government ordinances are also sometimes imposed in the USA to prohibit demonstrators from wearing helmets, gas masks, or other protection from police assaults (Szczesny, 2000b), thereby ensuring police brutality has the maximum effect.

At any rate, since most East Germans watched West German TV, their opinions of the events were strongly influenced by the Western anticommunist interpretation of the actions of October 7-8 (that naturally emphasized police repression and put East Germany in a negative light). As a result, many East German supporters of the demonstrators attended candle-laying ceremonies to show their solidarity against violent attacks on innocent people, and the movement began to gain momentum (Bahrmann and Links, 1994).

THE LEIPZIG AFFAIR

Shortly thereafter, on Monday, October 9, 1989, one of the stranger events of this weird episode occurred. On that day in a town with over four hundred thousand residents in the southwestern portion of East Germany, there was a threat of another large demonstration, and the background to and actions of that day remain a mystery to most investigators (Joppke, 1995).

Since 1982, small demonstrations had periodically occurred around a church (Nikolaikirche) in the center of Leipzig at approximately 6 P.M. on Monday (Scheider, 1990). For many years, young East German dissidents had figured out that the East German government's guarantee of religious freedom allowed them some rights to freedom of assembly and expression there, after a "peace prayer" was issued at 5 P.M. I myself interviewed some of the participants who indicated that most of the demonstrators had no religious beliefs but merely used the church as a protective cover for expressing their discontent. Such demonstrations usually consisted of several dozen dissidents at the most, and the demonstrators were always dispersed shortly after leaving the church. Suspected ringleaders of the demonstrations were usually arrested and sometimes given jail sentences of up to several years for slander or plotting against the state.

On September 4, 1989, in keeping with this tradition, several youths began to demonstrate with placards "For an open country with free people," as reported by Tetzner (1990). Their signs were torn down immediately by secret police but not before Western reporters had taken pictures. On September 18, 1989, this action was followed up with a demonstration of several hundred people, with some demanding the right to leave the country. This demonstration was also quickly dispersed by police, and approximately one hundred people were arrested. These incidents were followed by a similar demonstration of over a thousand people on September 25. As usual, this latter demonstration was also broken up by police, and numerous suspected ringleaders were arrested for taking actions against the state (Schumann, 1990).

On Monday October 2, 1989, another demonstration ensued in the center of Leipzig, as also reported by Tetzner (1990). This time the demonstrators did not yell anti-government slogans. Instead, they chanted Gorbachev's name to demonstrate their support for their communist ally. They also shouted "We're staying here" to show that they were not people who wanted to illegally emigrate. Such slogans did not give the police adequate cause to make arrests and disperse the demonstrators. The failure of the police to act and the supportive nature of the slogans also gave the demonstrators a sense of legitimacy. As a result, as the demonstrators walked peacefully around the plazas and parks in the center of Leipzig, many other people who were strolling in the area joined the group. The crowd soon grew to approximately three thousand people. Although police cordoned off some areas and roads to prevent the demonstration from blocking all traffic, no violence or arrests occurred. The slogans remained supportive of Communism (as opposed to demanding reforms), with the most militant cries to the police on that day being "Shame on you for not letting us through." Only after most of the demonstrators had gone home did verbal and physical provocation of the police occur, which resulted in a few arrests.

On October 7, 1989, normal official festivities were held in Leipzig to celebrate the 40th anniversary of East Germany. Several well-known dissidents used the opportunity to speak to masses of people gathered for the festivities. The East German police were already prepared and quickly dispersed the crowds with water cannons and numerous arrests (*Schnauze,* 1990).

The Decisive Day

Renewed arrests and violent dispersal of demonstrators in Leipzig on October 7, combined with the news of violence in Dresden on October 4 and in East Berlin on October 7, led many to fear the worst for the Monday October 9 demonstration in Leipzig (Bahrmann and Links, 1994). As a precaution, a large number of East German police, soldiers, and tanks had been called into the city, and orders had been issued by the East German leader (Erich Honecker) and by the secret police chief (Erich Mielke) not to allow the demonstration to occur (Kuhn, 1992). There were rumors in Leipzig that a slaughtering of demonstrators might occur, as it had in communist China in June of 1989 (Bahrman and Links, 1994). People were warned not to go toward the center of the city after 5 P.M., and some schools and businesses in the center of the city were closed early to allow the people to go home before then (Kuhn, 1992). In this situation, there may have been only a very small number of people brave enough to join in the demonstration on that day, and the police might have been able to disperse the few courageous demonstrators as usual.

However, a series of events then occurred that dramatically changed the course of history but has rarely been reported by anyone except Kuhn (1992), who interviewed many of the key participants. To begin, early on the morning of October 9, Walter Friedrich, a professor for youth culture at the University of Leipzig, drove to East Berlin to confer with his old friend Egon Krenz, who held an important position in the East German government's policy-making committee called the politburo. In addition to his position in the politburo, Egon Krenz was also in charge of security and was the head of the East German youth organization called the Free German Youth. Friedrich convinced Krenz to check to make sure that the police and other troops had been given orders not to shoot. In addition, he pleaded with Krenz to try and have the security forces show restraint, unless the demonstration turned destructive or violent. He also suggested that Krenz replace the old sick leader of East Germany (Erich Honecker) and take charge of the country himself.

After Friedrich left, Krenz attempted to contact the East German leader, but the old man was in meetings all day. Because Krenz was unable to reach Honecker, he called the various ministers of the central government in charge of the various police forces (such as the secret police chief Mielke) and convinced them not to employ violence.

After talking with Krenz, Friedrich returned to Leipzig and spoke with his friend Roland Woetzel, who was a communist party member with an influential political position in Leipzig. In conjunction with five other local dignitaries, Woetzel then recorded an announcement requesting the demonstrators in Leipzig to remain nonviolent and promising to have the government listen to the opinions of the demonstrators. The cassette with the recording was given to various administrators in the center of the city, as well as to the Leipzig radio station, with instructions to play the cassette on the radio in the afternoon and on the city's loudspeakers at the time of the church "peace prayer" between 5 P.M. and 6 P.M.

There were several thousand people gathered around the central church for the "peace prayer" between 5 P.M. and 6 P.M. Included among them were over a thousand communist party members who had been ordered by the local communist party to inhibit a demonstration from occurring afterwards. Because of the large number of people attending the church ceremony, many had to stand outside the church, even though three nearby churches had been opened up to handle the overflow. After the church ceremony ended peacefully (around 6 P.M.), the church leaders recommended that the people go home in a direction away from the city center in order to avoid a confrontation. However, this recommendation was ignored in the face of the public announcement condoning a demonstration that was being broadcast on local loudspeakers and on the radio. The thousand communist party members in attendance at the "peace prayer" also perceived the public announcement played on the loudspeakers to be a rescinding order of the command to break up any post-ceremony gathering. As a result, after the prayer services were over, many people moved uninhibited through the central plaza toward the main train station in the city center. They were observed there by an estimated thirty thousand people, many of whom were merely on their way home from work, school, or shopping.

About this time, Woetzel was busy explaining the unauthorized public announcement to his superior Helmut Hackenberg. Hackenberg was the overall political leader in charge of Leipzig and, as such, was responsible for coordinating the various police and other forces that were available to break up the anticipated demonstration. Faced with a local public announcement condoning the demonstration that conflicted with the order from the central East German government not to allow the demonstration, Hackenberg called the head of the central East German government, Erich Honecker, for instructions. Because Honecker was in a previously scheduled meeting, Hackenberg was only able to talk with Krenz. Krenz said to wait until he had checked with Honecker, after which he would call back. An hour passed without official orders. In the meantime, the police forces were frozen, the public announcement condoning the demonstration had greatly reduced tensions in Leipzig, many observers and bystanders joined in the demonstration, and about seventy thousand people peacefully demonstrated in Leipzig that day.[11]

SUBSEQUENT DEMONSTRATIONS

On the following Monday (October 16), there were over one hundred thousand demonstrators in Leipzig (Bahrmann and Links, 1994). Although demonstrations in the rest of the country had been inhibited by the arrests and violence in the early part of October, they had not been completely stifled, and the prior week's peaceful, semi-authorized demonstration had given the people in Leipzig renewed courage. On October 18, 1989, the previous leader of East Germany (Erich Honecker) was replaced by Egon Krenz, the man who had effectively allowed the crucial October 9 demonstration in Leipzig to occur without arrests (Krenz, 1990).

With Leipzig as an example, and with a new leader who had shown a willingness to allow demonstrations to occur, a larger wave of demonstrations broke out across East Germany in both large and small towns, with over a half million people participating in 145 different demonstration across East Germany in the week of October 23-30 (Hertle, 1996). These as well as the regular Monday demonstrations in Leipzig continued in ever growing numbers (Bahrmann and Links, 1994). On November 4, 1989, a demonstration was even formally authorized in East Berlin, and a crowd of over a half million people attended (Hertle, 1996) that was broadcast on East German government television (*Frankfurter Rundschau,* 1999). On November 6, 1989, a peaceful demonstration occurred in Leipzig with over four hundred thousand people present (Tetzner, 1990), which was approximately the number of residents in that city, although many of the demonstrators came from other East German cities to participate.

Opening the Berlin Wall

The new leader of East Germany, Egon Krenz, stated his openness to advice and change, and soon new reforms were initiated in response to many of the demands of the demonstrators (Krenz, 1990). For instance, prison terms for engaging in illegal demonstrations or for illegally attempting to cross the border into West Germany were eliminated, and past victims of these laws were freed (Schabowlski, 1990). Dialogue was continued with the demonstrators, and the state began to increase the freedom of the press by providing greater access to information and less censorship of reporting (Bahrmann and Links, 1994).

In addition, with increasing requests from demonstrators for travel freedom, and with the number of new applications to emigrate from East Germany running at about one thousand daily (to about 190,000 unfulfilled applications by the end of October), Krenz reinstituted the normal policy of unrestricted to travel to Czechoslovakia beginning November 1 (Hertle, 1996). By November 3, the area around the West German embassy there in Prague was filled up with over six thousand East Germans seeking the right to emigrate, but Czechoslovakia refused to open up refugee camps and instead demanded a solution to the crisis from East Germany (Maximytschew and Hertle, 1996). Although East Germany could have requested that either the overcrowded West German embassy in Prague be strictly cordoned off with Czech soldiers, or let Czechoslovakia itself close off its borders to East German tourists (if it wanted to avoid further incidents and problems), Krenz decided on the more humane course of allowing all East Germans to go to East Germany's own embassy in Prague and obtain legal permission to emigrate to West Germany from that office beginning on November 4.

Emigration to West Germany thereby became very possible via an unrestricted trip to Czechoslovakia. Over twenty thousand East Germans used this opportunity to emigrate to West Germany in the next few days, and only about one hundred of these returned to East Germany after a brief visit (Hertle, 1996).

With emigration now freely possible, with an enormous number of East Germans having already left the country in various ways since the beginning of the year, and with pressure then coming from Czechoslovakia to have the massive legal emigrations through Czechoslovakia be allowed more directly from East Germany itself, the leader of East Germany decided to open up all borders, including the borders to West Berlin and West Germany (Krenz, 1990). In particular, as of the morning of November 10 at 6AM, visas were to be provided promptly to all civilians who wanted them, except in unusual circumstances such as in cases of people being under criminal investigation (Hertle, 1996). This revolutionary development was initially planned to be announced early on the morning of November 10, but Krenz at the last minute changed the announcement time to between 6 P.M. and 7 P.M. on November 9, 1989 during a news conference (Maximytschew and Hertle, 1996).

At the news conference, a question about the possibility of new travel policies did not occur until 6:53 P.M. (Hertle, 1996). After a brief introduction on this issue, the East German responsible for answering reporters' questions indicated that a decision had been made to grant visas promptly for travel across all borders (Schabowski, 1991). When asked when the policy was to be implemented, he answered from the official document given to him with the word "immediately," but he failed to indicate that it would first be possible to apply for the visas the next day during normal business hours (Maximytschew and Hertle, 1994).

Few people actually watched East German TV, but the news spread anyway, especially after the announcement was repeated over the next few hours on West German TV stations, as documented by Hertle (1996). Many East Germans rushed to the Wall in order to be first in line to see the forbidden "West." By 9:20 P.M. on November 9, there were already hundreds of people in front of the Berlin Wall waiting for the monumental event that would end 28 years of travel restrictions. Although the border guards had been ordered to have the opening occur early the next day, they were also aware of the official East German television announcement somewhat ambiguously implying an immediate opening. In telephone conversations with their superiors (who in turn had spoken with the East German government leaders that were in contact with Krenz), the border guards were ordered to start letting a few of the most determined people cross through, while the others were to be held back peacefully until the next day if possible. By 10:30 P.M., suffering under great pressure to let the long line of people and cars through the Wall so that they could also return in time to sleep before work the next day, the guards at one of the Berlin Wall crossings indicated that they could no longer peacefully contain the crowd and obtained telephone permission to open up the border gate completely without any controls. Other uncontrolled border crossings into West Berlin were also subsequently made available prior to midnight, while additional gates into other parts of West Germany opened up somewhat later. By 4 A.M. on November 10, about 70,000 East Germans had crossed over into West Berlin (and 5000 into other West German cities), but more than half of these had already returned to East Germany by that time.

Although there were celebrations on the night of November 9-10, the bigger party occurred on the night of November 10-11 when millions of now informed East Germans entered West Berlin and other cities in West Germany on the originally scheduled date (Hertle, 1996). The West German leader (Helmut Kohl) came to make a nationalist propaganda speech to the celebrants, but he was drowned out by hecklers and jeering from the crowd of people who preferred to celebrate (Bahrmann and Links, 1994).

The celebrations continued throughout the month of November and into the early part of December. After an initial massive wave of emigrations in November, the average number of East Germans immigrating daily into West Germany fell in December to about one thousand, which was substantially lower than the rate just before the building of the Wall in August 1961 and was not that much higher than the levels of the 1950s that East Germany had previously survived (Murphy, 1990b). The average annual number of emigrations in the 1950s was 220,311, but there was a high point in 1953 of 331,390 emigrations, which was approximately the same as the 343,854 East Germans who emigrated legally or illegally in 1989 (Hertle, 1996), with many of the 1989 emigrants being people who would have emigrated in prior years but were prevented from doing so by the Wall.

While the parties continued, the politicians in East and West Germany continued to rant and rave throughout this period about issues of little immediate concern to the celebrating Germans. Many scarcely even noticed in late November when the West German chancellor Kohl indicated that any increase in aid and economic cooperation was dependent on East Germany initiating capitalist economic reforms and Western-style elections (dpa, 1989). Most were also not concerned when, in early December, the East German parliament (without consulting the East German people) succumbed to the pressure by removing the article of the East German constitution that guaranteed concentrated power in the hands of the communist party and by replacing Krenz with a more pliable economic reformist, Hans Modrow (Bahrmann and Links, 1994). Although West Germany initially responded somewhat positively by offering some limited financial aid (*Der Tagesspiegel,* 1989c), a decision was made before Christmas that would end the celebration and turn the widely-welcomed opening of the Wall into a catastrophe.

The Collapse of the Berlin Wall

Even after the November 9 event, the East Germans had always maintained strict control of West German tourist traffic into their country in order to protect their products from being smuggled out at cheap black market prices (Murphy, 1992b). However, after opening up the Wall for East Germans, the West German government was putting extreme political pressure on the East German government leaders to reduce controls on West German travel to East Germany. The East German government was also being pressured into allowing West Germans to freely convert their currency into East German money at an incredible exchange rate of 3 East German Marks per West German Mark. This exchange rate was absurd because the purchasing power of the East German Mark was approximately equal to that of the West German Mark. In fact, for many items (like food, books, clothing, rooms, and other consumer staples), the East German Mark could actually buy 5 to 10 times more consumer goods in East Germany than the West Mark could buy in West Germany (Collier, 1985). The 3:1 exchange rate thereby made it 15 to 30 times cheaper for West Germans to shop in East Germany than in West Germany, and such inexpensive purchases represented a form of legalized shoplifting that effectively reduced the East German standard of living by over 2/3.

Although the removal of controls on smuggling and the legalization of a ridiculous exchange rate would effectively make it possible for the richer West Germans to steal from the poorer East Germans (Arnold, 1990), the new, economically naive East German leader, Hans Modrow, succumbed to West German pressure in late December 1989 and agreed to the new policies along with other capitalist demands in return for

West German financial aid (*Der Tagesspiegel,* 1989c). January 1, 1990 was set as the date on which the new 3:1 exchange rate (*Der Tagesspiegel,* 1989f) and open borders with no visa fee, no minimum official money exchange, and no security check for visitors to East Germany (Hertle, 1996) were to go into effect. Prior to that, an unbiased mid-December survey of East Germans had indicated that over 70% were in favor of both socialism and the maintenance of a separate East German state (Bahrmann and Links, 1994).

There was one final enormous party on New Year's at the Brandenburg Gate with about a half million people enjoying the festivities and fireworks there (Bauer, 1990). After that celebration, the new economic reforms proceeded to destroy the East German morale, economy, and society. Already in early January 1990, the number of East Germans emigrating to West Germany had doubled from a somewhat manageable one thousand per day (Murphy, 1990b) to over 2000 per day (dpa, 1990a). By February 1990, most East Germans were in favor of unification as a means to avoid a further deterioration of their economy, although the majority still preferred a more left-wing government (*Der Tagesspiegel,* 1990g). However, by promising a 1:1 exchange rate if their East German representatives won an election scheduled for March 18, 1990, the conservative West German coalition parties were able to win the votes of a narrow majority of East German voters and impose their system on the East Germans (*Der Tagesspiegel,* 1990o).

It should be emphasized that the political collapse of East Germany was not inevitable. A more repressive government would have never allowed the demonstrations nor undertaken reforms of the system. In addition, a benevolent but more prudent government would have never have succumbed to Western pressure to open up their economy to a ridiculous and destructive exchange rate. Moreover, before adopting any Western-style elections (that enable the rich to buy the polling result), a wise East German leadership would have waited until reparations-induced wealth disparities had been eliminated (as could have been achieved within 2 years using the economic plan described in Chapter 5).

The Effect of the East German Revolution

The demonstrations and reforms in East Germany that occurred in the fall of 1989 spread quickly to the other communist countries of Eastern Europe. As the people in these countries saw that demonstrations could be successfully undertaken even against the most hard-line communist government (i.e., the one in East Germany), they followed suit (Weiss, 1990). Except in Romania, the governments of the remaining Eastern European countries gave in to the demands of the demonstrators without firing a shot (Ratesh, 1991). By the end of 1989, future Western-style elections had been declared in all of the previous communist countries of Eastern Europe in alliance with the Soviet Union, including East Germany, Poland, Czechoslovakia, Hungary, Bulgaria, and Romania (Weiss, 1990). Shortly thereafter in early 1990, constitutional reforms were also initiated in the Soviet Union (without the consent of the people) that permitted Western-style elections (Service, 1998). Such reforms opened up their countries to Western media manipulation (IAC, 1998a) and led to the break-up of the Soviet system the following year (Service, 1998), despite the fact that the Soviet people had voted earlier in 1991 to preserve the Soviet Union (Becker, 1999a).

East Germany had been the hardest and most crucial piece of armor in the Soviet Union's bloc of nations (Goertemaker, 1994). East Germany had the second largest army, the highest standard of living, and the strongest economy in the Soviet bloc (Krenz, 1990). And East Germany was at the forefront in high technology goods like electronics and computer chips (Mittag, 1991). The Soviet bloc desperately needed such products in order to survive in the Cold War against the capitalist nations which had restricted the export of high technology goods to the Soviet bloc (Parrott, 1985). Without East Germany, Eastern European leaders surrendered to Western pressure and allowed the Soviet bloc to simply collapse (*Frankfurter Rundschau,* 1999).

The collapse of the Soviet Union resulted in many former republics being transformed into outright capitalist dictatorships (Whalen, 2000). Even Eastern European countries such as Russia that have attempted to create a façade of political freedom have turned the words "democracy" into a farce by banning opposition parliament, political parties, and media (Ignatius and Rosett, 1993), by allowing organized crime to seize economic and political power (Raith, 1994), and by engaging in outright purchases of people's votes in elections (Hearst Newspapers, 1996).[12]

In addition, the transformation of Eastern Europe into capitalist countries did not bring the desired economic prosperity. Instead, the pressure that the capitalist West put on the Eastern European countries to destroy all vestiges of Communism merely brought unemployment, inflation, poverty, financial uncertainty, crime, and chaos (Cox News, 1995).

And Egon Krenz, the East German leader who had acted so quickly upon the demands of the peaceful demonstrators to open up the Wall and initiate political reforms in East Germany, was convicted and imprisoned in the united Germany for deaths at the Wall (Associated Press, 1999d). That conviction occurred despite the fact that Krenz (as an East German government minister merely carrying out the orders of the East German leader Erich Honecker at the time) was far less responsible than the West German government itself for the Wall and the tragedies there (Murphy, 1990b).

The economic destruction resulting from unification was to create social and economic divisions between East and West Germany that would take decades to mend (Dumas and Dumas, 1996). Although the differences between the two Germanies were not that great at the end of December 1989, the policy of unifying the countries by destroying East Germany greatly magnified those differences (*Frankfurter Rundschau*, 1999) and also contributed significantly to various economic crises of the 1990s, as will be explained later in Chapter 6.

Before engaging in a thorough analysis of the aggregate new world order in the post-cold-war era in Chapters 6 and 7, however, the German case is studied in greater detail in the next two chapters to provide more concrete perspective on communism. In particular, a comparative analysis of the East and West German financial systems prior to the 1989 revolution is conducted in the next chapter. This analysis demonstrates not only the similarities of the two systems and their potential compatibility (implying that the destruction of the East German system was unnecessary) but also shows that the East German financial system was actually superior and more efficient in many respects. One implication of these findings is that it was the capitalist West German system that should have been changed, not communist East German society. At the very least, the advantages of the East German system should have been preserved, as Chapter 5 shows was indeed possible.

CHAPTER 4

A COMPARATIVE ANALYSIS OF EAST AND WEST GERMAN FINANCIAL SYSTEMS IN LIGHT OF THE NEW EVIDENCE

The political reforms in the communist world led to a popular demand for the importation of the economic and financial system of the capitalist West. This political demand for capitalism was stimulated by academic propaganda on the theoretical efficiency of capitalism (e.g., Taga, 1984; and Goldfeld and Quandt, 1988). Unfortunately, such simplistic theories ignore many practical financial issues, and the result of the economic reforms in Eastern Europe since 1989 has been depression instead of the promised prosperity. For example, the IMF (1996) reports that Gross Domestic Product fell by over 40% in Eastern Europe over the interval 1990-95. A realistic appraisal of differences between capitalist and communist business financial systems is useful in order to mitigate future economic catastrophes.

Historical Evolution of the Divided German Financial Systems

As a divided country, East and West Germany prior to unification provide an interesting example for a comparison of East and West business financial decision-making systems. Although Germany was a capitalist country prior to its capitulation in World War II, the eastern portion of the country was put under Soviet occupation after the war, and this sector developed into communist East Germany.

Despite specifying four separate zones of occupation for USA, French, British, and Soviet occupation forces after the war (and four separate zones of Berlin which was isolated within the eastern zone), the original plan of the victorious allied countries (stipulated at Yalta in early 1945) was for a united Germany to be created out of the defeated Nazi country and for that united nation to pay reparations to the USSR for war damages (Harmssen, 1951). The exact amount of the reparations was set according to an agreement between the Soviet Union and the Western occupying countries at Potsdam in July 1945 (with $10 billion contracted to be paid to the USSR as partial compensation for the enormous destruction that Nazi Germany had inflicted on it during World War II), but the USA violated this agreement in May 1946 when it began to prohibit the Soviet Union from taking any reparations from the western sectors of the occupied country (Apel, 1966). As a result, the Soviet Union had to extract the entire amount from its tiny eastern sector of Germany, and the resulting reparations payments from that area averaged about 25% of its national income each year between 1946 and 1953 (Stolper, 1960). Other expropriations of wealth by the Soviet Union (to cover other war-related costs) made the total amount taken from East Germany sum to over 100 billion Marks (Merkel and Wahl, 1991), which represented many times tiny East Germany's annual output at the time. For instance, most of the capital stock in eastern Germany had been seized by the Soviet Union by the end of 1946 (Harmssen, 1951), including about 40% being carted off to the USSR (Apel, 1966) and a further 20% being kept in eastern Germany but under Soviet ownership (Ritschl, 1996).

By 1948, reparations-induced money printing and inflation in the Soviet sector caused the USA and its allies (Britain and France) to form a separate West German currency for its western zone of Germany and Berlin (Schwarzer, 1999). The Soviet Union reacted with a blockade of western Berlin which was isolated from the rest of western Germany (Apel, 1966). After the USA airlift had succeeded in "saving" western Berlin from having to pay its share of the reparations, the USA had a German government formed for the western sector of the country (also including the isolated West Berlin) in 1949. This West German government's constitution mandated the annexation of the eastern Soviet sector whenever possible (Ritschl, 1996). In reaction, the Soviet Union allowed a separate communist country to form in East Germany later in 1949 (Autorenkollektiv, 1966).

Meanwhile, the wealth of German war criminals and former Nazis had been expropriated by the government in East Germany over the period 1945-46 (Adler, 1980). As a result, much of the private capital there not seized by the Soviet Union had been put under local East German government ownership, including a large amount of industry as a result of a June 1946 referendum in which 72% of the people in the industrial Saxony portion of East Germany voted for nationalization (Ritschl, 1996). Later in 1946, local elections in all of East Germany resulted in slightly over 50% of the people there voting for the Socialist Unity Party, which represented a merger of the Social Democratic and the Communist Parties (Andrew and Gordievsky, 1990). Also in the meantime, large private landholdings had been nationalized (and redistributed to smaller farmers) during this immediate post-war period (Burant, 1987), although agriculture was not collectivized until the 1958-60 interval (Ritschl, 1996).

Most of the remaining major businesses in East Germany were nationalized by the state in subsequent years, with a large section of privately owned capital bought out by the government in 1972 (the year after Erich Honecker assumed power), at which time state ownership of industry rose from 82% to 99% (Weber, 1988). By the 1980s virtually all land and businesses with more than 10 employees were owned by the state (with most conglomerated into huge state businesses called *Kombinate* in the 1970s), which thereby directly controlled decision-making, and the state also regulated wages, prices, and many other business decisions in the rest of the economy (Behr, 1985). The official policy with respect to the remaining private enterprises was that they were allowed only if they served the better community interest (Filmer, 1985b). Other than having one state owner, which theoretically attempted to act in the best interests of all the people in the country (instead of for the good of a rich minority of shareholders), the East German financial system was similar to that of West Germany in many respects (with the stock market in East Germany existing solely in the form of the government having the *right* to buy up any private companies that grew to over 10 employees, with the "buyout" price being specified to be a legal formula based on profits).

A Comparative Analysis of Financial Decision-Making

To facilitate the comparison of the financial systems, business financial decision-making activities can be divided into several semi-separate functions, including making, funding, and managing investments. A comparison of how each of these functions was practically carried out in East and West Germany prior to unification is conducted separately in different subsections. This analysis is followed by an empirical evaluation of the relative efficiency of the two systems.

Financial decision-making in East and West German firms prior to unification was fairly similar in many respects. Differences in investment, funding, and control functions existed largely because of the differences in the financial environment.

Making Investments

In both East and West Germany, investment decisions were typically centralized for large organizations but decentralized for smaller investments. In East Germany, the final decisions for large investment projects were made by a centralized State Plan Commission (*Staatliche Plankommision*). However, the management of the East German economy was divided among a number of different firms that included People's businesses called *volkseigene Betriebe* (VEB) and VEB conglomerates (*Kombinate*), and each of these firms had some degree of independence in investment decision-making. For example, decisions on smaller projects, such as those under 5 million Marks in value and some financed within the individual firm from internally generated profits and cash flow, were made by the firm's management (DIW, 1989). Such a combination of centralized and decentralized investment decision-making was similar to that employed in firms in West Germany. In West Germany, lower-level management makes decisions on projects up to a specific maximum value, and top management makes the final decision on larger investments (Perridon and Steiner (1988: 27).

In addition, the criteria used to make investment decisions were similar, with the payback period of the investment and/or the internal rate of return (IRR) being widely employed in both countries (Knauff, 1983). The payback period (called the *Rueckflussdauer der einmaligen Aufwendungen* in East Germany) is computed as the time required for the expected cash inflows from the investments to pay for the initial outflow. For investments with perpetually constant cash flows, investments with payback periods less than the inverse of the required return on the funds tied up in the investment are considered worthwhile. The IRR (called the *Grundfondsrentabilitaet* in East Germany) is computed as the discount rate that sets the sum of the present value of the cash flows from the investment equal to the initial investment. Projects with IRRs greater than the required return are optimally accepted. However, other factors are also considered, such as type and quantity of inputs, type and quantity of outputs, and environmental factors (Knauff, 1983).

For both the payback period and the IRR, the cash flows from the investments have to be forecasted. In East Germany, prices for goods and services were centrally controlled and determined, and so cash flows were more easily forecast. Thus, there was less chance of error of making an investment that should not have been made, as well as a lower probability of not making an investment that should have been made. In West Germany, where prices are determined by the market and fluctuate greatly, the probability of making an investment that does not subsequently earn the required return (or of not making an investment that would have earned a return over that required) is greater. In addition, the price uncertainty in West Germany requires more forecasting and analysis, and thus more time spent on making investment decisions.

Investments in East Germany were also made with full knowledge of other investment and future resource allocation plans, and so excess investment that might have resulted in redundant capacity or dual research and development programs were minimized. Gorbachev's experiments with a market economy in the Soviet Union in the late 1980s also illustrated the fact that investment decisions tend to be suboptimal when made by the individual businesses without central government planning (Marcy, 1990).

Moreover, central financial planners were able to avoid the costs and agency problems associated with bankruptcy risk that can cause capitalist borrowers to make excessively risky, imprudent investments and to neglect more profitable, prudent investments (Myers, 1977). An example of capitalist incentives to make imprudent investments is the case of a firm gambling its last funds on a project with extremely high risk and very low (or even negative) expected returns but the remote possibility of a very large return that would save the company from failure (Murphy, 1992c). An example of a capitalist company being unable to make a prudent investment with a high expected return is the case of a company that has no funds left to initiate the investment and has such shaky credit that it can't even win the trust of potential customers much less suppliers or creditors (*Frankfurter Allgemeine,* 1998b).

While the advantages of central planning supervision of funding and investment for financially troubled firms would be lost if failed firms were allowed to make investments that were economically unviable (Goldfeld and Quandt, 1988), heavy interest penalties and stringent administrative interference by the state in cases of insolvency did create incentives and opportunities to minimize wasteful activity, as Granick (1974), Melzer and Stahnke (1986), and Autorenkollektiv (1988) document. Apart from being more efficient in mitigating agency costs, the communist system also avoids both the legal costs of bankruptcy and the negative domino effects of bankruptcy that lead to layoffs, further bankruptcies, and lower economic growth (Hudson, 1992).

One problem often mentioned with investment in centrally planned economies is that decisions were based on centrally planned prices instead of "market-clearing" prices determined by consumer purchases. As a result, prices and cash flows did not "efficiently" reflect true "rational" values (Erdmann, 1983). However, it is not clear that prices are more efficiently and rationally determined by a large mass of uninformed West German consumers who must spend a considerable amount of time price-shopping and who can be manipulated at great cost by expensive advertisements and highly paid sales people motivated to sell any goods at a price as high as possible (as explained in Chapter 2).

In East Germany, a small group of well-informed East German central planners, who had access to information on the East German supply and demand situation as well as on West German prices, established different prices for different levels of quality and service. Flexibility in pricing some goods was provided to many East German firms through the issuance of price range guidelines (instead of fixed prices). Adjustments in both fixed prices and price ranges were also permitted at the firm level in order to better balance supply and demand (Steudtner et al., 1988). Although East German central planners maintained fairly static prices (or price ranges) for consumer goods that did not fully reflect the supply-demand situation, a complex system of subsidies and transfer pricing adjustments were made in East German businesses in order to adjust prices toward value for purposes of measuring costs, profits, and firm cash flows (Erdmann, 1983).

While the East German transfer pricing system required a significant amount of administrative time, greater effort for accounting, valuation, and transfer pricing is required in West Germany. In West Germany, there are many more firms and product brands, and there are at least three separate bookkeeping systems in each firm: one for financial reporting, one for internal purposes, and one for taxes (Matz, 1975). Within the paperwork maze of the cumbersome West German bureaucracy, West Germans expend an extraordinary amount of time to merely try and figure out (as well as avoid) tax liabilities (*Der Spiegel*, 1992a), which were computed more automatically in East Germany.

Funding Investments

Funding for investments came from sources internal and external to the firm in both East and West Germany. In both countries, internally generated funds came from business profits after taxes and after dividends to the owner(s) of the business, where the business owner in East Germany was the government (Steudtner et al., 1988). East German firms were automatically forced to pay 50% of net profits as dividends to their central government owner, and the government could also control the investment of the remaining profits as well (Melzer and Stahnke, 1986). The actual amount of funds retained in East German businesses was set as a function of both the profitability of the firm and its investment needs (Steudtner et al., 1988). On the other hand, in West Germany, amounts retained in businesses could be arbitrarily set by rich owners based on their idiosyncratic consumption and investment desires, with this decision being made for consumers by professional managers in large West German corporations (Perridon and Steiner, 1988: 302-319).

For decisions on internal financing, one advantage of the East German system was that the central planners did not have the same capacity to have excessive amounts of internally generated funds retained in the business to finance suboptimal investments, which Jensen (1986) has cited to be a major problem for managers of Western corporations. This problem is present in all capitalist economies because managers are motivated to inefficiently hoard assets to protect their salaries and jobs. The problem is compounded in West Germany because West German banks, as the major stock brokers who vote most shares owned by retail customers, and as equity investors (Whitney, 1994), tend to control the voting shares of many large industrial firms to which they also make large loans. To protect their loans from default, German bankers have an incentive to force the corporations they control to hold on to far more assets than are optimal for maximum productivity.

If more financing was needed, external funding was available in both East and West Germany. In East Germany, the external funding market consisted of a state bank (*Staatsbank*) that issued credit (Autorenkollektiv, 1988) and a state planning commission (*Staatliche Plankommission*) that provided equity capital (Melzer, 1983). The interest rate charged on credit from the Staatsbank was 5% (for both private and public firms), although a subsidized rate of 1.8% was offered for investments in technology (or other areas deemed to be vital to the economy), and the rate increased 2% (or more, up to a maximum of 12%) in any case of late payments (Autorenkollektiv, 1988). The return on the equity capital investments of the Staatliche Plankommission was set as a minimum of 6% (which automatically had to be paid annually to the state owner as a sort of preferred stock dividend that was deducted before computing the state's effective common equity claim or net profit) and was allowed (via the setting of prices controlled by the state) to be as high as 18% for the most efficient firm in an industry (Melzer, 1983). On the other hand, in West Germany, external funding comes from rich individual and institutional investors, to whom firms sold securities (debt and equity) that had to offer the expected returns arbitrarily demanded by those investors (Perridon and Steiner, 1988). In both countries, the pricing of the securities was important for allocating funds at the appropriate cost to the businesses, so that they could make their investment decisions rationally using this cost of funds.

Because external funding in East German firms came from a central planning body that had access to full inside information, the cost of funds could be more precisely priced, and funds could be allocated to the most efficient users of the funds. On the other hand, in the capitalist

West German securities market, prices differ from value by a random error term that may be known only to insiders (Myers and Majluf, 1984). The size of this error term and the corresponding difference in rational funds allocation to the most efficient users can easily be quite large (Summers, 1986). Causes of discrepancies include excessive securities price speculation through technical analysis (Beja and Goldman, 1980), price manipulation that "Wall Street insiders readily concede ... is rampant" (Stern and Fritz, 1987), mafia fraud and extortion in the securities industry (Smith and Schroeder, 2000), large security order imbalances (Blume, Mackinlay, and Terker, 1989), inadequate fundamental valuation analysis due to investor incompetence, neglect, and/or emotional swings (Oppenheimer, 1984), investor overconfidence and regret (Barber and Odean, 1999), biased reporting on companies because outside (and allegedly "independent") security analysts are under constant threat of companies withholding useful information (and even launching libel lawsuits) if negative statements about companies are made (MacDonald, 1999b), a short-sighted perspective on the part of investors (Zarowin, 1989), and general institutional psychological factors that cause market prices to deviate from intrinsic value (Haugen, 1999). According to Summers (1986), corrective arbitrage of such situations might prove unsuccessful even in a well-developed securities market. As a result of such mispricings, funds are allocated irrationally in capitalist economies, instead of to the most efficient users.

To the situation of reduced rationality of funds allocation in the West German securities market is added the problem of increased resources being applied to security analysis (and funds allocation) than were necessary in the centrally planned communist capital market. A centrally planned economy permitted decisions on fund allocation in East Germany to be made by a small, well-informed group of analysts, who were theoretically well-trained in socially useful financial analysis (Autorenkollektiv, 1988). That compares favorably to the situation in West Germany, where funds are channeled to businesses by a large, less well-informed group theoretically composed of price speculators and individuals who happen to have large amounts of wealth (through inheritance, crime, sales ability, acting ability, etc.). Even when "professional" managers are chosen to invest money in capitalist countries, the evidence does not indicate more intelligent investment decisions, as money managers are generally selected based on sales ability and personal contacts (O'Barr and Conley, 1992). Such a situation implies even less rational and less efficient investment in West Germany.

In addition, in Western capital markets, the costs of trading and analyzing the value of a security often result in investors requiring a premium return over that normally required (Halle and Stoll, 1989). This liquidity premium is larger for smaller firms because of the inability to spread fixed costs of trading and analysis over a large trading volume (Dubosfsky and Groth, 1986). The existence of liquidity premiums in Western capital markets implies a higher cost of capital, especially for smaller firms (Stoll and Whaley, 1983).[1] In an effort to reduce these liquidity premiums, an extensive financial infrastructure can be built up, but the fees and commissions from the banking, brokerage, and insurance components of that infrastructure alone exceed 5% of GDP in some countries (Stopa, 1999), and these deadweight costs don't even include other major costs of liquidity trading (like differences between buying and selling prices), nor do they include all the costs of shopping around for the best deal and analyzing investments (Murphy, 2000).

Moreover, because of the existence of central planning in East Germany, greater stability in consumption there might have been expected than in West Germany. As a result, a lower return premium could be required for systematic risk as measured by a consumption beta (Ahn, 1989), thereby magnifying the discrepancies between the costs of capital in the two countries.

It should also be mentioned that required risk premiums on securities fluctuate wildly in Western capital markets (Chan, Chen, and Hsieh, 1985). The result is uncertainty as to the cost and availability of funds, socially unproductive speculation on the future course of the risk premium, and more mispricing and wasted analytical resources (Murphy, 2000). In addition, a further risk premium may be required in Western capital markets for the variation in the risk premium (Chan, Chen, and Hsieh, 1985). The resulting higher cost of capital results in less investment projects being acceptable and therefore lower economic growth in capitalist countries (although the higher returns required mean faster income growth for the rich).

There is also some evidence that rich capitalists and corporate bureaucrats are more difficult to persuade to fund innovative and productive long-term investments than governments (*Der Spiegel*, 1998), as previously discussed in Chapter 1. In particular, the desire to protect jobs, salary, and the status quo contributes to the fact that capitalist corporations "don't tend to be great foundations of independent thinking" in the USA (O'Barr and Conley, 1992) or in Germany (Rhoads, 1999). Moreover, "innovative" capitalist heroes (such as Bill Gates) glorified by the Western press often create nothing on their own but instead copy the innovations of others and then monopolize the market through special deals arranged through rich relatives (and social contacts), buyouts, and predatory pricing made possible only because of their riches (Wilson, 1998a). Even true innovators and entrepreneurs are not really made happy by enormous amounts of accumulated personal wealth but are instead motivated more by the lure of "creating something," "having a mission," and "connecting with other people...in a team" (*Wall Street Journal,* 2000a). Further evidence on this issue is provided by the fact that, despite technology embargoes and despite having less capital, the communist countries were fairly successful in staying fairly close to the technological level of the richest capitalist countries (Smith, 2000), often strictly through local development because of the technology embargoes (Parrott, 1985). An example of East German technological advances can even be found in their much maligned auto industry, which developed a world class car (the Trabant) in the late 1950s (Schroeder, 1995), and which also designed a new car model that was years ahead of West German development in the 1970s although East Germany did not have the resources to justify further development for its small market (Bauer, 1999). Adler (1980) has cited evidence indicating that communist countries were able to motivate more innovation (and participation) among workers, and he logically drew the conclusion that "the type of production technology associated with the communist mode of production is being engendered in the scientific and technological revolution."

Managing Investments

Once an investment decision is made and financed, the project must be managed. Good financial management requires monitoring of problems, making adjustments to the plan because of changes in the environment, and undertaking proper measurement of, and setting incentives for, good performance.

It is often assumed that efficiency in monitoring and changing plans was lower in East Germany. In particular, because pricing was more static and centralized in East Germany, shortages were more frequent than in West Germany, where firms often have more flexibility to correct problems of being out of stock with marketing manipulation (McCarthy, 1975) and changes to the usual cost-based prices (Erdmann, 1983). Burant (1987) has also mentioned the problems in the East German system of fixed prices that did not readily adjust for technological and factor cost changes. Product black markets, hoarding, speculation, wastage, and production stoppages (caused by machinery breakdowns and a lack of spare parts) thrived in this environment. Subsidies and transfer pricing corrections were often too complicated and inflexible to completely remedy these problems (Melzer, 1983).

However, there is little evidence that the supply-demand imbalances in East Germany caused more inefficiency than the potentially more onerous problems in West Germany. As explained in Chapter 2, the more flexible West German pricing system created problems such as product price uncertainty, extra time spent planning for an unknown future, decisions made incorrectly due to lack of knowledge regarding future prices and the aggregate economic situation, time lost shopping around for the best price, inconvenience associated with the financial incentives to wait for the next "special" or coupon, and misleading marketing tactics that create annoying disinformation and discrepancies between price and rational value (Furlough and Strikwerda, 1999). A particularly large amount of time is lost in capitalism while negotiating or bartering over the price that can range widely depending solely on relative negotiating skills. Although some laws restricting the size of discounts in West Germany reduce some of this inefficient use of time for consumers, such time expenditures are still required for the very frequent inter-business purchases in order to maximize the chance of negotiating the best possible price.

In addition, the lack of perfectly competitive markets in capitalist countries results in prices being chronically too high to clear. As a result, waste and inefficiency such as unused industrial capacity, unemployment, apartment vacancies, and unpurchased and spoiled goods are historical norms (Marx and Engels, 1988b). The current existence in the USA of an extraordinary number of homeless not geographically dispersed from a large oversupply of housing is a typically perverse case of capitalism in practice (Johnson, 1990). A similar example of the perversion caused by capitalism is the perceived need to reduce agricultural output (or even destroy food "surpluses"), so that agricultural prices (and profits) can be increased (with the help of a capitalist government), even when there are domestic citizens suffering from hunger and malnutrition (Hobhouse, 1989).

Berliner (1957) has mentioned problems in socialist enterprises arising from managers having incentives and capacity to conduct unreported transactions and falsify records (MacDonald, 1999a). However, similar problems exist in capitalist corporations and are likewise minimized in socialist enterprises with proper auditing and control through interfirm comparisons (e.g., Steudtner et al., 1988). In addition, the organizational and human problems of bureaucracy, waste, and judgmental errors existing in socialist societies (Shmelov and Popov, 1989) are equally prevalent in capitalist firms (Schwartz, 1990). Moreover, while corruption and bribery may occur in government operations of all types, most such bribery is initiated by rich capitalist businesses bribing poor country officials (Tanzi, 1998). In addition, such activity may actually be much more prevalent in capitalist systems, given that bribery between business representatives is rarely prosecuted, is not always illegal, and is "just accepted" as a normal business activity even in well-developed (and allegedly less corrupt) economies like the USA (Gerlin, 1995), and given that "flagrant" cases of extortion (including death threats for failure to do deals) also exist even among the largest and most prestigious companies (Simpson, 2000). Corruption may be far more widespread in West Germany where bribery (literally translated from the German word "Schmiergeld" as "lubrication money") is not only legal but also tax-deductible (Celarier, 1995). The capitalist reforms of Gorbachev's Perestroika in the Soviet Union in the late 1980s indicated that the capitalist system of controls tends to be inferior, as indicated by the larger number of administrators required, the higher amount of crime that results, and the compounding of problems compared to under the earlier, more centrally-controlled government system (Marcy, 1990).

In addition, in East and West Germany, except for small companies (which had a potentially more serious problem of overall management skills), there existed the agency problem of motivating non-owner managers and workers to achieve organizational goals such as improving efficiency (Jensen, 1986). In both East (Steudtner et al., 1988) and West (Perridon and Steiner, 1988: 344-367) Germany, similar variables were used to measure, motivate, and reward good performance. For instance, actual revenue and profitability levels achieved were examined in both countries, and special emphasis was placed in East as well as West Germany on cost reductions (*Kostensenkungen*) and return on investment (*Rentabilitaet*). In addition, in both countries, the performance measures were compared to past performance, to competitors' performance, and to targeted results. Actual performance above expectation was often rewarded with bonuses and recognition, while sub-par performance could result in demotion.

In East Germany, the ability to compensate managers for good performance was limited by ideological directives that restricted differences in pay (Hof, 1983). In addition, job security rules inhibited laying off managers and workers for poor performance (Thuet, 1985). However, similar limitations also existed in most companies in West Germany, where the labor force is heavily unionized (including a large portion of white-collar workers). Where incentive systems do exist in capitalist firms, they are usually of a monetary form that can be manipulated for personal gain to the detriment of business or society as a whole (Schwartz, 1991). For instance, employees often have a greater incentive to play office politics than perform productive work in capitalist systems (Sherman, 1993). In addition, commission salespeople often "push" overpriced, unnecessary, and poor quality products that frequently have no positive value to the consumer (e.g., Shapiro, 1994). One German high-tech industrialist bluntly summarized the capitalist world with the statement, "Life is selling" (Orth, 1998).

The often somewhat arbitrary nature of capitalist pay-incentive awards can cause wasteful frictions, rivalries, jealousies, frustration, and short-sighted behavior that is counter to both company and societal interests in the long term (Murphy, 1989). Although the existence of stock incentive plans in West Germany can theoretically help to enhance the motivation to work toward a common goal of maximizing the company's stock price (Diamond and Verrechia, 1982), it is not clear that maximization of stock price maximizes company value and efficiency.

For instance, DeFusco, Johnson, and Zorn (1990) have found evidence that stock option plans only provide an incentive to transfer wealth from bondholders to stockholders and do not result in any increases in firm efficiency. In addition, Larcker (1983) has found empirical evidence that stock incentive plans are no more effective than other long-term incentive plans in increasing stock prices.

Moreover, because stock prices are not determined by insiders with full information, stock prices often behave extremely irrationally (Krueger and Kennedy, 1990), may fluctuate around short-term events and ignore long-term prospects (e.g., DeBondt and Thaler, 1985, and Jacobs and Levy, 1988), can deviate greatly from true value for significant periods of time without detection (Summers, 1986), and can therefore provide distorted signals for performance purposes (Froot, Scharfstein, and Stein, 1992). Because such distortions in stock prices exist in Germany as well as in other countries like the USA (Schiereck, De Bondt, and Weber, 1999), compensation based on such prices can lead to distorted performance by employees. Even if the common goal of company valuation maximization could be attained, individual company maximization is often inconsistent with value maximization of a larger whole (Eiteman, Stonehill, and Moffett, 1998) and is frequently at odds with the welfare of society (Marx and Engels, 1988a). For instance, even the capitalist philosopher Adam Smith stated that profit-maximizing business owners are often naturally engaged in a "conspiracy against the public, or in some contrivance to raise prices" (Strobel and Peterson, 1999).

Regardless of whether employees are paid in stock or cash, it should also be mentioned that promotions and the highest compensation in capitalist countries are often allocated to those who are best at playing office politics as opposed to those who are the most productive (Schwartz, 1990). What club(s) a person belongs to can also factor in as being very important in determining pay and employment status (Knight, 1983). In capitalism, jobs themselves can take a great deal of time just to find (if they can be found at all) and are typically allocated based on physical beauty, sales skill, self-promotion, and personal contacts instead of on skill and productivity (*Los Angeles Times,* 1996). It isn't what you know but who you know that often counts most in capitalism (Sesit, 1995). Although West German capitalism was somewhat more regulated than in other countries (like the USA), about 40% of all West Germans got their jobs through social connections such as via relatives (Wegener, 1991), with the percentage being significantly higher for private company positions than for government jobs (Noll, 1985), and with better positions being obtained by those who used their social connections to obtain their jobs (Noll, 1984).

Although about 40% of all East Germans also used social contacts to choose where they were going to work, there was no significantly higher prestige and pay for employment obtained through connections in East Germany (Voelker and Flap, 1999). Since jobs (and regulated wages) commensurate with a person's skill and education were effectively guaranteed by the East German state (so that there were no additional job search costs associated with not having social contacts in the right places), the capitalist concept of "social capital" and artificial "contact networking" had far less material employment value in East Germany (as contacts in East Germany were used merely to allow people to work with others they already knew and liked, and not to ration off scarce jobs). Perhaps as a result of knowing that they were working for the good of society as a whole (as opposed to slaving to maximize the profits of the rich), social pressure and awards to work together for a common goal were stronger in East Germany (Hof, 1983). As a result, an atmosphere existed that permitted greater cooperation among workers than in West Germany, with most East German workers welcoming innovation and new technology, and with 5 times as many East German workers finding their work increasingly interesting as those finding it less so over time (Adler, 1980).

Empirical Comparison of Efficiency

The analysis of practical financial decision-making indicates that the East German system may have been superior for purposes of investment decision-making, funds allocation, and financial management efficiency. Some evidence on the overall comparative efficiency of the two systems can be obtained from national economic growth statistics reported in *Das Statistische Jahrbuch der Deutschen Demokratischen Republik* and in the IMF's *International Financial Statistics.* As explained by Stolper (1960), "the differences in the concept of national income between East and West Germany are surprisingly small."

Comparative Aggregate Economic Performance

In 1989, Net National Income per capita in West Germany was 31,774 West German Marks, while Net National Income per capita in East Germany was 16,712 East German Marks. Although the East German Mark was inconvertible, research indicates that it had a purchasing power equal to between 75% (for the reasonably affluent) and 150% (for the less affluent) of the West German Mark for average consumers in the early 1980s (DIW, 1984). The average higher purchasing power of the East German Mark was confirmed when average prices rose by about 13.8%-8.6%=5.2% more in eastern Germany between 1989 and 1991 when the East German Mark was replaced with the West German Mark (and prices in eastern Germany moved close to the market levels in western Germany), as documented by various West German professional research estimates (Osmond, 1992). Given the subsequent phasing out of rent controls, and given other factors that caused consumer prices in eastern Germany to rise another 16% more than in West Germany between 1991 and 1996 (Statisticshes Bundesamt, 1997), it can be assumed that the average purchasing power of the East German Mark was equal to at least 1.15 West German Marks in 1989.[2]

Deflating the 1989 West German incomes by the average 15% higher prices that existed in West German Marks, East German income per capita appeared to be about 40% lower than in West Germany in 1989.[3] However, since the East German National Income figures do not include some "unproductive" services that are incorporated into the West German figures, as noted by Stolper (1960), a more comparable National Income for East Germany might be over 10% higher than reported (Collier, 1985), making East German income per capita about 2/3 that of West Germany. On the other hand, given that a larger number of East Germans were in the work force because a larger percentage of the females (over 60% of the female population) was employed (Schwarzer, 1999) and given that unemployment did not exist in East Germany, the disparity in income per employed worker was probably greater at about 50%. A similar conclusion was reached by a major economic research institute in West Germany (*Handelsblatt,* 1990).

Nevertheless, the cause of the disparity between East and West German incomes was a function of the post-war treatment of the two Germanies and can not be traced to different levels of efficiency in the two systems. As previously mentioned, East Germany had to pay over 100 billion Marks to the Soviet Union after the war (Merkel and Wahl, 1991), while West Germany was receiving substantial foreign aid (Marshall Plan) from the USA that largely offset its minor payments for Nazi Germany's war crimes (Apel, 1966). Studies have indicated that reparations (such as those paid by France after that country's defeat in an 1871 war that helped finance Germany's industrialization) do lead to a permanent decline in the relative level of economic prosperity of the paying country, as well as typically inhibiting economic growth rates because of lower levels of investment and depressed morale (Gavin, 1992).

With income levels in West Germany already substantially higher than in East Germany, approximately 15% of the population of East Germany, or about 3 million people, chose to move from East to West Germany in the 1950s, while only about a half million Germans moved from West Germany to East Germany (Apel, 1966). The emigrants provided further wealth gains in the West and losses in the East (Behr, 1985), with the cost to East German society as a whole of the net emigrations (in terms of lost taxes and investment, i.e., the output that the emigrants otherwise would have created for East German society as a whole net of the emigrants' own expected consumption) being estimated at another 36 billion Marks (Apel, 1966). This figure combined with the reparations losses of 100 billion Marks represented an enormous value in the 1950s and would have grown to an even larger sum today if invested at normal rates of return.

In particular, given an average real growth in Net National Product of 4.5% on an average aggregate investment equal to 27% of Net National Product between 1961 and 1988,[4] East Germany was able to earn a rate of return on its investments equal to 17%, which is similar to the East German return on investment estimated over different time periods by Mueller, Murphy, and Sabov (1993), Naumann and Truempler (1990), and Mueller (1978). Assuming that East Germany had been able to invest the 136 billion Marks at that normal 17% rate of return starting as late as 1961, it would have grown to a value of $136(1.17)^{28}$=11,034 billion Marks by 1989, or over 11 trillion Marks (over $6 trillion). Assuming just the 17% interest rate on this money was finally paid to its people in 1989, Net National Income per capita in East Germany would have been higher by 11.034x.17/.000016=117,236 Marks annually thereafter. As a result, East German incomes would have then been over four times the level of West German incomes per capita in 1989, if there had been nominal compensation in 1961 for all the different costs associated with post-war reparation payments (i.e., if West Germany had paid East Germany for the share of the reparations payments that it was really morally obligated to pay). If compensation had only been made for the nominal reparations payments (and not for the emigration-related losses), East German income per capita would have still grown to over 3 times that of West Germany by 1989.

Another way to evaluate the effect of reparations is to assume that the average annual 100 billion/9=11 billion Marks of East German National Income paid in reparations between 1945 and 1953 (see Chapter 2) was invested each year at a *real* 17% interest rate (which is well below what it probably could have earned given the severe shortage of capital in East Germany at that time caused by the reparations), and then assume a 17% rate of return on this extra wealth accumulated by 1953 was earned and paid out to East German citizens as higher wages that could be consumed and saved in normal proportions thereafter (so that it would also grow after 1953 at the same rate as the rest of East German National Income). The result would have been East German National Income per capita in 1953 that would have been about 2.5 times as high as otherwise and would have thereby resulted in East German wages being similar to (and perhaps slightly in excess of) those in West Germany at the time. That fact would have likely resulted in far less East Germans emigrating to West Germany, thus enabling East Germany to avoid a substantial portion (if not all) of the emigration-related loss of 36 billion Marks. Because real economic growth was historically faster in East Germany than in West Germany in the 1950s even with those losses, East German income per capita would have no doubt been higher than in West Germany in 1961, especially since West Germany's own income per capita would have been lower as a result of it not having the millions of valuable East German emigrants they were able to exploit.

Given faster economic growth in communist East Germany thereafter (because of the greater efficiency of the system, as will be documented empirically in this section for the post-1961 situation that was not distorted by reparations and emigration losses), East German income per capita would have far exceeded that in West Germany by 1989 (almost double). In that situation of fairness in reparations payments, West Germany might have been motivated to build a wall to keep its own workers from emigrating to the higher incomes of East Germany (especially given the higher quality of life in East Germany with respect to nonfinancial factors, as documented in Chapter 2).

However, East Germany was never compensated for its huge reparations-related losses, and so it constructed the Berlin Wall in 1961 to stem its already considerable economic losses. As a result, the resettlements stopped after 1961, and the different economic systems in the two Germanies were allowed to function semi-isolated from each other.

In this separated environment between 1961 and 1989, real East German Net National Product per capita increased by an average 4.5% whereas real West German Net National Product per capita increased by only 2.7% per year. For this comparison, the National Income accounts reported in constant prices were used,[5] so that the nominal growth figures were effectively deflated by inflation (averaging 0.5% and 4.0% for East and West Germany, respectively).[6] Backcasting the 1989 estimated value of the East German Mark (at 1.15 West German Marks in 1989) by the relative aggregate economic inflation rates reported for the two countries (the 0.5% and 4.0%, respectively) indicates that the East German Mark had aggregate purchasing power equal to 0.44 West German Marks in 1961.[7] These results imply per capita East German income was about 2/5 that of West Germany in 1961 compared to almost 2/3 in 1989. The latter two ratios are identical to those reported by the Western researchers Merkel and Wahl (1991) and Gregory and Stuart (1995), respectively, for the two different time periods.[8]

Analysis of Variance (ANOVA) tests revealed that the higher economic growth rates for East Germany between 1961 and 1989 were statistically significant from those of West Germany at the .001 level (with a t-statistic of 4.4). In addition, as previously hypothesized, income and consumption per capita in the planned East German economy had lower annual standard deviations (of 1.1% versus 2.1% for income, and 2.1% versus 2.6% for consumption), with Chi-squared statistics of 53.5 and 43.9, respectively, indicating the difference to be statistically significant at the .005 and .05 levels.

Moreover, even in the 10 years before its collapse, East German economic growth was faster than in West Germany, at 4.0% versus 2.0%, respectively. A listing of economic growth rates in East Germany in its final decade is provided in the following Table 4 along with the comparative numbers for West Germany:

TABLE 4

REAL ECONOMIC GROWTH IN EAST AND WEST GERMANY BEFORE THE END (1980-89)

	1980	1981	1982	1983	1984	1985	1986	1987	1988	1989
East	4.4%	4.8%	2.6%	4.6%	5.5%	5.2%	4.3%	3.3%	2.8%	2.1%
West	1.8%	0.0%	-1.0%	1.9%	3.3%	2.0%	2.5%	1.5%	3.7%	4.0%

Source: Statistisches Amt (1990) and Statistisches Bundesamt (1992).

These aggregated results occurred despite higher social spending and lower investment spending in East Germany than existed in Western capitalist countries (Schwarzer, 1999), despite the advantages that West Germany had in superior access to the capital, trade, and technology of the richer Western countries, and despite the substantially higher military expenditures that East Germany felt obliged to make (6-8% of National Income versus only 3% in West Germany) to defend itself (Merkel and Wahl, 1991).[9] Thus, aggregated statistical evidence indicates that the East German system was more efficient in spurring economic growth.[10]

Causes of Collapse in the East

Like the Berlin Wall, the cause of the collapse of East Germany can be traced to the income disparities in the two countries (Dieckmann, 1991). As explained in the previous subsection, the income disparities resulted from the contrasting postwar treatment by the occupying victors (i.e., despite faster economic growth, East Germany never caught up). Even greater income disparities existed for skilled positions, and heavy economic incentives were provided by the much larger and wealthier West Germany to East Germans for migrating to the West (like above-average income, preferential housing, and enormous guaranteed loans). This economic situation not only induced massive migrations to the West and thereby sabotaged the East German economy (Murphy, 1990b), but it also enabled West Germany to market capitalism as the religion of prosperity, just as it continues to do (Christ, 1991). With the use of heavy West German propaganda that portrayed the communist system as inferior, enough East Germans were convinced to vote in March 1990 for an end to their system. The ruling conservative parties in West Germany also used a combination of promises and threats to ensure electoral success. For instance, 10% annual real economic growth in the first two years after unification was forecast if the conservatives won (*Berliner Allgemeine*, 1990b). In addition, because the permission of the conservative ruling parties in the West German parliament was needed for any unification agreement or aid (*Wall Street Journal,* 1990), they had a great deal of leverage to offer rewards (like a 1:1 exchange rate) for a vote favorable to capitalism and "free trade" (Nelson and Du Bois, 1990).[11]

A final factor influencing the March 1990 election results was a very destructive West German currency strategy. In return for limited economic aid, the West German government persuaded the East German government to change the official exchange rate from 1:1 to 3 East German Marks for 1 West German Mark in January 1990 and to eliminate strict import and export controls. This action effectively reduced East German wealth and income by 2/3 (Murphy, 1992a) and totally demoralized the East German population, as Cote (1990) illustrates. Then, in the week before the March election, the ruling West German party promised a return to the 1:1 exchange rate, if it was elected (Fisher, 1992).[12] Many left-wing East Germans indicated that they voted for the right-wing political parties merely so that the money would come (*Der Taggesspiegel,* 1990d).

The importance of expensive marketing in defeating communism should not be underestimated. Through effective advertising, distribution, sales manipulation, and economic clout (Von Dohnanyi, 1991), and through gross exaggeration of any quality problems for communist products (*Zeitmagazin*, 1992), a superior "Western" image was created (Fox, 1991). As a result, despite the fact that East German products were frequently demonstrated to be superior in unbiased scientific analysis (like taste tests without brand names), more expensive West German products were preferred (Labs, 1991). Also contributing to the rapid increase in West Germany's market share of the East German market shortly after it was opened up in 1990 was the normal practice of capitalist penetration pricing (McCarthy, 1975), whereby West German exports to East Germany were priced low enough to bankrupt their

East German competition (*Der Spiegel,* 1993a). Once the East German firms (which, in addition to suffering image problems, also had inadequate liquidity, experience, and preparation for the capitalist competition) were bankrupted, prices were raised to West German levels (in order to maximize West German corporate revenues and profits). Some evidence of this phenomenon can be found in the fact that prices rose less rapidly in eastern Germany than in western Germany in 1990, whereas inflation in eastern Germany was over 13% in 1991 compared to just 4% in western Germany after the widespread bankruptcy of East German firms, which was reflected in the 40% decline in economic output in eastern Germany in 1990 and 1991 (Statistisches Bundesamt, 1992).

Evidence on the Economic Inefficiency of Capitalism In the East

Despite their current popularity, past capitalist reforms in poorer countries have never produced any evidence of a material increase in efficiency (Seib and Murray, 1991), neither for Eastern Europe (Gey and Quaisser, 1989) nor for other areas of the world like Latin America (Prebisch, 1982). The indications from the most recent capitalist reforms in Eastern Europe have demonstrated even more negative indications. In particular, as previously documented, GDP fell by over 40% over the interval 1990-95 in the former communist countries of Eastern Europe and the USSR.

In eastern Germany, the capitalist reforms also led to a catastrophe despite hundreds of billion of Marks in aid from western Germany. For instance, output was estimated to have fallen by about 10% in eastern Germany in 1990 (Kempe, 1991a) and substantially more in 1991 (Aeppel and Roth, 1991), although transfer payments (like unemployment checks) from the western German government amounting to 70% of the output of eastern Germany (Kempe, 1991b) increased their income substantially above the level under communism (and thereby kept them content enough not to rebel). Production fell by more than 60% in the 1990-91 interval (Kempe, 1991b), GNP fell by over 40% over that short time period (Osmond, 1992), and unemployment in eastern Germany reached 40% if the mass of part-time workers were counted as unemployed. In addition, despite sizable unemployment checks and higher wages for those able to find work, early surveys indicated only a third of the population in eastern Germany felt better off economically than before (*Junge Welt*, 1991).[13] Even after western Germany had poured over $100 billion annually into eastern Germany from 1990-96 (equal to about half East Germany's pre-1989 Gross National Product), the economy of eastern Germany remains a disaster zone that requires similar continued high welfare payments from the west just to maintain a minimum standard of living (Rohwedder, 1996).

Despite the ending of the large special subsidies paid to eastern Germans for fleeing to western Germany and despite the heavy economic aid now being given to eastern Germany, the number of Germans fleeing from the eastern part to the western part continued to run over 10,000 per month into the early 1990s (which matches pre-1960 levels), and this figure did not include the nearly one million eastern Germans who commuted to jobs in western Germany daily in the early 1990s (*Wochenpost*, 1992b). However, noneconomic factors as well as the dismal economic conditions contributed to the dissatisfaction and desire to leave the eastern part of Germany. For instance, Garrettson (1991) compared the situation in eastern Germany in the early 1990s to the southern United States after the American Civil War: the area was flooded with opportunistic West German "carpetbaggers" (like consultant and financial swindlers) seeking "shameless exploitation" of the eastern Germans, who had limited knowledge of the New Order and who were persecuted for any part they may have played in the old system.[14]

Nonfinancial Considerations

The analysis in this chapter so far has focused totally on financial efficiency. However, a complete comparison of two systems and living standards should include not only monetary and consumption figures but also qualitative factors like political freedom, environment, and other factors not incorporated into economic output (Lippe and Heese, 1983).

For instance, the higher level of pollution in East Germany (Buck, 1996) should be accounted for. One possible methodology is to take into consideration the fact that West Germany typically spent about 1% more of National Income on the environment than East Germany (Welfens, 1992), assume this 1% differential could be eliminated by reducing productive East German investment by that 1%, and then reduce real East German economic growth by the 1% times the typical 17% return on East German investment. The implication is that real East German growth may have been overstated by about 1%x.17=0.17% per year (although it would remain almost 2% higher than in West Germany).

The social disutility of consumption good shortages and black markets in East Germany should also be considered. Although some of this disutility could be avoided through the use of Exquisit shops where high quality goods in short supply were sold for high prices denominated in East German Marks (*Der Spiegel*, 1962, 1987), some negative utility may have remained as a result of deviations between price and value (Feiwel, 1980). However, as explained in Chapter 2, these qualitative disadvantages of communism were probably more than offset by various odious capitalist factors such as general consumption uncertainty related to marketing manipulation. For instance, price bickering, price shopping, and waiting for the next "special" or coupon may create the same (or even a higher) level of disutility as product shortages in East Germany. Although there was less time wasted on price negotiation in West Germany than in other countries like the USA for big ticket items like car sales (Sedgwick, 1993), capitalist marketing still created significant annoyances to consumers. In particular, the negative utility of misleading marketing tactics that can create undesirable disinformation, uncertainty, and discrepancies between price and value in capitalism (Furlough and Stirkwerda, 1999) is so great that many people expend a significant amount of effort and money to avoid it (Kaufman, 2000). Although some West Germans may enjoy price shopping and advertising, it is also true that some East Germans enjoyed searching for (and finding) scarce items, playing the black markets, and innovating in cases of shortages.

Similarly, the freedom from high rates of crime and drug usage, the freedom from unemployment anxiety, and the freedom from life sustaining money anxieties (through low stable prices for essentials, free health care, and a secure social security system) in East Germany should be measured against the limited political freedom there (Burant, 1987). In January 1990, I conducted a limited survey of emigrants from East to West Germany in an attempt to compute values for the some of the qualitative factors. However, harassment and threats from the West

German secret police hindered efforts sufficiently to prevent procurement of a large enough sample to conduct statistical analysis (only 5 surveys were completed before I was blatantly told that there would be no further cooperation, and that I was endangering myself and anyone involved in the survey). The limited sample collected did indicate emigrants would on average be willing to pay 3.13%, 6.15%, 6.82%, 1.89%, and 3.05% (cumulating to 21.04%) of their annual West German income to eliminate unemployment, drugs, crime, uncertain prices, and life-sustaining money anxieties (like for food and shelter) in West Germany, respectively.[15] The emigrants were found on average to have been willing to have paid 3.06% of their East German income in return for free elections in East Germany according to Western standards.

Separately, the emigrants also were found to have been willing to pay an average 3.63% of their East German income to eliminate the East German secret police. This number may be much higher than for most East Germans, most of whom were not harassed by the Stasi for wanting to leave the country (Henke and Engelmann, 1995). In addition, a similar question on the West German secret police was unfortunately not included in the survey (my own neglect in this respect resulted from me still being partially under the incredibly strong influence of Western propaganda about the "kindness" of the West).

From my personal experiences in East Germany prior to and during the revolution, from stories from individuals, and from anticommunist books on the subject, such as by Gauck (1991) and Furian (1991), the East German secret police appears to be less heinous than the West German secret police, whose organization, leaders, agents, and laws were inherited from Hitler's fascist Germany (Schulz, 1982). Although both secret police forces tend to come into play only when one has the "wrong" political opinion, the West German secret police probably operates more negatively, as explained in Chapter 3. For instance, the West German secret police may be much more active in opening mail without justification (*Berliner Allgemeine*, 1990a) than their East German counterparts ever were (Diedrich, Ehlert, and Wenzke, 1998). In addition, the total extent of their other illegal activities like engaging in arms smuggling activities (*Wochenpost*, 1991) and harassing peaceful environmentalists and leftists in West Germany (including tailing, infiltrating organizations with spies, and spreading information to damage the careers and personal lives of people with the "wrong" political opinion) is unknown (*Der Spiegel*, 1992b, 1993b), but the number of victims of West German secret police harassment is definitely in the millions (Schulz, 1982). It is possible that domestic spying, harassment, and assassinations by the secret police in "free" countries like West Germany may exceed that of the former eastern bloc countries, just as it may in the USA itself (Cockburn, 1993). A 1993 survey is consistent with the latter hypothesis, as it indicated that more East Germans felt safe from encroachments by the state in their lives in 1988 under East German government rule than they did under united West German government rule in the 1990s (Northoff, 1995).

Moreover, the socially undesirable predominance in pure capitalism of naked self-interest and monetarization of personal worth, family, human relationships, and life itself should also be factored into the analysis (Marx and Engels, 1988a). Besides contributing to huge black markets for sex (Falck, 1998), narcotics (Dietz, 1983), weapons (Schmidt-Eenboom, 1995), and tax evasion (McGee, 1999) in West Germany, these factors also contribute to a much higher level of social dissatisfaction, sexual misuse of children and women, and violence in capitalist countries (*Nordeutsche Neueste Nachrichten*, 1992). Although some of these capitalist variables might have positive utility to some people (such as to perverts and criminals), and although monetary considerations also existed to a lesser degree in East German life, the relative desirability of such variables might significantly affect conclusions on relative quality of life and living standards. In addition, a nonfinancial analysis of relative living standards should also incorporate an evaluation of the fact that the communist East German system created a "nourishing" cultural life about which Olshausen (1996) states, "Those who lived it do miss it."

The superiority of the communist system with respect to nonfinancial considerations is further verified in a 1999 survey of East Germans which indicated that, despite a significantly higher standard of living after the merger with the richer West Germany (and despite greater travel freedom), over 40% of East Germans were happier under the old communist system (CNN, 1999a). The superiority of communism on nonfinancial issues would have reinforced its financial superiority if East Germany had not had such adverse postwar treatment.

Outlook for Reform

An alternative to the capitalist solution for Eastern Europe might be a politically-reformed socialist system. Political reforms relating to press and election freedoms actually might further enhance the efficiency of a centralized system. Such reforms might stimulate the flow of innovative ideas and reduce the possibility of an inept and/or corrupt central planning commission from becoming entrenched and/or working for personal gain as opposed to societal goals (Gey and Quaisser, 1989).[16]

Such political reforms would, however, also necessitate some economic reforms. For instance, the opening of the borders in East Germany in 1989 created a very real danger that the country would be cheaply sold to West Germany through the migration of well-trained and well-educated East Germans to the higher-paying jobs in the West and through the sale of subsidized East German goods and wealth via a ridiculously cheap exchange rate. As a result, a wage and price reform of the East German system was unavoidable. The lifting of some restrictions on wage differentials might have also enhanced incentive systems, and a more flexible pricing system might have also created the groundwork for a more efficient flow of goods and services. The possibility of expanded trade, capital, aid, and technology from the West because of such reforms might have provided a further impetus to growth (*Der Tagesspiegel*, 1990a). However, the fact that reforms cause uncertainty and thereby inhibit the inflow of beneficial foreign capital should also have been considered (Reuter, 1989). An effective framework for reform that would have preserved stability (and the advantages of communism) has been described by Murphy (1992a), and details for the German case are provided in the next chapter.

CHAPTER 5

AN APPLIED INVESTIGATION INTO A PLAN FOR EASING THE TRANSITION TO ECONOMIC COMPETITIVENESS USING EAST GERMANY AS AN EXAMPLE

Although the West German government originally forecast economic prosperity for all (including equal wages and very low unemployment) as a result of winning the vote for the annexation of East Germany on its own terms in 1990 (*Ostseezeitung,* 1990a), the economic unification of Germany in 1990 actually led to a large drop in economic activity by over 40% in the eastern part of the country (Kempe, 1991b). In addition, despite wealth transfers from the western part of Germany that have accumulated to almost one trillion Marks (over $500 billion), the problems continue, with nearly half of eastern German income still representing transfer payments from western Germany in 1996 (Rohwedder, 1996). While real output per capita in East Germany before unification was 2/3 of that for West Germany (Gregory and Stuart, 1995), and may even have been over 80% of West German output per capita according to some estimates (Summers and Heston, 1988), output per capita in the eastern part of Germany is now only about 1/2 that of western Germany, and many believe that such large differences will persist into the long-term future and may even be magnified significantly if the transfer payments are reduced (*Der Spiegel,* 1997b).[1]

While many now claim that there was no way to avoid the enormous economic difficulties of unification (Ritschl, 1996), there was in fact a realistic economic plan available at the time that could not only have avoided the catastrophe (Murphy, 1990a) but that could have actually led to the prosperity which many (including the West German leader Helmut Kohl) were forecasting in 1990 (Ritschl, 1996). As the designer of the idea, I gave copies of the plan to various media and government officials in December 1989, although the plan was not published until 1990 (Murphy, 1990a) and did not appear in an academic journal until 1992 (Murphy, 1992a). The plan essentially focused on a transition from a state-controlled protected economy to a competitive market-oriented economy and from an inconvertible currency (the East German mark symbolized by M) to a convertible one (the West German mark symbolized by DM). As stated by Czege (1989) and many others, both previously and subsequently, alternative plans to integrate a protected economy into the world market have generally been counterproductive.

This chapter simulates the economic events that would have transpired if the Murphy plan had indeed been used. The results of the investigation are important for demonstrating how useful the plan can be to ease a country's transition to economic competitiveness and how unnecessary economic catastrophes like the one that occurred in eastern Germany in the 1990s really are.

The Plan for Transition to Economic Competitiveness

According to the plan, the subsidized prices of East German goods could be kept in a market economy by giving each resident a limited amount of a special currency every month (perhaps called the Karl Mark and symbolized by KM) that would effectively allow them to pay for things like rent, food, monthly mass transportation tickets, some cultural events (such as theater, sports, and vacation trips), child care, and children's clothing at very low M prices. Sellers of necessities produced in East Germany would be able to price their goods in M at higher market-clearing prices, but they would be required to accept KM for up to 90% of the price from East Germans who purchased such goods produced in East Germany (and the selling state businesses would then be able to exchange their KM so received for an equal amount of M from the East German central bank). This system is similar to giving all residents coupons or food stamps, except that these coupons could be used to pay for any necessities (the KM could also be made more like food stamps by allowing 100% of the price to be paid in KM).

In addition, the plan called for the state to agree to exchange M for DM at a set exchange rate like the 1:1 ratio estimated to be appropriate given the relative purchasing power of the two currencies (Collier, 1985).[2] However, a shortage of capital in East Germany (stemming from the enormous reparations payments it had to make, as previously explained in Chapters 2-4) made its industry too uncompetitive relative to other countries like West Germany to earn enough DM to be able to afford an unlimited amount of exchanges at that rate. As a result, the plan mandated restricting the exchanges only to cases where an individual or business agreed to invest a fixed number of M into savings accounts in state banks, such as M5 saved per M1 exchanged into DM. Withdrawals from the savings accounts might be restricted for a fixed number of years, which was set as 5-10 years in the original plan (although the number of years could be varied between 2 and 10 years, depending on the amount of foreign capital and financial assistance that could be obtained). Given limited wealth and income in East Germany, the amount that could be exchanged would be severely restricted by such a rule.

The money from the special long-term savings accounts could then be used by East Germany to invest into modern capital, either through direct government investment or indirectly through the government investing into private businesses just as Japan has successfully done in the past (Blejer and Cheasty, 1986). Such investment would allow East German industry to become more competitive. The rate of return paid on the savings accounts could be contracted at 3%, which was 0.25% less than the rate available on East German checking accounts, and which would represent very cheap financing for the capital. The ratio of exchanged M to mandatory saved M could be reduced in subsequent years depending on the success of the plan in promoting domestic productivity and production.

This currency exchange system would encourage the purchase of East German goods, since necessities produced in East Germany would be cheaply priced in KM. In addition, excessive spending on imported goods would require prohibitively high levels of savings that would give East Germans an incentive to buy "East German" as opposed to

West German goods, which were more prestigious and better marketed but not necessarily better, as documented by Von Dohnanyi (1991), Fox (1991), *Zeitmagazin* (1992), and others. The restricted demand for imported goods would require foreign firms to produce in East Germany if they wanted to generate significant profits from that potentially lucrative market. The plan would thereby prevent the large decline in East German output and employment that resulted from the actual economic unification. Moreover, the freezing of prices for necessities using KM would reduce inflationary pressures, while still permitting market-clearing prices for foreigners and excess domestic demand so that there would be less waste. The overall system would also promote confidence in the East German economy and thereby enhance morale, which was important not only for productivity but also to motivate workers to stay in East Germany (as opposed to emigrate to West Germany, where they were freely welcome as citizens).

In addition, the Murphy plan also called for putting East Germany's state businesses into a mutual fund owned by all citizens of the country. The citizens could vote for management of the mutual fund, but shares in the mutual fund could be sold only after 2-10 years (and perhaps only incrementally and/or with a sales fee) in order to prevent a cheap sell-out of the nation's wealth (Murphy, 1992a).[3] The book value of East German capital was over M100,000 per capita (Statistisches Amt, 1990), and so the market value of each share would clearly be nontrivial in a healthy local economy (and might be far in excess of the book value, especially if the shares paid an annual growing dividend). The possibility of accessing cash in the future from such shares might provide further encouragement for East Germans to stay in their country, since leaving would result in forfeiture of shares. Once domestic and foreign investment had generated sufficient economic growth and competitiveness, unrestricted sale of securities and currencies could be allowed to occur (at future market prices that would obviously give East Germans communal motivation to work productively). The East German people could then vote independently on whether they wanted to preserve some or all the advantages of their socialist society without economic pressure/blackmail.

THE ECONOMIC MODEL FOR EXAMINING THE 1989 EAST GERMAN SITUATION

To evaluate what would have happened if the Murphy plan had indeed been used, a basic economic model is employed by applying well-accepted theory (Byrns and Stone, 1995) to the situation in East Germany at the end of 1989. In particular, National Income is set equal to gross East German disposable income (that equaled M168 billion in 1989) plus government revenue from taxes and profits to East German government-owned firms (that equaled M107 billion in 1989), which summed to M275 billion in 1989. National Income, plus any change in credit issued to East German entities or any net withdrawal from East German savings (which consisted of M160 in money market checking accounts in 1989), is spent as consumption (for both domestically produced goods and for net imports) and investment (government spending is incorporated in the form of consumption or investment here). National Income in the following period equals consumption plus net exports (i.e., exports minus imports) plus investment plus the return on investment. The general framework of this simple economic model and its parameters/functions are described in this section, while the exact mathematics will be delineated in the relevant subsequent empirical sections for ease of understanding the discussion as it goes.

Inflation equals last year's price increase plus any growth in National Income that is not earned by return on investment or by an increase in the number of workers employed. Because East German firms are run by the state, there can also be a tradeoff between profits to East German firms and inflation. Since there was actually deflation of 1.1% in East Germany in 1989 (as computed from the fact that real and nominal economic growth were 2.1% and 1.0%, respectively, in 1989), and since the state can simply avoid further deflation by not having its owned companies lower prices, inflation at the beginning of the simulation (at the end of 1989) can be assumed to be 0%.

Wages are determined by the number of workers and the annual wage per worker. The annual wage per worker can be increased with economic growth. In addition, wage increases above the economic growth rate can be offered in order to keep labor in East Germany and possibly also motivate workers to greater productivity improvements (albeit at the cost of lower investment). On the other hand, lower wage increases might not only increase the chance of labor strife and strikes but would also motivate more workers to leave East Germany.

Because there was no net population growth in East Germany (where the birth rate approximated the death rate), the number of workers are a function of the ability of the East German economy to keep its current labor force. The number of workers are therefore affected by real income levels in East Germany relative to West Germany (as well as by future expected income and wealth), which in turn are affected by any subsidization of East German consumption goods.

Consumption is a function of East German wages, the historic savings rate from East German wages, and the real interest rate (i.e., the yield above inflation rates) paid on savings. However, consumption is also a function of the amount of goods imported from West Germany, with higher imports forcing increased savings under the Murphy (1990a) plan. Imports are a function of relative prices in East and West Germany (given any subsidization of East German products) at the given exchange rate.

Investment in East Germany equals savings from wages plus profits to East German firms plus net foreign investment. Non-foreign investment can be made into low-technology capital using East German production or high-tech capital imported from Western industrialized countries. The amount of foreign capital coming into East Germany is set as a function of the profit that can be earned there relative to what can be earned by exporting to East Germany (e.g., if exports to East Germany are restricted by government policy, there will be increased capital investment into East Germany). The amount of high-tech capital that East German firms can import equals the lesser of zero or exports plus foreign loans and transfer payments minus consumption imports.

Exchange rates are determined by the supply and demand for foreign currency. The supply of foreign currency is initially given as the amount of East German exports, but this amount can be increased with higher capital investments, loans, and transfer payments from other countries such as West Germany. The demand for foreign currency is set at the point where it is cheaper or more desirable to purchase foreign goods at the margin, but relative cheapness must also incorporate government restrictions on foreign currency purchases, which can actually be used to fix the exchange rate and restrict imports as in the proposed plan.

Parameters and functions for the model can be estimated using actual historical information, with much of the raw empirical data on East German national accounts being obtainable from various years of the annual *Das Statistische Jahrbuch der Deutschen Demokratischen Republik.* Use of parameter estimates based on the actual economic events that did occur should ensure that the simulation results are consistent with reality and should avoid the problems associated with other simulations of Eastern European economies that employed unrealistic assumptions about parameter values and that were therefore far too optimistic in predicting capitalist reform would result in high positive growth in post-revolutionary Eastern Europe (Cohen, 1991).

For purposes of estimating profits to East Germany, the historic average return of 18% earned by East Germany is assumed on old capital investments, while the average return of 21% earned by West Germany is used on new capital imported by East German firms from Western industrialized countries (Naumann and Truempler, 1990). These rates of return figures are probably fairly reliable, given similar numbers reported over different time intervals by Mueller (1978) and Mueller, Murphy, and Sabov (1993), and given a similar estimate for East Germany derived from dividing that country's real economic growth by its average gross investment (as explained in Chapter 4). Although foreign capital investment into East Germany is assumed to earn the rate available in West Germany (21%), the return will be split among the foreign investors and East Germany according to rules that must be relatively attractive to the foreign investors.

Net exports equal exports minus imports of both consumption goods and capital. East German exports can continue to be encouraged through government subsidization of export industries (Kusch et al., 1991), which on average needed M4.4 to generate DM1 of exports in 1989 (*Die Marktwirtschaft,* 1990). This expenditure of M4.4 to earn DM1 can be reduced through capital investments in export industries that equal normal 18% rates of return on East German investments.

Some of the other parameter values or ranges can be estimated from the results of the actual unification plan that was used. The implemented economic policy immediately replaced the M with the DM and exchanged existing M at a 1:1 exchange rate (although amounts above

M6000, M4000, and M2000 per person had to be exchanged at M2:DM for East Germans aged over 60 years old, 15-59, and under 15, respectively). While domestic wages and investment followed normal patterns of increase (relative to aggregate income) after unification, there was a drastic change in net exports, which turned into a huge negative as East Germans used over half their DM to import previously forbidden goods from the Western industrialized countries, mostly from West Germany. For instance, in 1991 (the first full year after unification), imports from western Germany amounted to DM207 billion, which was only minorly offset by DM38 billion in eastern German exports to western Germany (Osmond, 1992). Thus, it can be assumed that East Germans will spend over half of their money on imports if their currency is made convertible.

The result of the use of the actual disastrous unification plan was over a 40% drop in National Income in the annexed provinces of eastern Germany in 1990-91 as there was little demand for East German goods, and employment fell over 50%.[4] Although output in eastern Germany did eventually increase from this low level in subsequent years, as Western capital finally spurred some production, the country has still not fully recovered from the economic shock of 1990 that the head of the West German central bank indicated was entirely predictable given the catastrophic plan that was employed (Osmond, 1992). A decade later, eastern Germany's output still remains below that of 1989, despite the fact that the united German federal government provided DM191 billion in infrastructure investments (including DM 146 billion for roads and railways, and DM45 billion for the telephone system) to eastern Germany over the first 6 years after unification, and despite the fact that it provided DM100 billion in investment assistance which attracted DM500 billion in private investment into eastern Germany, in addition to DM200 billion invested there without state assistance (*Der Spiegel*, 1997b).[5] As a result of the economic collapse in East Germany, another DM899 billion from the unified German government was spent (net of taxes collected from eastern Germany) as social transfer payments to the unemployed, early retirees, and similar distressed people in eastern Germany (*Frankfurter Allgemeine*, 1998a).[6]

Because of these historical facts, it is assumed that private foreign investment equals DM700 billion in the first 6 years, just as it actually was, as long as there are incentives to invest. As found empirically by Wheeler and Mody (1992), direct government incentives provided to encourage investment provide much less motivation to private investors than a growing market that can only be accessed by investing there. Thus, the plan's indirect incentives to foreign investment (by restricting access to the market except for those producing in East Germany) are likely to draw at least as much foreign private capital as the German government subsidies were able to solicit in the actual depression scenario that unfolded with the disastrous unification policies. In order to illustrate that the plan is not dependent on foreign government assistance of any type, no foreign government infrastructure investments, foreign aid, or additional foreign loans are assumed initially.

Except for the initial shock year when restrictions on imports of Western consumption goods are removed, and income spent (and/or saved) for imports is assumed to rise to over 50% of National Income, international trade will have stable relationships to the prior year. In addition, it is assumed that, barring external influences or specific policy variables, East German consumption, wages, profits, and investment all rise with National Income growth, and that all other domestic parameters values will be the same as in 1989.

The results based on these assumptions are reported in the next section. The effects of alternative possibilities (and other parameter values and functions) are explored (and analyzed) in the subsequent section.

THE MODEL'S FORECASTED RESULTS

As mentioned in the prior section, the empirical finding from the actual unification plan implies that East Germans prefer to spend at least half their money on Western goods and services at a 1:1 exchange rate. With East German National Income at M275 billion in 1989, it can be estimated that DM138 billion is spent on imports in 1990. However, using the Murphy plan, the need to save M5 for every M1 that is exchanged into DM1 to purchase imported goods would result in a total of only

M138 billion/(1+5)=M23 billion

available to actually exchange into DM, with the other M138-M23=M115 billion having to be put into the special savings accounts.

Since it took M4.4 to earn a DM of exports in 1989, East Germany would have to expend DM23(M4.4/DM)=M101 billion to generate such exports. Of this amount, M23 billion was expended by the importers themselves at the 1:1 exchange rate, leaving M101-M23=M78 billion of the exports to be subsidized, so that M115-M78=M37 billion of the M115 billion in savings would be available for investment. Given East Germany's average 18% rate of return on invested capital, it would take about 9 years to earn the necessary amount to pay back the savings accounts in full, with $M37(1.18)^9$ - $M115(1.03)^9$ = M14 billion being left over for additional wage or profit increases at that time.

Gross investment in East Germany normally averaged about 27% of National Income, or M74 billion, in 1989. If this amount were funneled in the future entirely into export-oriented industries, the savings on exported goods would be M74(.18)=M13 billion. Assuming that imports and this type of investment both grew with the economy after 1990, it would take about 6 years to permit a termination of the export subsidies. These savings could be passed on to those who imported West German goods in the form of lower required amounts that had to be put into M savings accounts after the first year, so that there might be no savings requirements for money exchanged after 6 years.

In the meantime, given the foregoing investment policies of concentrating on making the export industries competitive enough to enable an unrestricted 1:1 exchange rate in 6 years, East German National Income available for equal distribution to workers would only grow to the extent of foreign investment. In addition, the change in wages would actually be somewhat less in the first year because the difference between the assumed 27% gross investment figure and the actual 22% net investment undertaken by East Germany in 1989 (net of depreciation or the replacement of depreciated fixed assets) would reduce real wages by .05xM275=M14 billion that year (1990). This reduction would be at least partially implemented by the increase in prices for all purchases beyond those paid for with KM, with such effects only being felt by foreigners and excess consumers of essentials, so that most domestic residents would not be materially affected. However, if additional amounts were needed, a special tax (such as an additional payroll or consumption tax, or some special social security withholding designed to enable greater pension income at retirement) could also be levied to transfer a portion of National Income from consumption to investment (perhaps explained to the public as a tax to pay for the prior year's deflation as well as to enable the investment needed for international competitiveness and future rapid growth in wage and pension incomes).

While a reduction in real wages in the first year of the plan is not required for its success, it could help enable movement to an unrestricted 1:1 exchange rate in a faster time period (6 years). This possibility might offset the disutility of the real wage decline sufficiently to inhibit emigrations. Alternatively, any such amount taken out of wages could be set up as a form of forced savings that could go into private investment or into a public mutual fund. Regardless, emigrations would still be inhibited by the fact that emigrants would automatically forfeit their right to sell, or receive dividends from, their mutual fund shares in existing East German industry. Although wages could only grow to the extent of foreign investment in the first 6 years, it is likely this growth would actually be very high (including in the first year). In particular, if the assumed 21% return on foreign capital were taxed at a 50% tax rate (competitive with the 56% corporate tax rate in West Germany), half of this amount would accrue to East Germany in the form of higher taxes, which could be passed on to East German workers in general in the form of higher wages and salaries.[7] It seems reasonable to assume that at least DM700 billion in private capital would be invested in the first 6 years, as happened in actual fact under much more adverse economic circumstances relative to those that would exist under the Murphy plan where there are far greater incentives to invest just to access the growing East German market. This amount of about DM117 billion per year would permit an annual increase in distributable National Income of DM117x.21x.50=DM12 billion, which represents an annual 12/275=4% growth in income at a 1:1 exchange rate. Given that such investments would create products that could either be exported or substitute for imported Western goods, they would permit East Germany to save even more on export subsidies, as much as DM12(M4.4/DM)=M53 billion, which represents 19% of National Income. Such savings would allow output for domestic consumption and real National Income to grow at high double digit rates (as that M53 billion not expended for export subsidies could be consumed domestically), although consumption would grow at a lower rate (at about 13%) in the first year because of the assumed increase in the net domestic investment rate.

The extremely high economic growth would slow as the number of M required to generate a DM of exports fell. In particular, after the most modern and valuable Western capital was imported (that had a value equal to at least 4.4 times that of domestic East German capital), the marginal value of the Western capital (relative to East German capital) would decline. Given that there were an annual M78 billion in export subsidies needed without foreign investment, the annual M53 billion in savings related to exports created by foreign investment replacing domestic exports would disappear in about 1.5 years. At that point, every DM1 of Western capital would have the same value as M1 of East German domestic capital, and the multiplicative effect would dissipate (although the slight 21%-18%=3% difference in rate of return might persist).

In any event, modern Western capital could have easily been used to replace the expensive East German investment required to make East Germany's export industry competitive at a far lower cost, thereby allowing the country's normal domestic investment to alone keep the East German economy growing at its past average rate of 2% higher than in West Germany, plus possibly an extra 1% more because of the higher domestic investment rate assumed (27% versus 22%). At the same time, the enormous Western investment (whether invested for export-related production or for domestic consumption) would increase this growth rate by at least 4% (as previously explained). The resulting real East German economic growth rate would be a minimum of 2%+4%+1%=7% higher than existed in West Germany.

Given that East German per capita National Income was already two thirds that of West Germany's in 1989, even the lower 7% higher real economic growth rate would allow East German income per capita to catch up to the level in West Germany in about 6 years. However, this computation does not consider the very powerful effect of the potential savings in export subsidies (from the DM117 billion in foreign capital possibly producing export goods or import-substituting goods that would replace imports). If the East German economy grew 19% faster for 1.5 years (as is more likely given the aforementioned savings in export subsidies) and then 7% faster for the next 1.5 years, it would catch up in just 3 years. Since all these calculations are based on a potential underestimate of the true amount of Western investment (DM117 billion annually), it is possible that the East German economy would catch up faster than in 3-6 years.

Under these circumstances, the high unemployment rate, the inequality in incomes, and the enormous West German transfer payments (that have averaged DM150 per year through 1996 with no end in sight) never would have been necessary. In present value, the plan could have easily saved Germany over $1 trillion.

RISKS OF DEVIATIONS FROM MODEL EXPECTATIONS

The foregoing results assume specific values for various parameters. While the estimated parameter values are based on historical data (and are therefore probably consistent with reality), the implementation of a new economic policy can change parameter values, and such deviations from assumed parameter estimates can cause different economic results. However, as the subsequent analysis shows, the initial assumptions employed are reasonable even within the context of a changed economic policy, and many possible deviations from assumptions may actually have a positive effect on the foregoing results reported. In addition, any negative effects can possibly be offset by other policy variables to keep the economic results at least as favorable as found in the previous section.

Risk of a Different Level of Western Imports Under the Plan

The foregoing results were based on an assumption that the East Germans will spend slightly over half their income on Western goods and services under the plan. Although this assumption may be conservative given that each DM1 of imports essentially mandated M6 in reduced consumption, the mandatory savings accounts could certainly lead to different spending decisions.

If a greater amount were spent on Western imports, East Germany would have to transfer even more resources from production for domestic consumption to production for export. However, as shown earlier, the mandatory additional savings conditional on such Western imports enable East Germany to subsidize production of sufficient additional goods for Western export to cover the cost of the higher imports.

It is really more probable that the import of Western goods would be lower than originally assumed. For instance, 39% of National Income was directly controlled by the East German state through government and government-owned business spending (for public consumption and investment), and the portion of that income which was used to purchase DM could be simply directed to be below 50%, if desired. Only if it was more efficient in the aggregate sense to import for public consumption and investment purposes would this income be directed at all to imports.

Moreover, it is very improbable that the East German people would spend more than 50% of their income on the purchase of DM. Instead, it is likely that the typical East German would only purchase the most wanted Western imports of luxury goods (or services such as tourism) that were either extremely expensive or unavailable in East Germany. In particular, if it were assumed that East Germans would spend about half their disposable income of M167 billion on imports, that would leave about M83 billion for consumption (plus the M84/M6/DM=DM14 billion in luxury goods/services that would be imported). With 16.4 million people in East Germany, that would come to scarcely M5000 (and less then DM1000) in spending per person (which represented about $3000). Although the prices of essentials such as food and rents were low enough in East Germany for retirees to live comfortably on the minimum annual pension of M4800, it would be difficult for the average East German to live on much less, and so most would probably choose to spend more than half their disposable income on East German goods and services to maintain a reasonable standard of living.

As a result, it is probable that East Germany would have had to transfer far less resources into expensive production for export than originally assumed. Moreover, although East German consumption in total Marks would still be less to the extent that there were some of the 1:1 exchanges that mandate increased savings, total consumption utility would undoubtedly increase. In particular, each East German would only voluntarily conduct the 1:1 exchanges if the satisfaction from the purchased imports more than offset the lost utility resulting from having to replace some current domestic consumption with future consumption (because of the mandatory savings required for each 1:1 exchange).

Risk of Different Savings Rates

One risk is that the M160 billion of savings accounts existing in East Germany in 1989 could be drawn down, such as for consumption or to invest into the new savings accounts to access more DM. East German savings accounts consisted solely of their money market checking accounts that allowed unlimited withdrawals and paid 3.25% interest annually (there were no other checking or savings vehicles in East Germany).

If all M160 billion in savings were used to purchase imports, East Germany would need M160/(5+1)=DM27 billion in external funding. A portion of the needed amount could come from Western industrialized countries (especially West Germany and the European Community) seeking to support the political and economic reforms in East Germany and the opening of the Berlin Wall (*Der Tagesspiegel,* 1989c, 1990a). The rest could be financed by the sale of assets in East Germany, such as real estate (which would reduce the claim of East Germans on their own country's capital, thereby possibly having a collective impact on inhibiting excessive savings withdrawals). For instance, existing apartments could be sold to Western investors or countries who might be enticed by a stable revenue stream derived from low rents that were strongly supplemented by guarantees of continuing East German government subsidies. Alternatively, part of the amount could be paid for by the previously mentioned private capital inflows of DM117 billion a year, although this amount is uncertain, and any use of a portion of such flows to pay for consumption imports would reduce the otherwise extremely high real growth rate that would arise from it.

It is actually unlikely that much of the M160 billion in savings would be drawn down, since everyone needs some liquidity. The ratio of the East German checking/savings accounts combined with M17 billion currency in circulation totaled only M177/M275=64% of East German National Income in 1989. This ratio is lower than the level of liquidity available even in Western industrialized countries that have a more developed financial system with far easier access to loans and security sales, which can substitute for some of needed cash liquidity. For instance, the ratio of checking and short-term savings accounts to National Income was 65% in West Germany in 1989 according to data reported in the IMF's *International Financial Statistics.*

The hypothesis that withdrawals from East German savings accounts would be limited is buttressed by the behavior of East German accounts in 1989-90. For instance, although the opening of the borders in November 1989 allowed unlimited East German purchases of West German goods for the first time in decades (albeit at high black market exchange rates), there was only a M2.5 billion increase in withdrawals from East German savings accounts in November 1989 compared to November 1988 (and only a M2.1 billion increase in withdrawals compared to October 1989), and the amount of currency in circulation actually fell M0.1 billion from the prior month. In December 1989, there was only a M0.8 billion increase in withdrawals compared to the prior December, and the amount held in savings accounts actually increased net of these withdrawals (as a result of a higher level of money deposited into savings). Even the complete replacement of the M with the DM in July 1990 resulted in East Germans withdrawing only DM4.5 billion in the first week of the event (*Ostseezeitung,* 1990b) and, overall, did not lead to a enormous spending spree or a sizable decline in savings balances in East Germany (Osmond, 1992).

However, if there was perceived to be a need to bolster savings (perhaps because too much was withdrawn in the early months of the plan implementation), it would be possible to offer new and more attractive savings accounts (Murphy, 1992a).[8] One such account could be set up to pay 3.25% plus 0.5% times the number of years the account was to be frozen (e.g., 7.75% for a 9-year savings account). In addition, to attract speculative money, a special 10-year account could offer to pay 3.25% plus 75% of real National Income growth. This additional interest cost would essentially transfer a portion of National Income from profits and wages to savings account holders, who at the maturity of their savings accounts might consume the amount and lower future investment. Nonetheless, in the meantime, their balances and interest would be invested, and, even at maturity, they might be more likely to reinvest their money than to spend it, especially if they are richer individuals.

Besides increasing the savings of East Germans, the existence of such new savings accounts that pay higher interest rates in M than exist on DM accounts in West Germany might attract a significant amount of money from West Germans, who might be willing to exchange their DM for M to get the higher interest rate if they perceived the likelihood of an eventual 1:1 convertibility of the M to be fairly high. Since each DM so exchanged would save the M4.4 that is normally required for each DM in export revenue (at least initially until East Germany could earn DM at more competitive M costs), such deposits would be especially useful to East Germany's economy. As a result, even if such accounts were not needed to prevent a decline in East German savings, they could be offered to West Germans and other foreigners (who might be enticed not only by the speculative value but also by feeling a social obligation to invest in and help out a reformed East Germany).

An alternative risk with respect to East German domestic savings accounts would be that too much money would be saved. However, such a scenario would permit greater investment and therefore faster economic growth and wage increases, although there might be some short-term costs associated with the transfer of resources from domestic consumption good industries to other industries.

Risks of Currency Black Markets

Some East Germans might prefer to exchange their M on the black markets for DM with West Germans and other foreigners, as opposed to lock up so much money for so long. However, such exchanges would merely substitute for the East German government's requirement to pay for DM1 of imports with M4.4 of East German production expenditures. If a black market exchange rate of less than M4.4/DM existed, there would be a lower cost of financing DM imports in this fashion than with normal East German export production. In addition, if some of the M obtained by foreigners on the black market were instead held by foreigners as an investment or for future possible purchases, the amount so held would be like an interest-free loan that would allow East Germany to invest the money as opposed to create goods for foreign consumption.

Given that East Germans could legally purchase DM1 with M6, the black market exchange rate could never be worse than M6/DM, and it would likely be far less than that amount since M5 of the M6 would be returned plus 3% annual interest in 9 years if legally exchanged. Even for an East German who could otherwise invest his/her net cash savings from using the black markets in some real commercial investment (like an ice cream stand) at the same 18% rate as the East German government (which strictly controlled prices, wages, and therefore return on investment), the maximum black market exchange rate X would have to satisfy the constraint

$(6\text{-}X)(1.18)^9 \geq 5(1.03)^9$, or

$X \leq M4.5/DM.$ (B-1)

If the exchange rate were in excess of M4.5/DM, the cash savings of M6-MX from using the black market, invested at 18% for 9 years, would not grow to an amount in excess of what could be earned from the alternative strategy of exchanging at the official 1:1 exchange rate and putting the mandatory M5 in the 3% savings account.

Thus, the black market exchange rate would be close to or less than the all-important cost of earning a DM in exports. This hypothesis is supported by Murphy's (1992b) empirical finding that, even without the unrestricted opportunity to exchange money legally, the black market exchange rate was strongly affected by the cost of earning a DM export. In addition, while Murphy (1992b) also found evidence that the black market value of the East German mark was negatively influenced by higher prices in West Germany (implying a high degree of inelasticity of demand for West German goods relative to price due to the existence in East Germany of a shortage of modern Western goods), such an effect might be alleviated under the current plan that allowed greater imports of Western goods (as the same Murphy study found that the demand inelasticity problem had been alleviated in the past by enhanced political recognition for East Germany, which opened up the opportunity for greater importation of high-tech Western goods, and by increasing the amount of legal imports from West Germany in general).

It is quite possible that the black market exchange rate in equation (B-1) greatly overestimates the number of East German Marks that would be needed to buy DM. In particular, a high tax rate was levied on profits in East Germany, whereas interest on savings accounts was not subject to tax (*Der Tagesspiegel,* 1989e), and so the return on a commercial investment would have to be put on a comparable after-tax basis. For instance, with a tax rate of 50% levied on profits in excess of M25,000 in East Germany (Buero des Ministerrates, 1966), the maximum exchange rate from the adjusted foregoing inequality would be

$X \leq 6 - [5(1+.03)^9/(1+\{.18x.5\})^9] = M3.0/DM1.$ (B-2)

Even the M3.0/DM exchange rate might overestimate the true black market rate that would exist. In particular, the tax rate on domestic company profits was as high as 90% on profits in excess of M250,000, which might be relevant to the richest East Germans who might be the ones most likely capable of investing their money commercially.[9] East Germans faced with that marginal tax rate would optimally invest any money saved from using the black market into the traditional tax-free money market checking accounts earning 3.25% (since the after-tax yield on commercial investments would be only 18%{1-.90}=1.8%, which is lower than 3.25%). As a result, the boundary exchange rate might be as low as

$$X \leq 6 - \{5(1 + .03)^9/(1 + .0325)^9\} = M1.1/DM. \qquad (B\text{-}3)$$

Thus, black market exchanges might be very close to the 1:1 official exchange rate. In addition, because most East Germans did not have the opportunity, know-how, or desire to conduct lucrative investments on their own, and because black market exchanges would be illegal (creating risk of imprisonment and/or fines, as well as possibly resulting in a negative criminal status and psychological worries), there might be very little black market activity at all. West Germans and other foreigners might therefore encounter some difficulty in finding East Germans from whom they could buy M, and so they (being also subject to similar risks) might decide instead to exchange their money legally with an East German bank at 1:1 when making purchases inside East Germany.[10] These extra DM so obtained would reduce the amount needed to subsidize East German imports and therefore increase the amount available for East German investment.

Risk of Different Costs of Earning DM Export Revenue

An in-depth time-series study by Murphy (1992b) indicated that the cost of earning a DM in exports was unaffected by increases in exports or imports from West Germany, as well as unaffected by increases in foreign trade in the aggregate. As a result, the constant M4.4 assumed to be expended to generate each additional DM1.0 in export revenue in the original model seems reasonable. However, it is possible that a very high increase in foreign trade (possibly mandated by excess demand at the 1:1 exchange rate) might result in additional costs, such as increased distribution and resource reallocation expenses, at least initially.[11] Such a situation would slow the ability of the East German government to phase out the mandatory savings associated with DM exchanges. For instance, if the amount needed to earn a DM of exports rose to M5, there would be required export costs of DM23{M5/DM}=M115 billion in the first year to pay for the originally assumed DM23 billion in imports. With the East German government receiving M6 for every DM1 in imports, only M138-M115=M23 billion could be invested in the first year to reduce the cost of future export revenue generation. If the higher cost to generate a DM of export revenue were not a one-time expense and instead continued, it would take 12 years of normal East German investment to enable the government to remove the plan's mandatory savings requirement associated with East German imports.

On the other hand, it is also possible that the enhanced capacity to import goods from West Germany would raise productivity and actually decrease the amount needed by East Germany to earn a DM1.0 of export revenue. In particular, East German firms would have greater flexibility to buy capital equipment from West Germany that could modernize East German industry and greatly cut the costs of earning export revenue. The probable elimination of the Western embargo on high-tech exports to East Germany (as a result of the opening of the Wall and the reduction in political tensions) might be especially important here (Parrott, 1985). For instance, despite investing over M10 billion in prior years into microelectronics, East Germany had in 1989 a cost of producing 256K semiconductors of M534 compared to the DM5 cost for such chips available on the "free" world market to Western countries (Hertle, 1996). If East Germany's political and economic reforms were rewarded with the removal of the embargo on computer chips, East Germany would be able to replace the M534 cost with the cost of DM5x[M4.4/DM]=M22 needed to generate the exports to pay for the import of such high technology goods and thereby save over 95% on the production costs of that important component of the modern economy (thus freeing up substantial sums of money, which could be used to cover additional export costs associated with the plan, as well as to increase investment or wages). Apart from any positive effect resulting from greater productive imports, the increased imports of consumer goods from West Germany might also enhance the morale of East German workers and spur productivity improvements. Such productivity increases would lower costs further.

In addition, the opening up of the East German economy and political system would probably reduce many of the government trade barriers set up against East German goods and thereby further facilitate an expansion of exports at a lower cost, especially to the European Community (EC), which included the richest countries of Western Europe. In particular, although East German exports to all EC members except West Germany had previously faced significant tariff barriers, and although West Germany itself had employed significant quota barriers that effectively prohibited East Germany from obtaining more than 5% of the market in any industry (Melzer and Stahnke, 1986), EC membership was offered to East Germany shortly after the opening of the Berlin Wall (*Der Taggesspiegel,* 1990a). Such membership would greatly reduce tariffs and thereby facilitate East German export sales at a lower cost to a larger market and enable East Germany to concentrate its exports in areas where it had a competitive advantage, such as in heavy machinery, auto parts, porcelain, salt mining, and food production where the cost of earning DM1.0 was less than M3.0 (Mueller, 1989). East Germany might also be able to realize further economy of scale cost reductions as a result of such increased production in specific industries, especially if it were able to expand exports of the various goods for which it already had production costs less than M1.0 for every DM1.0 earned (Schwarzer, 1999).

Also within this environment, Western distribution barriers and consumer biases against East German goods might evaporate, especially in West Germany where the government trade quotas might even be eliminated.[12] The resulting increased exports might lead to further economies of scale in both general distribution and manufacturing, especially as East Germany became more integrated with the entire world economy.

Besides a reduced cost of earning DM export revenue, an increase in tourist traffic, which would likely result from a reduction in Cold War tension and fear as well as from a heightened curiosity and desire to assist (brought on by East Germany's reforms), might also facilitate the earning of hard currency revenue. For instance, without the plan, foreigners spent billions of DM in East Germany in the first 2 months of 1990 alone, although a lack of controls against black market exchanges resulted in few of these DM being exchanged officially with the government (*Der Tagesspiegel,* 1990i). In addition, without the plan, the cost of earning a DM equaled the exchange rate, which was 3:1 for official exchanges and 7:1 for black market exchanges (*Der Tagesspiegel,* 1990d), times the unsubsidized price divided by the subsidized price (which often implied a high double digit M cost for earning a single DM). Given the plan to raise prices to market-clearing levels for foreigners, and given the greater likelihood of official 1:1 exchanges and very low black market exchange rates (as explained earlier in the subsection "Risks of Currency Black Markets"), the cost of earning the billions in DM sales to tourists would be greatly reduced. It is also very probable that far more in hard currency tourist revenue would be earned by East Germany since goods and services would no longer be effectively given away for almost free at the subsidized prices and exchange rates (i.e., at such low prices, demand would likely be extremely inelastic with respect to price). As a result, it seems probable that the plan overall would decrease the cost of earning hard currency revenues as opposed to increase it.[13]

Risk of Different Amounts of Western Investment

It is possible that if there were not political support from West Germany or another Western country, the amount of Western investment might not even be as high as under the catastrophic economic scenario that actually developed. In that case, the great rise in output caused by such investment would not happen. However, if the Western capital that flowed into East Germany was only a third as much as the investment that indeed occurred, that should be enough to generate double digit growth rates for years.

In addition, even if East Germany had chosen a path politically independent of West Germany, its economic and political reforms would probably have been sufficient to attract a substantial amount of Western investment, as long as the economy were just reasonably healthy. The EC had indeed promised both political and economic support following the opening of the Berlin Wall in 1989 (*Der Tagesspiegel,* 1990a), and the USA had expressed its readiness to make substantial investments (*Der Tagesspiegel,* 1990l). It is therefore probable that, with strong international political support, with the strong incentives incorporated into the proposed economic plan for foreigners to produce in the country instead of just export to it, and with a healthy economy, East Germany would have attracted far more Western capital than it actually did with the depression scenario and limited incentives for productive foreign investment that unfolded without using the Murphy plan. Just to provide an example of the importance of a healthy economy and incentives for local production, communist China has attracted more direct foreign investment than any other country in the world (except the very rich USA) over the last few years (Wei et al., 1999), despite having far less international political support than East Germany in late 1989 and despite having a closed communist economic system for most of the country. Greater foreign investment would only add to the incredibly high double-digit growth rates projected in the original model (just as it has added to communist China's very high real growth rate).

The Risk of Economic Depression in Eastern Europe

Perhaps the greatest risk to the plan came externally from Eastern Europe, with which East Germany conducted much of its trade (M60 billion in exports and M57 billion in imports in 1989). If this area of the world suffered the over 40% decline in real GNP over the early 1990s that indeed did happen (IMF, 1996), there would likely be a commensurate decline in trade with this area. The actual 60% decline in East German exports to Eastern Europe that occurred in the early 1990s (Osmond, 1992) would represent a M36 billion drop in demand for East German goods (representing over 10% of East German National Income) that would require East Germany to replace this loss of production and goods with other markets.

However, the plan's 1:1 exchange rate with the DM would actually require a change-over to greater production to meet the demands of greater trade with the Western Europeans. The decreased demand for exports to the Eastern European market would free up resources for just this purpose (while the domestic East German demand for imported goods from Eastern Europe would be replaced by increased saving and spending on imports from Western Europe). Although this shift in production would entail significant restructuring expenses, the costs might be less because of the centralized control and planning that exist in the East German socialist system.

In addition, it is also possible that a robust East German economy would have helped prevent the huge economic catastrophe from occurring in Eastern Europe, both by providing greater demand than actually occurred for Eastern European products (from higher East German income) and by serving as an example to the other countries of Eastern Europe on how a successful transformation of their economies can occur. For instance, it might have been possible to avoid the disastrous policy of changing Eastern European trade from a system of multilateral barter on December 31, 1990 to a system where all trade was paid for strictly in hard currencies like the DM (Sabov, 1991). Besides thereby avoiding the resulting huge decrease in trade between Eastern European countries, the catastrophic policy of depreciating the Russian ruble enormously in 1991 to make it convertible (as will be discussed in Chapter 6) might also have been avoided (Hays, 1991).

Restructuring Costs

The analysis so far has not explicitly considered any special frictions or restructuring costs (including retraining expenses) associated with shifting investments and resources from one sector to another. Instead, any such costs have been assumed to have been incorporated into the rate of return on investment, which are measured net of such costs. However, in the case of massive investments in some sector or industries, such as the export sector, restructuring costs might be higher than normal. Such additional costs would reduce the return on investment. East Germany would incur such costs for its own investments, while, for foreign investments, East Germany would have to decide whether to bear the costs in order not to discourage foreign capital or suffer a lower level of foreign investment as a result of the lower level of profitability available to foreign investors.

Because there was no unemployment in East Germany, and workers were in fact guaranteed the right to a job for life, the costs of restructuring might be highest in terms of labor due to the lack of slack in this resource input. To attract workers into growing industries such as the export sector, it might be useful to have most of the wage increases concentrated in those industries (and especially for needed skilled workers to keep them from emigrating). In addition, a special payroll tax might be levied on all workers that could be used to further increase wages in critical industries with labor shortages and to pay for any needed additional training. This reallocation of wages might reduce the costs of restructuring born by the entire economy.

It should also be emphasized that incorporated into the historical 18% return on investment are the costs of restructuring normally incurred by East German investments in the past. These restructuring costs included those associated with about 2% of the population moving annually between the 15 different sectors or states of East Germany (Statistisches Amt, 1990). In addition, Eastern European socialist countries typically were involved in retraining over 5% of the work force each year in normal times (Marcy, 1990).

In any event, the costs of restructuring would only penalize the return on investment in the initial year and therefore would not materially affect long-term growth or long-term investment decisions. Even if the amount of such costs were as high as 30% of the first year's profit from each investment, that would only reduce National Income growth by about 2%, which is fairly minor compared to the double-digit National Income growth that would be expected to be caused by the massive investments.

In addition, it is likely that East Germany's greater openness to trade might actually increase the return on investment more than enough to offset any restructuring cost problems. In particular, expanded international trade allows a country to specialize in producing the goods and services that it produces most effectively and thereby permits concentrated investment in the sectors where it can earn the highest returns (Eiteman, Stonehill, and Moffett, 1998). For instance, the return on East German investment in the textile, consumer good, and electrical industries exceeded 40%, compared to under 10% in energy and construction (Mueller, 1978). Concentrated investment can also enhance economies of scale and scope, thereby lower costs, and further enhance returns.

The Risk of Inflation, Emigration, and Productivity Problems

As previously mentioned, to inhibit foreigners from being able to purchase East German products at subsidized prices, the prices of all goods and services in East Germany would be allowed to rise to market-clearing levels that cover costs. However, to avoid inflation, maintain consumer confidence in the economy (and thereby increase morale, as opposed to experiencing the productivity decline and emigration that actually occurred in early 1990 without the plan), avoid poverty, and encourage the consumption of East German products by East Germans, each East German citizen would be paid a fixed amount each month into special KM checking accounts. These checks could be written to cover 90% of the price of specified subsistence goods such as food, children's clothing, day care, monthly mass transportation tickets, cultural events, and housing. The annual amount paid into each person's KM account would be set to equal the per capita amount of subsidies paid out by the East German government in 1989, which approximated the M70 billion/16.4 million people=M4268 in per capita subsidies reported to be paid in 1988 (the M70 billion in subsidies would continue to be financed by higher prices for nonessential goods and services that are essentially taxed more heavily by the government).

Although the existence of the additional KM currency/account/pricing would create some administrative costs and bureaucratic difficulties, such problems would probably be far less than those imposed by commercial coupons (of which there are so many different types in capitalist societies) and likely even less than with buyers' clubs or cooperatives which also give a select group of people special discounted prices (Furlough and Strikwerda, 1999). Because the KM coupons could only be used by East German citizens, the subsidies would not be available to foreigner tourists, whose cheap purchases of goods and services in East Germany in 1987 were effectively subsidized by an estimated M1.3 billion (Schwarzer, 1999), and who were in the process of stealing many billions more in the first 2 months of 1990 alone after the removal of effective border controls (*Der Tagesspiegel,* 1990i). Thus, the plan allows the M price of essentials to rise to market-clearing levels while still permitting limited subsidized purchases for domestic residents to shield East German citizens from the effect of the one-time inflation.[14] By thereby maintaining such advantages of living in East Germany (i.e., a very low and stable cost of living), this policy should keep the morale of the East German workers high. As a result, there should be no decline in productivity, and the incentive to emigrate to higher-paying jobs in West Germany should be reduced. The vast majority of East Germans were very content with their socialist system, and, only once it became clear that the January 1, 1990 opening to West German exploitation would destroy the system economically, did the East Germans decide to vote with their feet and ballots for West German capitalism.

To provide an example of the important interaction of these factors, it can be observed that East German real economic output actually rose 2% in 1989 despite the emigration of 343,854 East Germans (over 2% of the population) during that time period as travel restrictions were eliminated (Hertle, 1996). The productivity of the remaining East Germans was so boosted by the positive morale effects of the opening of the Berlin Wall that the disruptive influence of the movement of so many East German workers was partially offset. In addition, by December 1989 as the initial flood of emigrations had subsided, daily East German emigrations had fallen drastically to a much more manageable level of one thousand per day, which was significantly less than the rate just before the building of the Berlin Wall in 1961 and was similar to that experienced by East Germany in the 1950s (Hertle, 1996) when annual real growth in National Income averaged over 10% (Statistisches Amt, 1990). East German production first declined significantly in 1990 when travel restrictions and border checks of West Germans were eliminated, an official M3:DM1 exchange rate was established, and West Germans thereby not only received the same opportunities for bargain purchases with M as East Germans but effectively only had to pay 1/3 of their own DM. Within this environment, daily emigrations doubled (to an annual rate of over 500,000) in early 1990 despite continuing political reforms and promises of a unified economy (Murphy, 1990b).

Without the proposed plan to maintain East German morale, it is quite likely that productivity would drop, and some disruptive effects of a high level of emigrations would occur, possibly reducing GNP growth by as much as several percent. While such problems would only slightly reduce the very high growth rates possible under the narrower aspects of the plan, lower growth rates would increase the time required for East German incomes to reach West German levels, thereby prolonging the negative effects.

On the other hand, by combining the advantages of East German communism with the right to a 1:1 exchange rate and all the positive aspects of a very rapid economic growth rate (which includes good employment opportunities and an optimistic outlook), it is likely that the number of net emigrations would have tapered off considerably, especially as time, confidence, foreign investment, and incomes grew.[15] Also contributing to lower emigrations would be the allowance in the plan for direct ownership of shares in East German state enterprises that would be lost upon moving to the West. Emigrations would be especially inhibited if West Germany discontinued its program of offering aid and loans totaling over DM160,000 to each immigrating worker, as it indeed finally did early in 1990 (*Der Taggespiegel,* 1990f). This situation would compare very positively to the very large number of East Germans (an average of over 200,000 annually) who, in the depression scenario that actually unfolded, continued to move to western Germany long after the actual unification of the two Germanies in 1990 (Statistisches Bundesamt, 1996).

The maintenance of low prices in East Germany, along with expanded employment opportunities and other advantages associated with the broad plan, might not only stem the outflow of East German emigrants but actually entice many West Germans into moving to East Germany. As infrastructure and incomes became more equal, there might have been a net inflow of people into East Germany.

Different Spending on Infrastructure and the Environment

Although the results discussed so far have assumed ordinary infrastructure investments by East Germany into industries such as communications and transportation, it is possible that Western European (or USA) telephone companies, railroads, and other infrastructure organizations might have been attracted enough by the profit potential in a more open and vibrant East Germany to undertake important investments. Such capital could have modernized the East German telephone, rail, and road system within a few years (as the West German infrastructure investments actually did) and could have further increased the productivity and growth of the East German economy. In addition to increasing productivity, the return on investment, and therefore National Income growth (even more so than estimated originally), such investments would improve the quality of life for the average East German (and thereby lower emigrations and even increase immigrations).

The East German government had estimated that its telephone system could be expanded and brought up to a standard comparable to that of West Germany for M12 billion (*Der Taggespiegel,* 1989b), which would also meet the backlogged demand for about one million new telephones (Schwarzer, 1999). However, East Germany had forecast that it did not have enough construction capacity to completely satisfy all demand for phones at least until 1995 (*Der Taggespiegel,* 1989b). As a result, a deal with a foreign telecommunications firm might be useful in order to be able to import some additional foreign materials, machinery, and services needed to modernize the phone network more quickly, with the foreign firm being offered future telephone revenues in return.

Since the cost of DM45 billion that was actually incurred to totally rebuild the East German telecommunication system was unnecessary, it might have been possible to have the foreign telephone firms paid with higher telephone charges on new installations. Assuming DM10 billion in foreign investment needed to meet all backlogged demand immediately, and assuming a 21% required return on that investment, there would have to be an annual DM2.1 billion increase in telephone rates to satisfy all current demand. With the backlogged demand for one million new phones in East Germany, the annual telephone fees would have to be about two thousand marks (or just under DM200 per month). Because the fee was only about M200 per year for those who waited for East German telephone construction (Schwarzer, 1999), it is likely that most would choose to continue to wait, and only the most urgent demand for telephones would be met with foreign investment. Alternatively, the East German government could subsidize telephone usage in order to improve the quality of life there (with the cost being DM2.1 annually, which would replace other productive investment and thereby decrease economic growth by 0.6% initially and 0.1% thereafter as the shortage of DM was alleviated).

Similarly, as reported in *Der Taggesspiegel* (1990h), a West German opposition party (the SPD) estimated that it would cost DM2 billion annually to upgrade the East German transportation system to a reasonable level of quality. Since it was not necessary to spend the DM146 billion actually incurred to overhaul the whole system, it might have been possible to obtain attractive financing (using gasoline and railway taxes as collateral) from Western infrastructure firms seeking the DM2 billion in annual business, but only to the extent that the return on such transportation system investments (or the quality of life improvement) was expected to be high enough.

In addition, it is possible that East Germany would choose to spend more on the environment to improve the quality of life there. In 1989,

East Germany spent only 0.5% of National Income on environmental protection, compared to 1.6% for West Germany. Increasing the spending on the environment to the same level as in West Germany would have cost East Germany .011xM275=M3 billion. Investing M3 billion more into the environment would have reduced productivity investments and therefore real economic growth by .18xM3 billion/M275 billion=0.2%. Although this effect on growth would be fairly small, the East German government estimated a need to spend as much as M100 billion long term (half for air and about half for water pollution clean-up) because of past neglect (*Der Taggespiegel,* 1990k). However, if the extra M100 billion in pollution control spending were spread over 20 years, the impact would remain fairly limited, with a further reduction in annual economic growth of less than 0.3%.[16]

Foreign Aid and Loan Factors

The original modeling results assumed no net external financial aid, and so deviations from assumptions for this final factor could only have contributed to the success of the plan. In fact, some amount of aid was likely just to encourage the political and economic reforms in East Germany. Indeed, shortly after major political reforms were announced in Eastern Europe, the EC proposed a 5-10 year program of giving *annual* aid of DM39 billion to East Germany and 5 other Eastern European countries (*Der Tagesspiegel,* 1990a), which comes to about DM6 billion per year to East Germany if split evenly. Such a grant would have saved East Germany over M20 billion initially in export subsidies (or over 5% of National Income).

With respect to loans, East Germany already had hard currency debt of about DM20 billion that cost it under DM2 billion in interest payments annually (*Der Tagesspiegel,* 1990b).[17] The modeling results have assumed no net foreign loan payments, but this assumption seems reasonable given that Western commercial banks had rated East Germany as being in good enough credit standing to merit additional credit (*Der Tagesspiegel,* 1990j) and would have been willing to loan it the annual interest due (if not far more). The World Bank also indicated its willingness to loan Eastern Europe billions of DM, which East Germany could tap into along with International Monetary Fund (IMF) loans as soon as it joined that organization (*Der Tagesspiegel,* 1990c). In addition, shortly after the opening of the Berlin Wall, West Germany offered East

Germany DM12 billion in additional credits on favorable terms (*Der Tagespiegel,* 1989c), which could have been drawn down if there were any short-term problems with the plan. Additional net loans, especially ones at subsidized rates, might have helped significantly if used to import Western capital, thereby supplement private Western investment in East Germany, and thus further increase East German economic growth rates.

In addition, hard currency loans would have permitted a more gradual orientation of production toward export industries and thereby reduce some of the costs associated with a rapid restructuring. For instance, the DM12 billion in loans from West Germany would have enabled East Germany to avoid having to reallocate DM12xM4.4/DM=M53 billion to earn the export revenue otherwise necessary to pay for much of the imports that would occur under the 1:1 exchange rate plan. The loans could then be paid back after East Germany had time to gradually restructure and invest enough into the export industries to drive down the cost of earning hard currency exports.

Far larger and longer aid programs were very possible, given that western Germany in fact has already given about DM1 trillion to eastern Germany (and continues to give about DM150 billion per year). Even without West Germany's support, many of the other Western European countries themselves were delighted enough with the ending of the Cold War (which the opening of the Berlin Wall symbolized) and fearful enough of a reunited Germany that they appeared ready to provide extensive financial help (which they could justify financially insofar as they felt the need for less military spending in a more friendly external world). Combined with the plan, a significant amount of aid and loans could have easily helped East Germany grow fast enough to catch up with West Germany within a matter of 2 years (instead of the original estimate of 3-6 years, depending on the productivity and amount of private foreign investment). In fact, the initial 1989 Murphy plan called for a total of DM40 billion in aid or loans (to expand the telephone network, import up to a million inexpensive used cars, improve pollution control, purchase technology, and buy foreign machinery to enhance export and import-substituting production). When combined with the aspects of the plan described in this chapter, DM40 billion could have potentially accomplished in 24 months what it might, at current rates of growth and aid, take more than 24 years and over DM4 trillion to achieve: income parity between eastern and western Germany (Osmond, 1992).[18]

Conclusion

The simulated results indicate that implementation of a unique economic plan for transition to international competitiveness could have avoided the economic catastrophe that occurred as a result of German unification. The simulated model shows that the plan could have saved or earned Germany trillions of dollars. In addition, by providing an incentive for capital and jobs to move to people (as opposed to vice-versus), the plan may also have resulted in a far lower level of other social costs.

Although Germany already has adopted an alternative plan for unification and currency union (which has caused an economic catastrophe), there are still many countries in the world with currencies that are not totally convertible and that could benefit from the plan. For instance, many Eastern European countries might be able to adopt the plan, as they attempt to integrate into the European Union.[19] The idea might also be usable in the many countries of Asia, Africa, and Latin America that do not have a completely convertible currency. In addition, some form of the plan might be employed in countries that experience rapid real declines in the value of their currencies, so that a currency crisis similar to that recently experienced in Southeast Asia might be avoided. The plan could be especially useful for countries like Russia that moved from having minimal foreign consumption imports in the 1980s to over half of all consumption goods being imported in the 1990s (Associated Press, 1998).

In addition, a component of the plan could still be utilized today in some form in countries with strong convertible currencies. For example, in Germany, various different groups of people could be issued a new KM currency or coupons, which could only be used to purchase goods from the still poorer, eastern part of Germany. The coupons could be given to all those receiving state welfare payments (in lieu of the normal currency), and a special tax could be levied by the state (perhaps on the rich) that would provide a refund in the form of the new KM currency or coupons with a nominal value equal to the special DM tax. The size of the coupon distributions could actually be set, so that a fixed amount of production had to occur in the eastern part of Germany, enough to greatly reduce unemployment there (or the coupons would go unspent and be lost to the recipient). To access this potential revenue, a large amount of *productive* private capital would be expected to be invested into the eastern part of Germany, which might finally spur the long-awaited catching-up process there. Italy could potentially implement a similar idea for its poor southern region, and even the USA could possibly use such a plan to spur economic development of its inner cities (or poor southern rural areas), where the coupons could only be spent for products or services produced there.[20]

Thus, besides enabling socialist countries to prosperously co-exist in a capitalist world, the plan may also be used to mitigate some of the economic problems of capitalism itself. It might be especially useful in helping avoid one of the biggest problems of global capitalism, currency crises, which are analyzed in the next chapter.

CHAPTER 6

A DETAILED EVALUATION OF CURRENCY CRISES AND BALANCE OF PAYMENT PROBLEMS IN THE NEW WORLD ORDER

The USA's Cold War victory represented an enormous coup for capitalism. In particular, the defeat of the Soviet Union has led to the discrediting of communism and government activities in general and has resulted in a worldwide trend toward "free markets" (Wysocki, 1999). Countries that don't open up their markets fast enough face the risk of capital flight and a reduction in foreign capital investment, as investors rush to the many other countries with more "desirable" systems (Schlesinger, 1999). Because investors not only want more open markets but also cheaper labor and lower taxes, increased competition among workers and governments to attract job-creating capital tends to result in a steady decline in wages and business taxes that enables wealth to be ever more in the hands of the rich providers of capital (Strobel and Peterson, 1999).

In addition, the USA government itself is pushing countries ever harder to open up their markets or face barriers to exporting to the very large USA market (Marshall, 1999). Moreover, with no counterbalancing superpower anymore, countries that refuse the trend toward a purer capitalist system are faced with an increasing likelihood of potentially severe damages from the USA in the form of embargoes, CIA terrorism, aerial bombings, and invasions (Griswold, 1999b).

The new era of freer markets has generally meant a reduction in government regulation, government enterprises, government subsidies, government taxes, government welfare, and government services at the same time that "free market" charges are levied on health care, education, and other essentials that make it impossible for the poor to meet their most basic needs (Chossudovsky, 1997). While some of these changes have promoted greater economic efficiency short-term, and while the privatization of many government-owned firms has indeed tended to make the privatized companies themselves more profitable (D'Souza and Megginson, 1999), the gains have generally accrued to the richer elements of the world and been at the expense of the poor, especially in less developed countries (Chossudovsky, 1997).[1] Even within the victorious USA itself, the gulf between the rich and the poor has widened significantly, as most if not all of the spoils of the USA's Cold War victory have accrued to the rich (Teepen, 1999), and even the USA middle class has experienced a large reduction in their share of the loot (Strobel and Peterson, 1999). In addition, the effects of global capitalism on macroeconomic growth or efficiency have often been quite negative (Friedland, 1999), as the case of Russia so clearly shows, where aggregate productivity and output have dropped about 50% since the introduction of a free market system in the early 1990s (Whalen, 1999).

Potentially one of the most explosive effects of the trend toward freer markets has been related to the removal of government restrictions on international trade and currency markets (Chossudovsky, 1997). Although the elimination of such restrictions can cause an expansion in trade and capital investment, which in turn can promote greater worldwide efficiency and output (Soedersten and Reed, 1994), it can also lead to currency crises and large pockets of economic chaos and destruction, as the 1990s clearly demonstrate. While there are other attributes of capitalist globalization, such as the spreading of megamergers and stock option plans, as well as a "reverse Robin Hood" society (Kamm and Vitzthum, 2000), currency crises have been especially notable for the widespread suffering that they have imposed on the world.

The various currency crises of the 1990s, especially those in Southeast Asia in 1997 (Lim, 1997), have brought these issues to the forefront of relevance (Gibson, 1999). Attempts have been made to explain at least some of the events that represent catalysts for, or symptoms of, international currency crises (Miller, 1998), but existing theories have not been very successful in explaining even more stable situations

(MacDonald, 1990), much less the root structural causes of the currency volatility of the 1990s (Berg and Pattillo, 1999). Because these crises cause so much economic suffering, especially for the less fortunate, and because they are not well-explained or understood by capitalist economists, they merit detailed study here. A general evaluation of currency crises (and solutions thereto) is provided in this chapter.

Currency crises are caused by balance of payments problems that are generally related to trade and current account imbalances. Such crises have occurred frequently since the USA won the Cold War, as more countries have been "persuaded" to follow the "free" market model "recommended" by the victors and have found themselves with severe balance of payments (BOP) problems. Such problems, and especially imbalances in the international *current account* (which include the net balance on trade, services, investment income, and transfer payments), represent a serious situation that must eventually be addressed (Root, 1990).

One classical solution to a current account deficit is to allow the domestic currency to fall in value and thereby discourage imports and encourage exports to eliminate the imbalance (Afesoglu and Dutkowsky, 1997). Unfortunately, this solution ignores two problems: elasticity of demand (Hufbauer and Schott, 1992) and inflation induced by currency depreciation (Abuaf and Jorion, 1990). Various alternative solutions designed to avoid these problems exist, but some merely postpone and magnify the negative effects of current account deficits, while others may not be feasible in the New World Order.

CURRENCY CRISES AFTER THE COLD WAR

The 1990s have been marred by one currency crisis after the other. Although there were international economic crises prior to the 1990s, such as the Latin American debt crisis of the 1980s (Witcher, 1999), there was nothing like the frequency and severity of the currency crises of the 1990s, largely because of the existence of government regulations on international trade, capital movements, and currency exchanges before then (Soedersten and Reed, 1994). However, as governments around the world began to reduce or eliminate their regulation of the international markets after the USA's Cold War victory, trade and capital flows as well as exchange rates were allowed to fluctuate more freely (and often completely) at the whims of the marketplace, and the 1990s have demonstrated that free markets can cause large fluctuations in currency values which can have very serious effects on the international balance of payments, inflation, and economic output.

A good example is provided by Yeltsin's capitalist Russia, which (at the suggestion of its primary USA economic advisor, Harvard University Professor Jeffrey Sachs) made its currency, the ruble (Rb), freely convertible in December of 1991 (Hays, 1991). Although the average purchasing power of the ruble in terms of what it could buy in real goods and services was approximately the same as the dollar before 1991 (and therefore approximated the official government exchange rate between dollars and rubles that was about 1:1 at that time), Russia did not have the products, reputation, and distribution system to be competitive in international markets (Williamson, 1991). In addition, there was enormous pent-up Russian demand for foreign products, including not only for electronics goods that had long been in short supply in Russia under communism but also for foreign brand-name versions of what was much more cheaply available in Russia such as blue jeans, cigarettes, and cola.

This situation represented one of extreme inelasticity of demand relative to price for Russian imports and exports (Caves, Frankel, and Jones, 1996). In particular, Russians were willing to pay almost any price for foreign goods in 1991, and the demand for (or addiction to) foreign goods continues strong even many years later (Associated Press, 1998). On the other hand, foreign countries were unwilling to pay any price for Russian goods, which had not yet been adapted to sell in foreign markets, which had a poor reputation (from Cold War propaganda) if they were known about at all, and which were not even being internationally distributed yet on any large scale (with the marketing necessary to "sell" and distribute products in capitalism being a very costly and time-consuming process).

As a result, when the ruble went from being almost fully inconvertible (in terms of severe restrictions on any currency trading) to suddenly being fully convertible in December of 1991, there was an enormous demand for foreign currencies like dollars and almost no demand for rubles. Not surprisingly, the currency immediately fell from about Rb1/$ to about Rb100/$.

Such an enormous devaluation had an effect similar to making the currency worthless, which would reduce hard currency exports to $0 if prices in the domestic currency remained the same. For instance, a vodka exporter selling bottles at Rb5/bottle would have the amount of dollars earned per bottle fall from $5 to $.05 when the exchange rate changed from Rb1/$ to Rb100/$. At the same time, the dollar retail price in an export market like the US might only fall by about a third because transportation costs, tariffs, liquor taxes, and distribution costs such as dealer mark-ups typically make up more than 2/3 of the final retail price, and these costs may be largely independent of exchange rates—as is also typical for many other products (such as textiles) produced in less developed countries, where even non-transportation distribution costs (i.e., rent and capital costs incorporated into wholesale and retail mark-ups) easily make up over 2/3 of the retail value (Chossudovsky, 1997). Even if the 33% drop in the retail price could lead to a doubling of sales to 2 million bottles from 1 million, the amount of export revenue would fall from $5 million to 2,000,000x$.05=$100,000. In the meantime, "needed" technology and Western brand-name imports might only be halved despite 9900% higher Rb costs (caused by the 99% devaluation), resulting in a 4900% increase in Rb imports that can not be paid for with a 100% increase in Rb exports. In this situation, there was virtually no exchange rate that would balance the payments for trade (or the international current account). Only investors seeking to buy up Russian real estate and fixed assets at some extremely low prices (like 1/100 of the prior cost) could bring the supply and demand for rubles into the equilibrium at 100 rubles per dollar.

However, such a situation could not and did not last long. Exporters prefer not to maximize revenue in a worthless currency, and so they naturally increase their domestic currency prices in such a predicament (perhaps using collusion), unless there is both perfect competition and sufficient capacity to meet the higher unit demand. With importers also having to raise ruble prices to pay the same dollar price but with far more rubles (and with those competing with importers doing likewise), almost immediate hyperinflation in Russia was the natural result, with inflation rising from 5.4% in 1990 to about 100% by the end of 1991 and to about 1300% in 1992 (IMF, 1993). At the time of the devaluation in 1991, the chairman of the Russian central bank (who disagreed strongly with Yeltsin and the imposed policy) predicted the effect "would be something much more destructive than an atomic bomb" (Hays, 1991).

In fact, the resulting chaos permitted organized crime to seize a vast portion of the economy in Russia, as such rich criminals were among the few willing to take the risk and enter into the uncertain Russian market to seize many assets whose prices were close to zero at the going exchange rates for those with foreign currency (Raith, 1994). Organized crime in the form of drug trafficking and black market activities (including in previously illegal foreign currency transactions) had already begun to seize significant economic power in the Soviet Union under Gorbachev's market reforms in the late 1980s (Marcy, 1990), with a claim on annual revenue in excess of $100 billion by 1990 (*Der Tagesspiegel*, 1990p). However, Russian mafia groups were able to utilize the chaotic economic environment of the 1990s to greatly expand their activities and wealth. For instance, after the convertibility of the currency in late 1991, they increased their smuggling activities on a potentially far grander scale than was possible under communism, with the profitable purpose now being the avoidance of government tariffs (Davis, Cloud, and Becker, 2000), as opposed to the avoidance of currency controls under communism. In addition, organized criminal groups in Russia have begun to extort most businesses in that country (including foreign ones) to pay them 15-30% of their revenues as "protection" against violent attacks and murder (Roth, 1996). As a result of this huge increase in income, the Russian state prosecutor's office estimates that mafia wealth has grown to the point where about half of the entire Russian economy is now under "mafia control" (Dominion, 1999).

Besides causing hyperinflation and laying the groundwork for mafia seizure of economic power, the removal of currency controls also created the opportunity for imports from Western countries to win a very large share of the Russian domestic market. While the Western goods were very expensive at the ridiculously low market exchange rate, the pent-up demand for such goods (along with their quality image and superior technology) motivated significant purchases. Much of this demand for foreign imports came from the growing Russian mafia, whose criminal activities gave them an ever-increasing share of disposable income in Russia, and whose riches enabled them to pay almost any price for foreign luxury goods. The increased demand for foreign luxury imports reduced real demand for domestically produced goods, thereby forcing many Russian companies to cut back domestic production and employment (thus creating unemployment in Russia). With gross revenues for Russian companies reduced by falling demand for their production and with their net revenue further reduced by the mafia extortion payments, the amount of money left to pay wages and government taxes was greatly reduced. The result was lower real wages and even a suspension of wage payments altogether at many Russian companies (*Economist*, 1998), while the drop in tax revenues reduced the financial power of the government to provide economic aid to the increasingly large number of poor Russians at the same time that it reduced the ability of the government to fight the mafia which was causing many of the problems.

In actual fact, the growing economic power of the mafia increased its political influence to the point where it virtually controls an increasingly corrupt Russian government (Roth, 1996).[2] The government therefore can no longer even make a meaningful attempt to terminate the criminal cycle of reduced domestic demand causing reduced domestic income causing reduced domestic demand. It would have theoretically been possible to stop such a vicious circle (even without government intervention) if sufficient private investments had been made into new Russian production facilities that would have domestically met the demand for luxury goods in the new capitalist order (i.e., if new factories had been created to produce for those with a significant amount of spendible income and wealth, which is concentrated in the hands of rich Western countries and the mafia). However, the economic chaos, crime, and corruption in Russia scarred off most investors, including not only Western companies but also to some extent the Russian mafia itself, which invested an estimated $500 billion of its loot outside of Russia in the 1990s (*Barron's*, 1999).

The economic chaos, crime, and related cycle of ever-falling real demand for domestic goods certainly contributed greatly to the productivity and output decline in Russia that approached 50% in the 1990s (Murphy, 1998). More specifically, relatively greater income in the hands of the mafia reduced the demand for (and output of) Russian industries producing non-luxury goods for the masses (and thus impoverished most Russians, whose own limited purchases of imported goods also contributed to the decline in domestic demand, output and income). This uncertain and depression-like environment greatly decreased domestic investment into new productive capital assets, thereby resulting in a reduction in demand for (and output of) Russian heavy industries that not only caused a further reduction in demand but also led to a significant decline in productivity and competitiveness.

There was also a serious worker morale problem, which caused a further deterioration in productivity. The morale problem was associated not only with an inability of firms to pay wages but also by a worker realization that wealth was obtained via crime and not by productive activities. As one of the largest Russian businessmen, Boris Berezovsky, stated, "There is no doubt that any person who did business in Russia over the last 10 years broke the law" (Cullison, 2000c).

The chaotic mafia-controlled economy also made possible (and encouraged) a fraudulent decline in tax payments (Himes, 1999). The resulting decrease in government tax revenues (combined with outside pressure from the IMF and others to reduce government budget deficits) reduced the ability of the Russian government to create much real domestic demand via transfer payments or spending on the Russian defense/aerospace industries (the latter of which also reduced Russia's ability to resist foreign pressures for further destructive reforms).

The large real income declines in Russia were also partially caused by the Russian central bank's successful attempts to eventually bring the devaluation-induced inflation under control with monetary tightening, dropping it from 1353% in 1992 to under 15% by 1997 (IMF, 1999). In particular, monetary tightening increased interest rates, thereby reduced borrowing for purchases, and therefore further decreased domestic demand for real output that in turn reduced real incomes and increased unemployment (at the same time that it successfully contributed to the central bank's goal of lowering inflation via reduced upward pressure on the prices of real goods and services).

Besides being used to help stop the inflation caused by the currency depreciation, the very large real income decline in Russia also solved the balance of trade problem. In particular, it reduced the demand for foreign products (as people had less income with which to import goods) and made Russian exports more competitive (as unemployment drove down real wage demands). This pattern of reducing real income in order to solve inflation and balance of payments problems (which themselves were caused by opening up the domestic market to foreign imports) had also been followed in other formerly communist countries of Eastern Europe (such as Poland and Hungary) that had been transforming themselves into capitalist societies, albeit generally in a less rapid fashion and therefore also on a less extreme scale (Williamson, 1991).

In addition, because the Eastern European countries had previously (under communism) conducted most of their international trade (via a type of multilateral barter) with each other (Gwiazda, 1986), the decline in real income in each country contributed to a decline in demand for imports from the other Eastern European countries and further magnified the depth of the economic depression throughout the area. The process of opening up their economies to Western imports, thereby causing declining economic output and declining trade with each other (which caused further declines in economic output), had actually begun in 1990 in the other Eastern European countries with the election of capitalist governments there in that year, but the Soviet Union had also already contributed to furthering this reduction in trade and real income in early 1991 (even before it made its currency fully convertible in December 1991) when it switched from a system of multilateral barter trade with its Eastern European neighbors to a system of requiring hard currency payments, which few there could afford to make (Williamson, 1991). The mafia seizure of economic power in most of the other Eastern European countries was a natural occurrence in this environment, just as in Russia (Raith, 1994).

The result has been a long-lasting decline in real annual economic output and income in this area of the world of almost 50%, as previously mentioned in this book. Although some modest economic growth has been recorded in some Eastern European countries in the late 1990s (such as in Poland, Hungary, and the Czech Republic, which have successfully attracted significant amounts of real foreign investment), the region's real output remains very far below that of the level of 1989 (IMF, 1998: 171).

The economic crisis in Eastern Europe in the 1990s is actually very similar to that in other countries around the world (both before and after 1990), with crime and poverty increasing significantly after an initial opening of the domestic market to imports forced a large currency devaluation (Chossudovsky, 1997). The major reason for the growing frequency and intensity of the currency crises of the 1990s is the fact that the Cold War winners (the USA and its allies) now have relatively greater political, propaganda, and military power to put more pressure on countries with protected markets to open up their markets faster.

In addition, the sheer magnitude of the Eastern European catastrophe itself contributed in part to the currency crises in the rest of the world in the 1990s. For instance, while the opening up of the Eastern European markets to foreign imports initially increased demand for production outside that area, the subsequent drop in real income in Eastern Europe eventually resulted in a decrease in demand that contributed to a worldwide economic slowdown in the early 1990s that was most deeply felt in Western Europe and that eventually spread. In addition, the reduction in real wages in Eastern Europe made exports from that region more competitive in comparison to the production of less developed countries whose real wages and income also had to fall to remain competitive in a cycle that spread the crisis and income decline far beyond the initial time and place (Chossudovsky, 1997).

THE SPECIAL EFFECTS OF THE DISASTROUS GERMAN UNIFICATION POLICIES

Perhaps the economic catastrophe in Eastern Europe that had the greatest negative effect worldwide was that in East Germany. In particular, a significant contributor to the various economic crises of the 1990s was Germany's disastrous unification policy, which resulted in the destruction of the East German economy.

Under the terms of the 1990 unification treaty, the united Germany effectively had to pay for any resulting unemployment and social costs resulting from the capitalist unification policies. Those policies indeed caused unemployment in East Germany to effectively rise from 0% to about 40% (Sherreff, 1996), and Germany was thereby sacked with an enormous debt load to pay the welfare benefits of over $100 billion per year (Aalund, 1999). To maintain a stable currency value for the German mark in this situation, the German central bank had to raise real interest rates to their highest levels since the country's founding in 1949.

Increased rates in Germany pressured interest rates higher throughout the rest of Europe, as a European currency treaty (the European Monetary Union) obliged other Western European countries to maintain exchange rates within a fixed 2.25% band against the German mark at that time (Eiteman, Stonehill, and Moffett, 1998). These higher interest rates slowed economic growth in Western Europe so much that speculation arose about the ability of some of the countries to maintain such high real interest rates and keep their currencies within the contractual 2.25% band. This speculation was concentrated on countries whose current account deficits had to be financed with the capital inflows of international investors. As currency investors and speculators demanded to be compensated for the increasing risk of the currency values falling below their lower bound in the European Monetary Union, interest rates rose even higher in such countries. With interest rates being forced ever higher in the countries with the weak currencies, the perceived likelihood of them being able to maintain the high interest rates (which were deepening an economic slowdown) was reduced further still. As the probability of devaluation rose, so did interest rates and vice versus in a never ending spiral, until, despite single-digit inflation, interest rates reached 100% and higher in some countries in the face of enormous speculative attacks. Finally, in this European currency crisis of 1992, a number of countries (e.g., Britain and Italy) dropped out of the currency agreement, while the other countries were forced to widen their exchange rate band to 15%.

Although European interest rates subsequently fell, rates had been high enough for long enough to force interest rates higher in Japan (to stop excessive capital outflows there) and to cause a general recession in Europe in the early 1990s. The higher Japanese interest rates (combined later with the recession in Europe which reduced the demand for Japanese exports) caused a recession in Japan that burst its speculative stock market and real estate bubble (Peterson, 1990). Despite much lower Japanese interest rates subsequently (falling even to 0% in the late 1990s), Japan has been remained mired in a serious economic slowdown throughout the 1990s as a result. At least part of the reason for the prolonged nature of the economic slowdown in Japan has to do with the fact that Japanese bank lenders have been unable to foreclose on or repossess many of the recession-related bad real estate assets because about 40% are controlled by Japanese organized crime, which purchased them on credit in the 1980s speculative bubble (Kaplan, 1998), and which has gained enormous power through violence and threats, including extorting major Japanese companies for over $1 billion a year in return for just not disrupting their annual meetings (Becker, 1997b). Without being able to obtain a liquid recovery of their enormous bad debts, whose book value is estimated to be about $1 trillion (Desmond, 1996), the banks have been reluctant to lend money to productive entities, and so the economy has stagnated without the domestic investment of an adequate amount of capital.[3]

In turn, the economic slowdown in Japan negatively affected exports from Southeast Asia (both through reduced Japanese imports from Southeast Asia and through greater competition from Japanese firms seeking to export their excess production to the rest of the world) and therefore contributed to the balance of trade problems there that led to the Asian currency crisis of 1997 (Henderson, 1998). The Asian currency crisis in turn led to the Russian currency crisis of 1998 and the Brazilian currency crisis of 1999 by slowing world economic growth and by making the production of countries like Russia and Brazil relatively less competitive (i.e., countries like Russia and Brazil were pushed over the brink, as they already were only marginally competitive internationally before the crisis, and the devaluation of the Asian currencies made their products even less competitive). Even the currency crisis in Mexico in 1994 could be partially blamed on this chain of events as the economic slowdown in Europe and Japan (as well as lower priced competition from Eastern Europe) had a negative impact on that country's international current account, which in turn led to the collapse of the Mexican peso in 1994.

The Spreading Currency Crises

In and apart from the fact that the major currency crises later in the 1990s at least partially spread from the initial Eastern European crisis of the early 1990s, these later crises also had other similarities in terms of being fundamentally caused by the same economic forces (which in turn related to the imposition or existence of global free markets or capitalism). In particular, in all the crisis countries but Russia in 1998, the current account deficits had for years been very large as a percentage of GDP (8% in Mexico and Thailand, 5% in South Korea and Malaysia,

3% in Indonesia, and 4% in Brazil), while the current account deficit in Russia had just turned negative before its newest currency crisis in 1998 (to an annualized amount equal to 4% of its GDP in the second quarter of 1998). In all but Malaysia, the current account had deteriorated in the year before the crisis, at least in some cases because of an earlier reduction in relative protectionism in the crisis countries (just as in Eastern Europe in the early 1990s). For instance, Mexico had long had a relatively higher level of protectionism compared to its major North American trading partners, and it had been reducing this level gradually (and significantly) in the years prior to 1994 and then proceeded to do so more quickly with the imposition of the North American Free Trade Agreement (NAFTA) in 1994 (Murphy, 1995).[4] In addition, the increase in the current account deficits in Asian countries prior to their crisis in 1997 was at least partially caused by increases in protectionism (especially by the developed countries) against their imports (Chandrasekhar and Ghosh, 1998) at the same time that a prior world trade agreement (under GATT), along with a local trade agreement (ASEAN), had forced them to open up their own markets more (Vatikiotis, 1995).

A large decline in the currency value or real income was therefore necessary to bring the account back into balance. In each situation, high real interest rates (over 5% above the domestic inflation rates) had been postponing a needed devaluation until there occurred some event or catalyst, which significantly raised investors' subjective estimate of the probability that a currency devaluation would be used to solve the BOP problem. The interest rates required by investors to compensate them for the higher risk of the expected devaluation-related losses therefore rose, and the crisis countries were forced to devalue because they could not maintain such prohibitively high interest rates.

While the fundamental economic situation prior to each crisis was the same, the catalyst that triggered the crisis was different in each case (i.e., the event that motivated investors to greatly raise the interest rate required to finance the current account deficit varied). In Mexico, a leading politician's statement in late 1994 indicating an intention of the Mexican government to crack down on organized crime resulted in a very heavy outflow of mafia capital from Mexico (Murphy, 1995) that depleted Mexico's foreign exchange reserves (which were expended to keep the capital outflow from causing a large immediate devaluation) and caused investors to question whether Mexico could continue to be able to afford to postpone a devaluation solution to its enormous current account deficit (Agenor and Masson, 1999).[5] In Southeast Asia, it was 1997 revelations of excessive bad loans at many local banks (which had increased with the rising current account deficits) that caused investors to question whether the high real interest rates needed to postpone an immediate devaluation could be maintained in an environment where cleaning up the large banking problem might result in substantially reduced lending and economic growth (Miller, 1998). In Russia, it was widespread production stoppages and political unrest in 1998, caused by an inability to pay current or past wages for a large number of workers (*Economist,* 1998), that reduced investor confidence in Russia's ability to solve its growing BOP problem without a devaluation. In Brazil, although real interest rates in excess of 30% and sizable IMF financing had protected the currency from a devaluation for some time despite a severe BOP problem (Bennett, 1999a), a January 1999 default of a local Brazilian government on its debts to the national government virtually eliminated any investor confidence in the country's ability to avoid an immediate devaluation solution to its current account deficit (Goldstein, 1999).

Once the catalyst created the first signs of capital flight (as evidenced by declining foreign exchange reserves for the country with the BOP problem, for instance), herding behavior amongst investors magnified the effect, as a belief spread that the initial capital flight was being undertaken by knowledgeable investors (Calvo and Mendoza, 1994). As some investors increased their estimate of the probability of a devaluation, downward pressure on exchange rates occurred that could only be stopped with higher interest rates and/or expenditure of further foreign exchange reserves to prop up the currency value. These events provided a signal to other investors to raise their own estimates of the probability of devaluation, further raising investor expectations of a devaluation being used to solve the BOP crisis (which in turn put further pressure on exchange rates in a rapid cycle). Once the perceived probability of an immediate large devaluation increased toward 100%, the interest cost of funding the current account deficit became prohibitively large from a domestic economic and political perspective, and the countries allowed their currencies to fall substantially. Thus, investor expectations of an increased chance of devaluation essentially resulted in a self-fulfilling prophecy.

In addition, devaluation in one or more countries increased the likelihood that competitor countries would also have to devalue just to prevent their own current accounts from deteriorating, and so the crises spread. For instance, the 1997 Asian crisis actually began in Thailand and then spread to other competing Asian countries. Moreover, the crisis in Russia in 1998 and in Brazil in 1999 were partially caused by the 1997 Asian currency crisis, as the devaluation of the Asian competitors led to larger current account deficits for Russia and Brazil. In cases where competitor countries did devalue, the size of the devaluation needed to solve the BOP problem in the original crisis country or countries increased, and this cross-contagion effect also contributed to the large size of the currency declines (which equaled over 50% in Mexico, over 70% in Indonesia, over 40% in South Korea, over 30% in Thailand and Malaysia, over 70% in Russia, and over 40% in Brazil).

In each of the devaluing countries, interest rates had to be raised significantly after the currency depreciation to prevent hyperinflation and further currency declines, and, as a result, a significant real income decline occurred (which reduced the need for further currency devaluations). For instance,, the monetary tightening caused real GDP to fall by 6% in Mexico in 1995, while real GDP also fell by over 5% in Thailand, South Korea, and Indonesia in 1998.

The currency crises, and subsequent economic decline, caused an increase in bankruptcies and loan defaults that exasperated any existing banking problems in the countries, which in turn magnified the extent of the economic downturn as banks saddled with bad debts were not in a good position to lend and support economic growth. Banking problems were further magnified in this environment if the banks had been heavily financed with foreign currency debt that rose in value in domestic currency terms as the domestic currency depreciated (Henderson, 1998). In cases where the banking system had been relatively healthy and free of foreign currency debts to begin with, the real income declines were not as severe. For instance, before the 1997 currency crisis, the Philippines had a large current account deficit of 4.8% but a banking system with fewer bad loans and foreign currency debts than other Asian countries (Tanzer, 1999). While it suffered a devaluation of over 35% during the 1997 currency crisis, its real GDP fell by only 0.5% thereafter. The developments in the Philippines provide particularly strong evidence that the banking problems were not the cause of the Asian crisis but merely a catalyst (and were perhaps also a symptom that magnified the negative effect on real GDP, which was naturally reduced as the currency crisis intensified the lending problems of the banks with foreign currency debts). Moreover, although the banking and debt problems of many of the devaluing Asian countries have still not been solved, and in some cases have intensified (Orr, 1999), the currencies have stabilized (and even reversed their declines) as the very large devaluations have enabled the current account deficits to disappear (or even turn into surpluses).

The Asian crisis also affected countries without extremely large current account deficits but proportionally less. For instance, even India with a minor current account deficit of only 1.5% suffered a mild currency devaluation of about 15%. Although capital controls in India may have aided that country in avoiding an artificial currency decline related to speculative capital flows, the fairly small current account deficit did require some exchange rate adjustment. On the other hand, an Asian competitor like communist China with a current account surplus did not suffer any devaluation at all, even though it had very serious banking problems and even though the widely touted currency controls in China were not strict enough to prevent a capital outflow of over $10 billion there (Lachica, 2000).

In some of the crisis countries (such as in Asia in 1997), the currency depreciated more than enough to balance the current account. While these countries also raised interest rates significantly and thereby caused a deep economic downturn in their countries, the governments of these nations did not feel it politically feasible to raise interest rates to the level needed to maintain an exchange rate that would just balance the current account. In particular, capital outflows and the probability of the initial devaluation causing a very rapid increase in domestic inflation (and forcing further devaluations) rose so much after the devaluation that the interest rate required to maintain an exchange rate high enough to just balance the current account became prohibitively high. For instance, in Indonesia, a political crisis (caused by the inflation and real income losses that were brought on by the devaluation itself) made it socially impossible to raise interest rates sufficiently to stop the devaluation-inflation-devaluation spiral, as the political crisis itself lowered investor expectations that the cycle could be avoided (although the cycle was eventually stopped, and hyperinflation avoided, by a democratic solution to the political crisis and a credible monetary tightening).

The currency crisis in Malaysia deviated slightly from the rest because of a particular policy option it selected. In particular, Malaysia imposed capital controls after the onset of its currency crisis in 1997 that allowed interest rates to fall more rapidly than otherwise (at the same time that the currency depreciation was minimized to the approximate point necessary to just eliminate the current account deficit), and the country thereby minimized the short-term negative effects of the crisis on real income (Phillips, 1999).

The Russian crisis of 1998 developed characteristics similar to those of both Indonesia and Malaysia. The 1998 Russian crisis was partially related to the earlier devaluation/hyperinflation crisis there that occurred when the capitalist Yeltsin government transformed the inconvertible Russian ruble into a convertible currency in 1991. Although inflation and currency stability were eventually contained by Russia's tight monetary policy in the mid-1990s, the current account went into deficit in 1998 after the Asian currency crises (and devaluations) slowed world economic growth and demand (and made Russian products less competitive). Because of the prior hyperinflation and because the continuing depression in Russia had caused a very serious political/social crisis, investors perceived the probability of an immediate devaluation to resolve the BOP problem in Russia to be so high that the country was unable to stabilize the situation, even with real interest rates over 100% and even with substantial funding from institutions like the IMF. In particular, the prior problems in Russia had made investors especially sensitive to signs or fears of devaluation and inflation (Choudhry, 1998). In addition, the continuing economic depression and social chaos made investors increasingly skeptical of the ability of the country to pay its workers the enormous amount of overdue unpaid wages and therefore raised the risk of the government using currency depreciation to solve its BOP problems and printing money to pay the back wages due (*Economist,* 1998). Continued inelasticity of demand relative to exchange rate changes (Associated Press, 1998) and capital flight (*Economist*, 1998) made the needed currency decline especially large. Following the 70% devaluation in 1991, Russia has used capital controls to stabilize the situation (*Economist*, 1999b), insofar as excessive currency depreciation was avoided.[6] As a result, while GDP in Russia fell initially after its crisis in 1998 (*Barclay's Economic Review*, 1999), it has since recovered strongly for the first significant upturn since the 1980s.

Although Brazil was widely expected to fall into the same pattern as the other crisis countries, with a decline in its GDP initially expected to be over 5% in 1999 shortly after its currency devaluation (Bennett, 1999b),[7] it undertook an alternative strategy that led to significantly different results. In Brazil, the replacement of the central banker with someone with close connections to large foreign investors resulted in such enhanced investor confidence that the country was able to avoid having to raise interest rates as much as otherwise (Katz and Cohn, 1999), at least not to the level needed to cause a deep recession and real GDP decline of sufficient size to eliminate the current account deficit. As a result, Brazil was the only country in the group of examples whose current account deficit continued as a significant percent of GDP (*Wall Street Journal,* 2000b), as opposed to turning into a balanced or surplus current account in the case of the other crisis countries. Note, however, that Brazil has merely succeeded in postponing a solution to the current account problem into the future, and, in the meantime, the real interest rates charged to consumers are over 100% (Fritsch, 2000).

THE REAL EFFECTS OF CURRENCY CRISES

Current account deficits are endemic to global capitalism for reasons related to heterogeneous preferences for the timing of consumption (Obstfeld and Rogoff, 1995), changes in the terms of trade (Stulz, 1988), temporary productivity and government spending shocks (Glick and Rogoff, 1995), and optimization of investment outlays (Dellas and Galor, 1992). Regardless of the cause, current account deficits must be reversed so that the financing for the deficits can be repaid (Obstfeld and Rogoff, 1995), and chronic current account deficits represent an especially serious situation that has to be addressed (Yusoff, 1997). The classical capitalist solution to a current account deficit can only lead to a devaluation-inflation-devaluation cycle that must eventually be stopped with a real income decline in the country with the BOP problem.

The decline in real income necessary to balance the international trade and current accounts in free market capitalism is invariably concentrated in the lower income groups (Catalinotto, 1998d). For instance, in Eastern Europe, unemployment rose from 0% to about 10%, and it is estimated that 50-80% of the population have fallen long-term below the poverty line (Becker, 1997a). Real wages fell by about 50% in Mexico after its crisis in 1994 and still have not completely recovered (*Wall Street Journal,* 1999). This concentration of the negative effects on the poor is often considered to be economically necessary because upper income groups tend to be more mobile internationally, and so a reduction in their income can lead to the emigration of the most skilled labor and capital flight (Bhagwati, 1977), which can cause real productivity declines and result in further BOP problems (Soedersten and Reed, 1994).

To make the necessary income losses for the poor politically more palatable, evidence is often spread purporting to support an assertion that the richest are entitled to an even large share of the pie because they are the most productive and employ their wealth in the wisest fashion, allegedly for the benefit of all (Strobel and Peterson, 1999). This argument (besides being socially undemocratic) breaks down in the cases of people who obtain their riches via inheritance (Morgan, 1999), via crime (Klebnikov, 1999) or via other unproductive and counterproductive means. This argument also ignores the fact that the rich get richer simply because they save and invest more (Deardorff, 1994). Nevertheless, the trickle-down elitist doctrine is heavily marketed by those with more wealth (Foerstel, 2000), even in countries with enormous current account surpluses (like Japan) where fears are spread of future BOP problems (Bloomberg, 1999). To divert the attention of the poorer members of society from the reality of their further impoverishment (and thereby make the rich stealing from the poor more politically palatable), racial/ethnic/religious/sex conflicts are often stirred up, so that the attention of the less affluent elements is distracted by pure non-economic issues and/or by competition on how the small portion of the GDP pie allotted to them is divided up (Strobel and Peterson, 1999).

Even without a deliberate intent to force the most negative effects of a real income decline on the poor, tight monetary policies by themselves naturally have an especially negative effect on the poorer members of society. In particular, tight monetary policies tend to increase unemployment (and create more poor people) and thereby also lower labor demands and real wages (Chossudovsky, 1997). Although this unbalanced effect on the poor is typically explained, or disguised, as a collective effort to stop inflation, more overt measures to soak the poor are frequently undertaken in conjunction (such as to reduce welfare, or "reform the labor market" via a reduction in the power of labor unions), even though empirical evidence indicates that it is tight monetary policy and the reduction in real economic growth alone that usually slow inflation (Leybourne and Mizen, 1999).

The heavy concentration of negative effects on the poor and less mobile elements of society is also often facilitated by policies suggested (or mandated) by the IMF (Chossudovsky, 1997). The IMF, which is controlled by the superior voting rights of the developed countries that provide most of the funding for the organization,[8] offers loans to countries with balance of trade and current account problems (Eiteman, Stonehill, and Moffett, 1998). It thereby permits countries to delay the currency devaluation-inflation-depression spiral. However, IMF loans have to be paid back and therefore only delay the occurrence of that spiral, and they actually eventually magnify the problem as the borrowed amount has to be paid back plus interest (Chossudovsky, 1997). Moreover, the IMF typically provides loans to temporarily fund a current account problem only if the recipient country increases regressive taxes (such as sales or value-added taxes), decreases benefits to the poor (such as reduced welfare payments and government subsidies for essentials), and reduces regional wealth reallocations to poorer areas (Mufson, 1992). Often enough, the IMF has even mandated restrictions on nominal wage increases in the debtor country (IMF, 1986). As a result, these measures tend to increase poverty and suffering even in showcase countries where some real overall economic growth is eventually exhibited (Konadu-Agyemang, 1998). IMF lending conditions can have especially dire consequences on average people's lives in nations that are already afflicted with extreme poverty and that can ill-afford the typical real income decline which IMF policies typically cause (Chossudovsky, 1997). In addition to their negative effect on the welfare of capitalist countries (or countries in transition to capitalist systems), IMF-imposed conditions have also been very successful in causing very serious economic problems in communist countries, such as Poland before its collapse (Marcy, 1982) and more recently in countries like Vietnam and Yugoslavia (Chossudovsky, 1997).

An alternative (or supplement) to delaying the resolution of a balance of trade problem with an IMF loan is to attract foreign capital funding for the payments deficit. However, like the IMF, private investors require repayment, and generally at a real market rate of return in excess of what the IMF might charge (Root, 1990). This rate of return may be fairly high because it must compensate the investors for the expected eventual depreciation of the currency (King, 1998). Even if foreign investors reinvest their capital and investment income in the country, the effect is merely postponed and compounded to some future date when real payments (such as in exports) begin to be required. The day of reckoning can not be postponed indefinitely, as eventually the foreign providers of financing will effectively own the entire country, and there will be no more capital or collateral to offer them.

In addition, although private investors might have less clout to directly force draconian policies on a country within a loan contract, they can indirectly create the need for such policies by refusing to provide (or renew) credit at a reasonable rate (or at all) unless such policies (often labeled "fiscal and monetary responsibility") are indeed followed (Solomon, 1999). To appease foreign investors, many countries even appoint people to key positions of power (such as central bankers and ministers of finance) who have been indoctrinated with a USA education in capitalist economics (Torres, 1999), who have connections with large foreign investors (Katz and Cohn, 1999), and/or who have actually come from prior employment at foreign creditor institutions like international banks (Chossudovsky, 1997).

Regardless of whether external financing is obtained from private investors, foreign governments, or international lending agencies like the IMF, it can only postpone the negative effects associated with a country having to eventually reverse a current account deficit, at which time the negative effects will occur in a magnified form. However, if such financing reduces the need for (and chance of) an immediate devaluation, real interest rates do not have to be excessively high, and so the necessary devaluation and real income decline (required to eventually solve the BOP problem) can be made gradually. Such a gradual solution can easily result in 0.5% lower annual real economic growth for many decades (and may thereby be worse than an immediate devaluation solution).

Policy Options to Avoid Currency Crises in the New World Order

The negative effects of BOP problems, and the resulting currency crises, are not necessarily inevitable, even in a capitalist world, as numerous policy instruments can be employed in an attempt to avoid or mitigate those effects. However, the standard policies for doing so, including adopting a rigid monetary policy (like a gold standard or currency union), imposing capital controls, increasing relative protectionism, and improving productivity, are often ineffective or can not be implemented in the new order of global capitalism. On the other hand, the economic plan proposed in Chapter 5 may represent a viable solution to BOP problems even in the USA's New World Order.

Gold Standards and Currency Unions

One proposal for directly avoiding currency crises is to eliminate fluctuations in exchange rates through a rigid currency system, such as via a gold standard or a currency union (whereby different countries or regions adopt the same currency). A similar monetary policy that is not supposed to permit exchange rate fluctuations can be imposed by establishing fixed exchange rates between paper currencies and/or defining a precise anti-inflation monetary policy (Flood and Garber, 1984).

One major touted advantage of rigid currency systems is that a current account deficit can be theoretically financed with an infinitesimally small increase in domestic interest rates in such a situation (Ishiyama, 1975). In particular, with all countries effectively using the same currency, it is not necessary for a country with a current account deficit (and a weaker currency) to pay investors higher interest rates to compensate them for the risk of a currency devaluation (King, 1998). However, such financing can only continue until foreigners effectively have a claim on all the capital in the country, at which time the real income/consumption decline (needed to balance the current account) would still have to finally occur if the monetary policy is to be continued. Thus, while a rigid system may lower the costs of financing a current account deficit (and may therefore not result in as large a magnification of the problem as without the rigid system), the overall effect is not materially different from subsidized IMF financing.

In addition, as explained by Flood and Garber (1984), despite promises and guarantees, governments historically have quit gold standards and other rigid monetary policies (like maintaining fixed exchange rates between currencies), usually well before the ending point of having no further capital or reserves to pay off investors speculating against the rigid system. The mere possibility of such a devaluation at any time can cause investors to require a significantly higher interest rate to continue to finance a current account deficit. If the needed increase in interest rates is extremely large because investors believe the probability of a devaluation is very high (as happens whenever the central bank lacks sufficient credibility, and investors engage in a "speculative" attack on the currency), the government is often "forced" (effectively by the investor expectations of a devaluation) to abandon the rigid monetary policy (as the alternative of a deep economic depression caused by prohibitively high interest rates might be politically infeasible).

Note that the probability of a devaluation in a fixed exchange rate system, is affected by the legality of a devaluation (as is therefore the existence of significantly higher interest rates). For instance, states under one federal government such as the 50 states of the USA are not very likely to be able to change from the use of a common currency because it is not lawfully possible without a revolution or secession from the system. However, it should be mentioned that revolutions and secessions do occur even in a very fixed federal system, as history has indicated in the USA in the 1860s and in the Soviet Union more recently. In addition, it is more feasible for a currency change in a looser federation, such as in the 11 states of the European Monetary Union (Sims, 2000), and completely separate nations can do so even more easily. Moreover, countries with separate currencies can readily break a fixed exchange rate system and float or devalue their currencies. Thus, in no case does a common currency or fixed exchange rate completely eliminate the chance of a devaluation.

Moreover, even with a common currency, differences in default premiums and therefore interest rates can occur to the extent that the debts of individual states and entities within the currency union are not guaranteed by the centralized federal system (Sims, 2000). Such higher interest rates in one area can force real income declines there earlier than otherwise, as in the case without a currency union. Regardless, unless a current account deficit is permanently subsidized by other states in the currency union with surpluses, or unless some other solution to a BOP problem is employed (such as the one explained in Chapter 5), a current account deficit must eventually be addressed with a decline in income/consumption (with the decline still being magnified by postponing it.

It should also be mentioned that, even without any devaluation and even with approximately the same interest rates throughout a currency union, use of the same currency does not naturally lead to equal prosperity across the union. In particular, once an income differential exists, it can persist over many decades (or even centuries) even within a common currency area, as the poorer sections of the USA and Italy so well illustrate empirically (and as eastern Germany is expected to further verify with the disastrous unification experiment). One reason income differentials tend to persist is because income-raising investment tends to be more attracted to areas nearest to the bigger markets, which consist of people with higher incomes, as such nearby production facilities reduce the transportation/distribution costs of delivering the products/services to those areas of high demand. Although capacity-increasing investment might be attracted to the lower income areas, this income-narrowing process would cease once the wage differentials declined to the point where they no longer offset transportation cost differentials. Another reason for persistence in income differentials is that productivity-enhancing investment and mechanization tends to be especially concentrated in areas with higher incomes, as the benefits of such investment is higher in the wealthier areas with higher wage costs. Finally, the most valuable "human capital" (i.e., the most skilled workers) is attracted to the areas of higher wealth, which can afford to provide higher wages, more skilled jobs, and better living conditions through more investment in mechanization and infrastructure (thereby leaving mostly the less skilled and lower-paid workers in the poorer areas and thereby "naturally" magnifying differences in regional incomes).[9] While some of these problems can be mitigated with central government subsidy, tax, and other policies, it is important here to point out that a currency union (or other rigid monetary policy) does not solve

BOP problems and, by itself, does not represent an optimal method of avoiding currency crises.

Capital Controls

Another solution to a BOP problem often proposed is to impose capital controls (Giovannini, 1992). Capital controls were extensively employed by almost all countries after World War II to restrict capital flight (and inhibit the resulting downward pressure on exchange rates which might result in inflation or require higher domestic interest rates to counteract), although these controls have now been removed in many rich, developed countries that have accumulated sufficient capital to be internationally competitive (Dooley, 1996).[10]

Capital controls can be used to stop the investment outflows that will normally occur when investors perceive an increased chance of a currency depreciation, as so often happens after an initial devaluation (Agenor and Masson, 1999). In particular, capital controls are useful for allowing a country to maintain interest rates below those that would otherwise be required to prevent a currency depreciation beyond the minimum devaluation necessary to create a balanced current account. As a result, an excessive devaluation (and the resulting inflationary spiral) can be avoided without incurring the excessive real income losses that are caused by extremely high interest rates. In addition, if currency controls are used to restrict capital outflows while, at the same time, incentives (such as tax breaks, contracts guaranteeing investors access to foreign exchange for repatriation purposes, trade barriers that encourage local production, etc.) are provided for direct foreign investment, it may be possible to fund a current account deficit with private capital investment without having to raise interest rates (thus without immediate real income losses) and without having to allow an immediate currency decline (thus without increasing future inflation near-term).[11]

Capital controls are also useful for stemming capital flight for factors that are not directly related to a current account deficit. For instance, capital controls can be used to prevent an artificial currency devaluation which is caused instead by an exogenous shock (such as a random capital outflow). While an artificial devaluation in such a situation might have only a temporary effect (as the resulting fall in the exchange rate might create a current account surplus which would eventually pressure the currency back up), an inelasticity of demand can sometimes result in a currency devaluation actually causing a deterioration of the current account situation (Goldstein and Khan, 1978), as explained earlier in the chapter with the Russian ruble devaluation in 1991. In addition, the inflation induced by the currency depreciation (Abuaf and Jorion, 1993) may eventually offset any competitive advantage created by the initial devaluation, so that the same devaluation-inflation-devaluation cycle explained earlier may occur (even when the initial devaluation happens in a situation with a healthy current account). As a result, capital controls can be very useful for avoiding such negative effects in these cases, just as they can be employed to inhibit capital flight which sometimes arises from investor fears of capital controls themselves (Dellas and Stockman, 1993)

Malaysia has provided an empirical example in the 1997 Asian currency crisis that at least some form of restriction on capital movements can reduce the severity of a currency crisis (Phillips, 1999), just as Russia had some success in averting another major economic catastrophe by using informal capital controls after its second currency crisis in 1998 (*Economist,* 1999b). China has demonstrated that currency crises may be avoided altogether with permanent capital controls as long as there is not a deficit in the balance of trade or current account (Roach, 1999).

However, under normal circumstances, capital controls only postpone a real income or currency decline to a future date when the controls are removed (or when all the local capital is owned by foreigners), and they generally can not be used to solve the problem of an existing current account deficit. In the meantime, capital controls may create inefficiencies in capital allocation and counterproductive black markets as well as discourage some productive foreign investment (Sheikh, 1976). As a result, capital controls can also cause an increase in the current account deficit longer-term.

Changes in Relative Protectionism

One possible way to avoid a currency or real income decline when the current account is in deficit is via a change in relative protectionism (Borkakoti, 1998). Protectionism includes not only the classical barriers of tariffs and quotas (Winkelmann, 1998), but also currency controls imposed for trade transaction purposes, multi-tiered exchange rates (designed to discourage the imports of non-essentials), and subsidies provided to domestic businesses competing against foreign competitors (Kindleberger, 1968), as well as technical standard requirements and business/legal systems that inhibit the distribution of imports (Hine, 1994). The developed countries of Western Europe (as well as Japan) had used protectionism (especially currency controls) very effectively after World War II to generate fast economic growth without suffering the negative side effects of current account deficits (Williamson, 1991), but they have now achieved a level of wealth that enables them to have sufficient capital and mechanization to be internationally competitive without needing such severe restrictions on imports (and have therefore recently moved to a system of fully convertible currencies). On the other hand, the level of protectionism for less developed countries that have not yet achieved an adequate level of international competitiveness (because of inadequate wealth and capital resources) remain generally higher than for developed countries (Anderson, 1995). In order to solve a BOP problem in those less developed countries, such trade barriers must be increased relatively further (or be reduced relatively less than in their export markets).

The removal of trade barriers is usually negotiated multilaterally through organizations such as the World Trade Organization (WTO), the European Union (EU), and NAFTA, or bilaterally (Bowen, Hollander, and Viaene, 1998). Such negotiations generally result in greater overall reductions in protectionism (which increase trade and productivity in the aggregate world economy) than would unilateral actions (Bagwell and Staiger, 1999).

Countries with lower levels of protectionism benefit more from any general agreement to proportionally reduce trade, but, since such countries have less in trade barrier reductions to offer, they have less bargaining power in instituting such agreements. A good example of this negotiating problem is provided by New Zealand, which has been one of the least protectionist countries in the world since the mid-1980s (McLoughlin, 1993). As a result of New Zealand's free trade policies, its 1999 request to join NAFTA was rejected by the USA because New Zealand essentially had nothing to put on the table or offer in return (Barber, 1999). In other words, the reduction in North American trade barriers against imports from New Zealand that would occur if it joined NAFTA would be far larger than any reduction in New Zealand's barriers against imports from North America because New Zealand already has removed most of its barriers.

Bargaining power in negotiating advantageous changes in protectionism is also affected by country size, wealth, and military power. Access to the export markets of larger and richer countries is relatively more important to smaller and poorer nations (for whom each dollar of trade represents a larger portion of their smaller incomes), and so the smaller, poorer nations are willing to offer such countries more concessions to obtain access.

In addition, a strong military can always provide the last word in any political negotiations. Perhaps as a result, the major multilateral trade organization, the WTO, is widely perceived to be controlled by the USA (Cooper, 1999), which attempts to open up trade in industries where it is competitive while keeping other industries protected, just as other countries such as the European nations and Japan also try to do (*Economist,* 1992). For instance, while the USA maintains trade barriers in many industries against imports from poor less developed countries with serious BOP problems (Moffett, 1997), it uses its clout to have the WTO force some of those same less developed countries to open their markets to exports from the USA in some of those same industries (*Wall Street Journal*, 2000e).

While a country can undertake a unilateral increase in protectionism against imports, there exists a significant risk of retaliation from trading partners or other penalties according to bilateral or multilateral agreements especially in the 1990s (Wong, 1997). Even attempts to exclude products with scientifically proven health risks can result in retaliation under the WTO system (Reuter, 1999).

A beneficial unilateral reduction in trade barriers is sometimes undertaken by a foreign country (or countries), but such reductions are usually limited. One example is provided by the USA, which unilaterally lowered subsidies to sheep farmers in the early 1990s. This reduction in subsidies allowed New Zealand to double its real exports of sheep meat to the USA by the mid-1990s (de Lacy, 1999). However, market share increases beyond this point led to USA threats of retaliation, and there is little prospect that significant unilateral reductions in protectionism would occur in potentially more important industries such as USA dairy farming (de Lacy, 1999) or European farming in general (Moran, 1999).

Thus, although a relative increase in protectionism against imports into a country compared to any change in protectionism against that country's exports may seem to be a painless way of correcting a current account problem (and avoiding the negative effects of a currency or real income decline), this solution requires the cooperation of trading partners and is often not feasible (Staiger, 1995). In addition, as Beltrame and Millman (1999) have practically pointed out, even for countries with a current account problem, there is always the risk of adverse changes in relative protectionism due to the political economy of businesses lobbying for protectionism only in industries where they are directly hurt by import competition, while local businesses naturally lobby for more free trade (and less domestic protectionism) in industries where they benefit from cheaper imported components and products (e.g., industries that service foreign tourists like motels would generally lobby for more free trade to lower both their own costs and those of their customers). Business enterprises can apply a significant amount of political pressure to ensure that their interests (for or against free trade) are served (Rodrik, 1995). When a change in relative protectionism is unfavorable (due to a poor negotiating position or strategy, or due to business pressure put on political negotiators), it can magnify a BOP problem (as has happened over the last 15 years in New Zealand, which has reduced its trade barriers both absolutely and relatively more than other countries).

Improving Productivity

Another way to avoid an immediate (or eventual) currency depreciation or real income loss is to improve the productivity of exporters or businesses that compete against imports. Such an increase in productivity may be attained via increased investment in these industries, which can be encouraged with tax policies in capitalist countries and with increased government capital allocations in socialist countries. Special trade zones such as in China that attract foreign investment for export purposes (through tax breaks and other incentives) are also very useful (Hu and Khan, 1997).

However, excessive investment subsidies or encouragement to businesses that compete with firms in foreign countries could lead to retaliation by those foreign countries in the form of protectionism or offsetting encouragement for their own businesses (Wong, 1997). Anis and Ross (1992) have noted cases where export subsidization can benefit both the importing and exporting countries, but they also admitted that retaliation may occur in many circumstances.

To reduce the chance of some form of protectionist retaliation, proposals are sometimes made to increase investment and savings in the economy as a whole, such as with tax policies to encourage general investment in capitalist countries or direct increases in allocations of GDP to investment in socialist countries. Such policies will have a positive effect on the trade sector to the extent that they also improve the productivity of industries which compete in international trade. However, such policies can also increase real GDP growth, and the resulting higher real income can increase the demand for imports, therefore offsetting the productivity effect and sometimes even exasperating a BOP problem (Obstfeld and Rogoff, 1996).

In addition, the policies that encourage investment in capitalist systems are ones that tend to make the wealthy investors richer and so may cost the less fortunate shorter-term, especially since the increase in investment is at the cost of lower current consumption. Moreover, while investment can also be increased by attracting foreign capital, Wheeler and Mody (1992) have empirically found that merely offering foreign investors tax and other incentives has relatively little effect on foreign investment decisions, as the factors of most concern to foreign investors are good infrastructure, special input advantages, and an expanding domestic market.

It should also be mentioned that simply lowering income tax rates and imposing a free market economy in a country are often especially counterproductive solutions to a BOP problem. For instance, such policies may simply result in increased consumption spending (including on imports) and thus increase a current account deficit (Peeters, 1999). In particular lower personal income tax rates decrease the incentive to engage in business investment (Gordon, 1995) and provide less incentive for the rich to engage in tax dodges that require investment (such as purchasing real fixed assets to obtain depreciation tax deductions and engaging in buy-and-hold strategies with reinvestment of earnings to avoid taxes on investment income and capital gains).[12] Moreover, Zinn (1995) and Strobel and Peterson (1999) have reported evidence from the USA of a positive relationship between corporate income taxes and investment, implying that lower corporate taxes may merely permit more consumption of returns to capital. Privatization of state assets can also reduce the level of investment if the proceeds from the sale are consumed by the government, or by individuals if rebated to them in the form of tax reductions (Mackenzie, 1998). In fact, there is actually little evidence of the efficiency and productivity of the overall economy being improved by imposition of free market systems, as real growth has historically been higher in socialist countries (Murphy, 1998), implying that the synergy of state control tends to enhance productivity more than market decentralization.

For instance, New Zealand has undertaken a free-market, low-tax strategy since the mid-1980s (Quaintance, 1998), and the result has been economic stagnation, with very low capital formation, low R&D spending, and low infrastructure investment (McCoughlin, 1993). At the same time, there has been a large increase in New Zealand's current account deficit, which has been magnified by the country's own unilateral removal of protectionist barriers in the 1980s. The free market model has actually resulted in the New Zealand government reducing spending in productive areas like education and infrastructure at the same time it provides none of the traditional productive business subsidies like export financing (Barber, 1996) and general business assistance (Brockett, 1999).

In addition, New Zealand's movement toward the privatization of state companies has led to myopic business policies that do not benefit its economy or its BOP. For instance, the privatization of New Zealand's government airlines has resulted in air fares that make it far cheaper for New Zealanders to travel abroad than for foreigners to visit New Zealand. Assumedly, the airlines have set prices that maximize their own profits irrespective of the effect on New Zealand as a whole (as is normal for a private company). As a result, there are as many New Zealanders spending their tourist money in foreign countries as there are foreign tourists in New Zealand (*Massey News,* 1999), despite the fact that New Zealand is one of the most attractive tourist locations in the world (Turner et al., 1998). Given that the high cost of travel to New Zealand is one of the most important deterrents to greater tourism revenues for the country (Allport, 1999), given that tourism is New Zealand's biggest export industry (with foreign currency revenues approximately equaling New Zealand's current account deficit), and given that there exists sufficient capacity for the number of tourists to New Zealand to double from its present low level of just over one million (Purdue, 1999), the opportunity cost of lost tourist business as a result of artificially high airfares to New Zealand may be enormous.

Moreover, as previously explained, New Zealand's unilateral reduction in protectionism could only cause the current account situation to deteriorate. New Zealand's overall free market activities are well summarized by a Brazilian minister seeking to avoid similar mistakes, "One thing is opening the economy; another thing is being a sucker" (Moffett, 1997).

An Effective Solution to Current Account Problems

While most of the widely proposed methods of resolving a BOP problem (including capital controls, increased protectionism, and improving productivity) may not be feasibly employed to cure a current account deficit in today's world, there is one solution that can be effectively implemented, as explained in Chapter 5 of this book. The economic plan explained there can be adapted to any country by merely offering domestic consumers coupons that give them the right to purchase domestic goods at a discounted price (or giving them the right to purchase goods from a particular area of the country with relatively low income). By also allowing the consumers to turn the coupons into the country's convertible currency in exchange for a fixed number of such coupons being invested into a long-term government savings account, a convertible currency can be maintained (for trade purposes) at the same time that domestic savings and consumption is encouraged. This form of protectionism may be subtle enough to avoid retaliation by trading partners, as some domestic policies, which are effectively protectionist but are considered more of a domestic policy issue, are allowed by the world's major multilateral trade regulator (Hufbauer and Erb, 1984).[13] In addition, if a country's current account deficit is large, even the WTO does allow some unilateral increases in protectionism (Edlin, 1999).

Once a current account problem has been solved, a country can lower domestic interest rates and thereby spur faster real economic growth without causing a devaluation and currency-related inflation. On the other hand, if the domestic central bank wanted to maintain high real interest rates even after the BOP problem had been solved, it would continue to attract net foreign capital inflows and thereby permit an accumulation of foreign exchange reserves if it chose to maintain a stable currency value with open market purchases of foreign currencies. An alternative to accumulating foreign exchange reserves in this situation would be to allow the currency to appreciate. The latter option of increasing the international purchasing power of the domestic currency would help the country in its battle against brain drain and domestic inflation. Although the latter strong-currency policy might also cause a short-term return of a current account deficit, the downward pressure on domestic prices caused by an appreciation in the domestic currency would eventually result in a balancing of the current account.

Thus, while the standard policies for dealing with a BOP problem may often not be feasible or effective, a viable solution does exist. This solution provides some hope for avoiding some of the negative aspects of the post-Cold-War era of USA world domination.

CHAPTER 7

A SUMMARY POLITICAL ANALYSIS OF USA WORLD DOMINATION

This book has conclusively demonstrated that the "bad guys" won the Cold War, resulting in a far more evil world that is both crueler and more inefficient than before. This final chapter provides more facts on the resulting New World Order and briefly describes the outlook for changing it.

Global Americanization

The triumph of the USA and capitalism in the Cold War has cleared the way for undisputed world domination by the country documented in the introduction to this book to be the most evil on the face of the earth. The Cold War victory has indeed enabled the USA to even more successfully portray "free markets" as a superior religion and to paint its ideological communist enemy as the "evil empire." The term "evil empire" was originally applied by USA President Reagan to the Soviet Union, which did indeed conduct some killings of civilians in a brutal civil war in Afghanistan (Cordovez and Harrison, 1995), as documented in Chapter 1. However, even a peaceful priest like President Aristide of Haiti has recently been widely labeled "a psychopath" and "bloodthirsty little socialist" by USA capitalists for refusing to go along with USA exploitation of his country (Dupuy, 2000) and for offering resistance to a USA-backed dictatorship that murdered 5000 innocent Haitian civilians (Dunkel, 2000). Although it is pretty clearly documented in Chapter 1 that communism did not collapse because it was evil (but instead because it took root in poorer countries with less resources and power), and although Chapter 2 documents the fact that communism is superior to capitalism in virtually all respects for virtually all people except the super rich, most are still swayed by the very successful USA propaganda to the contrary.[1]

In addition, the USA propaganda is so powerful that many ignore the fact that the USA itself only advocates "free market" capitalism when it is to its own advantage to do so. For instance, the USA itself was historically one of the most protectionist countries in the world (Bairoch, 1993), and its protectionist unfair trade strategy (combined with its successful imperialist policies) greatly facilitated its wealth accumulation (Smith, 2000). Now that it has accumulated such a large amount of capital from plundering the world for so long (through both trade and military conquests, which complemented one another), the USA currently advocates "free markets." In particular, the USA's higher productivity per worker (relative to that of most workers of less developed countries, whose lack of loot results in them having far less capital and technological equipment with which to operate) enables USA corporations to be extremely competitive in most industries (insofar as the greater mechanization of production in the USA enables it to have lower overall costs even with much higher hourly labor costs). Nevertheless, even today, whenever USA industries are threatened by foreign imports, the USA government either subsidizes its domestic industry (Matthews, 1999) or engages in all kinds of protectionist policies, including imposing quotas, tariffs, and artificial technical standards against foreign imports in many different industries like citrus, sugar, meat processing, steel, and textiles (Moffett, 1997).

There is therefore a great deal of hypocrisy in the USA advocating free trade at the same time that it itself employs protectionism, including against imports from countries that are more oriented to free markets than the USA and that have larger balance of payments problems (Hilsenrath, 1999). Such unfair trading practices are engaged in not only by the USA but also by other wealthy countries (like Western Europe and Japan), and they are typically directed against even the poorest countries (whose income per capita is less than 1/60 that of the richest countries), which are thereby hindered from earning the export income they need to finance growth and attract foreign investment and technology (*Economist,* 1992). Although the WTO is supposed to be a worldwide organization that represents the world in terms of promoting and enforcing fair trade practices, the WTO is widely acknowledged to be run by the USA, albeit with some minor input from its Western European and Japanese allies in worldwide exploitation (Cooper, 1999). One USA think tank itself has stated, "There is a widespread view abroad that globalization is being forced on the world by American corporations, that globalization is Americanization" (Washington Post, 1999).

Besides serving as a very valuable tool for the USA to propagandize the superiority of its capitalist system (and motivate its globalization to the USA's advantage), the USA's Cold War victory now enables the USA to more easily slaughter people of countries that refuse to submit to USA wishes and demands (such as nations refusing to submit to capitalist globalization), as there is little hope of outside help from a more benevolent, balancing power like the Soviet Union. Although there is some competition for economic power in some regions from other exploitative capitalist countries such as those of Western Europe (Griswold, 1999a), the USA's strategy for world domination was confirmed in a February 18, 1992 policy statement issued by the Pentagon in conjunction with the National Security Council and in consultation with the USA President (Tyler, 1992). Reflecting on "the fundamentally new situation which has been created by the collapse of the Soviet Union ... and the discrediting of Communism as an ideology," the Pentagon document states, "our strategy must now refocus on precluding the emergence of any potential future global competitor," and "we will retain the pre-eminent responsibility for addressing selectively those wrongs which threaten not only our interests, but those of our allies or friends, or which could seriously unsettle international relations" (*New York Times,* 1992). Secretary of Defense William Perry spoke even more to the point in 1997, "Since we are the only superpower in the world, every country is in our national interest" (IAC, 1998a), and there are now USA occupation troops and military bases in more than half the countries of the world (Catalinotto, 1997).

The USA's world dominance is often subtly referred to as a mandatory internationalism, which, however, is very one-way insofar as Americans "find it quite natural to pressure the Japanese to make life better for their consumers, the South Koreans to abandon crony capitalism, the Russians to collect taxes" (Grunwald, 2000), but it goes without saying that no country can put pressure on the USA to change its system or to rectify its wrongs (some of the most atrocious of which are mentioned in this book). The USA empire has become such an accepted fact that one *Wall Street Journal* writer forecasts much of the world will become ever more like "little Americas," with foreign middle classes being totally "Americanized" (even speaking English and "consuming the same media, goods and services"), although "regional instability forces the USA to install permanent armies (known as peacekeepers) in both Africa and Russia" (Zachry, 2000). While USA politicians (such as the Bush family) often propagandize USA control of foreign countries as being required because of "a world that 'depends on America to reconcile old rivals and balance ancient ambitions'" (Calmes, 1999), they fail to mention the fact that the foreign rivalries used to "justify" USA interventions are often deliberately promoted by the CIA and general USA policies themselves (Blum, 1995). As *New York Times* writer Thomas Friedman (1999) stated in the middle of the USA bombing of Yugoslavia, "The hidden hand of the market will never work without the hidden fist."

This USA "strategy" of world domination has had a murderous effect on the people of the world, as the Soviet Union is now no longer around to inhibit the USA's subversion and attacks on other countries. For instance, the number of wars and armed conflicts in the 1990s has doubled from the level of the 1980s (Associated Press, 1999h), with these violent conflicts having caused the deaths of 60 million children in the 1990s (*Deutschland,* 2000). Some, especially those who do not have an adequate knowledge of USA history and gullibly believed USA President George Bush's propaganda about a "kinder" America (Greene, 2000), predicted that the USA's Cold War victory would result in the USA becoming more benevolent once its primary enemy of the post-World-War-II period had been defeated. However, it is actually only necessary to see that the USA was founded (and stolen) via genocide[2] to be able to realize that the foundations of the country are criminal and to be able to forecast a continuation of that core evil,[3] especially after examining all the millions of people killed in the hundreds of countries attacked by the USA in the past.[4]

In fact, the USA in the 1990s has continued its murderous, imperialist policies that it has practiced almost continuously throughout its history. The costly maintenance of the "kind" embargo against Iraq, which still kills thousands of innocent civilians each month from preventable diseases, represents just one obvious example (Flounders, 1998b).[5]

The various wars and embargoes launched against Yugoslavia by the USA (and its NATO tool) in the 1990s represent further evidence of USA "kindness" in action after the ending of the Cold War. The IAC (1998a) has documented the background and context of the war in Yugoslavia, demonstrating that it merely represents a continuation of imperialism by the USA and other NATO powers. For instance, West Germany gave the local ruler of the Yugoslav province of Croatia $2 billion in 1988 in order to assist in recreating "a new independent State of Croatia with international borders in the form originally set up by the German chancellor, Adolf Hitler, in 1941." In addition, despite the fact that "during World War II, Croatia was a Nazi puppet state in which the Croatian fascist Ustashe murdered as many as one million Serbs, Jews, and Romani (Gypsies), [the resulting newly 'independent'] Croatia adopted a new currency in 1994, the kuna, the same name as that used by the Ustasha state, and the new Croatian flag is a near-duplicate of the Ustasha flag."

Nevertheless, most of the world has come to believe that the Serbs are the "bad guys" in Yugoslavia (Independent Commission of Inquiry, 1999), even though Serbia itself (with its democratically elected coalition government) had exhibited only very limited signs of repression until after the USA's overt attempts to overthrow the government (Block, 1999b). One cause of this general misperception was a USA public relations firm, which "was paid to turn Serbs into monsters, fascists, and beasts" in the public eye, and journalists seeking out the "bad guys" willingly cooperated to invent evidence of Serb atrocities even though most such evidence has been disproved (IAC, 1998a). While Serbia was being demonized by the Western media in the 1990s, Western powers were busy arming anti-Serb terrorists in Bosnia and Kosovo as well as in Croatia (Oberg, 2000), Croatia was renaming the "Square of Victims of Fascism" the "Square of Croatian Heroes" (Levene and Roberts, 1999), and "800,000 to 900,000 Serbs" were being "ethnically cleansed from Croatia, Bosnia, and Kosovo" (Oberg, 2000).

The outright war launched by the USA and NATO against Yugoslavia in 1999 is especially illustrative. Despite all the absurd propaganda about the "kind" intent of the USA (and NATO) to stop the alleged atrocities of the Serb "bad guys" in the Kosovo province of Yugoslavia, there had actually been very little evidence of Serb atrocities or human rights violations committed against the Albanian ethnic population there (Johnstone, 2000). In addition, although a terrorist civil war was launched in Kosovo by the USA-backed Kosovo Liberation Army (KLA), which was financed by the Albanian mafia, the CIA, and German "intelligence" (Independent Commission of Inquiry, 1999), allegations of mass murders in Kosovo by the Serbs have been disproved (Dunkel, 1999). In fact, only 2108 bodies have been found in "mass graves," which contain people of all nationalities who appear to have died from many possible causes, including from the acts of terrorism committed by the KLA (Catalinotto, 2000a). The KLA, many of whose leaders "trace their roots to a fascist unit set up" by Axis occupiers during World War II (Feinberg, 2000), had long engaged in a strategy of threatening and assassinating Albanians participating in Yugoslav elections and other democratic processes in order to create the appearance of repression (Johnstone, 2000).

Regardless, any Serb atrocities in Kosovo that did exist should be seen in the light of Hitler's forcing Serbs out of Kosovo in the 1940s in order to create a Greater Albanian puppet state (at the time when the Serbs were a majority there) and in light of the KLA's 1998 terrorist attacks on Serbs, gypsies, and non-Albanian Muslims (Wilson, 1999c). It was within this context that NATO conducted its 1999 terrorist bombings, which deliberately attacked civilian targets but almost ignored the Serb military (Wilson, 1999d), and which directly killed thousands of civilians but only 571 Serb soldiers and police (Independent Commission of Inquiry, 1999). Western investigators indicated that the NATO bombers hit just 14 tanks and 18 artillery/mortar pieces, and that "Bombing civilian targets worked best" (Catalinotto, 2000b). *Newsweek* (2000) reported that although "air power was effective in the Kosovo war not against military targets but against civilian ones, military planners do not like to talk frankly about terror-bombing civilians ('strategic targeting' is the preferred euphemism)." Given NATO's deliberate targeting of facilities vital to civilian life (Becker, 1999b), including attempts to eliminate healthy food and water supplies in Kosovo via NATO bombing of the power and transportation networks, the massive exodus of civilians out of Kosovo during NATO's terror bombings (including 70,000 Serb civilians going to Serbia and hundreds of thousands of Albanians going to Albania) may have saved many lives, as evidenced by the frightful living conditions created there by the bombing (Independent Commission of Inquiry, 1999). Even "the Western media now admit that the vast majority of refugees who left Kosovo last spring were fleeing the U.S. bombing" (*Workers World,* 2000a).

On the other hand, the forcing of 250,000 Serbs and other people (including many gypsies and non-Albanian Muslims as well as some Albanians who don't support the KLA) out of Kosovo later in 1999 under NATO occupation (via continued terrorist KLA attacks which have killed over 500 people in the ethnic cleansing process that NATO occupation forces have made no meaningful attempt to stop) can in no way be seen as defensive (Chin, 1999) or justified (Pearl, 1999a). Moreover, Kosovo Albanian terrorists have already begun making frequent terrorist attacks on targets in Serbia itself with the apparent tacit approval of the NATO occupation force in Kosovo (Block, 1999a). In addition, the KLA, which represents "a Balkan criminal network responsible for over 20 percent of Europe's heroin imports" (Goff, 2000), is no doubt benefiting from the opening of the sex-slave trade in Kosovo under NATO occupation (Feinberg, 2000). However, the mainstream Western press continues to largely ignore these facts and even has the audacity (without fear of losing credibility with a brainwashed audience) to blame the destruction of the civilian infrastructure in Kosovo and Yugoslavia on "lack of maintenance" by the Serbs (Associated Press, 1999e). In reality, despite NATO's "destruction of Serbia's electrical network," it was NATO-occupied Kosovo, and not Serbia, that had to endure electrical outages and water shortages nearly a year after the NATO bombings (Cirjakovic, 2000).

Although the mainstream media virtually ignored the existence of substantial mineral wealth in Kosovo (including the largest lead and zinc mines in Europe, as well as sizable coal deposits, not to mention cadmium, gold, and silver), access to that wealth certainly represented one motivation for the USA/NATO seizure of the territory (Flounders, 1998a). The USA/NATO's unstated purpose in the 1999 war to militarily occupy and seize that wealthy area of Yugoslavia is especially evident from the fact that all offers by Yugoslavia before and during the bombing to have the civil war mediated by neutral UN peacekeepers were refused by the USA/NATO aggressors (Independent Commission of Inquiry, 1999). Besides the attraction of the mineral wealth of Kosovo for their own exploitation, it is quite likely that the capitalist powers also saw an opportunity in Kosovo to divert the attention of neighboring Albanians, who had earlier engaged in armed rebellion as a result of a nation-wide capitalist pyramid scheme that essentially stole the life savings of many several years after communism was overthrown in that country (Griswold, 1997). The purpose here was obviously to have the Albanians hate Serbs instead of capitalism by giving them the potential chance to recreate a Greater Albania just as Hitler did in the early 1940s (albeit as a USA/NATO capitalist protectorate in the late 1990s, as opposed to a German/Axis capitalist protectorate in the 1940s). As noted by Wilson (1999b), the USA/NATO strategy is not much different from that employed by Hitler (who also "justified" some of his invasions of other countries as "liberations" of some ethnic group that he had incited to riot to draw repression), by Mussolini (who invaded Ethiopia in 1935 in order to "free" Ethiopians from their monarchy government), and by the fascist Japanese (who sought to "protect" the Chinese in the 1930s).

The totally unjustified bombing of a badly needed pharmaceutical factory in Sudan in 1998 represents another clear-cut case of USA "kindness" after its Cold War victory, albeit on much a smaller scale. The plant had been important for producing medicines (especially against malaria) that could have saved many lives in that impoverished country, and numerous investigations of the destroyed Sudanese factory indicated absolutely no evidence of the biological or chemical weapons claimed to be there by the USA, but, in spite of these facts, the USA has refused to allow a UN investigation (Parker, 1999). Consistent with this "kind" action committed by the USA against Sudan, the USA has also tried to disrupt serious proposals to end a Sudanese civil war because the proposed peaceful solution of allowing the Sudanese people to vote on the issues might not result in the side the USA has been backing to gain power, although the propaganda explanation for this attempt to disrupt peace is that the USA "is stepping up efforts to hold Sudan's opposition together amid an increasingly successful push by the Sudan regime to make peace with its exiled opponents" (Pearl, 1999b).

Other examples of USA "kindness" in the 1990s include the USA's continued embargo and terrorist attacks on Cuba (Gutierrez, 1999), and the embargoes against North Korea (Griswold, 1999b) and numerous other countries that refuse to open up their economies to the USA's capitalist exploitation (Marshall, 1999). Today, about 2/3 of the world's population faces a USA embargo of some form or degree (Smith, 2000). While the USA's capitalist propaganda machine may be sufficient to convince many foreign country leaders to embrace the USA's new world order (with many foreign leaders in countries such as in Latin America actually having been educated in the USA), the USA threat of financing "internal" terrorist attacks on disobedient foreign countries (using "covert" operations), imposing or intensifying embargoes, conducting bombings of civilian targets, and militarily invading foreign countries is also useful for ensuring a high level of compliance with the USA's "kind" wishes.

RICH CRIMINALS' PARADISE: CAPITALISM WITHOUT GOVERNMENT

It should be noted that the role of the USA government itself is not essential for the enforcement of the new capitalist world order. In particular, many of the CIA's covert actions themselves have long been financed by private money and carried out by the private mafia, especially the attempts to overthrow the Castro government in Cuba (Furiati, 1994). In addition, ever more "defense" services are starting to be put into the hands of corporate owners, some of which directly hire foreign armies to defend their interests (Chatterjee, 1997) instead of using the more indirect traditional procedure of having the USA government (under the pressure of corporate lobbies and political donations/bribery/other pressure) make the world safe for USA commerce and acquisitions (Copeland, 2000). In addition, there is a growing private "defense" service industry (Wolf, 1999), which is currently separate from the armaments production that is already largely corporate-owned, and which goes far beyond the private secret police and terrorists owned by USA corporations before the creation of the CIA (Schulz, 1982). The market for such private "defense" services is forecast to grow so rapidly that some believe they may even one day replace government armies, at which point "military and economic functions will be reunited" as they were before the creation of the modern capitalist state (Chatterjee, 1997). Given that there are numerous billionaires, each of whom is richer than many countries (Foerstel, 2000), such a prediction is not all that far-fetched.

There are also serious movements to privatize the police/judicial/prison system (Reynolds, 1994). Prisons in the USA are already in the process of being privatized in order to create a virtual slave market of nearly two million prisoners that corporations can exploit (Phillips, 2000). The privatization of the police system is also proceeding quickly, with private police or security guards outnumbering public police by 3 to 1 in the USA (Reynolds, 1994). In addition, the private law enforcement system is bolstered by incredible Orwellian technology, which permits the private employment of a massive number of "security" cameras that not only spy on people in private buildings, but also increasingly in public areas (Ramirez, 1998). At work alone, 20 million employees are watched with cameras by the corporate "Big Brother," 5 billion phone calls are recorded annually, and employee email is read by 36% of all employers (Dowd, 1997). Moreover, while technology has also long provided the capacity to photograph people almost anywhere with satellite cameras (Zimmerman, 1988), technology now exists for cameras to see through buildings and clothing (Hansen, 1997). Even if controls are placed on government misuse of this technology, the potential for unregulated private abuse is enormous.

Similarly, although government spokespeople are very effective in spreading the message of global capitalism (Smith, 2000), and although the CIA itself was one of the biggest publishers and disseminators of pro-capitalist "information" (more appropriately labeled misinformation or disinformation) in the world during the Cold War (Schulz, 1982), the USA's capitalist propaganda machine is not at all dependent on the USA government. For instance, instead of quoting capitalist government leaders for opinions and descriptions of events, the capitalist media can provide more analysis and reporting direct from corporate executives and other capitalist leaders (Smith, 2000), whose opinions on events the media already accepts and reports as fact (Phillips, 2000). In addition, many of the CIA's prior publishing activities can now be sponsored by think-tank institutions that are well financed by rich conservatives to spread the capitalist gospel (Strobel and Peterson, 1999). Corporations already use public relations (PR) firms extensively to ensure that public opinion is manipulated to their liking (Phillips, 2000).

Moreover, much of the USA's propaganda continues to be perpetuated by the same mainstream press whose ownership is even more heavily concentrated in the hands of anticommunist rich owners than it was in the Cold War times (Foerstel, 2000). In particular, less than 20 media/entertainment conglomerates currently control the bulk of the worldwide "information, entertainment, and mass culture" (Flounders, 2000), with Time Warner, Disney, Rupert Murdoch's News Corp., Viacom, Sony, Seagram At&T/Liberty Media, Bertelsmann, and GE being the dominant players in the USA (McChesney, 2000). In the USA, the most recent increase in media concentration was made possible by the deregulation of the Telecommunications Act of 1996, which the media elite requested to be passed by USA politicians who themselves are dependent on the media for their popularity and reelection (Phillips, 2000). Such deregulation of the media has also occurred elsewhere under the pressure of capitalist globalization. For instance, the IAC (1998a) reports, "In Eastern European countries, the first institutions to undergo the transition to privatization seem to be the media, both in ownership and content. Western capital helps to subsidize the media in Poland, Hungary, Romania, the Czech Republic, and Slovakia. The political views which are reported are virtually indistinguishable from those of the U.S. media. *Blitz*, a newspaper funded by German capital, appeared in Serbia on September 16, 1996. The paper, which at nineteen cents is the cheapest in the country, sells raffle tickets and gives away cars. Within a month after its first printing *Blitz* had a circulation of 100,000. This process of moving toward a pro-capitalist, pro-imperialist ideological monopoly is described straight-faced by U.S. leaders and media commentators as the 'democratization of Eastern Europe.'" On the other hand, when confronted with an anti-USA media, NATO has actually come in with occupation troops (as in Yugoslavia) and closed such undesirable media as a cynical means of "silencing broadcasts to encourage freedom of speech" (Parenti, 2000). As one journalist summarized when referring to censorship in the USA itself, "In the era of U.S. triumph, is even one alternative, sometimes radical, voice too many?" (Bernstein, 2000)

The pro-USA/pro-capitalism bias in this concentrated media is often attained by very subtle tactics (Herman and Chomsky, 1988). For instance, the media widely accepts and spreads the lies of corporate and capitalist government leaders as facts without permitting many (if any) contrary opinions (Parenti, 2000). In addition, simple and repetitive slogans, such as "The rich will save and invest and create jobs for Americans," are very effective in making people believe in trickle-down economics, even when the trickle is really in the upward direction and actually increases the poverty of the poor (Strobel and Peterson, 1999). Labels are also employed to subtly take sides, such as by referring to union leaders as "bosses" but to corporate executives as "leaders" (Parenti, 2000). Such tactics are especially useful for purposes of distracting people's attention from the dire need for infrastructure investments (like transportation) and productive investments (like equipment) that corporate leaders and the rich are not making in sufficient quantities because of their own excessive consumption and unproductive real estate investment (Strobel and Peterson, 1999). Moreover, anti-USA/anti-capitalist stories or facts are frequently omitted or scarcely reported (Parenti, 2000). As the owner of the *Washington Post* owner once told the CIA, "There are some things the general public does not need to know and shouldn't" (Jackson, 2000). Possibly as a result of the latter opinion of the media elite, there has been a large deterioration in the quantity and substance of reporting of foreign events, about which Americans have a great deal of interest, and of which they should be aware in the era of globalization, but about which corporate media elites believe they are better off not knowing (Phillips, 2000).

The result is a worldwide propaganda machine that "has developed an ideology of individualism based on destroying the resistance of the individual [insofar as] it glorifies the individual hero, the star," and it thereby "destroys" the idea of resistance to this ideal, especially "collective resistance" (Foerstel, 2000). It foments "a self-centered careerist outlook of life, an apathy to social problems, a fascination with sex, violence, and commodities that sell well, but rob people of morality, ethics, zeal and the determination to fight against injustice and exploitation," and generates "a culture that dehumanizes mankind into 'robots' with no morality, ethics, or any vision for humanity" (Mukherjee, 2000). Consistent with this effective brainwashing system, the mainstream media limits political reporting to "mindless speculation about campaign tactics and the regurgitation of mainstream politicians' sound-bites" (McChesney, 2000).

As Smith (2000) summarizes, "With government information services, intelligence services, and think tank press releases; with foundation, corporate, and intelligence service funding of the propaganda process; and with negligible resources among the impoverished and politically weak, the belief systems of the world stay to the right of the political spectrum. There is no left and no functioning middle. There is only a right and an extreme right, which, because there is no true left or true middle, are viewed by the people as a political right and a political left."

CONCLUDING PERSPECTIVES ON THE CAPITALIST WORLD ORDER

It should also be mentioned that, even without considering the effect of the most deadly embargoes and violence of the USA and its puppet governments, the new capitalist world order is very deadly. In particular, while the capitalist system ensures that there is sufficient money to buy the grain needed to fatten cattle so the more affluent can eat fatty expensive meat in relative luxury, the system provides insufficient jobs and money to the poorest of the world to enable them to buy enough food just to avoid starvation (Smith, 2000). As a result, 35 million people suffer starvation-related deaths annually in the "prosperous" 1990s under the USA's capitalist world order (Flounders, 1998b), including 19,000 children under the age of 5 daily (*Deutschland,* 2000). This annual catastrophe occurs despite the fact that the UN has estimated it would only cost $13 billion annually (about 0.1% of the USA's annual income) to have a minimum level of both nutrition and health care extended to all people worldwide (Catalinotto, 1999).[6] The capitalist market is similarly responsible for the fact that pharmaceutical companies concentrate so much of their research on cures for ailments that are not threatening to human life (such as baldness and pet animal diseases), while very little research is conducted into cures for life-threatening diseases (like malaria) that are concentrated in poor tropical countries which can't afford to pay for any drugs that are created (Phillips, 2000).

As Chossudovsky (1997) has documented, this human tragedy of unnecessary mass deaths can be blamed on the international capitalist system, which not only causes periodic economic catastrophes naturally (as explained in Chapter 6) but also more generally intensifies poverty (and related deaths). For instance, as previously mentioned, pressure is often put on less developed countries (LDCs) to open up their markets to imports. These imports (mostly from the rich developed countries whose higher level of mechanization and technology, as well as greater marketing resources, makes them more competitive despite higher labor costs) tend to result in widespread bankruptcy of the LDCs' local industry and agriculture that used to produce for the domestic market. As a result, incomes in the LDCs, especially those of the poor, fall dramatically.

Meanwhile, to enable the LDCs to pay for the imports, the LDCs are typically given loans from the richer countries (or from their representatives at the IMF or World Bank), and those loans are usually made subject to stringent conditions on further capitalist reforms, which require reducing or eliminating subsidization of essentials like food and health care, thus intensifying the impoverishment process. In order to be able to pay back the loans, the LDCs are forced to focus on the production of goods such as illegal drugs, tobacco, cheap commodities, and labor-intensive manufactured products, which can be exported to those with the most money (i.e., the richer countries). This process further lowers the amount of domestic output available for domestic consumption in the LDC, further impoverishing the poor, and results in a concentration of the LDC's remaining wealth in the hands of a small elite including narcotics dealers, swindlers who take advantage of the economic chaos, and corrupt politicians and "business people" who profit from the "free trade" with the rich capitalist countries via bribes or special deals. With reduced production for the domestic LDC market and with export earnings going largely to make debt service payments to rich foreign lenders and to pay for luxury imports for the LDC's rich elite (who increasingly become the only ones in the LDC able to afford imports), there are increasingly less resources available to keep the poor alive. As Chossudovsky (1997) also shows, the economic chaos, poverty, and increasing competition for decreasing resources often leads to regional or ethnic violence and civil wars that cause further suffering and poverty.[7]

This process of the rich getting richer, and the poor poorer, is magnified by other characteristics of global capitalism. For instance, free markets and fully convertible currencies tend to result in richer developed countries having high real exchange rates for their currencies, implying a relatively low purchasing power for the currencies of the LDCs on the international markets compared to what they can buy from domestic production (Froot and Rogoff, 1995). As a result, expanding trade results in the LDCs effectively paying more for the same products (and thereby getting poorer in real terms) while the richer developed countries pay less (and thereby get richer).

This situation of unfair terms of trade is a natural outgrowth of the capitalist system, with or without different currencies and currency crises, as Smith (2000) has shown. For instance, assume a worker in an LDC earns $1 per hour to produce a T-shirt that takes one hour to produce, but a worker in a rich country earns $8 per hour and can produce the same T-shirt but with a different brand name or label for $8. If marketing and name-brand fetishism (created via expensive advertising, psychological manipulation, and control of market distribution channels) can create demand for the $8 T-shirt, it takes the poor workers 8 hours of work to buy the brand-name T-shirt, while the rich worker can produce enough to be able to buy 8x$8=$64 of the generic T-shirts (i.e., $64/$1=64 of them) in the same 8 hours. Thus, the rich workers accumulate the square of the wage differential in products (or capital, since they probably don't need 64 T-shirts) and enrich themselves exponentially the greater is the level of trade.[8]

Note that this phenomenon of capitalism magnifying exponentially the effect of wage differentials does not require the rich worker to buy only generic products. In particular, name-brand products can be built in the LDC for a trivial amount of money (like $1) and then sold for many times that amount (like $8) in a rich country, with most of the final retail price being paid to distributors (like wholesalers, retailers, and sales people), landlords (i.e., renters of retail and wholesale real estate), and investors (i.e., creditors and the rich owners of the capitalist system), as Chossudovsky (1997) illustrates. In addition, as long as most income in LDCs is concentrated in the hands of a rich few, most of their own countries' demand will be from the wealthy who can afford to pay for name-brand fetishes (like exotically labeled/packaged T-shirts), and so there will be limited monetary demand for inexpensive products (resulting in production being so focused on the name-brand goods with marked-up prices and far superior profit opportunities that it might be difficult to obtain economies of scale for production and distribution of inexpensive goods).

Already by 1992 the quintile of people living in the world's richest countries had 82.7% of the world's income and were 60 times better off than the people in the poorest quintile of countries (*Economist,* 1992). Within many of the poor capitalist countries themselves, this enormous difference is magnified even further. For instance, the quintile of the richest people in Latin America have 150 times the income of the poorest 20% of the Latin Americans (Smith and Ratner, 1997). Any attempt by workers (or the poor) to obtain a larger share of the economic pie is openly attacked worldwide by central bankers, who meet such attempts to redistribute wealth with threats of higher interest rates (Aalund, 2000), which cause unemployment, a reversal in any trend toward rising wages, and eventually more poverty (Chossudovsky, 1997).

While the USA's brand of violent domination (and exploitation) of other peoples is more atrocious than any other in history (as documented in the Introduction), it should be reemphasized that the cruelty of capitalism itself is nothing new. For instance, it was capitalism that transformed all people into objects to be exploited, so that the rich could accumulate ever more wealth at the expense of others (Marx and Engels, 1988b), especially in colonies like India (Gopal, 1963). The capitalist economic system also caused the Europeans together with the USA to initiate an enormous and profitable slave trade (DuBois, 1965) that killed tens of millions of Africans, who not only died in massive numbers on land and sea in transit to their new jobs but also during their initial "seasoning" at those jobs (Stannard, 1992).[9] The extent of the overall exploitation here can be seen from the fact that today's third world nations had average per capita incomes in 1750 that exceeded the average of today's developed countries at the time, but the imposition of several centuries of colonialism (or the forced removal of protectionist barriers against imports from today's developed countries) has resulted in their average per capita incomes being less than 1/8 that of the developed nations (which maintained protectionism until they had gained sufficient income/technological superiority) in 1990 (Bairoch, 1993). Although the enormous current income differential makes exploitative trade with the third world relatively insignificant to the developed countries today, that contrasts greatly with the situation in 1750 when incomes in the two areas were more equal, and trade with the developed countries remains a very important component of the low incomes of the poor third world (putting them in a very weak and even desperate bargaining position relative to the richer developed nations, even without considering the daunting military situation).

It is interesting to observe that the Europeans used an economic strategy to colonize Africa several hundred years ago that was very similar to that employed worldwide by the USA today. In particular, European capitalists exported a flood of cheap manufactured goods (like textiles) to Africa, thereby reduced the demand for goods produced locally, and thus destroyed the African economy (DuBois, 1965). Nevertheless, even after their economies were destroyed, Africans were able to continue to make payments for the goods imported from Europe by offering raw materials and slaves in return. Today, the USA no longer engages in outright exploitation of slaves and no longer transports labor units to a new work place in the Americas, but it does continue to accept raw materials and the production of cheap labor as payment. This exploitation of the cheap labor in less developed countries today is not much different from the exploitation of slaves earlier, except that the cheap workers can now stay in their own country and receive wages that are just enough to buy what slaves in the past were provided with by their masters (i.e., the people of many less developed countries are transformed into wage slaves who must work for the equivalent compensation of slaves just to stay alive, and that is for the lucky ones who can find a company that will offer them the "right" to be a slave so they won't have to starve to death or die of related disease).[10]

In direct contrast to the holocausts caused by capitalism, communism (in the countries where it was instituted) saved many millions of lives annually not only by having a more even distribution of food, shelter, health care, and work (Davies, 1997), but also by generating faster growth rates than under capitalism, as previously explained in Chapter 1 of this book and as admitted by the IMF (1993) itself. It should also be emphasized that the faster growth rates in communist countries were generally achieved with 7-hour work days and reasonable living conditions (Davies, 1997) that were in stark contrast to the terrible work and living conditions endured by most during the capitalist industrial revolution where many males and females (many starting as young as 6 years old) were forced to work 100+ hours per week just to survive just for instance (Marx and Engels, 1988b).

As an especially clear contrast of the deadly effect of the imposition of the USA's capitalist new world order, it is possible to examine post-communist Russia of the 1990s. GNP per capita there has fallen by about half since communism was overthrown there in 1991 (IMF, 1997a), and death rates have significantly risen, mostly due to increased stress, illegal drugs, and less access to sanitation and medical care for many (Cox News, 1995). Also contributing to the increased death rate has been an enormous increase in the number of murders and mafia executions, which exceeded 350,000 in the first four years of the return to capitalism (Roth, 1996) and continues to be far above the level of even that in the violent USA (Wiedemann, 1997). The USA think-tank Brookings Institution, heavily sponsored by USA corporations (Strobel and Peterson, 2000), has estimated three million more deaths than normal in Russia in the 1990s (Wilson, 1998b).

However, given that Russian death rates have risen from 1.1% in 1990 to 1.6% in the mid-1990s (Becker, 1997a), the reimportation of capitalism in Russia in the 1990s has actually caused about 1,000,000 extra deaths there annually. So many extraordinary deaths in Russia represents a worse catastrophe than if a large number of nuclear bombs had been dropped on the country, but they actually represent a mere normal symptom of the very deadly disease called capitalism. In fact, the catastrophe in Russia should not be surprising, given its capitalist system, which has been labeled "democratic" and "civil" by Western capitalist leaders who praise its founder Yeltsin (Wayland, 2000a).

Western capitalist leaders' idea of a civil democracy can be clearly seen from just a few of Yeltsin's more notable "civil" and "democratic" acts. For instance, Yeltsin declared peaceful strikes by unpaid workers in 1998 to be unconstitutional (*Ostseezeitung,* 1998) according to a constitution that he himself had created (Ignatius, 1993). He had been able to design this constitution after he had effectively made himself Russian dictator in 1993 by ordering military tanks to fire on an elected parliament (which opposed his new capitalist order), killing hundreds of members of the opposition in the process (Wayland, 2000a). Shortly after this "civil" and "democratic" action, he suspended the country's supreme court that had opposed his decision to close down the elected parliament (*Wall Street Journal,* 1993), banned opposition political parties and media (Ignatius and Rosett, 1993), and refused to even create a law allowing for a possible transfer of power if the controlled media were not successful in obtaining a subsequent confirmation "vote" for himself (Rosett, 1996).[11]

HOPE FOR THE FUTURE

Despite the horrible worldwide situation created by the USA's Cold War victory, the future does not necessarily have to be as bleak as the past. There is always the chance that the American people themselves will be able to see the evil of their capitalist system, see that most of the loot from the USA's crimes continues to be owned by a very small rich elite (Strobel and Peterson, 1999),[12] and see fit to vote to end the system.[13]

Currently, no major political party in the USA advocates an end to the country's atrocities. Liberal *New York Times* writer Thomas Friedman (1999) has adequately summarized the only significant differences between the various capitalist political parties today to be their opinions on how much (and whether) the poor should be bribed with a larger share of the income pie (to keep them from revolting) and how fast (and whether) capitalism should be spread throughout the world system. For instance, USA Democrats tend to favor giving the poor a larger share of the loot than USA Republicans, while there is some mixture of opinions among individual Democrats and Republicans on how much, how fast, and in what manner the USA should force international capitalism on the world. However, even the small differences between the Democrats and Republicans in terms of sharing the loot have been almost eliminated in the 1990s (coinciding with the ending of the Cold War), so that the Democrats are now so similar to the Republicans that some call them "Republicrats" (Strobel and Peterson, 1999).

Historically, as documented by Copeland (2000), the Republicans have generally represented the party of big business and the rich (and pure trickle-up economics), while Democrats have represented the party of small family businesses (including family farms that employed slaves) and the "average" citizen (who was offered small bribes for not revolting). Although the policies of individual candidates of the two main USA parties have varied somewhat both geographically and temporarily depending on the interests of their main supporters (Zinn, 1995), it is no coincidence that the Democratic Party is not only the party that tends to "bribe" the average American with a larger share of the pie but is also the party that has engaged the USA in more extensive wars, as the "bribes" are very useful to maintain the support of the masses needed to successfully fight those wars (Copeland, 2000).

Note that while the Republicans and Democrats have been the two parties in power that have engaged the USA in its horrible inhuman acts over the last 150 years, alternative parties such as the Reform Party and the Libertarian Party in no way advocate an end to USA atrocities. The Reform Party is merely more nationalistic (and therefore potentially more militaristic) in maintaining USA world domination at the same time that it is less wedded to the ideology of global capitalism (somewhat similar to the ideas advocated in Adolf Hitler's *Mein Kampf*, which also promoted nationalism, strong encouragement of domestic business, and protectionism, as well as restrictions on international stock exchange speculation). On the other hand, the Libertarian Party is less nationalistic but more extremely oriented toward global capitalism (which can theoretically be enforced in the "ideal" world of Libertarianism via private armies of the rich instead of government military forces that serve the same end).

Despite the political monopoly of a few capitalist parties in the USA, the possibility exists that some anti-capitalist political party will some day attract sufficient support so that a majority of Americans can vote to terminate the crimes and create a true democracy. The likelihood of such an event is greater the sooner Americans actually become aware of the extent of their country's atrocities. Awareness may help them realize that they are tacitly approving a continuation of USA atrocities unless they vote for political candidates who explicitly state their intention to end all USA exploitation, aggression, and mass murder of innocent civilians. Although candidates from anti-capitalist parties (like the Workers World Party, which does advocate terminating USA atrocities) are not on the ballot in all states, people can always cast a write-in vote as a protest and as a way of developing needed momentum for the anti-atrocity movement (one write-in possibility is the long deceased,

American socialist Eugene Debs, who might be delighted to run under the slogan "Better a dead red than another mass murderer").

Hope for such a drastic change in national attitude does exist. For instance, one survey indicates that American participation in demonstrations is about as high as it was in the Vietnam War, "although today's lack of media coverage renders GenYers' social consciousness invisible," i.e., people are less aware of the protests of the American people because they are covered less in the mainstream media (Buss, 2000). Based on past history, it seems quite likely that, once Americans become aware of the crimes committed by their country, a natural outrage may spark Americans' innate and ingenious culture of rebelliousness at being so badly manipulated for so long, and the desire for change may spread very rapidly. The internet provides a wonderful opportunity here, as it can be used to spread news that is otherwise effectively censored by the mainstream media (Foerstel, 2000). For instance, although TV and cable continue to be controlled by a concentrated few who attempt to distract Americans from important political issues with a barrage of sexual and personal subjects (Strobel and Peterson, 1999), the influence of the internet on that mainstream media is already apparent. In particular, the internet provides enough alternative outlets for "interesting and sophisticated" entertainment and knowledge that the mainstream media's lock on American minds is being reduced, as evidenced by the growing demand in the USA for information beyond the "formula comedy, feel-good tales and big budget he-man adventures" with which Hollywood has saturated people's minds in recent decades (New York Times News, 2000).

Nonetheless, there even exist risks of big business obtaining centralized control of the internet (just as it controls the rest of the media), such as through advertising and payment for top placement in internet searches through browsers (e.g., see footnote 3 of Chapter 2). Possibly the best solution to the general problem of centralized control of the media/entertainment business would be to create a number of different government media companies (perhaps 1000) whose administrators would be elected by the people in a single periodic vote. Candidates for these positions would be allowed to have their resumes, opinions, proposals, and promises available for reading at polling places (and permitted equal free access for engaging in media debates), but there would optimally be a prohibition on spending money on political advertising or campaigns. The top 1000 or so candidates in the election would be entitled to an administrative post, so that there would be room for many media firms in which only a small minority of people are interested. Although the government could still sell commercial advertising time on these media (perhaps, however, subsidizing the advertising of smaller firms with new products to level the playing field and to encourage innovation), the advertising revenue would optimally go to the overall federal government (which would centralize such sales separately from the independent programming of the media companies) in order to eliminate any financial pressure the advertisers might be able to put on the media companies. In addition, in order to further democratize the media, it would also be necessary to outlaw the information-repressive effect of allowing big businesses to pay for top placement on an internet search engine (that should be done more randomly or independently of money considerations).

Once Americans recognize that the USA's wealth was stolen via horrible crimes against humanity, they might also see the justice in ending any further domestic or foreign exploitation. While reparations to the USA's victims might also seem appropriate, it might be sufficient (and more practical) to merely give the poor the freedom to grow out of their poverty using some economic plan such as proposed in Chapter 5. Such growth might very well benefit all, including the USA itself.

In addition to sparking faster worldwide economic growth, an enlightened American people might also decide to have a system that shares the existing loot more evenly. In particular, it would seem only fair that the surviving Indian victims of possibly the worst holocaust in history (i.e., the virtual genocide of the native Americans) should be provided with jobs that give them close to an equal share of the income from the land that was stolen from them by force. While the native Americans have clearly been the people most abused by the USA's capitalist system, other victims of USA capitalist crimes like the Afro-Americans (i.e., the former slaves) should also be entitled to a fair share of the income from the wealth that they helped create while being exploited. In addition, since a very large percentage of white Americans initially came over to the USA as indentured servants and were forced to effectively work as slaves for a limited number of years (Zinn, 1995), the ancestors of the majority in the USA have been exploited and should really be entitled to an equitable portion of the loot/income of the USA.[14]

Moreover, it must be remembered that American workers in general (hourly or salaried) have always received compensation that was less than the value created by their work (and that often represented a form of wage slavery) in order to ensure a good profit margin to rich investors (Marx and Engels, 1988b). One result of this exploitation is a significant amount of poverty among many Americans (Strobel and Peterson, 1999) that is so severe that the rich USA ranks 24th in the average healthy life-span of its residents even though it spends more than any other country in the world on health (Associated Press, 2000i). It would thus seem just and humane to have all Americans be provided with jobs that pay approximately an equal share of the USA's national income (or GDP), which would come to about $70,000 per worker in 2000. Note that incomes in such a socialist system could still be allowed to vary somewhat for differences in skill and performance (e.g., ranging between $50,000 and $150,000 in the USA). Thus, although the USA capitalists have shared some of their loot with the average American (as a form of bribe or diversion to keep them from investigating or complaining about USA crimes and exploitation), and although most Americans today (at least the middle class) therefore have a higher standard of living than people in most of the rest of the world (and thus profit from the USA's past atrocities), over 95% of the American people earn less than the value of their work created and would therefore benefit from a more equitable socialist system (the only exceptions being those currently with an abnormally large share of the USA capital/loot). That benefit could come from higher wages and salaries or a shorter work week, or both.

Note that incomes would also grow faster under a socialist system than under capitalism, as documented in Chapters 1 and 4. Note also that taxes for social security and government services in a socialist system would be less than under capitalism because unemployment could be eliminated, wasteful and destructive defense spending could be reduced to an extremely low level, and a more efficient government could be created, as explained in Chapter 1. As documented in Chapter 2, a socialist system would also be advantageous for many non-economic reasons, permitting greater personal individuality (as socialism prevents rich individual owners of capital from repressing the individuality of others) and greater personal freedom (as socialism prevents "free" markets from economically repressing personal freedoms).

Regardless, since the analysis in Chapter 3 of this book shows that the fall of socialism in Eastern Europe was not inevitable, and since Chapters 4 and 5 demonstrate that a socialist system can function and even integrate in a capitalist-dominated world, there is also hope for other countries even if the USA's new world order is not overthrown by USA voters. In particular, other countries can vote in political parties promising to attempt to create more just socialist systems that are immune from the USA's capitalist exploitation and atrocities. While socialism may not be perfect (and while an even better system could perhaps be developed, maybe by developing further some of the ideas presented in Chapter 5), it has clearly been shown to be superior to capitalism in practice.

In the meantime, while waiting for the majority of voters to wake up to the reality of the USA's Cold War victory, this book provides perspective on the hypocrisy of individuals, organizations, and nations that refrain from doing business with countries for "ethical" reasons. Such a refusal to engage in peaceful international cooperation is often based on citations of terrorist acts or other atrocities committed by those countries. It is true that some of the peoples and countries against whom the USA has committed its own extermination tactics have also engaged in morally criminal acts. For instance, Nazi Germany and fascist Japan both made the top ten in civilian killings (as documented in the introduction), Cambodia executed as many as 150,000 people after the USA slaughtered about a half million innocent Cambodians (as already mentioned previously), Vietnam assassinated about 40,000 civilians during the USA occupation and extermination process there (Lewy, 1978), the American Indians killed thousands of civilians in retaliation for the USA mass murders (Utley and Washburn, 1985), and Iraq killed thousands of its own civilians (Andreopoulos, 1994).[15] Nevertheless, even though other countries have also engaged in terrible acts, none compare to the USA (and some of those terrible acts by others actually represented a form of revenge for much more horrible USA atrocities committed against them). A consistent policy of refusing to interact with countries that commit terrible atrocities would therefore also mandate a refusal to do business with the USA itself.

In summary, this book irrefutably documents the fact that capitalism is a much less efficient and much crueler system than communism. While further worldwide suffering can be expected as long as the USA is able to enforce its power and capitalist religion on the rest of the world,[16] the situation today in the year 2000 is probably not more hopeless than it was in 1941 at the height of the triumphs of Nazi German capitalism (which then also seemed invincible). Just as some have speculated that Hitler's rule of Germany could have been "aborted" with "mass protests" (Associated Press, 2000h), so too could widespread demonstrations and other political actions terminate the rule of the criminal USA leaders. In particular, the USA's own democratic façade (which it currently uses so successfully for propaganda purposes, much more so than Hitler did for his own elections) creates an opportunity to overthrow the USA tyrants peacefully via the ballot box.[17]

NOTES

Introduction

1. Besides being incompletely documented, there are a number of procedural problems with Mooney's (1928) estimates. For instance, many of Mooney's own base figures were derived from other sources that had already subjectively discounted actual sightings of Indians for no apparent reason, and Mooney arbitrarily reduced these figures even further (Jennings, 1975). In addition, many of Mooney's estimates are based on just multiplying four by the number of warriors claimed to have been seen after extensive contact had been made with the white invaders (Denevan, 1976), whereas observed warrior numbers should have been multiplied by a more normal 12:1 military mobilization ratio for Indians (Dobyns, 1983). Moreover, Mooney even ignored many of the tribes encountered (Denevan, 1976), possibly in part because his work was not completed at his death (Jennings, 1975). Finally, Mooney failed to make any allowance for Indian warriors who were never directly counted (because they fled from the deadly whites) or who were met (and killed) only before extensive military contact was made (Thornton, 1987). The uncounted numbers might be especially large given rumors that there was a widespread frontier practice of giving Indians gifts infected with smallpox (Jennings, 1988), and given that the Indians quickly learned to avoid the superior firepower of USA by engaging in guerrilla warfare that avoided massing warriors for observation (and counting) by the deadly whites (Jennings, 1975). Despite Mooney's methodological flaws, bias, and obvious underestimation of Indian population in the USA, the USA government publication of Mooney's numbers gives them an aura of authenticity. Possibly as a result, many twentieth century researchers tend to report similar low numbers (Wax, 1971).

2. While Indians did have more vacant land to allow for more hunting, it is not clear whether such practices resulted in more underutilization of land than the European system of concentrating land holdings in the hands of the rich (Thomas, 1976).

3. Mexicans also stole a great deal of land from Indians via fraud, but, unlike the USA, Mexico generally allowed the Indians to continue to live on the land as serfs (Atkin, 1970). In addition, unlike the USA which did not provide Indians with citizenship until the twentieth century after they had been virtually exterminated (Churchill, 1994), Mexico automatically granted citizenship to all Indians immediately upon achieving independence from Spain in the 1820s (Jennings, 1993). Perhaps for these reasons, Indians were known to migrate from the USA to Mexico (Mallery, 1877), as well as to Canada, to escape the USA's attacks (Jennings, 1993).

4. This estimate of the USA's short-term kill rate may actually be far too low, as Wax

(1971) indicates that the California gold miners killed nine-tenths of the Indian population in the space of a few years after it was annexed by the USA.

5. The body count for these countries may actually be seriously underestimated. For instance, some estimate the number killed in El Salvador to be in the hundreds of thousands (Catalinotto, 1998b). A group of Catholic religious orders (the Inter-Congregational Commission of Peace and Justice) provide evidence that over 50,000 people may have been assassinated by USA-backed Colombian government forces or their death squads over the 1988-95 period alone (Javier, 1996), and Colombian rebels claim the anticommunist government in Colombia has been killing 30,000 people annually for some time (FARC-EP, 1998). In addition, although the USA puppet Pinochet was only able to slaughter about half the 20,000 civilians he planned to execute outside of battle in the initial weeks of his terroristic rule of Chile in 1973 (Sandford, 1976), and although only 2700 political executions have been verified since then (Javier, 1996), there are estimates that tens of thousands of unarmed Chileans were killed over the course of his long and brutal dictatorship (*Workers World,* 1998).

6. The number of civilians killed by the USA in these other countries may be enormous. For instance, the Shah of Iran, who was put into power by the CIA in 1953, killed nearly 50,000 people just in the final year of his reign of terror that had lasted until he was overthrown in 1979 (Clark, 1998). In addition, the CIA-sponsored mercenary wars launched against Nicaragua killed an estimated 75,000 (Flounders, 1998b). Moreover, the CIA-financed terrorist war launched against Angola has killed an estimated 300,000 people (Blum, 1995). Although many of the latter died in battles between government troops and the CIA-backed terrorists, the CIA-financed terrorists were responsible for a large number of deliberate civilian murders (Minter, 1994), and the *Wall Street Journal* has actually estimated over 600,000 killings in Angola (mostly of civilians) since 1975 (Block, 1998). In addition, the USA-sponsored atrocities listed in the text is far from all-inclusive, as it does not formally mention many other countries with murderous USA-backed (or USA-installed) governments like Bolivia, Brazil, Haiti, Peru, Uruguay, and so many others (Blum, 1995), which have all killed a significant number of people for political reasons although the estimates of the number of victims vary. For instance, in Argentina, executions and arranged "disappearances" caused by USA-trained terrorists and USA-installed government thugs range from 9000 (Javier, 1996) to 30,000 (Mathiowetz, 1999).

7. Although the USA (as well as other countries) has been using embargoes to impoverish people of countries that do not submit to the capitalist world order at least since 1804 (when Haiti was punished with a 60-year embargo for its slaves revolting and seizing power), the embargoes were not as effective when the Soviet Union was still around to support oppressed peoples (Flounders, 1998b).

8. Some additional information on some of these mass murders is merited. For instance, while the British directly exterminated tens of thousands of unarmed civilians in Germany with its terror bombings in World War II (Markusen and Kopf, 1995), and while it directly slaughtered thousands of natives in its colonies (Kiernan, 1998), including in Ireland (Levene and Roberts, 1999), in the Caribbean (Daunton and Halpern, 1999), in India (Gopal, 1963), and in Kenya (Maloba, 1993), most of those killed by Britain in Ireland and Australia died of hunger and disease as the British deliber-

ately destroyed or stole the food of the local inhabitants (Levene and Roberts, 1999) or forcibly removed the natives from their food sources (Reynolds, 1995). Similarly, although czarist Russian soldiers directly massacred thousands of Circassian civilians, many more died of hunger and disease while fleeing from this onslaught to refugee camps in Turkey (Levene and Roberts, 1999). For France, Smith (2000) reports about a million people killed by the French in its war to keep Indochina colonized over the period 1946-54, and Bodard (1967) provides evidence that ½ to ¾ of those killed by French ground forces were civilians and that possibly even a larger percentage of civilians were killed by French aerial attacks that focused on peasant living quarters and largely ignored the rice patties and jungles in which the armed guerrillas tended to hide. This massive slaughter is alone sufficient to put France in the number 9 slot, but France engaged in other atrocities in its other colonies as well, such as in Algeria where it conducted tens of thousands of executions (Horne, 1977) and employed widespread torture (Maran, 1997). Although the number of dead resulting from France's 1954-62 war against Algerian independence fighters is estimated as high as one million if losses of human life caused by hunger and disease (largely stemming from France's forced resettlements of Algerians) are included (Horne, 1977), only about 300,000 people were clearly deliberately killed, with many being murdered by armed Algerian nationalists and with many more of the dead being armed Algerian nationalists themselves (Ruedy, 1992). France also committed major atrocities in its Madagascar colony, where it is estimated that it killed as many as 100,000 people in conquering the country during the 1896-1897 period (Ellis, 1985), and where it may have massacred an additional 50,000 or more in a 1947 revolt there (Heseltine, 1971).

9. Besides not counting capitalism-induced deaths unless obviously deliberate, other dead bodies, such as the starvation deaths of three million residents of India that resulted when Britain destroyed Bengali agriculture upon the approach of the Japanese army in World War II (Markusen and Kopf, 1995), are not incorporated into the analysis because there was no explicit intent to kill them.

10. The exaggerated numbers reported by the capitalist press to have been killed by communist governments are frequently based on outright CIA fabrications or absurd logic (Blum, 1995). For instance, the numbers might be based on an allegation from a refugee (perhaps even a CIA agent) that, say, 10% of the people in his village disappeared, it is assumed that all were executed, and then this percentage is extrapolated to the entire country (Rummel, 1991).

11. Cambodia would not even come close to being in the top ten in mass murders. For instance, it definitely killed less than Uganda, which slaughtered 250,000 of its own civilians under Idi Amin at about the same time (Decalo, 1989), although Idi Amin doesn't get nearly as much publicity as Pol Pot today (possibly because he was a capitalist). Cambodia also certainly murdered less than Burundi, which (under dictatorial rule by a government army dominated by minority Tutsis) slaughtered potentially in excess of 100,000 Hutu civilians in a 1993-98 civil war (Uvin, 1999), as well as another 250,000 Hutus in an earlier 1972 extermination campaign (Chalk and Jonassohn, 1990). The Tutsis' mass murder of Hutus no doubt helped motivate the conflict in neighboring Rwanda, which (under Hutu rule) exterminated about 500,000 of its ethnic Tutsi civilians in 1994 (Klingerhoffer, 1998), and which therefore would also rank far above Cambodia. Cambodia also killed less than communist China, which is discussed later

in the Introduction, and less than the Soviet Union, which is evaluated in Chapter 1. Note also that if the rankings were based on the existence of an actual state, there might be others ahead of Cambodia (and possibly in the top ten), such as Mongolia due to Ghengis Khan's medieval practice of killing unarmed civilians (Chalk and Jonassohn, 1990). In addition, if Nationalist China (now only existing on the island of Taiwan) were held responsible for all the people killed (including many communists) under a combination of warlord and foreign domination before the communist takeover in 1949 (Ho, 1959), it would undoubtedly also easily beat out Cambodia, although many of Nationalist China's atrocities might actually be more appropriately attributable to the Western colonial powers that to some extent controlled the country into the first half of the twentieth century. Besides the major colonial powers already mentioned, Portugal also had a stake in Nationalist China, engaged in the killing of tens of thousands of people in its own colonies that continued into the 1970s (Kiernan, 1998), and might therefore also merit investigation for a high ranking. Similarly, Belgium might be deserving of consideration here for its atrocities in its Congo colony (Galvez, 1999).

12. For instance, while there were no doubt hundreds of innocent civilians killed in the guerrilla war launched against communist China by Tibetan feudal warlords and slaveowners financed by the CIA, the USA State Department itself has privately called claims that China killed 65,000 Tibetans in a civil war in the 1950s "wild exaggerations" (Grunfeld, 1996).

13. In addition to the 1950-52 executions and the 1960s killings, there were undoubtedly hundreds of demonstrators killed at Tiananmen Square in 1989 and at various other times (MacFarquhar, 1993), but these numbers are not significant in the history of mass murders. The 1950-52 mass executions and the 1960s killings, however, would certainly put communist China in the top 20 (see footnote 11 of this Introduction for the country's other competition, which would also include Nationalist China itself if its mix of deadly warlord and foreign rule of mainland China before 1949 was considered a true independent state).

14. The death rate in pre-communist China reported by Deleyne (1974) is consistent with other estimates for peaceful years with normal harvests in the 1930s (Eastman, 1974). The estimated death rate in pre-communist China is also consistent with the fact that the Chinese population growth rate was about 0.5% in the first half of the twentieth century, as that growth rate implies a death rate of over 3.2% given that the annual birth rate (which has been trending down) must surely have exceeded the 3.7% rate of the early 1950s (Deleyne, 1974).

15. While Chapter 1 provides sufficient information to refute the overall allegations against the Soviet Union, that analysis of Soviet killings concentrates on Stalin's most notorious decade, the 1930s. In fact, demographic data alone are sufficient to disprove the conjecture of Rummel (1990) and others that Stalin and his successor murdered millions of people in the 1940s and 1950s. In particular, Chalk and Jonassohn (1990) report census data indicating that the population of the Soviet Union had risen to 209 million by 1959, of which 75 million had been born since 1940, implying 209-75=134 million of these living in 1959 having been in existence before 1940. Combining the early 1939 Soviet population of 168 million with 24 million new Soviet citizens (who were added as a result of Soviet re-annexations of formerly Russian territory later in 1939)

implies a population of 192 million at the end of 1939. Given Rummel's (1990) own estimates of 20 million Soviets killed by the Nazis in World War II, there are a total of 192-20-134=38 million people left who could have died from deaths not related to the Nazis. That number of deaths represents only 38/20=1.9 million per year over the 1940-1959 interval, or under 1.0% of the population annually. Such an annual death rate is far less than the over 3% Russian death rate under the czar even in peacetime in 1913 (Wheatcroft, 1990), is less than the 1.9% Soviet death rate in 1928 before Stalin took full control (Buck, 1937), is even below the 1.1% death rate in the final year of communism in 1990, and is significantly less than the 1.6% death rate under Yeltsin's capitalist Russia (Becker, 1997a). Thus, although there was some guerrilla warfare between Soviet troops and Nazi collaborators (i.e., "freedom fighters" in CIA terminology) after areas of the Soviet Union seized by Hitler were liberated in World War II, and although the Soviet Union had hundreds of the Nazi collaborators executed and many others deported (Associated Press, 2000e), there is no evidence of Stalin having killed a significant number of people in the 1940s and 1950s. Similarly, while there were numerous executions in other Eastern Europe countries under Soviet military occupation after World War II, they numbered only in the hundreds (Parrish, 1996).

CHAPTER 1

1. Given that the pre-communist relative GNP estimates quoted here are higher than most other research estimates (Gregory, 1982) and given that other estimates of per capita Soviet GNP in the final years of communism are closer to 50% of the USA (Gregory and Stuart, 1995), it is possible that the numbers listed in the text understate the magnitude by which the Soviet Union caught up. Stalin himself stated in 1931 that the USSR was "fifty or a hundred years behind the advanced countries" (Harrison, 1994), making what was accomplished economically by the USSR truly amazing.

2. As admitted by the former National Security Council member Richard Pipes (1993), the Foreign Interventionist Civil War would not have been possible if it had not been for the extensive military and other support given to anticommunist mercenaries by Great Britain and over a dozen other capitalist powers that invaded the USSR between 1918 and 1921. The destruction of this war, as well as that of the Nazi invasion, was therefore not inherent to communism but inflicted upon the Soviet Union by outside capitalist powers.

3. That includes its final decade (IMF, 1993), during which the Soviet Union experienced its slowest peacetime growth (Gregory and Stuart, 1995). With respect to other subintervals, Maddison (1969) estimated that real GNP growth per capita in the Soviet Union cumulated to 25.8% more than in the USA between 1913 and 1953 (or 0.6% faster annually), despite the Foreign Interventionist Civil War and the Nazi invasion (each of which set back Soviet output levels by about a decade) and despite including 4 years of negative Russian growth under the czar during the German invasion in World War I. This estimate combined with the figures stated in the text implies that real Soviet growth between 1953 and 1991 must have cumulated to be 124% greater than in the USA (implying 2.1% faster annual growth over that time interval). Such a finding is consistent with the growth figures reported by the IMF (1993) and is substantially higher than various estimates based on pre-1990 studies cited by Gregory and Stuart (1995) that indicate only 0.8% higher annual Soviet growth between 1950 and 1990.

In addition, Maddison's (1969) estimate that Soviet growth per capita was 2.4% higher between 1953 and 1965 implies from the foregoing information that Soviet growth must have been 1.9% higher annually between 1965 and 1991. The latter information, along with IMF (1993) data, refutes the hypothesis cited by Gregory and Stuart (1995) that the rate at which Soviet output had been catching up had not only slowed significantly but had actually reversed itself in recent decades.

4. Anticommunist propaganda certainly played its part in the overthrow of communism. Herman and Chomsky (1988), Blum (1995), and Foerstel (2000) provide some details on how the capitalist propaganda machine functions without many people even being aware that it is biased propaganda. For instance, attempts to portray pre-communist Russia as relatively efficient and affluent by drawing attention to the fact that Russia was a major grain exporter in 1913 but had turned into a major grain importer under communism (Pipes, 1993) convinced many Soviets, including Gorbachev himself, that communism was inefficient, and Gorbachev even purged people who expressed contrary, pro-communist opinions (Marcy, 1990). However, data provided by Gregory (1982) and Goldman (1991) indicate that, despite almost a 2/3 reduction in the number of workers employed in Soviet agriculture compared to 1913, Soviet grain production nearly doubled by 1990 compared to the 1913 level. While the transfer of labor from agriculture to industry helped enable the Soviet Union to greatly increase industrial production and consumption, consumption of grain also rose significantly under communist rule, both indirectly (through greater meat consumption, which requires large amounts of livestock fodder) and directly (Marcy, 1990). Moreover, it should be emphasized that aggregate Russian agricultural production was lower than that of the USA in 1913 despite employing over six times as many people and despite 1913 being a bumper year for Russian farmers with abnormally high agricultural production (Gregory, 1982). Although some estimate Russian per capita income to be as high as ¼ that of the USA in 1913 based on a backcasting of very subjective growth estimates (Maddison, 1995), backcasting leads to a compounding of errors and biases over time that can cause huge distortions in past output estimates. For example, it is impossible for output per capita in Russia to have been ¼ that of the USA in 1913, given that Russia produced less with 6 times as many people in agriculture even in a good year, and given that Russian industry was even less competitive relative to the USA than Russian agriculture (Gregory, 1982).

5. In a 1988 survey of East Germans who sought to emigrate to West Germany, 69% listed limited consumption and travel opportunities in East Germany as the major reason for wanting to leave (Falck, 1998).

6. The anticommunist propagandist Rummel (1990) alleges 250,000 outright communist killings of civilians in Afghanistan, based on his typical method of effectively multiplying by ½ the highest possible number reported from any source, in this case an unsubstantiated 500,000 killings cited by Klass (1987). Given that Rummel's (1990) methodology typically results in an estimate that is too high by a factor of 10-100 times (as demonstrated previously and subsequently in the text for different alleged communist atrocities), the true number of deliberate communist killings of civilians is more likely to lie between 2500 and 25,000. For instance, of the largest communist atrocities mentioned by Khan (1991), which included the killing of over 1000 civilians during the Soviet Union's 1984 combined air/artillery/ground assault on rebel-controlled posi-

tions in the Afghan city of Herat, the killing of almost 300 civilians in an air/ground attack on three Afghan villages in the Shomali region, and the killing of two hundred civilians in a pure aerial bombing on the outskirts of Qandahar, only one action (the latter one) resembled USA terrorist tactics in Vietnam (and as mentioned in the text, the Soviets, unlike the USA, had an official policy of providing adequate warning to civilian residents before an aerial bombing). Other alleged communist atrocities have been mentioned by Urban (1990), who cites a 1989 communist air/artillery shelling of rebel-held villages that the USA claimed killed 600 civilians, and who also specifically mentions two separate air/ground campaigns in which communist bombings killed a total of several hundred civilians according to rebel sources in 1987. Given the proximity to ground/artillery forces in these latter attacks, the civilian deaths appear to be more related to actual military battles with armed rebels (as opposed to aerial terrorism), and, in any event, the numbers of deaths may have been exaggerated (as are most others). To provide some perspective on the relative number of civilian casualties involved in military battles, Girardet (1985) cites rebel claims that more than 6 times as many civilians (an estimated 1200) were killed as armed rebels in one big Soviet ground offensive (that included tactical aerial bombings and strafing, as well as heavy artillery fire, to directly support Soviet ground troops) into a key rebel-controlled area in 1982 (that reportedly resulted in thousands of communist casualties). However, it should be mentioned that, since many of the rebels were part-time civilians, it is not clear if the estimate of 1200 civilian deaths is supposed to represent only innocent civilians or not. Moreover, it should be mentioned that "resistance groups rarely acknowledged significant casualties in battle" (Cordovez and Harrison, 1995). In another air/ground battle (in 1984), Urban (1990) cites a rebel estimate of twice as many civilian as rebel deaths. Another perspective is provided by Amstutz (1986), who cites the estimates of one French journalist indicating that there were about half as many civilians killed (several hundred) as deaths of armed troops (on both sides) for one province of Afghanistan during one month of air/ground battles in 1982.

7. As noted in the Introduction, even Vietnam's invasion of Cambodia could have been at least partially and indirectly caused by USA policies. In particular, communist Vietnam invaded and occupied communist Cambodia in 1979 after a significant amount of border warfare that had been initiated by Cambodia with the support of China and possibly also the USA (Klinghoffer, 1998). Cambodia's provocative border incursions had earlier led to an attempted coup against Cambodia's leader Pol Pot, who retaliated with massive killings of ethnic Vietnamese and Vietnam sympathizers (Kiernan, 1996). Given the USA's history of using diplomacy, extortion, and bribes to create conflicts between communist China and the Soviet Union (Griswold, 1972), it would not be surprising if the USA had also played a significant role in stirring up the war between Cambodia and Vietnam, which were allied with China and the Soviet Union, respectively. Some evidence of such a scheme is provided by the fact that the USA did indeed eventually recognize the Pol Pot government and directly supported his guerrilla activities against Vietnam after his fall from power (Blum, 1995). Communist China itself actually attacked Vietnam militarily after the Vietnamese occupation of Cambodia, but the scale of the attack was very limited (Klinghoffer, 1998), so it is not counted as an actual invasion, just as the minor border skirmishes between the Soviet Union and China several decades ago (Bradsher, 1983) are not counted as invasions.

8. When Nazi Germany did invade the Soviet Union in the early 1940s, it did indeed put many czarists into power in its occupied territories, and although the greater efficiency of collectivization and communism inhibited them from immediately transforming the occupied areas into a capitalist system while the war was continuing, there were some experiments along those lines, and there was a long-term plan to do so for political reasons that were consistent with the Nazi capitalist ideology (Schulte, 1989). Hitler's long-term plans were to colonize Russia with Germans while killing off the native Russians in a manner very similar to (and based on) the genocidal methods employed by the USA to take land from the Indians, and, in the meantime, he hoped to enslave and fragment the Russians as much as possible although he planned to allow them to keep their local communes if absolutely necessary (Cook, 1973).

9. Although there have been some capitalist countries (such as in southeast Asia) that grew faster than Eastern Europe (IMF, 1998: 171), communist Eastern Europe did grow faster than the average capitalist developing country even in its final years, as well as faster than the average capitalist developed country (IMF, 1993). In addition, it should also be mentioned that many of the developing capitalist countries (such as in southeast Asia) had special advantages that Eastern Europe did not, as the USA encouraged their economic development as a defense against the further spread of communism (Smith, 2000). The advantages offered by the USA to its strategic capitalist allies included facilitated exports to the USA market at the same time these allied countries were permitted to use a substantial amount of protectionism against imports, were given easy access to Western capital and technology, and were not required to spend so much on defense. Despite these advantages, many of the southeast Asian countries are now facing a very severe economic crisis that has reversed some of the previous income gains, as is discussed later in Chapter 6.

10. While China has conducted numerous capitalist reforms of its economy in special coastal zones to attract foreign investment, encourage exports, and ease the transition to unification with Hong Kong (Adams, 1997), most of industry remains state-owned and controlled (Mok and Hui, 1998), and "no large enterprise has been completely privatized, with most permitted to sell only a small stake on overseas capital markets" (Chang, 2000). In addition, it should be mentioned that real economic growth in communist China was relatively high even in earlier periods, as admitted by Gregory and Stuart (1995), who cited sources indicating real average annual growth to be 7.9% in the 1950s, 5.6% in the 1960s, and 7.0% in the early 1970s. Although some have asserted that the real growth rates in the aggregate economy reported by China of 7.8% in 1998 and 7.1% in 1999 were overestimated and were closer to the nominal 5% wage and tax growth reported in those years (Johnson, 2000), such lower estimates ignore other factors such as profits and net export income, and because they apparently ignore the effect on real income increases of the commodity price deflation incurred during those years (Leggett, 2000). In addition, as explained by Roach (1999), if growth were in fact lower than China reports, there would likely be a significant increase in unemployment which doesn't appear to have happened.

11. Stalin originally did not plan to implement forced collectivization (Campbell, 1974), but he changed his mind after there was a threat of another British invasion in 1927 (Meurs, 1999) and after farmers refused to make mandatory sales of food to the state at low prices in the late 1920s (Conquest, 1986). This scenario had its roots in the

brutal war that was launched against the Soviet Union practically from the moment of its creation in October 1917. The war was made possible only through the extensive armaments support, embargo, and military invasion by Britain, and the control and withholding of food supplies were strategic weapons used in this war that killed millions by starvation over the period 1918-22, as the rich farmers simply murdered the thousands of Soviet tax collectors sent out to the farms to obtain food for the cities (Pipes, 1993). After an effective multi-year cease fire in most of the Soviet Union except Turkestan (Krivosheev, 1997), much of the civil strife in the 1930s was, to some extent, merely a continuation of that conflict (Viola, 1993). The armed guerrillas often used the same weapons in the 1930s to fight the Soviet government as they used, and obtained from Britain, in the earlier civil war (Conquest, 1986). While capitalist countries now often glorify people as "clever" for cornering a market in essentials like food (or for avoiding taxes and government regulations in order to be able to maximize their own profits/income at the cost of others like the poor), only a few hundred years ago people engaged in such acts even in capitalist countries like Britain were considered morally and legally criminal (Furlough and Strikwerda, 1999).

12. The growth rate in the population was actually abnormally high in the late 1920s compared to prior and later times (Wheatcroft, 1993).

13. Data supporting these facts on lower birth rates are provided by Davies (1997) and Conquest (1990) himself. The 1.5% lower annual birth rates in the 5-year interval of 1932-36 imply 5x.015x169=12 million less babies, while the 0.5% lower birth rates in the other four years imply a further 4x.005x169=3.2 million reduction in babies. Thus, all 15 million "missing" people were caused by a lower number of births.

14. Including 1933, the average death rate in the 1930s was 2.1% per year, which remained far below the annual death rate in normal peacetime in Russia before communism (Wheatcroft, 1993). The 1930s average includes a horrible 6% death rate in the leading agricultural region of the Soviet Union (the Ukraine) in 1933 (Wheatcroft, 1990), implying one million deaths above the normal 2% death rate there that year. While this figure itself is tragic, it refutes the allegations of Conquest (1990) and Antonov-Ovseyenko (1981) that Stalin murdered millions there. In addition, while the Soviet archives do indicate widespread food shortages and disease in the Ukraine during the 1932-33 interval, as well as serious conflicts and economic warfare between striking farmers and the government, there is little evidence of a deliberate attempt to starve people to death, and the Soviet government undertook strong measures to relieve the food shortages when and where they were discovered (Koenker and Bachman, 1997). Conquest's (1986) allegation that real wages fell by over 80% during this time period is ludicrous, since the estimate is probably based on an illegal black market exchange rate, which was rarely used (except for luxury goods), and which was fairly meaningless (especially given the subsidized price of essentials in the Soviet Union), and since less ludicrous studies indicate real consumption fell only a few percent in the USSR in the 1930s as production was shifted more toward investment (Maddison, 1969).

15. For example, Bergson (1987) conducted a study that indicated output in certain Eastern European countries in one particular year (1975) was inefficient in relation to the amount of capital employed (implying that Eastern European growth was largely

achieved through heavy investment as opposed to the efficiency of central planning). However, Bergson (1992) later admitted that his results may have been biased by his overestimate (and perhaps very large overestimate) of the value of the Eastern European capital stock (among other things). In particular, he made no adjustment for the much higher cost of technology and high-tech capital goods in Eastern Europe resulting from the technological embargo (Parrott, 1985), and he used gross capital stocks that do not take into consideration the higher level of depreciation that exists on Eastern European capital due to their tendency to keep it in service longer (instead of depreciating the capital over time, he increased its value with price indexes). He also failed to adjust for differences in the quality of agricultural land and weather factors in all countries except the Soviet Union, he excluded services such as education and health from the analysis although socialist countries may be more efficient in these areas (which are priorities in many socialist countries), and he attempted to arbitrarily factor a portion of government administration and capital out of the model although he admits the importance of government infrastructure that communist systems are more efficient in administering (Campbell, 1974). In addition, by effectively measuring output per employed worker, he failed to adjust for overall system efficiencies in communist countries related to a higher level of employment that is made possible by the existence of guaranteed jobs (which greatly reduce or eliminate unemployment) and extensive childcare networks (whose economies of scale may permit more women to be more productively employed as opposed to individually having to take care of children). Moreover, Bergson (1987) made no adjustment for the effect on labor effort of differences in worker protection, environment, and satisfaction, which may be higher in communist countries compared to other nations at similar levels of development due to the communists' pro-worker philosophy (Adler, 1980). For instance, Bergson (1987) did find that an adjustment for the quality of labor related to the number of hours worked per worker increased the estimate of the productivity of communist labor.

16. Although corruption (including tax evasion and bribery) does exist in communist systems, communist governments frequently engage in widespread efforts to root it out (through imprisonment and expelling corrupt bureaucrats out of the communist party), as in the Soviet Union under Stalin (Getty, 1985) and in China under Mao (Gong, 1994). Corruption does tend to rise when communist countries initiate capitalistic market reforms, as in China in the late 1970s (Kwong, 1997) and in the Soviet Union in the late 1980s (Marcy, 1990). It should also be mentioned that corruption also existed before communism, especially in China, which had a substantial amount of corruption prior to the communist seizure of power in 1949 (Gong, 1994).

17. Although the Soviet Union spent a higher percent of GNP on defense than the USA, the absolute dollar amount was substantially less. It is therefore likely that the USA could also exist on far lower defense expenditures if it maintained a more defensive foreign policy like the Soviet Union did (especially since there would be no other world power to threaten it), thereby further lowering the tax bite. Moreover, given the USA's enormous nuclear arsenal and overwhelming military power, it is very unlikely that there would be any foreign invasions to prompt the type of destructive civil war which occurred after the communist revolution in Russia in 1917 and which reduced national income there by about half. Instead, if the USA were to choose a communist path, there would be no more USA economic, military, political, and subversive (i.e.,

CIA) pressure for the rest of the world to remain capitalist (Blum, 1995), and it is quite possible that a large number of other countries would turn toward a communist system.

18. For example, the Soviet Union typically spent only 1% of GNP on government administration vs. 3% for the USA (Campbell, 1974). It should also be noted that the lack of unemployment in communist countries would eliminate the taxes that have to be paid under USA capitalism for the unemployed. Further evidence on these issues is provided by communist China, whose government spending (including not only for administration but also for defense and various government services) represents only 16% of economic output, and the overall tax burden there is one of the lowest in the world (Forney, 2000).

19. The nontrivial risk of falling into poverty can be illustrated by the fact that there are Americans who go quickly from very good-paying jobs (such as $125,000 annually) to being unemployed and homeless, and by the fact that even working people earning over $30,000 per year often live in poverty and sometimes go homeless because landlords require a good credit history as well as high current income to ensure payment of rent (Washington Post, 2000). It should be noted that the latter figure is the approximate median income for USA families (Phillips, 2000).

CHAPTER 2

1. While West Germany did eventually pay out DM72 billion for war-related crimes and debts, including for some pre-war debts of Nazi Germany that were largely forgiven by the rich West (Faber, 1990), and while the united Germany continues to make some war-related payments (Winestock, 2000), the amounts were spread over very many years (Merkel and Wahl, 1991) and therefore amounted to only a small portion of West German GNP each year. Assuming an average payment of DM2 billion per year beginning in 1953 were invested at 18% instead of paid out for war-related crimes and debts, and assuming the earnings (based on the same 18% interest rate) from the capital accumulated after 36 years were paid out in 1989 (and each year thereafter), West German income per capita would have been only about 1/3 higher. Comparing this figure to the per capita East German figures estimated to have existed without reparations indicates East German per capita income in 1989 to still have been far higher at 5-10 times the level of West German per capita income. In order to provide just compensation here, it would be necessary for the West Germans to pay the East Germans an annual amount that exceeds their own current GNP. For the very reason that an annual payment in excess of GNP would not be possible, it would be necessary for the West Germans to establish a more efficient economic system (like communism) so that they could increase their GNP sufficiently to be able to afford fair compensation to the East Germans.

2. Inflation first appeared in East Germany after the currency union that replaced the East German Mark with the West German Mark in 1990. According to the German central bank, prices were 14% higher in eastern Germany with the West German Mark in 1991 than they were under the old system with the old East German Mark in 1990 (*Neues Deutschland*, 1991), and these figures do not even include the effect of the multifold increase in rents that occurred subsequently (and other factors that are analyzed in Chapter 4 in more detail).

3. Theoretically, one way a true unreported inflation could be hidden from the official figures would have been via a process of East Germany massively increasing its foreign debt to enable it to import more than it exported and then to artificially value those imports. However, East German foreign debt actually changed little between 1980 and 1989 (Haendcke-Hoppe-Arndt, 1996), and East Germany had to export more than it imported in the 1980s to enable it to make payments on its existing foreign debt (which itself was actually a fairly low percentage of the country's National Income). On a somewhat more serious note, Schwarzer (1999) has hypothesized that East German official inflation figures were understated because East Germany introduced new products at premium prices in order to be able to finance subsidies on essentials. However, this practice is not much different from that occurring in capitalist countries where profit margins on newer products are higher, and where greater marketing expenses (which further increase their prices) are incurred to manipulate people to buy such products (regardless of any true advantages of the "new" products). In any case, the result of the East German practice was merely an increasing level of subsidization of consumer essentials over time (Schwarzer, 1999) so that East German consumer price inflation could be kept at 0% while aggregate East German economic inflation was 0.5% annually.

4. Some might also assert that the West German system of unlimited private wealth might encourage innovation, but the evidence indicates that capitalism is actually innovation-unfriendly (for the same level of economic development) because it is often easier to persuade governments to take long-term chances than rich capitalists or corporate bureaucrats, as previously explained in Chapter 1. Adler (1980) has shown how and why East German communism is actually more compatible with decentralized decision-making and with the technological and scientific revolution in general than capitalism. It is true that government development of the internet has increased the potential for greater innovation in capitalism through more decentralization of marketing and distribution of innovative goods, thereby transferring some of the power to exploit innovations away from static corporate bureaucrats to individual small innovators (Associated Press, 1999f). However, the capitalist system itself may succeed in crippling the potential of this democratic, decentralized, and innovation-friendly medium (Phillips, 2000), which was originally developed by the government but later assigned to the private sector. For instance, some (including apparently the average investor from stock market valuations of the largest internet firms) forecast a trend toward greater concentration of market control of the internet into the hands of a few large businesses, where consumer habit of using the biggest (and richest) sites can result in less established sites, companies, and products remaining undiscovered and unused (Ip, 1999). In addition, the less established internet sites can't afford the necessary expensive advertising and payment for top placement on internet search engines that allow people to find sites (Foerstel, 2000). Moreover, less known sites may not be trusted (because insufficient marketing resources make them unfamiliar, unknown, and riskier due to the lack of an established reputation and due to insufficient assets that could be seized by lawsuits in the case of fraud) and don't have sufficient economies of scale (because of inadequate volume caused by not being able to afford sufficient marketing expenditures), just as it is with traditional retailing and wholesaling activities (Associated Press, 1999f). The internet in that sense is not dissimilar from radio, TV, and cable, which also created the opportu-

nity of reaching a mass audience, but the advertising cost (for a sustained and effective marketing campaign) can generally only be borne by the rich and powerful (Foerstel, 2000). The internet is also not substantially different from the telephone, which also permits interactive communication and marketing (such as telephone sales pitches). Although internet chat groups do have some potential for increasing the scale of interactivity, especially with increased availability via libraries and other free services, as well as via cheap internet terminals (Wingfield, 2000), access to the internet currently is still a luxury mostly reserved for the world's more affluent/educated.

5. Use of black market exchange rates would imply even far less East German spending on security at about $30 per citizen, or one ninth that of West Germany, although there would be little theoretical justification for using such an exchange rate for the comparison (just as it would be meaningless to use some traded-weighted exchange rate that would indicate East German spending on security to have been about $50 per capita).

6. Although the East German secret police did use a large number of unpaid informants and witnesses (as do all police forces worldwide) to assist in its information-gathering tasks (which included obtaining very general information on the economy and public sentiment that is gathered by journalists in Western countries), there were only 4450 undercover East German agents in 1989 (about 0.03% of the population), and a large number of these were spies in foreign countries (Diedrich, Ehlert, and Wenzke, 1998). In addition, given that there were annually over hundreds of millions of letters and tens of millions of phone calls from West Germany (Edwards, 1985), which had a constitutional goal of annexing East Germany by unspecified means, the several hundred Stasi members involved in opening mail or listening in on phone calls (Wiedmann, 1996) had time to monitor only a small fraction of the communication with the country's ideological enemy (Diedrich, Ehlert, and Wenzke, 1998), much less intercept any significant amount of communication between East Germans.

7. The hypothesis that the lack of a market economy in communist countries resulted in them becoming less and less efficient over time, with continued growth only occurring due to excessive investment (Gregory and Stuart, 1995), is not born out by the facts. For instance, the real growth rates in per capita income in East Germany reported by the Statistisches Amt (1990) were higher in every decade from 1950 to 1989 than those reported for West Germany by the Statistisches Bundesamt (1993). In the meantime, East Germany's ratio of national income to capital stock rose from 7.2% in 1950 to 15.7% in 1989 despite over a 10% drop in its population over that time period (Statistisches Amt, 1990) and despite the fact that the East German capital stock started out at an extremely low level because of capital seizures by the Soviet Union after World War II (Harmssen, 1951).

8. While the united capitalist Germany did not place much value on cleaning up the environment in East Germany, it did find it important to "clean" out communist political monuments. For instance, an expensive (and popular) recreational building in East Berlin (Palast der Republik) was closed down ostensibly because of asbestos in the structure, even though the chance of a person being hit by lightening was three times higher than the chance of someone living in the building for 20 years being inflicted with an asbestos-related disease (von Schnitzler, 1992).

9. While pollution per capita was substantially higher in East Germany than in West Germany with respect to sulfur oxide (largely due to East Germany's heavy use of its domestic coal resources to meet much of its energy needs), pollution per capita with respect to nitrogen oxide and hydrocarbons was on about the same level, and extremely high smokestacks in East Germany dissipated some of the concentrated effects of East Germany's pollutants (Buck, 1996). While East Germany spent about 1% less of National Income on pollution control and environmental protection than West Germany (Welfens, 1992), it also had developed a system that in some respects caused less pollution. For instance, because of East Germany's emphasis on rail and mass transportation, there were fewer automobiles per capita to cause pollution than in West Germany (Welfens, 1992). Moreover, the typical East German car (the Trabant of older design vintage) emitted only 1/10 as much nitrogen oxide as the average West German car, and although the Trabant did produce far more hydrocarbons (Kusch et al., 1991), which contribute to dangerous global warming, hydrocarbons have been shown to actually have a beneficial effect on the all-important earth ozone layer that blocks out the sun's ultraviolet rays, and it is nitrogen oxide which has the more long-term damaging effects (U.S. Congress, 1987). Although the anticommunist Buck (1996) was able to find evidence of fluorocarbon (FC) pollutants emanating from East Germany (probably caused by its heavy chemical industry), it is chlorofluorocarbons (CFCs), emanating especially from air conditioners as well as Western chemical and electronics industries, that cause especially heavy and long-term damage on the ozone layer (U.S. Congress, 1987), and East Germany's lack of air conditioners certainly limited its CFC pollution. While water pollution in East Germany probably did exceed that of West Germany (Buck, 1996), it should be mentioned that many pollution problems exist in West Germany (especially with respect to chemical pollution) that have not been widely investigated (Welfens, 1992). In addition, it should also be noted that East Germany was probably the most polluted of the Eastern European communist states, as the rest of Eastern Europe (especially the USSR) had placed a relatively greater emphasis on the environment and nuclear power than East Germany which had emphasized economic growth (Medvedev, 1991), at least partially in an apparently futile attempt to reduce the ability of West Germany to buy its workers with the allure of greater wealth.

10. The rights of citizens to protest against government policies and against government bureaucrats or politicians were fairly widespread in communist Eastern Europe, and the communist systems not only allowed such protests but actually encouraged them to reduce the occurrence of "departures from legality," "arbitrary acts," and "abuse of power by agencies of public administration" (Bader and Brompton, 1968).

11. Hitler employed a similar procedure to essentially outlaw German Jews in the 1930s (and thereby caused several hundred thousand of them, or about half, to emigrate from Germany) by forbidding Jews to work for anyone but Jews and by destroying most Jewish businesses (Chalk and Jonassohn, 1990). Hitler's system was similar to the West German one in other respects as well, insofar as "ordinary Germans" (who were not Jewish, communists, or otherwise hated by the Nazi leaders) "had little to fear from the Nazis" (Associated Press, 2000h), just as "ordinary Germans" (who are not communists or otherwise hated by the West German capitalist leaders for some reason) have little to fear from direct persecution by West German leaders.

12. The difference in the views of the various East German political parties in parlia-

ment was about as small as that between the main political parties of West Germany, the CDU and the SPD. The situation in the USA is not much different, with the Democrats being so similar to the Republicans that they are often called "Republicrats" (Strobel and Peterson, 1999).

13. This finding is consistent with a statement made by a former centrist prime minister (of Italy) in reference to a scandal about secret illegal financing of conservative political parties in Germany, "Democracy is the system that is most exposed to corruption, simply because it's the one that is most expensive" (Kamm, Rohwedder, and Trofimov, 2000). The worst excesses of the East German leaders have been stated to be their use of East German state land for hunting purposes during vacations (Krenz, 1990), as well as their consumption of some West German goods, some of which may have been given to them as presents. For instance, the leader of East Germany from 1971-89 was given gifts of 14 Western cars from Western European governments and firms, but he handed them all over to the East German government (Honecker, 1994). There was one East German who was rumored to have looted billions of Marks of wealth from East German investments in Western countries, but West Germany protected him from prosecution, possibly because he had been engaging in any such illegal activities with the cooperation, encouragement, and active participation of West Germany (*Super*, 1991).

14. Even many East German communist leaders ignored, and continue to ignore, the all-important reparations issue (Krenz, 1990), possibly earlier out of fear of causing discontent with their former Soviet ally and protector, and possibly now out of belief in (and/or fear of repression if they espouse opinions contrary to) the ruling Western propaganda, through which the anticommunist rich attempt to control the overall opinions of the German people just as in the rest of the world (Foerstel, 2000). As mentioned in the text, the West German press (both right-wing and moderate left-wing) has long been manipulated by the CIA (Agee and Wolf, 1975). In addition, although capitalist Germany has many "independent" newspapers (Hintereder and Zips, 2000), they tend to be owned by rich capitalists, and even the capitalist press itself has pointed out the enormous control exerted over the media by rich conservatives (*Der Spiegel*, 1994). Capitalist German television and cable themselves are in the hands of the capitalist government and two large corporate media conglomerates, and all of the major media of former East Germany has naturally (and strategically) been taken over by large West German companies (Hintereder and Zipf, 2000).

CHAPTER 3

1. *Webster's* (1992) cites Soviet World War II deaths of 7 million civilians and 11 million soldiers. As explained in the Introduction, the former numbers may greatly underestimate the total civilian deaths from all causes. Of the latter, over 6 million Soviet soldiers were killed in action, a further half million Soviet soldiers died of disease and other causes, and over 4 million Soviet soldiers died in Nazi captivity or remained missing after the war (Krivosheev, 1997). In spite of these losses, the Soviet Union never conducted terror bombings or mass murder of unarmed German civilians (Urlanis, 1971), whereas the USA (itself untouched by war) savagely bombed the civilian populations of both Germany and Japan in terrorist aerial attacks that included both firebombings and atomic bombs designed to inflict maximum civilian casualties (Marku-

sen and Kopf, 1995). It should also be mentioned that the USA's terror bombings of civilian targets only increased the fascists' will to resist (Schulz, 1982). For example, despite several years of intensive aerial attacks, German armaments production was at its highest level ever in July 1944, and it declined thereafter only because of lost production and raw materials from territories seized by ground forces (Speer, 1970). In addition, it must be remembered that the USA essentially only entered into World War II to protect its Pacific colonies and not for any humanitarian reasons (Copeland, 2000). Even Hawaii at the time of the Japanese attack on Pearl Harbor in 1941 was not yet a state, and the seizure of that territory in the late 1800s by USA businessmen backed by Marines was so blatantly imperialistic (even by USA standards) that it continues to be challenged legally (Associated Press, 1996c). Similar to the USA's terrorist war on the German civilian population, the USA's terror bombings of Japanese cities and the USA's widespread killing of Japanese prisoners of war merely increased the will of the Japanese to fight to the end (Dower, 1986). Japan finally surrendered about a week after being attacked militarily by the Soviet Union (Werth, 1964), which confronted the main body of the Japanese army in Asia and thereby suffered in a brief time about 10,000 battle deaths (Krivosheev, 1997), which represented over 1/30 of the losses of the USA for the entire war on all fronts from all causes.

2. One of the most important weapons was the media, which was probably more successfully, and definitely more subtly, employed by the West. For instance, the distorted, one-sided reporting by the most influential Western press is especially effective because most aren't even aware of how they are manipulated by the Western mainstream media, which is owned by a rich concentrated few, which relies heavily on the reports of government agencies like the CIA, which can be pressured by rich corporate advertisers to disseminate only anticommunist views, and which reflects the natural self-interest of the most valuable rich advertisers and "customers" who have been indoctrinated since birth with anti-communism, but which allows for some "dissent" in the form of negative reporting on some controlled and relatively unimportant issues (Herman and Chomsky, 1988). In addition, the USA dominates the media in most countries of the world not only through Hollywood's market share of movies (*Economist,* 1999a) but also via the extensive use of USA TV programs in countries outside the USA, translated or subtitled in countries that don't use English, and the "independent" media of other countries (whether private or government controlled) is becoming more and more like the USA media (Foerstel, 2000). Exploiting this control, television and Hollywood films (as well as even cartoons) tend to always show the capitalist USA to be the "good guy" that always wins in the end, even if the "good guys" have some minor correctable problems or suffer temporary setbacks. Possibly as a result of this brainwashing system, Harvard University professor Cornel West has concluded, "the mainstream population is looking for happy endings, like in Disneyland. America is growing old and big without growing up" (Murray, 2000). Moreover, the violence of Hollywood films and TV promote the perception that the USA's long history of continuing violence is justified to overcome evil villains (with the true comprehensive evil of the USA itself explained in this book never being portrayed). Because of the hypnotic power of such media and the extensive amount of time Americans and others spend watching television, the repetitiveness of the theme causes many people to believe in such even when they might be aware that individual shows or films are fiction. The media thereby create what Hast-

ings (1999) calls a "gullible electorate" that can be easily manipulated to support USA terrorist attacks on countries like Yugoslavia in 1999. Media portrayal of violence also more subtly serves the purpose of encouraging violence in defense of USA capitalist "morals" and helps to develop the soldiers, police, and right-wing terrorists that are needed to keep repressed those who disagree with USA capitalist world domination, while violence programming (along with sex and sports shows) also achieves the goal of channeling youth protest away from anti-capitalist activities (Saadawi, 2000). The media also more generally provides a distraction from issues that might lead to anti-capitalist political discussions (Foerstel, 2000).

3. One of the primary battlefronts was the propaganda war, which was probably waged more deceitfully and successfully by the West. For instance, when the Eastern bloc of countries started to win an extraordinary number of medals at the Olympic games in the 1970s due to superior motivation (as the communist athletes enjoyed the process and challenge of the sport, which has been found to spur 6 times more effective performance than the incentives offered Western athletes in the form of fame and money), the Western bloc of nations blamed the communist successes on doping the athletes with drugs, even though drug tests revealed less than 0.01% of the athletes had used drugs of any sort, and even though the test finding of two athletes having drugs in their body was consistent with them having taken only harmless antihistamine tablets (Williams, 1995). In comparison, steroid and other illegal drug use by athletes in the Western countries appears to be much more prevalent (Rozin, Flynn, and Durcanin, 1995). Nevertheless, Western countries are generally still considered to be the "good guys" on this issue, in spite of other negative facts like the existence of a huge worldwide narcotics trade sponsored by USA intelligence services (Stich, 1994), and like the close connection between British capitalists and the drug trade in their colonies prior to USA world domination (Gopal, 1963). One reason for the continued belief in the USA as the "good guy" is the fact that those Americans who have called the official anti-communist religion into question (including professors) have often been fired (Smith, 2000).

4. Besides outright mass murder and other blatant atrocities (as previously documented in the Introduction), the USA also victimized many people using more discrete methods, such as clandestine assassinations, druggings, and hypnosis, which are often implemented through religious cults that they use as fronts, and that they typically finance with profits made from distributing illegal narcotics in the USA and elsewhere (Constantine, 1995). Bowart (1978), Schulz (1982), and Stich (1994) provide substantial documented evidence of these facts. Books by Agee and Wolf (1975), Stockwell (1978), Prouty (1992), and Reed and Cummings (1994) provide inside information on these issues presented by former CIA agents, while Milan (1989) and Giancana and Giancana (1992) provide some personal accounts of important mafia connections with the USA secret police. Furiati (1994) has provided very interesting documentation and perspective on how the Mafia/CIA alliance assassinated an elected USA President (JFK), who wasn't right-wing enough for that criminal consortium, especially on policies related to the criminals' desire to overthrow the Castro government in Cuba. In an attempt to discredit such facts that are in conflict with the mainstream lies and propaganda spread by the capitalist press and USA government officials, the CIA itself covertly promotes the spreading of some very absurd conspiracy theories (Constantine,

1995), such as invasions by aliens and other nonsense reported in publications like the *National Enquirer* (Associated Press, 1999b). However, despite the CIA's disinformation campaign, it has not been possible to totally dupe Americans. For instance, surveys indicate that the majority of Americans believe that the CIA has engaged in various actions against its own people, such as murdering President Kennedy and importing narcotics (Scripps Howard News Service, 1997). In addition, even though the CIA is able to use bribes, extortion, and arbitrary mention of "national security" reasons to purge any damaging evidence from being admissible in court (Stich, 1994), some conspiracies between the CIA and organized crime (such as the assassination of Martin Luther King Jr. in order to stop his anti-war activities during the Vietnam War) have been proven beyond a reasonable doubt in court (Associated Press, 1999g).

5. Even the very limited choice provided by West German elections tends to be controlled by money, marketing, and personalities (Schumacher, 1998). Some of the money used to finance the "election" of conservative political leaders like Helmut Kohl (the "unification" chancellor) has been contributed illegally and secretly, and Kohl himself would rather pay a multimillion dollar fine than reveal the actual source of the money (*Wall Street Journal,* 2000d). Although I have not been able to provide any documentation to support the claim (and so it may not be true), I heard from one Neonazi several decades ago that Kohl (who was not yet chancellor at the time) was being financed (and controlled) with Nazi money in the 1970s. This hypothesis is consistent with some of the rumors that have been publicized indicating the West German secret police as the source of some of the money, especially since some contributions to Kohl's party have been documented to have been bribes to facilitate German weapons exports (Schulte, 2000), and since the West German secret police has long used both weapons smuggling and Nazi money to fund its operations (Schmidt-Eenboom, 1995). Also magnifying the shadiness of the affair has been an official accusation that a good attorney friend of Kohl's has been helping drug traders, dictators, and the Russian mafia launder their illegal money through Liechtenstein (AFP, 2000).

6. The USA has continued to influence West German politics via CIA propaganda and manipulation (Agee and Wolf, 1975). Political machinations (whether controlled by outside powers or domestic capitalists) have long characterized capitalist countries and ensured their continued rule, as documented by Zinn (1995). For instance, in order to deflect attention away from any proposals for a more complete redistribution of wealth and power away from the rich, capitalists are motivated to channel disagreement and conflicts into issues relating to how to divide up the tiny amount of wealth not owned by the rich few, and racism often results, as poor and middle class whites struggle with others for a larger share of the tiny portion of the pie allotted to them (Strobel and Peterson, 1999). Besides detracting discussion away from more important issues to less important ones, many capitalist "democracies" are also very effective in concentrating public attention on candidate personalities as opposed to real issues (Foerstel, 2000). By doing so, politicians who promise to undertake policies less attractive to voters often win elections because of their charisma or personality, or because enough dirt on opposing candidates is either dug up or fabricated to make them undesirable for many voters. In addition, representative "democracy" (as opposed to direct democracy where the people directly vote on important issues) creates the potential for candidates to either camouflage or lie about the true policies they intend to carry out, with one survey indi-

cating that over 80% of the American people believe that their leaders don't tell the truth (Zinn, 1995). This fact creates a further distraction from the issues, as many vote for those who are thought to be most honest in keeping their promises, regardless of the actual content of their policies. This "democratic" system often results in elections representing nothing more than a choice between rival rich factions, which use their wealth to manipulate voters to give them control of the government so that they can obtain even bigger relative shares of the aggregate pie (Copeland, 2000). As a result of this manipulated political system, the winner of the 1998 Fulbright prize for "International Understanding" has stated that many people in capitalist "democracies" have lost faith in the political process (and no longer vote) because they perceive little difference between the policies of different candidates (or political parties) and "feel that the really important issues are not in their power to decide" (Azocur, 1998).

7. As previously mentioned in Chapter 1, one reason why the USA and other industrialized capitalist countries were wealthier in 1917 is the long history of imperialism, colonialism, slavery, and other forms of exploitation (enforced by technologically advanced military forces). One of the most important forms of exploitation (imperial, colonial, or otherwise) was carried out using unfair trade practices that were militarily enforced to extract resources from countries for low compensation and that even reduced areas like India and China which were previously relatively rich (with China actually having had a higher standard of living per capita than that of Europe in 1800) into abject poverty (Smith, 2000). Also contributing to income disparities between countries was the failure of many nations (such as Russia) to replace their inefficient feudal systems fast enough (Meurs, 1999). The relative wealth of the Western countries continues to increase by further exploitation in the form of destructive unfair trade policies that inhibit the ability of less developed countries to compete in industries where they have a comparative advantage (*Wochenpost*, 1992a). A general discussion of neocolonialist exploitation can be found in Morgan (1992), while Smith (2000) provides a much more comprehensive analysis of the issue. Ways to overcome neocolonialism can be found in Murphy (1992a) and are further analyzed in Chapter 5.

8. Despite the very negative effect that this treatment had on the East German economy, an association of West German bankers estimated East German GNP per capita had grown to be the eighth highest in Europe by 1989 (*Berliner Morgenpost*, 1990), although it remained significantly less than that in West Germany.

9. Even fairly rich capitalist countries, which have incomes very close to that of the richest countries (and whose citizens, instead of being offered sizable government rewards for leaving, are faced with severe legal restrictions against obtaining a job in the richest countries because of visa and citizenship requirements), can suffer substantial losses in well-educated, costly "human capital" as a result of the richest countries' businesses providing enormous financial incentives for the best talents from the less rich countries to leave. A good example is provided by the large number of engineers from the relatively rich Canada who take jobs in the richer USA (Brenner, 1999).

10. Although it was somewhat cumbersome to cast a vote against the system in East Germany (which required having to draw a line through each candidate's name), the procedure for voting against the system has also been somewhat difficult in the past in the USA. For instance, I personally have made three efforts to register a write-in vote

against the presidential "party slates" in the USA. In two of the three attempts I required the assistance of the voter registration officials, who largely ridiculed my vote publicly, and in the third attempt, I doubt my vote was properly counted. My conversations with East German dissidents who attempted to vote against the party slate before the revolution indicate a similar system in East Germany, where simply marking a ballot with an "X" represented a vote for the candidate list, and where use of a closed voting booth to register a secret ballot was ridiculed by those in the queue who were anxious to return to their own business. In addition, it should also be mentioned that claims of outright fraudulent voter counts have also been alleged in the USA in recent times (Collier and Collier, 1992).

11. Opp and Gern (1993) have estimated 124,500 to 166,000 participants in the October 9, 1989 demonstration in Leipzig. In survey interviews conducted after unification, these investigators stated that the demonstration seemed to be fairly spontaneous without any apparent leaders, although it is interesting to note that their research did not allude at all to the public announcements played on the radio and on loudspeakers essentially condoning the demonstration (implying that either the two Western researchers conducted very superficial interviews, or they have a political agenda that motivated them not to report such seemingly important facts).

12. It is also instructive to see that Western-oriented "free" market advocates, who applauded the Soviet Union's movement to "democracy" under Yeltsin in 1991, provided no opposition to Yeltsin's appointment of his former head of the secret police, Vladimir Putin (who had been a KGB officer in the 1980s), as his successor in 1999 (Cullison, 2000a), although they did formally protest Putin's bringing people with left-wing opinions into the government (Chazan, 2000a). These "freedom" advocates (like the Ukrainians who collaborated with Hitler and who worked with the CIA to enact a violent return of the Nazi "freedom" to exploit and kill) thereby confirmed that their only real concern was about the "freedom" of the marketplace (which, as explained throughout this book, restricts people's freedom and creates an enormous amount of repression and suffering in people's lives).

Chapter 4

1. Many of these problems are magnified in West Germany because the financial markets are less liquid than more developed capitalist markets such as in the USA. However, for private firms in East Germany that operated outside of state control, the cost of capital was even higher than in West Germany because of heavy income taxation (90% for firms that do not supply services or essentials) and legal restrictions on the maximum number of employees (10), as explained in *Der Tagesspiegel* (1989a, 1989d).

2. This estimated purchasing power value of the East German Mark is also consistent with the consumer price inflation figures reported by the West German government, which showed eastern German inflation to be 2% lower than in western Germany in 1990 but 12% higher in 1991 (Statistisches Bundesamt, 1992). These numbers, when combined with the 16% higher inflation in eastern Germany after 1991, imply that the consumer purchasing power of the East German Mark was equal to about 1.28 West German Marks. However, given that such purchasing power might apply to no more than 80% of East German National Income, and given the fact that East German pro-

ducer prices fell by 50% in 1990 to a distressed level well below their true value (van Ark, 1995), the weighted-average aggregate inflation in eastern Germany was likely closer to 15% higher than in western Germany after 1989, implying the 1989 exchange rate of 1.15 West Germany Marks per East German Mark. This estimate may actually be too low, as one West German study indicated that, instead of insignificantly changing during the time around the transformation of the East German Mark into the West German Mark, consumer prices in East Germany actually rose by over 25% between January and July 1990 (Welfens, 1992). Such a figure (combined with the subsequently higher inflation in eastern Germany as its prices continued to rise to western German levels over time), might imply the consumer purchasing power of the East German Mark was equal to that of 1.60 West German Marks (although the latter estimate may not fully adjust for quality differentials).

3. Data inconsistencies on relative living standards (Shmelev and Popov, 1989) caused by the use of official or black market exchange rates can greatly distort real income comparisons because they are extremely poor indicators of true purchasing power, as shown by Sheikh (1976), Schmitt (1980) and Daniel (1986). Such distortions are avoided here because it is possible to use estimated purchasing power parity exchange rates that are verified by the much higher prices that appeared in East Germany when they were denominated in West German Marks compared to East German Marks earlier (*Neues Deutschland*, 1991). While Shmelev and Popov (1989) have hypothesized that the existence of shortages and other problems may make figures from some Eastern European countries suspect, Collier (1985) has found the East German figures to be fairly reliable, even after adjusting for shortages. In addition, although van Ark (1995) estimated East German industrial productivity to be only 30% of that in West Germany, his results are severely biased by an industrial purchasing power comparison that failed to adjust for East Germany's heavy levies on industry to finance consumption good subsidies.

4. Note that the 27% ratio of investment to National Income is measured gross of depreciation, i.e., it includes capital investment undertaken to replace depreciated assets. Investment net of depreciation averaged only slightly over 20% of National Income in East Germany.

5. While individual national account figures in all countries are subject to large error (Morgenstern, 1963), no significant overstatement of output has ever been found for the East German accounts, which Schwarzer (1999) has cited as being as accurate as national accounts for Western countries. Unbiased errors in national income should largely cancel out over the long time interval examined. Although Ritschl (1996) has cited a study indicating that East German output figures may have underweighted some service production (compared to West German weighting) and that East German economic growth may have therefore been overstated by 1% annually, such a reduction in East German growth would still indicate it to be significantly higher than in West Germany. It should also be noted that virtually all of this alleged neglected "output" growth effect is in the area of financial services, which the East German government continuously provided via a very simple, cheap, and efficient system of savings, pensions, and insurance (Merkel and Wahl, 1991), and which can correctly be considered to be a cost of real output (i.e., a cost of allocating funds to future consumption and needs) as opposed to being an output itself (and theoretically should therefore not be included

in the real output computations, since doing so results in an overstating of economic growth for capitalist countries that increase their spending on selling, repackaging, and unnecessarily complicating a basic service that communist systems provide so much more effectively and less confusingly, i.e., with less risk and analysis time lost to the individual). It should also be mentioned that official output accounts in all countries systematically leave out some economic activity, such as unreported output by tax dodgers and other law evaders (some of whom provide useful products or services). Also, official accounts don't take into consideration most of the output produced by individuals and families for themselves (this latter unreported output was probably much higher for East Germany, since shortages there motivated individuals to do many things on their own instead of purchasing them, as commercially sold consumer services made up a relatively small portion of National Income because the dominating state businesses put far more resources into production).

6. Some, such as Merkel and Wahl (1991) and Schwarzer (1999), have suggested that the actual prices paid for all goods should be adjusted for a price ratio determined by some very narrowly-traded products when estimating the actual inflation rate needed to deflate nominal output to compute real output growth. However, even an anticommunist propagandist like Ritschl (1996) has called such an arbitrary, biased, and inaccurate practice "obviously questionable," especially since the chosen traded goods did not include big essentials like housing, which East Germany heavily subsidized. The use of such exchange rates to evaluate relative income, living standards, and output is about as ridiculous as using the black market exchange rate, which had only a very narrow use and varied widely, being as high as 20 East German Marks per West German Mark on the day after the Wall opened up in November 1989 (Nawrocki, 1987), implying an absurd ratio of per capita income in the two countries of about 40 to 1 on that day.

7. This exchange rate is consistent with the cross-rate between East German Marks and West German Marks implied by Stolper's (1960) estimated valuation ratio of 1.748 West German Marks in 1950 per 1936 Reichsmark and his citation of a 1936 Reichsmark having the same purchasing power as 4.186 East German Marks in 1950. These data imply that the East German Mark was worth 1.748/4.186=0.42 West German Marks at that time. Although a drastic reduction in reparations payments permitted East German consumer prices to be lowered significantly after 1953 (Weber, 1988), the official economic statistics (reported by each country) indicate negligible aggregate inflation (on all output) in both East and West Germany in the 1950s, thus implying approximately the same relative purchasing power (0.42 West German Marks per East German Mark) in 1961 as in 1950. Despite the fact that both East and West Germany initially had the same Mark currency between 1945 and 1947, the USSR (in an attempt to circumvent the USA's refusal to allow West Germany to pay its share of the reparations) had caused East Germany to print excessive amounts of money to pay reparations (Schwarzer, 1999), and the USA reacted by causing West Germany to form a separate currency that was not subject to the reparations-induced inflation of East Germany. As a result, in 1948, after the establishment of separate currencies for East and West Germany, there were over twice as many East German Marks per East German resident as West German Marks per West German resident, and, despite a continued 1:1 official exchange rate (which was only honored for some specified currency trades), the black

market exchange rate was 0.27 West German Marks per East German Mark late in 1948 and fell below 0.2 West German Marks in the early 1950s (Schwarzer, 1999).

8. Many prior studies of relative income may have overestimated relative East German income at various points in the past, at least partially because of an overestimate of the value of the East German Mark in the aggregate (Gregory and Leptin, 1977). Previous research has shown the relative consumption purchasing power of the East German Mark to have generally exhibited a rising trend over time that is consistent with the higher inflation in West Germany, with the currency having been estimated to be worth 0.88 West German Marks in 1973 (Gregory and Leptin, 1977), 1.06 West German Marks in 1980 (Collier, 1985), and values averaging about 1.13 West German Marks in the early 1980s (DIW, 1984). However, these values may not fully incorporate quality differences, and they definitely do not include producer prices, which were much higher in East Germany because of the East German government's taxes on industry to finance subsidization of consumer prices (Schwarzer, 1999). As a result, such past figures overstate the true aggregate economic purchasing power of the East German Mark on those dates and therefore also result in overestimates of the comparative income of East Germany at those times. East Germany itself overestimated its relative per capita income in 1960 to be only 30% below that of West Germany, but this estimate was likely based on its clearly overvalued official 1:1 exchange rate (that it felt necessary to officially support and that also enabled it to make an apparently futile attempt to keep its work force in the country with optimistic statements about relative living standards), whereas actual East German income per capita was probably about 40% of the West German level at that time (Merkel and Wahl, 1991).

9. The relative pricing of goods and services in international trade may also have led to economic advantages for West Germany. For instance, because of superior marketing and protectionist trade policies in West Germany, the West German Mark was often overvalued in the currency markets relative to its purchasing power, and this overvaluation provided West Germany with terms of trade advantages with the rest of the world (Murphy, 1992a). On the other hand, East German terms of trade suffered not only from trade barriers erected by capitalist countries against communist countries (Melzer and Stahnke, 1986) but also from the negative worldwide propaganda leveled against products from communist countries (Szczesny, 2000a) that was both political and economic in content and purpose. East German terms of trade with their larger Russian trading partners, which were determined by negotiation, did not produce any offsetting advantages for East Germany, as slow adjustments to world market prices for many commodity trades provided East European countries with temporary advantages and disadvantages that tended to cancel out (Mendershausen, 1960), until the late 1980s when the USSR began to charge prices for oil that more reflected world market prices (Ritschl, 1996).

10. Whereas other studies have also shown economic growth in less developed countries to be higher under communism than under capitalism (Dietz, 1976), the finding of this chapter is especially important because it compares two relatively advanced, industrialized economies. This comparison of real economic growth measures relative efficiency in aggregate terms of mobilizing and managing resources. Comparative return on capital figures are not separately analyzed in this paper because marginal returns to capital are often more a function of the percent of national income allocated to invest-

ment, the amount of labor per unit of capital employed, and the quality of the capital (i.e., the technology level) than of financial efficiency.

11. This official economic blackmail was supported by a massive number of individual militant threats of physical violence made unofficially and illegally against representatives of other political parties, especially against the communists (*Der Tagesspiegel*, 1990n), who nevertheless mustered almost 20% of the vote, and who have continued to receive about 1/5 of the vote in eastern Germany throughout the subsequent elections of the 1990s (Autorenkollektiv, 1995).

12. An indication of the effectiveness of the West German election strategy is provided in surveys. In mid-December 1989, 71% of all East Germans were in favor of Socialism, and 73% were for preserving the East German state independent of West Germany (Bahrmann and Links, 1994). By February 1990, the number of East Germans in favor of unification had risen dramatically to 76%, although only 11% would have voted for the West German conservative parties at that time (*Der Tagesspiegel*, 1990g).

13. Surveys of other Eastern European countries reveal similar levels of dissatisfaction with capitalism, with at least half of all Eastern Europeans believing that they were better off under communism (*Investors Business Daily*, 1993). Capitalist media propaganda, the costs and risks associated with turning back, threats of Western boycotts, and political repression have so far kept Eastern European countries from returning to their prior system, as explained throughout this book.

14. The destruction of the economy in the eastern provinces is also used to make the residents there feel inferior, subservient, and powerless. A typical example of the misleading nature of this psychological warfare can be found in the agricultural sector, where heavy West German government subsidization of family farms (*Economist*, 1991) made it very difficult for the East German collective farms to compete in the New Order of "free trade." As a result, agricultural production fell by 1/3 in the eastern provinces in the year after unification (*Frankfurter Allgemeine*, 1991). According to conservative West German propagandists, this collapse of East German agriculture stemmed from the "inefficiency" of collective farms! While East German agricultural output per hectare of land and per farm worker was significantly less than in West Germany, even West German anticommunists admit that one contributing cause was the far lower level of mechanization of East German farms (Thiele, 1998). This situation in turn reflected the lower level of capital and wealth in East Germany in general (stemming, once again, from its reparations payments), so that East German agriculture and collectivization may very well have been very efficient for its level of resources. For instance, East Germany had only 1/6 as many harvest combines per acre as West Germany in the 1980s (Kusch et al., 1991) but harvested about ½ as much agricultural output per farm worker (Thiele, 1998). Some studies have indeed discovered Eastern European agricultural collectives to be relatively efficient (Meurs, 1999), including in East Germany (Gregory and Leptin, 1977), and even in cases where private farming has appeared to be more productive, the cause may well be better land and weather, more mechanization, and other input advantages, as Thiele and Brodersen (1999) found when comparing agricultural productivity in eastern and western Germany.

15. These figures represent additional amounts that would have to be spent over and above the costs that are currently being incurred for these undesirable characteristics

of capitalism. For instance, in the capitalist USA, over 10% of GDP is currently spent or lost due to crime. In particular, approximately 2% of GDP is spent on public law-enforcement (including for over half a million public police, as well as for criminal court and prison costs), approximately 3% of GDP is lost in the form of stolen property (largely paid for by higher insurance premiums), and about 5% of GDP is lost due to the medical costs, suffering, and lost wages of victims of violent crime (*US News & World Report*, 1994). Another 1% of GDP is spent on private security, including for well over a million security guards (Reynolds, 1994). Evidence of the fact that capitalism causes crime is provided by Japan, which has moved toward a more market-oriented society in the 1990s with all its side-effects of unemployment and homelessness, and the result has been an enormous increase in crime (Tyson, 1998).

16. Legal proceedings have actually found corruption among the East German leaders to be fairly trivial (in comparison to the corruption in West Germany or America), usually involving only privileged use of vacation spots in East Germany, or acceptance of gifts from the West, whose value could be measured in thousands of Marks (Krenz, 1990).

CHAPTER 5

1. Having first fallen by over 40% to under 2/5 that of western German output per capita between 1989 and 1991 (back to the 1960 ratio), output per capita in eastern Germany experienced a brief rapid spurt of growth in the mid-1990s (driven by tax-incentives provided by the united German government to invest into eastern Germany). However, this short-term rapid growth raised output per capita to only about half that of western Germany where it has since stabilized at a level well below the 2/3 ratio of 1989.

2. Deviations between market exchange rates and purchasing power parity exchange rates can occur not only due to barriers to trade (including transportation costs and marketing/distribution expenses, as well as artificial barriers such as tariffs and quotas) but also due to the existence of nontradable goods and services like housing (Kravis and Lipsey, 1988).

3. Simply giving citizens shares in state-owned companies that they can immediately sell may not only lead to mass sales at distressed prices but might also cause excessive consumption and inflation (Ciampi, 1998). The plan actually used in eastern Germany simply had the German government sell off all state-owned assets as soon as possible to private investors and utilized the very limited proceeds from this distressed sale of capital to slightly reduce the enormous costs of unification incurred. Although the overall plan used has led to a depression which resulted in less outside capital investment than initially forecast, almost all of the existing capital stock in the eastern part of Germany is now owned by entities outside eastern Germany (*Der Spiegel*, 1997b).

4. Osmond (1992) reports that the Deutsche Bank and five other German institutes estimated the decline in real GNP to be over 40% in eastern Germany in 1990-91. Although official German government sources indicate National Income in the former East German provinces to have fallen from only 275 billion Marks to 181 billion Marks between 1989 and 1991 (Statistisches Bundesamt, 1992), prices in eastern Germany rose by an estimated 13.8% over that same 2-year interval, as estimated by five West German financial and economic research institutions (Osmond, 1992). In real terms

then, national income fell by 1-[{181/1.138}/275]=42.2%. This measure of the decline does not even take into consideration the fact that, after unification, the German government expropriated East Germany's M1.7 trillion in government-owned capital stock, which theoretically belonged to the East German people (as did all the land of East Germany), and gave most of it (and much of the land) to investors outside eastern Germany, who made non-binding pledges (many of which were not fulfilled) of investing additional capital, and who took most of the existing East German capital out of operation due to their own excess capacity (*Der Spiegel,* 1990b). As a result, most of the profit portion of the remaining output no longer belonged to the eastern Germans.

5. After unification, the united German government also offered significant tax incentives to invest into eastern Germany, such as heavy depreciation tax shields, which permitted tax savings to the equity investors that exceeded the amount put up by them in cash in the first year. However, these incentives often led to uneconomic investments that rewarded investors with the greatest potential tax savings for expensive and unproductive but depreciable buildings (such as superfluous and expensive retail outlets) that were constructed on the cheapest land (*Der Spiegel,* 1997a).

6. The German government has estimated that each unemployed person costs the government DM38,000 annually in transfer payments and lost tax revenue (Schlitz, 1998). With over 5 million less people working in eastern Germany after unification than before, that alone costs Germany around DM200 billion per year.

7. Actual foreign investment rules in East Germany imposed a 25% tax rate on profits for joint ventures with foreign participation not exceeding 49%, while terms were negotiable for foreign ownership levels above 49% (Buero des Ministerrates, 1985). In either case, East Germany could take at least a 50% share of the profits via either taxation or profit sharing (in the joint venture form, East Germany would normally provide its share of capital in the form of free lease of land and permits to do business, as well as guaranteed trained labor at set prices).

8. Another possible way to reduce any extraordinary withdrawals from savings initially would be to treat all monies in existing savings accounts as a separate inconvertible M currency that could neither be used to convert into DM nor to invest into the mandated savings accounts required to exchange into DM (thus requiring all DM exchanges to be made only with future income until it was economically feasible to make the M fully convertible). Alternatively, the government could rule that anyone using their existing savings balance to purchase DM would have a proportionate reduction in their share of the East German government mutual fund. However, such procedures would add a potentially unnecessary layer of confusion and might reduce confidence in the system.

9. The tax rate on profits was actually 5% higher (at 95% on profits above M250,000) if the private business was involved in manufacturing (Buero des Ministerrates, 1970). Although the maximum tax rate on wages was only 25% (Buero des Ministerrates, 1966), controls placed by the state on wages limited the opportunities to avoid the high profit tax by paying out high salaries to relatives and friends. It is quite possible, especially within this environment, that, instead of investing the cash savings from utilizing the black markets, East Germans could use the money to purchase even more DM on the black markets in order to buy more Western goods and services. For reasons men-

tioned earlier in this subsection, the overall results of the plan would still not be affected because such imports would only replace some of the export subsidies that otherwise would have to occur (and at a cheaper cost to the economy).

10. It might also be possible to pay West German banks a fee in order to entice them to conduct 1:1 exchanges and turn over the DM so obtained (less the fee) to the East German government. Black market exchanges could be discouraged by threatening lawsuits and banning black market dealers and currency smugglers from entering or doing business with East Germany. Increasing the penalties for black market exchanges (especially imprisonment) would also inhibit such activities, as might some public relations effort by the government that spread the message of how damaging and criminal such theft activities are. In addition, the policy could be continued of requiring foreigners to make minimum 1:1 official exchanges with the East German government (DM25 in the late 1980s) for each day a foreigner was in that country, although that policy had been shown to decrease West German visitors by about 40% (Melzer and Stahnke, 1986). Alternatively, foreigners (including West Germans) could be required to pay for all goods and services in East Germany with DM (at a 1:1 exchange rate) and denote all such purchases with a DM sign on receipts (thereby ensuring that the cashiers and businesses did indeed turn over the DM to the government). To enforce the latter system of foreigners paying only with DM, East German businesses (and border guards) could be required to periodically request customers to show identity documents in order to increase the risk to the foreigners of getting caught trying to pay (or having paid) with M which they could only obtain on the black markets (increased acceptance of credit cards at East German shops would also help here). A somewhat similar identity control procedure was used before 1961 that prohibited West Germans from using East German ration cards, although the system at that time was designed to prohibit all West German purchases of subsidized goods, even with DM, and although the system was not totally effective due to inadequate controls of cashiers and businesses (Falck, 1998). East Germany also engaged in some spot identity checks at shops for a few weeks in 1990, but the procedure was made ineffective because the requests for identification were very infrequent, because the system allowed foreigners to pay in M as long as they showed a receipt indicating that they had exchanged money with an East German bank at the official 3:1 rate at any time in 1990 so that foreigners were able to avoid more than one official exchange by using the same receipt whenever asked (*Der Tagesspiegel,* 1990i), and because even the 1990 official exchange rate itself (3:1) tripled East Germany's cost of earning a DM (which was already high due to the fact that the foreigners typically purchased goods and services that were subsidized by the East German government to sell at very low prices).

11. There is also a risk that demand for East German exports might be inelastic relative to West German inflation and thereby require East Germany to expend more resources to generate exports sufficient to pay for the same level of real West German imports whenever West German prices rose. However, Murphy's (1992b) study indicated that the M cost of generating a DM1.0 of exports did fall significantly with West German inflation, even though it was not a full one-to-one drop. Given that East German imports of West German goods were generally concentrated in high-tech areas such as electronics whose prices tend to rise less than with the overall economy (and often even fall), it is actually more likely that the cost of paying for the same amount of real

imports would actually go down instead of up with changes in relative prices.

12. Many of the West German quotas were informally agreed to by East Germany whenever it attained a significant market share of over 5%, as West Germany threatened to impose formal binding quotas otherwise (Melzer and Stahnke, 1986). This imposed practice certainly inhibited East Germany from obtaining adequate economies of scale in exporting. In addition, the political and consumer biases against East German goods (and the restrictions on developing their own distribution channels) gave Western firms greater bargaining power when determining the prices paid to East German suppliers, whereas a shortage of (and need for) hard currency put the East Germans in a very poor bargaining position (Heimann, 1997). For instance, Western companies could extract a much higher portion of the final price of products for their Western distribution systems because consumers and retailers would normally prefer not to buy products "made in East Germany" (the ideological enemy) when they could obtain similar products for a similar price elsewhere (such as from Asia). An elimination of such biased and unfair treatment, along with the increased economies of scale that often are necessary to even get unprejudiced products in capitalist retail stores (Associated Press, 1999f), would further increase East Germany's net hard currency revenues.

13. Although the ability of East German firms to earn DM revenues was dramatically impaired by the rise in the DM after 1984 (Mueller, 1989), this negative trend could not be expected to continue and could easily have reversed itself (and did eventually). In addition, East Germany's M cost of earning US dollars actually was fairly stable over the 1984-1989 interval. As a result, despite a large amount of trade with West Germany, East Germany's overall terms of trade (export prices divided by import prices) only deteriorated by 2% over the 1985-89 interval (Statistisches Amt, 1990) because the rise in the DM also reduced the DM cost of goods imported into East Germany.

14. In East Germany, in early 1990, one retail business did successfully develop an official policy of requiring foreigners to pay higher prices (three times higher) than East Germans (*Der Tagesspiegel,* 1990d), but this policy was not widespread enough (nor lasted long enough) to have much effect. Historically, the Soviet Union had also had a very popular rationing policy in the 1920s and early 1930s that was somewhat similar, insofar as it allowed Soviet citizens to purchase a limited amount of specified items (such as bread) at below-market prices (Davies, 1997). Communist China's economy is also characterized by a system that allows for limited purchases of goods at low prices while permitting market prices for excess production (Lau, Qian, and Roland, 2000).

15. Some evidence of how much net emigrations would change once personal wage-differentials were no longer motivating factors is provided by the fact that there were only 25,000 more East German retirees who had decided to move to West Germany than West German retirees who had decided to emigrate to East Germany in the 1980s when there were no restrictions on retiree emigrations and when pension income was fixed to be the same for retiree emigrants in both countries (Melzer and Stahnke, 1986). Even here, however, it must be taken into account that a West German retiree would normally have much higher pension income (based on his/her prior wages) than an East German, and so emigration to East Germany resulted in a decline in West German retirees' income that certainly discouraged such emigrations. Also affecting pensionees' choice of residence was the existence of additional sources of retiree income, such as

payments from rich West German relatives (or others) for emigrating from East Germany.

16. A somewhat radical group of environmentalists was actually demanding that 200 billion Marks be invested into the East German environment over a period of 5 years, but their requests included many unrealistic (and counterproductive) demands such as the replacement of all nuclear power plants (*Der Tagesspiegel,* 1990e). Many countries with relatively low income per capita tend to spend less on the environment, and therefore have less clean air, water, and landscaping, because most people at low income levels generate more utility from higher income than from a cleaner environment.

17. Osmond (1992) has estimated the amount of East German hard currency foreign debt at $18.5 billion in 1989, which represents about DM30 billion, although his figures were not netted out with East German hard currency foreign assets (these assets included East German foreign businesses, export receivables, and assets obtained but not yet consumed by draw-downs of special credits offered by West Germany shortly after the opening of the Wall late in the year, as well as normal foreign exchange reserves). For instance, East German businesses in West Germany alone had annual sales of over DM3 billion at the end of the 1980s (*Der Spiegel,* 1991), and the value of these business along with the foreign currency assets of the East German export bank totaled over DM12 billion in November 1989 (Haendcke-Hoppe-Arndt, 1996). While Hertle (1996) reported total foreign debt of 49 billion Marks in 1989 for East Germany, this amount includes various amounts of soft currency debts owed to other Eastern European and third world countries (which were much easier to repay at a lower M export cost), and it is also not netted out with foreign assets. For instance, Mittag (1991) reported that most of the over 6 billion transferable rubles in Soviet debt to other Eastern European countries in 1990 was owed to East Germany, and this amount represented almost 30 billion Marks at official commercial exchange rates. Given that the substantial amount of money lent to East Germany after the opening of the Wall was spent in the first 5 months of 1990 (to cover the large trade deficit that had arisen because of the country's failure to use the policy recommended in this chapter), the cited text estimate of DM20 billion in net East German debt at the end of 1989 is consistent with the DM27 billion in East German debt reported by the West German central bank for the end of May 1990 (Haendcke-Hoppe-Arndt, 1996). These figures are also consistent with the DM28 billion in debt reported by the East German government in mid-1990 (Schwarzer, 1999), which represented a time after unification negotiations had been finalized with the newly elected East German government that was politically allied (and effectively unified) with the West German government.

18. One special problem not considered in the analysis was the West German government decision after unification to reimburse those whose properties had been nationalized by the East German government at various times. In this process, the original owners (many of whom were West Germans) were treated like anyone else in the bidding for such properties, but they received financial compensation if they did not win the auction that took into consideration the bidders' pledges of employment and additional capital investment (Osmond, 1992). This transfer of wealth does not seem necessary or justified although it alone probably did not materially affect output.

19. Note that Czechoslovakia (and later the Czech Republic) did indeed adopt some

economic policies similar to the Murphy (1992a) plan (a copy of the plan was given to Czech government officials early in 1990). Consumption imports were restricted, foreign capital investment was thereby encouraged, and consumption of domestic output was subsidized with a policy that was generally followed by most businesses to charge domestic customers a price (written in Czech and therefore unreadable for most foreigners) that was far lower than the price charged to foreigners (and was very popular with Czech citizens). Despite the bias against foreigners, the Czech Republic successfully attracted an enormous number of tourists and tourist spending (Wiedemann, 1996). Possibly as a result, Czechoslovakia was the most successful of the Eastern European countries in initially avoiding GNP declines (Kempe, 1991a). Extensive privatization of the Czech economy in 1991 (i.e., the importation of capitalism) and the failure to adopt the most important component of the Murphy plan (that would have mandated savings for each domestic currency conversion into hard currency), along with the collapse of Czechoslovakia's major trading partners elsewhere in Eastern Europe, did cause significant negative economic growth in Czechoslovakia in 1991 and 1992 (*Wall Street Journal,* 1992). However, in spite of economic performance more similar to the rest of Eastern Europe in those two years, the country has shown one of the most rapid economic recovery rates later in the 1990s (IMF, 1998: 181) at the same time that it has been able to eliminate the special pricing rules.

20. The plan may be especially desirable, since unrestricted markets tend to result in an increase in the disparity between the poor and rich, as shown by Deardorff (1994) and Murphy (1992a). In addition, it is far superior to some of the counterproductive strategies currently in vogue such as government welfare payments, which are clearly inferior to providing jobs and job-related support like subsidized child care (Mead, 2000), and such as government subsidizing the building of casinos and new sports stadiums, which also have no positive impact on job creation or economic growth but only transfer income to the rich (*Investor's Business Daily,* 1997).

Chapter 6

1. For example, in the USA, welfare reform was conducted to finance tax breaks to investors and the richer members of society (*Workers World,* 1997). In addition, the USA's welfare reform policy of the late 1990s often resulted in the replacement of existing workers with virtual workfare "slaves," who effectively had to work for compensation that was less than the minimum wage, and who put downward pressure on wages, while at the same time it did not provide for any childcare or medical coverage for parents forced into workfare (or other) jobs (Cheng, 1997), thus leading to questions about the long-term impact on future generations and their "efficiency." Moreover, while USA factory wages in the 1990s rose only 28%, compensation for the top two executives at the largest companies in the USA rose by nearly 500% (Associated Press, 1999a). About 40% of the enormous financial wealth of the USA is now concentrated in the hands of 1% of the USA's population (Strobel and Peterson, 1999), at the same time that over 10% of Americans "still face hunger as a regular fact of life" (Briscoe, 2000). Relative country poverty has also increased worldwide in this environment, with the UN reporting that nearly half of all the countries in the world have suffered a drop in real income per capita over the last few decades (Catalinotto, 1999), and "twenty-eight billionaires [now] own more than the population of half of the world's countries"

(Flounders, 2000). The growing gulf between rich and poor is expected to continue long-term into the future (Fishman, 1999), although a substantial change in government policies could potentially avoid such a socially disturbing trend (Strobel and Peterson, 1999).

2. The Russian mafia buys politicians themselves via bribes (and threats), and it also controls "democratic" elections of favored politicians with legal campaign donations and extensive media coverage (Raith, 1994). The controlled media typically ignores (or maligns) "undesirable" candidates like communists, while it positively portrays "desirable" capitalist candidates, and it is so successful with this strategy that most voters are often not even aware of negative facts about the "desirable" candidates (Banerjee and Rosett, 1996). Moreover, the Russian mafia engages in widespread outright purchases of votes in the "democratic" elections of politicians who conform to their wishes (Hearst Newspapers, 1996), and there have been allegations of ballots cast for communists being thrown into rivers or otherwise disposed of and not counted (Cullison, 2000b). The Russian mafia also works closely with the Russian government secret police to conduct its murders and other dirty work (*Toronto Globe and Mail*, 1996). Besides mortally wounding some political candidates' chances, the latter activities make threats of "upheavals" if undesirable candidates like communists are elected (Associated Press, 1996b) appear very credible, especially given Western threats of a return to the Cold War if the communists regained power (Griswold, 1996), and especially given the horrible civil war that Western powers caused after the 1917 communist seizure of power (Pipes, 1993). Interestingly enough, the mafia's activities in capitalist Russia are not really very dissimilar to the USA CIA/mafia (Furiati, 1994).

3. Many of the loans are now being sold for 10-20% of book value to foreigners (Rich, 2000), who (being out of the country) are not as exposed to Japanese mafia threats.

4. On the other hand, some have blamed the current account deficits in the crisis countries on prior increases in their real exchange rates, which in turn were caused by fairly inflexible nominal exchange rates not reflecting higher past inflation and wage increases (Dornbusch and Werner, 1994). However, the past real exchange rate changes in the crisis countries tended to be substantially lower than the subsequent real devaluations that were necessary to solve the BOP problem. In addition, Calvo and Mendoza (1996) have studied the Mexican case and found no evidence of the BOP problem being caused by past real wage increases.

5. Calvo and Mendoza (1996) showed that increased political risk had not been the catalyst, although it may have caused investors to require a larger portion of their Mexican debt holdings to be protected against peso depreciation (i.e., with bonds whose peso payments were contractually set to rise with a decline in the value of the peso).

6. China's economic success with capital controls has made financial experts ever more aware of the usefulness of that approach in situations where a current account deficit has been eliminated or does not exist at all (Roach, 1999).

7. It was also initially forecast that real wages would fall by about 10% at the same time that the Brazilian unemployment rate was expected to rise significantly (Katz and Cohn, 1999).

8. The new German managing director of the IMF has openly called the IMF a "for-

ward defense of U.S. interests" (Phillips, 2000b). The head of the IMF is generally a European, but the USA has sufficient voting power and influence over other countries to exercise veto rights over the actual choice (*Wall Street Journal*, 2000c). A European leader of the IMF helps ensure continuity in capitalist exploitation policies, insofar as the IMF effectively assists Europe in maintaining neocolonial control over the former European colonies (i.e., over the less developed countries that need IMF financing because European nations impoverished them during their colonial rule). However, the USA right to make the final decision is consistent with today's reality of overall USA world domination (and also represents a form of continuity given the USA's past and current exploitation of less developed countries, especially in Latin America).

9. One example of such a continuing phenomena in the USA is the Midwestern payment of salaries as much as $10,000 above those in the South for computer specialists, which results in one third of all new jobs in that area going to the Midwest (Stopa, 2000).

10. Capital controls are normally used to reduce capital flight, but they have sometimes been used (in countries like Germany) to maintain more autonomy over their economy and businesses and reduce unwanted currency appreciation (Caves, Frankel, and Jones, 1996).

11. In fact, capital controls can actually result in greatly increased foreign direct investment if the government restrictions lead to healthy economic growth (which attracts foreign capital) and prevent economic catastrophes (which scare off foreign investment). For instance, while Eastern Europe was rapidly reducing currency controls in the early 1990s (Williamson, 1991) and China was doing so only very slowly, the rate of direct foreign capital investment into Eastern Europe was less than 1/10 of the amount going into China (*Europaische Wirtschaft*, 1991). This situation had not changed much by the late 1990s (Liu et al., 1997), even though China still has capital controls (Roach, 1999), and even though over half of all foreign investors in China were not able to earn a profit in that very competitive but rapidly growing market (Smith, 1999). Direct investment into Russia did finally rise modestly by 1999 (Chazan, 2000b) after Russia had reinstituted capital controls and other government interference with free markets (*Economist*, 1999b).

12. Although tax dodges also sometimes create the potential for unproductive loophole schemes, such scams exist even with lower tax rates and simpler tax systems (Smellie, 1999). Regardless, any tax system should be evaluated not only for the negative effects of any incremental unproductive actions for which it creates opportunities but also for the economically productive behavior that it motivates.

13. For instance, one subtle method of protectionism that was allowed (without retaliation) by the forerunner of the WTO (i.e., GATT) is the use of sales taxes (primarily or completely) to finance government expenditures, as opposed to income taxes (Hufbauer and Erb, 1984). Sales taxes, or similar Value Added Taxes (VAT), act as a form of subtle tariff, insofar as such taxes are levied on imports into the country but exports out of the country are not so taxed (whereas income taxes are effectively levied equally on domestic entities producing for the domestic market or for export but are not at all levied on imports into the country). As a result, replacing sales taxes with income taxes makes domestic entities more competitive internationally. For example, assume a

German company and a USA competitor, each with the same costs of production of $7 per unit at current exchange rates, each with a 33% income tax rate, and each with a $2 net profit per unit required in order to cover its capital costs, implying a selling price of $2+$1+$7=$10 for their products. If Germany were to replace its income tax with a sales tax of 10%, the German company would suddenly be able to export its goods for $2+$7=$9, thereby undercutting the USA competitor (which would still have to charge $10 to cover all its costs). In addition, the USA company could not competitively export to Germany because the price it would need to charge would be $10x1.10=$11, whereas the German company could charge a price of $9x1.10=$9.90. In this situation, either the German currency would rise in value, or the German balance of payments situation would improve (or possibly some combination of both). Not only does a sales tax subsidize exports (by removing the tax burden on exporting businesses, as the sales tax is not owed on sales outside the country), it also discourages domestic consumption (by taxing it) and encourages domestic savings (by not taxing the earnings from savings). While such consumption taxes tend to negatively affect the consumption of the poor the most in relative income terms (if applied equally to all products), this regressiveness can be offset with transfer payments, or with the type of coupons proposed in Chapter 5.

CHAPTER 7

1. As explained earlier, the mechanics of the USA propaganda machine is fairly subtle (which is one reason why it is so effective). For instance, the CIA often directly (or indirectly through a front organization that it secretly funds) pays for the publication of a book by a noted person (possibly even with a Ph.D.) that cites mass atrocities committed by communists (or by other USA enemies) based on ridiculous evidence, and the mainstream press then accepts the fabricated events as fact and continually reports them (Herman and Chomsky, 1988). Although there is generally no penalty for printing anticommunist or pro-USA articles even when later proven to be false, and although there is not even a requirement to correct or retract such material once proven untrue, a far more severe system exists for those who print anti-USA or procommunist articles. For instance, two CNN journalists were recently fired for writing a story about the USA killing deserters with nerve gas in the Vietnam War even though the chief critic of the story admitted that the report was possibly true but lacked the enormous evidence that is normally required for printing such stories which put the USA in an unfavorable light (Pope, 1998). It should also be mentioned that the contested issue never was whether the deserters were slaughtered via aerial attacks but whether they were killed with nerve gas or not, and the claim of nerve gas usage was retracted only after CNN was put under heavy pressure by the CIA to accept its "investigative" interpretation of the events (Ayling, 1998). Other reporters printing negative facts about the USA have been fired from their jobs even though subsequent investigations have confirmed their stories (Zinn, 1995), and it only takes a few such examples (as well as positive pressure in the form of Pulitzer Prizes for spreading lies that unjustly vilify the USA's enemies) to ensure journalistic conformity to the system (Foerstel, 2000).

2. While the genocide of Indians is fairly well-recognized, some have argued that many of the Indians died of disease, and their deaths should not be labeled deliberate (Martin, 1978). That argument is comparable to saying someone who consciously

spreads AIDs is innocent since the original person with AIDs was largely just seeking personal enjoyment from the viral invasion (just as the USA only wanted the personal enjoyment of the Indians' land). More importantly, however, that argument ignores all the evidence of deliberate murderous intent on the part of the USA (including publicly announcing a national campaign to exterminate the Indians, USA laws providing rewards for the killing of any and all Indians, the gruesome cases of USA biological warfare, the USA's deliberate destruction of Indian food and water sources, and the USA's use of force to keep Indians away from food and water, as documented in the Introduction to this book). Deaths by disease tend to be maximized under conditions of extreme duress, forced migrations and overcrowding (Levene and Roberts, 1999), and war (Hobhouse, 1989), especially in a campaign of deliberate extermination (like the USA followed), as documented by Thornton (1997). To illustrate the importance of intent here, it is possible to examine the Polynesian peoples in New Zealand called Maori, who were very similar to Indians in terms of being very susceptible to deadly European diseases (as well as in terms of having some democratic communist tendencies), and yet there is some evidence that the European invasion of their country did not even result in a population decline for the Maori because the native people of New Zealand were recognized as humans whom (despite some land theft by the British and some wars with the British invaders) the British never attempted to exterminate (King, 1997). On the other hand, a malicious campaign that exhibited some intent (and effects) similar to (although not nearly as atrocious and deliberate as) that of the USA was Great Britain's policy in Australia, where about half the aboriginal population (or about 200,000 people) was exterminated (Reynolds, 1995). Although only about 10% of the Australian aborigines were killed directly (with most dying instead of hunger and disease as their livable land was stolen by brute force), and although there were never any laws in Australia providing rewards for the extermination of natives as there were in the USA, the deaths of the Australian aborigines can be considered deliberate because the British officially labeled Australia "uninhabited", effectively legalizing the extermination of the aborigines to make way for the settling invaders (Reynolds, 1995), who were effectively only compensated for such killings with free land (and not also with additional monetary rewards as in the USA).

3. Mass murderers have historically often attempted to portray their victims as the evil ones in order to try and justify their own atrocities (Daunton and Halper, 1999). For instance, Jennings (1975) has noted an old argument often made that the Indians in what is now the USA deserved to die because they were savages ruled by dictators who offered human sacrifices to pagan gods, and who even engaged in cannibalism. However, such allegations are generally either totally untrue (Sale, 1991) or based on some very speculative archaeological findings from the ancient past (*Der Spiegel,* 1998). The truth of the matter is that it was the Europeans who engaged in massive numbers of religious executions (Levene and Roberts, 1999), which some estimated numbered hundreds of thousands during the medieval Inquisition (Smith, 2000), and it was the earliest invaders from Europe who, despite gifts of food from Indians, engaged in cannibalism in order to survive the new environment in what is now the USA (Zinn, 1995). In addition, although there were Indians in Latin America who had a dictatorial political system that did offer human sacrifices (Chalk and Jonassohn, 1990), the Indians in what is now the USA did not, and they actually "were much more democratic and allowed

much more freedom to the individual" (Driver, 1961). Indian societies of what is now the USA were also characterized by more equal rights for women, besides exhibiting other widespread signs of social democracy and communism (Zinn, 1995). In fact, Novack (1972) argues that the existence of free communist democracies among the Indians was a primary underlying reason why the USA committed genocide, insofar as the native Americans were too different from the USA's capitalist system to be compatible with the invaders. Regardless, the logic of exterminating an entire people in order to "free" them (or stop a few human sacrifices) is morally incomprehensible to anyone but mass murderers.

4. Note that the figures reported in the Introduction to this book greatly understate the true number of deaths resulting from USA imperialism. In particular, even without considering the victims of pure capitalist exploitation, the number of innocent people killed by USA imperialism is much larger if one includes deaths from disease and starvation that were not deliberately inflicted but that stemmed indirectly from wars initiated and perpetuated by the USA. For instance, UNICEF estimates that over 300,000 children alone have died directly or indirectly as a result of the war in Angola that was begun and has been perpetuated by the USA (Minter, 1994). Moreover, as many as one million people may have been killed in the 1979-89 war in Afghanistan that was launched by terrorists who were financed with about $6 billion worth of weapons from the CIA and whose terrorist activities have now become threatening enough to provoke USA military attacks (Catalinotto, 1998c). Although the CIA-financed terrorists may not have been the only ones committing atrocities in the latter conflict, the Soviet Union had long offered to allow Afghanistan to become a neutral and independent country and to withdraw its troops as long as the foreign-supplied rebels discontinued their terrorist attacks (Girardet, 1985).

5. Despite the fact that even a USA congressional representative recently called the embargo against Iraq "infanticide," USA state department spokesman James Rubin continued with the worldwide propaganda line of blaming the USA holocausts on others, "Saddam is again pushing the canard that sanctions—rather than the misrule and the cynical manipulation of his own people that Saddam Husein propagates—are responsible for the suffering of the Iraqi people" (CNN, 2000a). While the absurd logic in the latter type of USA propaganda (i.e., blaming the leader of the victims for the suffering inflicted upon them by the USA) would seem to be all too apparent to anyone thinking it through, most Americans are already so convinced by the propaganda barrage that they are the "good" guys, they don't even stop to think about it (especially since to do so might cause some mental and social discomfort and distract them from their own personal lives). The result is Americans' tacit consent to a continuation of USA mass murders.

6. The UN has further estimated the cost of providing clean water and sanitation to all those people in the world who don't have such basic necessities to be just $12 billion annually, while the incremental annual cost of making it possible for everyone in the world to have a basic education was calculated to be only $6 billion (Catalinotto, 1999). As mentioned by Ashton et al. (1984), the needed money is not allocated to such important tasks partially because the rich capitalist countries (which could easily afford such aid that would amount to far less than 1% of the GDP of the USA alone, and less

than 15% of the USA's annual military spending) have political inhibitions about giving anything to people in countries whose governments are not agreeable to them (except potentially for propaganda purposes). In addition, the authors even mention a capitalist belief that providing basic necessities like food interferes too much with capitalist market prices and producer incomes (implying that free markets and profits are more precious than human lives).

7. It is not coincidental that one of the worst massacres in the 1990s, Rwanda's killing of a half million Tutsi civilians in 1994, occurred after the standard IMF policy of using tight fiscal and monetary policy to balance the current account had been imposed on Rwanda in 1990 and had greatly impoverished the poor there (Klinghoffer, 1998). The Hutu slaughter of Tutsi civilians had been precipitated by a fight against a band of armed Tutsi rebels whose leaders had been trained in the USA (Ray, 2000), who had received widespread aid from the USA's puppet government in Uganda (Ntamabyaliro, 1999), and who assassinated Rwanda's Hutu leader just before the massacre (Ray, 2000). The Tutsis themselves represented a very small minority group in Rwanda and had previously engaged in mass killings of Hutu civilians in Rwanda (Klinhoffer, 1998), as well as in neighboring Burundi where they, as military rulers, had earlier committed enough mass murders of Hutus in their own country to nearly make the top ten in human exterminations (as documented in footnote 11 of the Introduction). In addition, since 1993 when Tutsi soldiers assassinated Burundi's first elected president (a Hutu), the Tutsis have killed at least 200,000 people, mostly Hutu civilians (Associated Press, 2000a), and they have also massacred many Hutu refugees in the neighboring Congo (Ray, 2000).

8. Note that the theory of comparative advantage as well as supply-and-demand theory (Soedersten and Reed, 1994) can be easily incorporated into this illustrative analysis without affecting the conclusion. For instance, if the rich country is assumed to be the English-speaking USA, and if only a small affluent section of the LDC population is assumed to be educated in English, the English-speaking Americans will naturally have a comparative advantage in producing exotic English labels that are generally in higher demand not only by the richer, English-speaking Americans but also by affluent LDC residents (who may prefer them for status reasons and, despite their higher prices, may be able to afford them because of their higher incomes). On the other hand, the LDC has a comparative advantage in producing generic clothing, which may be preferred by more individuals worldwide, but for which there is very little monetary demand because the people preferring generics tend to be the poor who have very little money to pay for the products. As a result of the low monetary demand for the generic T-shirts, there will be no upward pressure on their prices to change the fact that an American can produce 64 times as much "market value" as an average LDC worker can in the same time period. However, it is important to point out that the illustrative example in the text does not incorporate the higher level of mechanization available to the richer countries that further magnifies real income and wealth accumulation differentials. In particular, assume that more capital-intensive production allows the USA to produce two $8 T-shirts in an hour, with half the income accruing to the worker and half to the investor provider of capital, so that the combined worker and investor can buy 16 generic T-shirts in an hour. Since it would still take the LDC worker 8 hours to create 8 generic $1 T-shirts to earn the money needed to buy one of the exotic $8

T-shirts, and since the USA residents can create 16 exotic T-shirts in the same 8 hours, the USA residents will be able to receive the equivalent of 16x8=128 generic T-shirts in the same 8 hours that it takes the LDC worker to earn 1 exotic T-shirt, for a 128:1 real income differential (versus *only* 64:1 before considering the effect of mechanization).

9. Despite the cruelty of the Europeans, with respect not only to Africans, but also in earlier Roman times (Brownlow, 1969), as well as in the Middle Ages with respect to the enslavement of Slavs (Bairoch, 1993), it should be reemphasized that it was the USA that imposed slavery in its most despicable and profitable extreme in the most recent era by making blacks and their offspring slaves for life. The cruelty of USA slavery laws is not surprising given that they are derived from capitalist commercial laws that turn everything, including people, into tradable commodities (Nicholson, 1994). It should be noted, however, that the Arab slave trade (lasting from the seventh to the nineteenth century) may have been larger (in terms of the total number of Africans enslaved), as well as crueler in the sense that Africans taken by Arabs as slaves were generally castrated (Bairoch, 1993).

10. This new form of colonialism and slavery also entails some of the same risks of major wars between major imperialist powers that existed centuries earlier, as rival capitalist countries rise up to compete with the dominating power for control of their own foreign markets, resources, and slaves (Collon, 2000). Today, the primary competitor for the USA is the EU, led by Germany, whose "natural" interest in colonies in Eastern Europe (as so clearly explained by Hitler in his book *Mein Kampf*) has certainly been a major factor in motivating NATO to expand eastward and attack Germany's long-time enemy Serbia (Foerstel, 2000). Note that it is not trade or foreign capital and investment that causes the evil, suffering, and war. Instead, it is the pure uncontrolled profit motive and the resulting exploitation and dehumanification of people. As explained in Chapter 5 (and as communist China itself has shown), controlled trade and foreign investment can lead to enormous benefits for all, whereas uncontrolled trade can retard the growth of even the mightiest power, as Britain demonstrated empirically after it removed its protectionist barriers in the nineteenth century and gradually lost its income/wealth dominance to the protectionist USA and continental Europe (Bairoch, 1993).

11. Such dictatorial actions help explain why, despite economic and social tragedy, Russia and the rest of the newly capitalist Eastern Europe have not yet returned to the more efficient and socially just communist systems they had. Although many of the former Soviet republics have created and continue to maintain outright capitalist dictatorships (Whalen, 2000), Yeltsin (at least more recently) and some other Eastern European countries have been able to develop some façade of democracy, partly because the capitalist seizure of control over the media there has created a very effective propaganda machine that is "unabashedly" one-sided in favor of anticommunist candidates and effectively censors negative information about capitalist candidates when confronted with a communist electoral opponent (Banerjee and Rosett, 1996). "Guns (discreetly) and money (blatantly) matter much more than ideas and party organization," and "there is no guarantee that the votes will be counted fairly, or that the election result will not be challenged in a suitably pliable court" (*Economist,* 1999). Whenever such control does not succeed in having the "correct" candidate elected, the capitalists can always seize

dictatorial control of a country again (such as via the unconstitutional shutting down of an elected parliament), just like in 1994 in Russia, which appears similar to the situation in the Ukraine in early 2000 (Wayland, 2000b).

12. For instance, since the USA's Cold War victory, workers have seen only a 1.9% real income increase despite a 12% increase in productivity, and the poorest 10% of the American population have seen their incomes drop by 15% in the last decade, while the richest 1% of Americans have increased their incomes to 40 times that of the bottom 40% of Americans (Teepen, 1999). Meanwhile, the average number of hours spent working on a job has risen to a higher level in the USA than in any other industrialized country (Associated Press, 1999a).

13. Once Americans are made aware of the facts and elect a government that reflects their will to end the atrocities, the guilty USA leaders could be tried by an International Criminal Court that those same leaders currently refuse to allow the UN to establish (Associated Press, 2000c). The criminal USA leaders currently permit the UN to only create special tribunals (such as in the case of the Bosnian civil war in Yugoslavia), after worldwide anger is aroused against USA enemies (such as Serbia in the case of the Bosnian war) by the fabrication of evidence (such as the portrayal of a Bosnian refugee camp as a fascist prison concentration camp by showing only pictures of the tiny portion of the camp flanked with barbed wire, when there was actually free entry and exit to the camp) that is then widely and repeatedly publicized long after it has been documented to be fraudulent (IAC, 1998a). Such deliberate imposition of one-sided and even fraudulent "justice" implies that the USA political leaders are aware of (and afraid of prosecution for) their own crimes, and so USA politicians may not be able to use the defense that they themselves have merely been brainwashed by the USA media to carry out their crimes (unlike the American people who can, until they are aware of this book or related documentation, legitimately assert that they were manipulated into electing the criminal USA government leaders). However, it might be appropriate at some point to offer amnesty to all those American terrorist leaders who surrender power willingly in order to maximize the chance of a speedy and peaceful revolution (although some form of reparations would have to be required from the mainstream political parties, the mainstream media, and the mainstream leaders who have inflicted so much suffering on the world-- the aim of such reparations would be to not only partially compensate their victims but also to reduce the power of those criminals who benefited so much from perpetuating the atrocities).

14. It should also be mentioned that many Americans were not even allowed to vote in the early decades of their country (Copeland, 2000). Although all American citizens now all have the right to vote, the majority are not even aware of the crimes committed by their country (Foerstel, 2000), just as the average American investor does not seem to be aware of how their optimism about the future is manipulated by politicians to cause the stock market to rise substantially on average (by about 10%) in the 6 months prior to each presidential election in the USA (Murphy, 2000). As a result, the American people as a whole should not be held responsible for the USA's past crimes against humanity unless and until they are made aware of the atrocities and of their moral obligation to vote out of power the criminal political parties and politicians who perpetuate those crimes.

15. Of these countries, the atrocities of only Germany, Japan, and Iraq were not directly motivated by prior USA mass murder (although Nazi Germany had used USA extermination of Indians as an example, as previously cited in the Introduction of this book). It should be mentioned, however, that the USA had no qualms about extensively using fascist Japanese soldiers and Nazis after World War II to defend (or create) brutal capitalist dictatorships in various countries (Blum, 1995). Despite the rivalry between competing capitalist powers that led to World War II, the previously warring capitalist powers (the USA, fascist Japan, and Nazi Germany) had a common interest in the repression of Marxists, unionists, and others with left-wing opinions (Feinberg, 1999). They also seemed to have a united belief that capitalists represent an elite group which knows best what to do with the world's wealth and is therefore entitled to it. The fact that the German stock market soared in value in the 1930s after Hitler's seizure of power (Bittlingmayer, 1998) represents an illustration of the latter capitalist philosophy in action. In particular, despite the Nazis' use of pro-worker slogans (such as by calling themselves the "National Socialist German Workers Party") as camouflaging demagoguery to help dupe the German public into supporting them (Feinberg, 1999), and despite Hitler's proposals for world disarmament, peace, and non-aggression that he formally offered in the early 1930s at the same time that he was making plans for German remilitarization and foreign subversion (Davidson, 1996), it was rich German capitalist imperialists (albeit non-Jewish ones) who financed Hitler's election to power and thrived under Nazi rule (Feinberg, 1999). It should also be mentioned that the Nazis also had substantial support from small business owners and the lower middle class in Germany (Winkler, 1972), and even many foreigners (such as the French) joined the Nazis in the oppression of Jews and the looting of Jewish businesses and wealth (Associated Press, 2000f). As documented by Copeland (2000), the rich have long and widely used the tactic of financing different anticommunist political parties (even ones with some left-wing demagoguery like the Nazis in Germany and the Democrats in the USA) in order to maintain their power and wealth. Financial aid for the more left-wing anticommunist parties is especially useful for appeasing the masses and taking support away from the communists, while at the same time it also serves as a means for the rich to hedge their bets, as political loyalty is thereby bought that ensures that any left-wing reforms to the capitalist system which damage the position of the wealthy are minimized (Agee and Wolf, 1975). Left-wing anticommunist parties are also often utilized as a means of winning the support of the masses for imperialist wars, which the masses must fight, but from which the rich profit so greatly (Copeland, 2000).

16. For propaganda purposes, the USA often emphasizes "human rights" as the religion it is protecting or spreading whenever it "wishes to replace local rulers with more compliant defenders of global financial interests" (Johnstone, 2000). The USA propaganda tends to associate "free markets" so very closely with "freedom," "democracy," and other "human rights" that it is able to successfully ignore actual human rights violations in countries that have free markets (like Kuwait) at the same time that it invents "human rights" problems in countries that don't have free markets (like Yugoslavia). In past centuries, Christianity represented the tool used by the USA (and Europe) to make the masses believe its extermination campaigns (and exploitation like slavery) were self-righteous attempts to eliminate (or civilize) pagans, with churches often working hand-in-hand with global capitalism to impose a Christian capitalism on the world

(DuBois, 1965). However, today, Christian churches tend to distance themselves from such activities, and the Pope has even requested forgiveness for Christianity's part in past violent oppression (Associated Press, 2000d).

17. As explained in this book, and in other research such as by Copeland (2000) and Foerstel (2000), the USA's democratic framework is largely a façade that it creates because it contributes greatly to the effectiveness of its propaganda machinery. However, as also documented in this book, as well as in other sources like Zinn (1995), the capitalist USA has a history of using extreme repression in cases where its propaganda machine (and other manipulation and pressure) is not successful in winning its own style of "elections." A statement by USA President Bill Clinton in 1999 may be illustrative here. In particular, in response to tens of thousands of Greeks demonstrating against his bombing of civilian targets in his unprovoked 1999 military attacks on Kosovo and the rest of Yugoslavia, Clinton stated, "they have a right to their opinion and I have a right to mine" (CNN, 1999b). In light of the facts provided in this book, this statement can be interpreted to reflect Clinton's belief that the masses around the world have the right to their opinion, but they should respect his opinion that USA leaders continue to have the "freedom" to commit atrocities whenever and however they choose (in the best interest of global capitalism and USA world domination of course). Actually, given that Clinton insisted Kosovo had to be occupied by USA forces and its "allies" (and refused Yugoslavia's many offers before and during the bombing to allow the USA-instigated civil war in Kosovo to be mediated instead with a neutral UN force), and given that Kosovo has an extraordinary amount of underground mineral wealth (Independent Commission of Inquiry, 1999), Clinton's use of the word "mine" in the foregoing quotation might actually be correctly interpreted to have a more subtle meaning. For instance, in the New World Order, it can be implied that people have a right to their opinions as long as they do not disturb the USA leaders' "right to mine" wealth from the rest of the world.

Bibliography

Aalund, D. "A Nation Still Divided." *Wall Street Journal* (September 27, 1999), R12.
Aalund, D. "ECB Head Discounts Inflation Concerns." *Wall Street Journal* (January 6, 2000), A17.
Abken, P. "Beyond Plain Vanilla: A Taxonomy of Swaps." *Financial Derivatives* (ed. by R. Kolb). Blackwell: Oxford (1998).
Abuaf, N. and P. Jorion. "Purchasing Power Parity in the Long Run." *Journal of Finance* 45 (1990), 157-174.
Adams, C. "China-- Growth and Economic Reform." *World Economic Outlook* (October 1997), 119-127.
Adler, F. "Work and Personality Development in the German Democratic Republic." *International Social Science Journal* 32 (1980), 443-463.
AND. "Trabi soll bei seinem hohen Preis bleiben." *Berliner Zeitung* (March 31, 1990), 1.
Aeppel, T. and T. Roth. "German Autumn Report Shows Unity Debt Was Less Than Feared." *Wall Street Journal* (October 22, 1991), A17.
Afesoglu, S. and D. Dutkowsky. "On the Dynamics of Balance of Payments Constrained Growth." *Applied Economics* 29 (1997), 1343-1351.
AFP. "Bild: BND-Bericht nennt Details zu Geldwaesche in Liechtenstein—Kohl—Freund Batliner soll Konten fuer Mafia gefuehrt haben." *Berliner Zeitung* (February 26, 2000).
Agee, P. and L. Wolf. *Dirty Work.* Lyle Stuart: Secaucas (1975).
Agenor, P. and P. Masson. "Credibility, Reputation, and the Mexican Peso Crisis." *Journal of Money, Credit, and Banking* 31 (1999), 70-84.
Agoncillo, T. *A Short History of the Philippines.* Mentor: New York (1969).
Ahn, C. "The Effect of Temporal Risk Aversion on Optimal Consumption, the Equity Premium, and the Equilibrium Interest Rate." *Journal of Finance* 44 (1989), 1411-1420.
Alexiev, A. *Inside the Soviet Army in Afghanistan.* RAND: Santa Monica (1988).
Aliber, R. "Credit Expansion in the Trouble Asian Economies: Domestic vs. Foreign Causes." Paper presented at the American Economic Association meeting (2000).

Allport, P. "Visitor Growth Doesn't Happen Just by Accident." *National Business Review* (March 12, 1999), 23.
Amstutz, B. *Afghanistan: the First Five years of Soviet Occupation.* National Defense University: Washington (1986).
Andersen, R. "Who is Killing the Press?" *Censored 2000.* Seven Stories Press: New York (2000), 165-171.
Anderson, K. "Lobbying Incentives and the Pattern of Protection in Rich and Poor Countries." *Economic Development and Change* 43 (1995), 401-423.
Andics, H. *Rule of Terror.* Holt, Rinehart and Winston: New York (1969).
Andreopoulos, G. (editor). *Genocide: Conceptual and Historical Dimensions.* University of Pennsylvania Press: Philadelphia (1994).
Andrew, C. *The Sword and the Shield.* Basic Books: New York (1999).
Andrew, C. and O. Gordievsky. *KGB: The Inside Story.* Harper Perennial: New York (1990).
Angenfort, J. "Grund des FDJ-Verbots war die Remilitarisierung." *Neues Deutschland* (July 1, 1996), 12.
Anis, A. and T. Ross. "Imperfect Competition and Pareto-Improving Strategic Trade Policy." *Journal of International Economics* 33 (1992), 363-371.
Antonov-Ovseyenko, A. *The Time of Stalin: Portrait of a Tyranny.* Harper & Row: New York (1981).
Apel, H. *Wehen und Wunder der Zonenwirtschaft.* Wissenschaft und Politik: Koeln (1966).
Arnold, K. *Die ersten hundert Tage.* Dietz Verlag: Berlin (1990).
Aston, B., K. Hill, A. Piazza, and R. Zeitz. "Famine in China, 1958-61." *Population and Development Review* 10 (1984), 613-645.
Associated Press. "Nationalists Halt Mainland Attack." *Pontiac Daily Press* (June 28, 1950), 1.
Associated Press. "Real Purge Reported in Western China." *Detroit News* (September 16, 1951), 2.
Associated Press. "Yeltsin Emerges to Quell Rumors of Bad Health." *Oakland Press* (July 2, 1996a), A9.
Associated Press. "Russians Decide Who Will be Leader." *Oakland Press* (July 3, 1996b), A-10.
Associated Press. "Native Hawaiians Face Court Battle." *Oakland Press* (September 1, 1996c), A-12.
Associated Press. "1-in5 Americans Below the Poverty Line." *Oakland Press* (June 12, 1997), A-12.
Associated Press. "Russians Strung Out From Import Addiction." *Flint Journal* (Oct. 1, 1998), A9.
Associated Press. "Report: Pay Raises Sharper for Executives." *Oakland Press* (August 30, 1999a), A-9.

Associated Press. "Elvis, Aliens Beware: National Enquirer Owner Buying out Rivals." *Oakland Press* (November 3, 1999b), C1.
Associated Press. "Cold War Leaders Mark Berlin Wall's Fall." *Oakland Press* (November 9, 1999c), A-7.
Associated Press. "Appeals Court Upholds Convitions in Wall Deaths." *Oakland Press* (November 9, 1999d), A-7.
Associated Press. "Oswald Impersonator Tapes May Exist." *Oakland Press* (November 22, 1999e), A-8.
Associated Press. "Kosovo Progress Slow Under U.N. Administration." *Oakland Press* (November 23, 1999e), A-10.
Associated Press. "Tiny Toymakers Find Success on Internet." *Oakland Press* (November 28, 1999f), D-1, D-2.
Associated Press. "Jury Sides with King Family, Blames Conspiracy in Killing." *Oakland Press* (December 9, 1999g), A-14.
Associated Press. "'Warm Wars' Lock Third of World in Strife." *Oakland Press* (December 30, 1999h), A-6.
Associated Press. "Defiant Protest Halted." *Oakland Press* (February 27, 2000a), A-8.
Associated Press. "Convictions Concern Kuwaitis Seeing More Creative Freedoms." *Oakland Press* (March 12, 2000b), A-7.
Associated Press. "War-Crimes Tribunals Seek to Strengthen Global Justice." *Oakland Press* (March 12, 2000c), A-12.
Associated Press. "Pope Asks Forgiveness." *Oakland Press* (March 13, 2000d), A-5.
Associated Press. "Communist 'Horrors' Prompt Baltic States to Try Accused Agents." *Oakland Press* (April 9, 2000e), A-14.
Associated Press. "French Report Concedes Wartime Looting of Jews." *Oakland Press* (April 18, 2000f), A-8.
Associated Press. "Police Negotiate Arrests at Protest." *Oakland Press* (April 18, 2000g), C-1.
Associated Press. "Author Argues 'Ordinary Germans' Could Have Aborted Third Reich." *Oakland Press* (May 14, 2000h), A-11.
Associated Press. "Japan Tops List for Healthy Lives, but U.N. Study Faults U.S., Africa." *Oakland Press* (June 5, 2000i), A-10.
Associated Press. "Ex-Communists Claim Win." *Oakland Press* (July 3, 2000j), A-8.
Atkin, R. *Revolution! Mexico 1910-20.* John Day: New York (1970).
Aus erster Hand. *Jung Sein in der DDR.* Panorama DDR: Berlin (1987).
Autorenkollektiv. *Geschichte der deutschen Arbeiterbewegung.* Dietz: Berlin (1966).
Autorenkollektiv. *1x1 fuer junge Eltern.* Verlag fuer die Frau: Leipzig (1973).

Autorenkollektiv. *Geld und Kredit.* Wirtschaft: Berlin (1988).
Autorenkollektiv. *Von den Anfaengen. Eine illustrierte Chronik der PDS 1989-1994.* Dietz: Berlin (1995).
Ayling, S. "CIA Made CNN Retract Story." *Workers World* (September 24, 1998), 9.
Ayling, S. "Survivors Recall Massacre by U.S. Troops at Sinchon." *Workers World* (March 23, 2000), 11.
Azad, A. "Why the U.S. is Seen as 'the Capital of Global Arrogance.'" *Workers World* (March 19, 1998), 7.
Azocur, P. "Fulbright Prize Address." *Fulbright Association Newsletter* 20 (1998).
Bacon, E. *The Gulag at War: Stalin's Forced Labour System in the Light of the Archives.* New York University Press: New York (1994).
Bader, H. and H. Brompton. "Remedies against Administrative Abuse in Central Europe, the Soviet Union, and Communist East Europe (Ombudsmen and Others)." *Annals of the American Academy of Political and Social Science* 377 (1968), 73-86.
Bagwell, K. and R. Staiger. "An Economic Theory of GATT." *American Economic Review* 89 (1999), 215-248.
Bahr, E. *Sieben Tage im Oktober.* Forum: Leipzig (1990).
Bahrmann, H. and C. Links. *Chronik der Wende.* Christoph Links Verlag: Berlin (1994).
Bairoch, P. *Economics and World History.* University of Chicago Press: Chicago (1993).
Bamford, J. *The Puzzle Palace.* Houghton Mifflin: Boston (1983).
Banerjeee, N. and C. Rosett. "Russia Barely Blinks as Yeltsin Returns to the Public View." *Wall Street Journal* (July 2, 1996), A10.
Barber, B. and T. Odean. "The Courage of Misguided Convictions." *Financial Analysts Journal* 55 (November/December 1999), 41-55.
Barber, D. "Frustrating Wait for Backer Financing." *National Business Review* (June 14, 1996), 24.
Barber, D. "Fat Chance of New Zealand Trade Agreement with US." *National Business Review* (February 26, 1999), 3.
Barclays Economic Review. "International Economy. Central and Eastern Europe." (1999), 23.
Barron's. "Peace Offerings." August 23 (1999), 5.
Bauer, A. "Berauschte Massen vor dem Tor." *TAZ* (January 2, 1990).
Bauer, R. *Pkw-Bau in der DDR.* Peter Lang: Franfurt am Main (1999).
Becker, B. "The Soviet Union in Perspective." *Workers World* 39 (May 15, 1997a), 31-35 (Section 2).
Becker, H. "Die Angst der Bosse vor der Unterwelt." *Focus* 21 (1997b),

280-281.

Becker, R. "The Link Between the Chechnya War and Caspian Oil." *Workers World* (December 2, 1999a), 8.

Becker, R. "International Panel Hears Indictment of U.S. and NATO for War Crimes." *Workers World* (November 4, 1999b), 6.

Behr, W. *Bundesrepublik Deutschland - Deutsche Demokratische Republik: Systemvergleich Politik - Wirtschaft - Gesellschaft.* Stuttgart: Kohlhammer (1985).

Beja, A. and M. Goldman. "On the Dynamic Behavior of Prices in Disequilibrium." *Journal of Finance* 34 (1980), 235-247.

Beltrame, J. and J. Millman. "U.S. Trade Gap's New Culprits: Canada, Mexico." *Wall Street Journal* (July 21, 1999), A-16, A-19.

Ben-Bassat, A. and D. Gottlieb. "Optimal International Reserves and Sovereign Risk." *Journal of International Economics* 33 (1992), 345-362.

Bennett, N. "Brazil Knells Wall Street's Bell." *National Business Review* (January 22, 1999a), 22.

Bennett, N. "Debt Spiral Adds to Currency Woes." *National Business Review* (March 12, 1999b), 29.

Berg, A. and C. Pattillo. "Are Currency Crises Predictable? A Test." *IMF Staff Papers* (1999), 107-138.

Bergson A. "Comparative Productivity: The USSR, Eastern Europe, and the West." *American Economic Review* 77 (1987), 342-357.

Bergson, A. "Communist Economic Efficiency Revisited." *American Economic Review* 82 (1992), 27-30.

Berliner Allgemeine. "BND schueffelte bis Februar in DDR-Briefen." March 7 (1990a), 1.

Berliner Allgemeine. "Wirtschaft koennte um 10 Prozent wachsen." March 7 (1990b), 1.

Berliner, J. *Factory and Manager in the USSR.* Harvard: Cambridge (1957).

Berliner Morgenpost. "Roeller: DDR auf Platz 8 im EG-Vergleich." February 25 (1990), 1.

Bernstein, D. "The Battle for Free Speech Radio." *Censored 2000.* Seven Stories Press: New York (2000), 235-252.

Bhagwati, J. (editor). *The New International Economic Order: The North-South Debate.* MIT Press: Cambridge (1977).

Bittlingmayer, G. "Output, Stock Volatility, and Political Uncertainty in a Natural Experiment, 1880-1940." *Journal of Finance* 53 (1998), 2243-2257.

Bittorf, W. "Der Raub der Neuen Welt." *Der Spiegel* 1-3 (1992).

Blejer, M. and A. Cheasty. "Using Fiscal Measures to Stimulate Savings in Developing Countries." *Finance & Development* 23 (June 1986), 16-19.

Block, R. "Angola Slides Back into a Bloody War With Rebels." *Wall Street*

Journal (December 17, 1998), A-19.
Block, R. "Old Hates Reignite and Blood Flows at Kosovo Border." *Wall Street Journal* (December 17, 1999a), A11.
Block, R. "Serbia's Ruling Couple Tighten Grip, Cracking Down on Opponents, Media." *Wall Street Journal* (December 13, 1999b), A27.
Bloomberg. "Japan's People 'Must Feel Pain'." *Dominion* (May 15, 1999), 13.
Blume, M., C. Mackinlay C., and B. Terker B. "Order Imbalances and Stock Price Movements on October 19 and 20, 1987." *Journal of Finance* 44 (1989), 827-848.
Blum, W. *Killing Hope: US Military and CIA Intervention Since World War II.* Common Courage Press: Monroe (1995).
Bodard, L. *The Quicksand War: Prelude to Vietnam.* Little, Brown and Company: Boston (1967).
Borah, W. and S. Cook. "Conquest and Population: A Demographic Approach to Mexican History." *Proceedings of the American Philosophical Society* 113 (1969), 177-183.
Borkakoti, J. *International Trade: Causes and Consequences.* Macmillan: New York (1998).
Boss, D. "The Entitlement Generation Wants it All—and They Want it Easy. How Dare They?" *Wall Street Journal* (May 22, 2000), R23.
Bowart, W. *Operation Mind Control.* Dell: New York (1978).
Bowen, H., A. Hollander, and J. Viaene. *Applied International Trade Analysis.* University of Michigan Press: Ann Arbor (1998).
Bradsher, H. *Afghanistan and the Soviet Union.* Duke University Press: Durham (1983).
Brenner, R. "Currencies Don't Lie." *Forbes Global Business & Finance* (March 8, 1999), 59.
Briscoe, D. "Problems of Hunger Persist." *Milwaukee Journal* (February 11, 2000), 4A.
Brockett, M. "NZ Risks Becoming 'Australian Colony'." *Dominion* (April 13, 1999), 2.
Brown, D. *Bury my Heart at Wounded Knee.* Holt, Rinehart & Winston (1970).
Brownlow, W. *Slavery and Serfdom in Europe.* Negro Universities Press: New York (1969).
Buck, H. "Umweltpolitik und Umweltbelastung." *Die wirtschaftliche und oekologische Situation der DDR* (edited by E. Kuhrt). Leske & Budrich: Oladen (1996).
Buck, J. *Land Utilization in China.* University of Chicago Press: Chicago (1937).

Buero des Ministerrates. *Gesetzblatt der Deutschen Demokratischen Republik* (March 23, 1966), 74.
Buero des Ministerrates. *Gesetzblatt der Deutschen Demokratischen Republik* (December 16, 1970), 676.
Buero des Ministerrates. *Gesetzblatt der Deutschen Demokratischen Republik* (May 31, 1985), 169.
Bullock, A. *Hitler and Stalin.* Knopf: New York (1992).
Burant, S. *East Germany: A Country Study*. Library of Congress: Washington (1987).
Burns, R. and M. Leitenberg. *The Wars in Vietnam, Cambodia and Laos, 1945-82.* ABC-Clio: Oxford (1982).
Butterfield, G. "Texas Prisoner is Defiant to the End." *Workers World* (March 23, 2000), 1, 5.
Byrns, R. and G. Stone. *Economics* (Sixth Edition). HarperCollins: New York (1995).
Calmes, J. "Bush Vows to Spend Political Capital if Elected for Social Security Overhaul." *Wall Street Journal* (November 22, 1999), B14.
Calvo, G. and E. Mendoz. "Mexico's Balance-of-Payments Crisis: A Chronicle of a Death Foretold." *Journal of International Economics* 41 (1996), 235-264.
Campbell, R. *The Soviet-Type Economies.* Houghton Mifflin: Boston (1974).
Campbell, R. *The Failure of Soviet Economic Planning.* Indiana University Press: Bloomington (1992).
Cassell, G. *Post-War Monetary Stabilization.* Columbia University Press: New York (1928).
Catalinotto, J. "U.S. Troops Spread to 100 Countries." *Workers World* (June 5, 1997), 1.
Catalinotto, J. "Protest Puts National Focus on Political Prisoners in U.S." *Workers World* (April 9, 1998a), 5.
Catalinotto, J. "U.S. Shields 1980 Killers of Nuns." *Workers World* (April 16, 1998b), 11.
Catalinotto, J. "Washington Reaps What It Has Sown." *Workers World* (September 3, 1998c), 8.
Catalinotto, J. "UN Report Shows Rich Richer, Poor Poorer." *Workers World* (Sept. 24, 1998d), 2.
Catalinotto, J. "Pentagon Gave Orders for War Crimes." *Workers World* (January 13, 2000a), 7-8.
Catalinotto, J. "Newsweek: 'Bombing Civilian Targets Worked Best.'" *Workers World* (May 25, 2000b), 9.
Cavaglia, S., W. Verschoor, and C. Wolff. "Further Evidence on Exchange Rate Expectations." *Journal of International Money and Finance* 12 (1993), 78-98.
Caves, R., J. Frankel, and R. Jones. *World Trade and Payments.* HarperCollins:

New York (1996).
M. Celarier. "Stealing the Family Silver." *Euromoney* (February 1996), 62-66.
Chalk, F. and K. Jonassohn. *The History and Sociology of Genocide.* Yale University Press: New Haven (1990).
Chan, K., N. Chen, and D. Hsieh. "An Exploratory Investigation of the Firm Size Effect." *Journal of Financial Economics* 14 (1985), 451-471.
Chandrasekhar, C. and J. Ghosh. "Hubris, Hysteria, Hope: The Political Economy of Crisis and Response in Southeast Asia." *Tigers in Trouble* (ed. by Jomo K.S.). Zed Books: London (1998).
Chang, L. "Marxist Ties Bind China's Tech Start-Ups." *Wall Street Journal* (April 5, 2000), A18.
Chatterjee, P. "Mercenary Armies & Mineral Wealth." *Covert Action Quarterly* (Fall 19997), 27-37.
Chazan, G. "Russia's New Parliament Erupts After Four Parties Leave in Protest." *Wall Street Journal* (January 19, 2000a), A18.
Chazan, G. "Investors Looking to Russia Try to Pin Down an Elusive Putin." *Wall Street Journal* (March 28, 2000b), A21.
Cheng, J. "'Stop Slavery, We Need Real Jobs.'" *Workers World* (January 16, 1997), 4.
Chin, P. "The Truth About NATO/U.S. Aggression in Yugoslavia.'" *Workers World* (December 2, 1999), 7.
Chin, P. "Africa's Gifts to Civilization." *Workers World* (February 24, 2000), 6.
Chittenden, H. *The American Fur Trade of the Far West.* Francis P. Harper: New York (1902).
Chitwood, O. *A History of Colonial America.* Harper & Brothers: New York (1948).
Chossudovsky, M. *The Globalization of Poverty: Impacts of IMF and World Bank Reforms.* Third World Network: Penang (1997).
Choudhry, T. "Another visit to the Cagan Model of Money Demand: the Latest Russian Experience." *Journal of International Money and Finance* 17 (1998), 355-376.
Chowdhry, B. and A. Goyal. "Understanding the Financial Crisis in Asia." *Pacific-Basin Finance Journal* 8 (2000), 135-152.
Christ, P. "das Land der Zwei Geschwindigheiten" *Die Zeit* (October 11, 1991), p.11
Churchill, W. *Indians Are Us.* Common Courage Press: Monroe (1994).
Ciampi, T. "Peru Dumps State-Owned Firms." *Pensions & Investments* (April 20, 1998), 14.
Cirjakovic, Z. "Milosevic, the Comeback Kid." *Newsweek* (May 15, 2000), 26.

Claessens, S. "Balance of Payments Crises in an Optimal Portfolio Model." *European Economic Review* 35 (1991), 81-101.
Clark, R. *The Fire this Time.* Thunder's Mouth Press: New York (1992).
Clark, R. "Fire and Ice." *Challenge to Genocide.* IAC: New York (1998).
Clark, R. "Media Manipulation of Foreign Policy." *War, Lies & Videotape* (edited by L. Foerstel). IAC: New York (2000).
CNN. "Ex-East German Nostalgia for Communism's Simpler Life." Internet (November 9, 1999a), http//cnn.com/WORLD/europe/9911/09/wall/nostalgia/
CNN. "Anti-Clinton Protests Erupt into Riots in Greece." Internet (November 19, 1999b).
CNN. "U.S. Says Iraqi Building Palaces, Ignoring People's Needs." Internet (February 29, 2000a), http//www.cnn.com/2000/WORLD/meast/02/09/un.iraq/
CNN. "Triumphal Parade Marks Anniversary of End of Vietnam Conflict." Internet (April 30, 2000b), http//www.cnn.com/2000/ASIANOW/southeast/04/30/vietnam.waranniversary/index.html.
Cockburn, A. "S. Africa: When States Are in Terror, They Often Resort to State Terrorism." *Detroit Free Press* (April 15, 1993), 15A.
Coe, M. *Mexico* (Fourth Edition). Thames and Hudson: New York (1994).
Cohen, D. "The Solvency of Eastern Europe." *European Economy* 2 (1991), 262-303.
Collier, I. "Connections, Effective Purchasing Power and Real Product in the German Democratic Republic." *Berichte des Osteuropa-Instituts* 135 (1985).
Collier, J. and K. Collier. *Votescam.* Victoria House: Bath (1992).
Connolly, M. and D. Taylor. "The Exact Timing of the Collapse of an Exchange Rate Regime and its Impact on the Relative Price of Traded Goods." *Journal of Money, Credit, & Banking* 16 (1984), 194-207.
Conquest, R. *Harvest of Sorrow.* Oxford University Press: New York (1986).
Conquest, R. *The Great Terror.* Oxford University Press: New York (1990).
Constantine, A. *Psychic Dictatorship in the USA.* Feral House: Portland (1995).
Cook, B. "Hitler's Extermination Policy and the American Indian." *Indian Historian* 6 (Summer 1973), 48-49.
Cook, D. *Born to Die.* Cambridge University Press: Cambridge (1998).
Cook, S. *The Struggle Between California Indian and White Civilization.* University of California Press: Berkeley (1943).
Cooper, H. "A Question-and-Answer Guide to Issues, Players at the WTO Meeting in Seattle." *Wall Street Journal* (November 26, 1999), A2.
Copeland, V. "How Big Business Picks the Secretaries of State and Defense." *Workers World* (August 27, 1998), 5.

Copeland, V. *Market Elections: How Democracy Serves the Rich.* World View Forum: New York (2000).
Cordovez, D. and S. Harrison. *Out of Afghanistan.* Oxford University Press: Oxford (1995).
Cosby, C. "America Taught My Son's Killer to Hate Blacks." *Workers World* (July 23, 1998), 3.
Cote, K. "Second-Class Citizens in their own Country." *Advertising Age* (February 19, 1990), 36.
Cox News Service. "Russian Population Drop Is a Political Time Bomb." *Oakland Press* (September 24, 1995), A-20.
Craven, W. *The Colonies in Transition.* Harper & Row: New York (1968).
Cullison, A. "Russia's Liberals, Left in Dark by Putin, Know Not to Cross Likely New President." *Wall Street Journal* (March 2, 2000a), A21.
Cullison, A. "At End of Russia Vote, Power Struggle Begins." *Wall Street Journal* (March 22, 2000b), A17.
Cullison, A. "Russia Arrests President of Big Private Media Company." *Wall Street Journal* (June 14, 2000c), C1, C2.
Curtin, P. *The Atlantic Slave Trade.* University of Wisconsin Press: Madison (1969).
Czege, A. "Ungarns Integration in die Weltwirtschaft: Vision oder Alptraum." *Aussenwirtschaft* 44 (1989), 425-452.
D'Souza, J. and W. Megginson. "Financial and Operating Performance of Privatized Firms During the 1990s." *Journal of Finance* 54 (1999), 1397-1438.
Darity, W. "A Model of 'Original Sin': Rise of the West and Lag of the Rest." *American Economic Review* 82 (May 1992), 162-167.
Daunton, M. and R. Halpern. *Empire and Others: British Encounters with Indigenous Peoples 1600-1850.* University of Pennsylvania Press: Philadelphia (1999).
Davidson, B. *Black Mother: The Years of the African Slave Trade.* Little, Brown and Company: Boston (1961).
Davidson, E. *The Unmaking of Adolf Hitler.* University of Missouri Press: Columbia (1996).
Davis, A., D. Cloud, and P. Beckett. "Bank of New York Defendants Likely to Cooperate." *Wall Street Journal* (February 16, 2000), B2.
Davies, S. *Popular Opinion in Stalin's Russia.* Cambridge University Press: Cambridge (1997).
De Lacy, H. "How NZ Ruined a Good Market." *The Press* (May 1, 1999), 10.
Deardorff, A. "Growth and International Investment With Diverging Populations." *Oxford Economic Papers* 46 (1994), 477-491.
DeBlasi, M. "Europe's Economic Engines That Can." *Bloomberg Personal Finance* (March 2000), 28-30.

De Bondt, W. and R. Thaler. "Does the Stock market Overreact?" *Journal of Finance* 40 (1985), 793-805.
Decalo, S. *Psychoses of Power.* Westview Press: Boulder (1989).
DeFusco, R., R. Johnson, and T. Zorn. "The Effect of Executive Stock Option Plans on Stockholders and Bondholders." *Journal of Finance* 45 (1990), 617-628.
Deleyne, J. *The Chinese Economy.* Harper & Row: New York (1974).
Dellas, H. and O. Galor. "Growth Via External Public Debt and Capital Controls." *International Economic Review* 33 (1992), 269-281.
Dellas, H. and A. Stockman. "Self-Fulfilling Expectations, Speculative Attack, and Capital Controls." *Journal of Money, Credit, and Banking* 25 (1993), 721-730.
Denevan, W. (editor). *The Native Population of the Americas in 1492.* University of Wisconsin Press: Madison (1976).
Denevan, W. "Carl Sauer and Native American Population Size." *Geographical Review* 86 (1996), 385-397.
Der Spiegel. "Bei Madeleine." November 24 (1962), 91-92.
Der Spiegel. "Heimlicher Handel." February 2 (1987), 90-92.
Der Spiegel. "Schatzkammer der Natur." March 9 (1988), 181-186.
Der Spiegel. "Das tut weh." Issue 21 (1991), 34.
Der Spiegel. "Ueberall sind Fallen." January 6 (1992a), 36-55.
Der Spiegel. "Spaetzle-Stasi." August 24 (1992b), 86-87.
Der Spiegel. "Hammer der Zerstoerung." Issue 34 (1993a), 18-23.
Der Spiegel. "Wo steht der Feind?" November 15 (1993b), 76-94.
Der Spiegel. "Kanzlers Machtkartell." Issue 31 (1994), 30-37.
Der Spiegel. "Fehl-Steuer Ost." November 10 (1997a), 30-44.
Der Spiegel. "Speerspitze des Wandels." December 29 (1997b), 22-28.
Der Spiegel. "Freibank der Natur." No. 13 (1998), 214-216.
Der Tagesspiegel. "'Zum biologischen Roboter verdammt.'" December 10 (1989a), 17.
Der Tagesspiegel. "Der deutsch-deutsche Telefonverkehr." December 13 (1989b), 6.
Der Tagesspiegel. "Bonn gibt DDR-Wirtschaft Kreditrahmen von zwoelf Milliarden DM." December 21 (1989c), 2.
Der Tagesspiegel. "Jedes Broetchen ueber dem Plansoll wird hoch versteuert." December 21 (1989d), 21.
Der Tagesspiegel. "Kredite in der DDR." December 24 (1989e).
Der Tagesspiegel. "Offene Grenzen und kein 'Ausverkauf.'" December 31 (1989f), 17.
Der Tagesspiegel. "Delors bietet der DDR Mitgliedschaft in der EG an." January 18 (1990a), 1.

Der Tagesspiegel. "DDR-Wirtschaft immer noch mit vielen Schwachstellen." January 19 (1990b), 17.
Der Tagesspiegel. "Weltbank zu Milliardenhilfen fuer Osteuropa bereit." January 25 (1990c), 24.
Der Tagesspiegel. "Am Mueggelsee sollen Westbesucher das Dreifache bezahlen." January 25 (1990d).
Der Tagesspiegel. "Umweltschuetzer fordern von Bonn 200 Milliarden DM fuer die DDR." January 30 (1990e), 7.
Der Tagesspiegel. "Leistungen fuer Aus- und Uebersiedler werden noch im Februar gekappt." February 2 (1990f), 7.
Der Tagesspiegel. "Umfrage ermittelte 54 Prozent fuer die SPD." February 8 (1990g), 6.
Der Tagesspiegel. "SPD schlaegt Milliarden-Programm zur Wirtschaftserneuerung der DDR vor." February 9 (1990h), 7.
Der Tagesspiegel. "DDR will Schwarzmarktkurs aus Gaststaetten verbannen." February 28 (1990i).
Der Tagesspiegel. "Reformen haben Kreditkonditionen verschlechtert." March 1 (1990j).
Der Tagesspiegel. "Umweltsanierung kostet 100 Milliarden Mark." March 9 (1990k), 8.
Der Tagesspiegel. "USA sind zu Investitionen in Osteuropa bereit." March 17 (1990l), 22.
Der Tagesspiegel. "DDR-Buerger sterben frueher." March 18 (1990m), 12.
Der Tagesspiegel. "CDU in der DDR strebt Grosse Koalition an." March 20 (1990n), 1.
Der Tagesspiegel. "Du musst rechter waehlen als du bist, damit das Geld kommt." March 20 (1990o), 15.
Der Tagesspiegel. "Moeglicherweise bis zu 30 000 Millionaere in der UdSSR." (August 1, 1990p).
Desmond, E. "Japan's Trillion-Dollar Hole." *Time* (April 8, 1996), 46.
Deutschland. "Tomorrow's World." April/May (2000), 40-51.
Diamond, D. and R. Verrecchia. "Optimal Managerial Contracts and Equilibrium Security Prices." *Journal of Finance* 37 (1982), 275-287.
Diane, K. and R. Bachman. *Revelations From the Russian Archives.* Library of Congress: Washington (1997).
Dickson, M. "John Govett Launches $100m Hungarian Fund." *Financial Times* (February 8, 1990), 18.
Die Marktwirtschaft. "Wettbewerbsvorteile durch mehr Aussenhandel." No. 3 (1990).
Dieckmann, F. "Konspiration mit der Vormacht." *Die Zeit* (October 11, 1991), 13-14.

Diedrich, T., H. Ehlert, and R. Wenzke. (editors). *Im Dienste der Partei.* Christoph Links Verlag: Berlin (1998).
Dietrich, C. *People's China* (Second Edition). Oxford University Press: Oxford (1994).
Dietz Verlag. *Fragen und Antworten zum Programm der SED.* Berlin (1983).
Dietz, R. *Die Wirtschaft der DDR.* Wiener Institut fuer Internationale Wirtschaftsvergleiche: Wien (1976).
DIW (Deutches Institut fuer Wirtschaftsforschung). "Das Kaufkraftverhaeltnis zwischen D-Mark und Mark der DDR 1983." *Wochenbericht* 17 (1984), 193-201.
DIW. "Eigenverantwortung versus Kontrolle -- der Zwiespalt in der Reformpolitik der DDR." *Wochenbericht* 21 (1989), 237-243.
Dixit, A. "Hysteresis, Import Penetration, and Exchange Rate Pass-Through." *Quarterly Journal of Economics* 104 (1989), 205-228.
Dobb, M. "A Note on Saving and Investment in a Socialist Economy." *Economic Journal* (1939).
Dobyns, H. "An Appriasal of Techniques With a New Hemispheric Estimate." *Current Anthropology* 7 (1966), 395-416.
Dobyns, H. *Native American Historical Demography.* Indiana University Press: Bloomington (1976a).
Dobyns, H. "Brief Perspective on a Scholarly Transformation: Widowing the 'Virgin' Land." *Ethnohistory* 23 (1976b), 95-104.
Dobyns, H. *Their Number Become Thinned.* University of Tennessee press: Knoxville (1983).
Domenech, A. *Deserts of North America.* Longman, Green, Longman, and Roberts: London (1860).
Dominion. "Russia Losing War Against Mobsters." February 10 (1999), 4.
Dooley, M. "A Survey of Literature on Controls over International Capital Transactions." *IMF Staff Papers* 43 (1996), 639-687.
Dooley, M. and P. Isard. "The Role of the Current Account in Exchange-Rate Determination: A Comment on Rodriguez." *Journal of Political Economy* 90 (1982), 1291-1294.
Dornbusch, R. "Equilibrium and Disequilibrium Exchange Rates." *Zeitschrift fuer Wirtschafts und Sozialwissenschaften* 102 (1982).
Dornbusch, R. and A. Werner. "Mexico: Stabilization, Reform and No Growth." *Brookings Papers on Economic Activity* 1 (1994).
Dowd, A. "Protect Your Privacy." *Money* (August 1997), 104-112.
Dower, J. *War Without Mercy.* Pantheon: New York (1986).
Downes, R. *Council Fires.* University of Pittsburgh Press: Pittsburgh (1940).
Dpa. "Kohls Zehn-Punkte-Plan zur Deutschlandpolitik." *Der Tagesspiegel* (November 29, 1989), 10.

Dpa. "Zahl der Aus- und Uebersiedler im Bundesgebiet 1989 stark gestiegen." *Der Tagesspiegel* (January 6, 1990a), 1.
Dpa. "Vereinigungsprobleme in deutschen Schlafzimmern." *Norddeutsche neueste Nachrichten* (July 9, 1990b).
Drazen, A. and P. Masson. "Credibility of Policies Versus Credibility of Policymakers." *Quarterly Journal of Economics* 104 (1994), 735-754.
Driver, H. *Indians of North America.* University of Chicago Press: Chicago (1961).
DuBois, B. *The World and Africa: an Inquiry into the Part which Africa has Played in World History.* International Publishers: New York (1965).
Dubosfsky, D. and J. Groth. "Relative Information Accessibility for OTC Stocks and Security Returns." *Financial Review* 21 (1986), 85-102.
Duca, J. and D. VanHoose. "The Rise of Goods-Market Competition and the Decline in Wage Indexation: A Macroeconomic Approach." *Journal of Macroeconomics* 20 (1998), 579-598.
Dumas, W. and A. Dumas. "Political Education in the Former German Democratic Republic." *The Social Studies* 87 (1996), 197-202.
Dunkel, G. "No Evidence of Serb Genocide." *Workers World* (November 4, 1999), 7.
Dunkel, G. "Tension and Violence Grow Because of U.S. Maneuvers." *Workers World* (May 18, 2000), 9.
Dupuy, B. "The Character Assassination of President Aristide." *War, Lies & Videotape* (edited by L. Foerstel). IAC: New York (2000).
Eastman, L. *The Abortive Revolution.* Harvard University Press: Cambridge (1974).
Eckart, G. *So sehe Ick die Sache.* Kiepenheuer & Witsch: Koeln (1984).
Economist. "Comeback. (Communists, Renamed Socialists Win)." (June 16, 1990), 54-55.
Economist. "German Subsidies." June 8 (1991), 70-73.
Economist. "Why the Poor Don't Catch Up." April 25 (1992), 48.
Economist. "Serbia: Roots of War." December 25 (1993), 63-64.
Economist. "Bulgaria: by Popular Demand." January 7 (1995), 43-44.
Economist. "Germany: Eastern Ghosts." August 12 (1995), 43-44.
Economist. "See No Evil." November 23 (1996), 55-56.
Economist. "Canny Survivor." November 22 (1997), 60-62.
Economist. "Russia Devalued." August 22 (1998), 14-15.
Economist. "Worrying Stastix." February 6 (1999a), 73.
Economist. "Russia's Economic Quagmire." April 24 (1999b), 73-74.
Economist. "Russia's Election." December 18 (1999c), 19-21.
Edison, H. and D. Pauls. "A Re-assessment of the Relationship Between Real Exchange Rates and Real Interest Rates: 1970-1990." *Journal of Monetary*

Economics 31 (1993), 165-187.
Edlin, B. "Central Bank Does Not Absolve Govt's Duty to Manage Monetary Policy." *The Independent* (March 31, 1999), 34.
Edwards, G. *GDR Society and Social Institutions.* St. Martin's Press: New York (1985).
Eisenfeld, B. *Die zentrale KoordinierungsGruppe Bekaempfung von Flucht und Uebersiedlung.* Der Bundesbeauftragte fuer die Unterlagen des Staatssicherheitsdienstes der damaligen Deutschen Demokratischen Republik: Berlin (1996).
Eiteman, D., A. Stonehill, and M. Moffett. *Multinational Business Finance* (Eighth Edition). Addison-Wesley: Reading (1998).
Elliot, G. *Twentieth Century Book of the Dead.* Penguin: London (1972).
Ellis, S. *The Rising of the Red Shawls.* Cambridge University Press: Cambridge (1985).
Erdmann, K. "Wirtschaftliche Rechnungsfuehrung im Kombinat -- Betriebswirtschaftliche Aspekte und Konsequenzen." *Das Wirtschaftssystem der DDR.* Stuttgart: Gustav Fischer (1983), 121-153.
Europaeische Wirtschaft. "In Osteuropa bleibt der erhoffte massive Investitionsfluss aus." December 13 (1991), 14.
Faber, M. "Renegotiating Official Debts." *Finance & Development* (December 1990), 19-21.
Falck, U. *VEB Bordell.* Christoph Links Verlag: Berlin (1998).
FARC-EP. "Letter From the FARC of Columbia." *Workers World* (May 7, 1998), 11.
Feinberg, L. "U.S. Intervened in Afghanistan First." *Workers World* (March 12, 1998), 11.
Feinberg, L. "The Class Character of German Fascism." *Workers World* (March 4, 1999). 13-14.
Feinberg, L. "NATO, UN Admits Women are Enslaved." *Workers World* (May 25, 2000), 9.
Feiwel, G. "The Standard of Living in Centrally Planned Economies of Eastern Europe." *Osteuropa-Wirtschaft* 25 (1980), 73-96.
Filmer, W. "Entlang der Saale." *Alltag im anderen Deutschland* (edited by W. Filmer and H. Schwan), 197-221. ECON Verlag: Duesseldorf (1985a).
Filmer, W. "Oberlausitzer Begegnungen." *Alltag im anderen Deutschland* (edited by W. Filmer and H. Schwan), 295-324. ECON Verlag: Duesseldorf (1985b).
Filmer, W. and H. Schwan. *Alltag im anderen Deutschland.* ECON Verlag: Duesseldorf (1985).
Finkin, M. *Academe* (July/August, 1997), 19-20.
Fisher, A. "Poehl Accuses Bonn of Risking D-Mark." *Financial Times* (May

15, 1992), 2.
Fishman, R. "The American Metropolis at Century's End: Past and Future Influences." *Housing Facts & Findings* 1 (Winter 1999), 1-15.
Fitzgibbon, L. *Unpitied and Unknown.* Bachman & Turner: London (1972).
Flood, R. and P. Garber. "Gold Monetization and Gold Discipline." *Journal of Political Economy* 92 (1984), 90-107.
Flounders, S. "The War is About the Mines." *Workers World* (July 30, 1998a), 9.
Flounders, S. (editor). *The Children Are Dying.* IAC: New York (1998b).
Flounders, S. "The Achilles Heel of Media Power: Loss of Credibility." *War, Lies & Videotape* (edited by L. Foerstel). IAC: New York (2000), 85-94.
Foerstel, L. (editor). *War, Lies & Videotape.* IAC: New York (2000).
Forney, M. "China Heralds Budget That Trims Deficit." *Wall Street Journal* (March 7, 2000), A18.
Forsyth, F. *The Biafra Story.* Penguin: Harmondsworth (1969).
Fox, S. "U.S. Pop Culture in Germany." *Funnel* (December 1991), 9-12.
Frankel, J. "Recent Estimates of Time-Variation in the Conditional Variance and in the Exchange Risk Premium." *Journal of International Money and Finance* 7 (1988), 115-125.
Frankel, J. and A. Rose. "Empirical Research on Nominal Exchange Rates." *Handbook of International Economics,* Vol. 3 (1995), 1689-1730.
Frankfurter Allgemeine. "Bauernverband in Ostdeutschland aufgeloest." December 23 (1991), 9.
Frankfurter Allgemeine. "Ifo nennt Wachstum im Osten beunruhigend." January 12 (1998a), 15.
Frankfurter Allgemeine. "Die Zeiten fuer die Werften Suedkorea sind schwierig." April 29 (1998b), 18.
Franklin, J. *The Cuban Revolution and the United States.* Ocean: New York (1994).
Freeze, G. *Russia: A History.* Oxford University Press: Oxford (1997).
Friedland, J. "The Have-Nots." *Wall Street Journal* (September 27, 1999), R22.
Friedman, T. "A Manifesto for the Fast World: From Supercharged Financial Markets to Osama bin Laden, the Emerging Global Order Demands an Enforcer. That's America's New Burden." *New York Times Magazine* (March 28, 1999), 40-95.
Frankfurter Rundschau. "So koennte ich heute fast das gleiche sagen wie damals." November 4 (1999), 7.
Fritsch, P. "Brazilian Central Bank Isn't Expected to Lower Interest Rates at Policy Session Set for Next Week." *Wall Street Journal* (March 16, 2000), A23.

Froot, K. and K. Rogoff. "Perspectives on PPP and Long-Run Real Exchange Rates." *Handbook of International Economics,* Vol. 3 (1995), 1647-1688.
Froot, K., D. Scharfstein, and J. Stein. "Herd on the Street: Informational Inefficiencies in a Market With Short-Term Speculation." *Journal of Finance* 47 (1992), 1461-1484.
Fullerton, T., C. Sawyer, and R. Sprinkle. "Latin American Trade Elasticities." *Journal of Economics and Finance* 23 (1999), 143-156.
Furian, G. *Mehl aus Mielkes Muehlen.* Das Neue Berlin: Berlin (1991).
Furiati, C. *ZR Rifle.* Ocean: Melbourne (1994).
Furlough, E. and C. Strikwerda. *Consumers against Capitalism.* Rowman & Littlefield: Lanham (1999).
Galvez, W. *Che in Africa.* Ocean Press: Melbourne (1999).
Garrettson, G. "Germany in the 1990s: Recovery or Reconstruction?" *Funnel* (June 1991), 27-32.
Gauck, J. *Die Stasi-Akten.* Rowohlt: Hamburg (1991).
Gavin, M. "Intertemporal Dimensions of International Economic Adjustment: Evidence from the Franco-Prussian War Indemnity." *American Economic Review* 82 (1992), 174-179.
Gerlin, A. "How a Penney Buyer Made up to $1.5 Million on Vendors' Kickbacks." *Wall Street Journal* (February 7, 1995), A1.
Getty, A., G. Rittersporn, and V. Zemskov. "Victims of the Soviet Penal System in the Pre-War Years: A First Approach on the Basis of Archival Evidence." *American Historical Review* 98 (1993), 1017-1049.
Getty, A. *Origins of the Great Purges.* Cambridge University Press: Cambridge (1985).
Gey, P. and W. Quaisser. "Planungssystem, Entwicklungsstrategie und Wirtschaftsreform im Sozialismus." *Osteuropa-Wirtschaft* 34 (1989), 33-48.
Giancana, S. and C. Giancana. *Double Cross.* Warner: New York (1992).
Gibson, N. "Author Aims at Market and Finance Culture." *National Business Review* (April 1, 1999), 30.
Gibson, R. and Y. Ono. "Cereal Prices are Cut by Philip Morris's Post." *Wall Street Journal* (April 16, 1999), A2.
Giovannini, A. "Capital Controls and International Trade Finance." *Journal of International Economics* 33 (1992), 285-304.
Giraldo, J. *Colombia: The Genocidal Democracy.* Common Courage Press: Monroe (1996).
Girardet, E. *Afghanistan: the Soviet War.* St. Martin's Press: New York (1985).
Glick, R. and K. Rogoff. "Global versus Country-specific Productivity Shocks and the Current Account." *Journal of Monetary Economics* 35 (1995), 159-192.
Glotzer, A. *The Case of Leon Trotsky.* Merit Publishers: New York (1968).

Goertemaker, M. *Unifying Germany.* St. Martin's Press: New York (1994).
Goff, S. "Is Colombia the Next Vietnam." *Workers World* (May 11, 2000), 12.
Goldfeld, S. and R. Quandt. "Budget Constraints, Bailouts, and the Firm under Central Planning." *Journal of Comparative Economics* 12 (1988), 502-520.
Goldman, M. *What Went Wrong With Perestroika.* Norton: New York (1991).
Goldstein, F. "Brazil and the Imperialist Banks." *Workers World* (January 28, 1999).
Goldstein, M. and Khan M. "The Supply and Demand for Exports: A Simultaneous Approach." *Review of Economics and Statistics* 60 (1978), 275-286.
Golub, S. "Foreign-Currency Government Debt, Asset Markets, and the Balance of Payments." *Journal of International Money and Finance* (1989), 285-294.
Gong, T. *The Politics of Corruption in Contemporary China.* Praeger: Westport (1994).
Goodhardt, C. "The Foreign Exchange Market: A Random Walk With a Dragging Anchor." *Economica* 55 (1988), 437-460.
Gopal, R. *British Rule in India.* Asia PublishingHouse: New York (1963).
Gordon, R. "Can High Tax Rates Encourage Entrepreneurial Activity." *IMF Staff Papers* 42 (1995), 49-80.
Granick, D. *Management of the Industrial Firm in the USSR.* Greenwood: Westport (1974).
Green, J. "Ford's Secret Art Weapon: Anthropology." *Oakland Press* (September 14, 1999), C-2.
Greene, J. *The Presidency of George Bush.* University Press of Kansas: Lawrence (2000).
Gregory, P. *Russian National Income, 1885-1913.* Cambridge University Press: Cambridge (1982).
Gregory, P. and G. Leptin. "Similar Societies under Differing Economic Systems: the Case of the Two Germanies." *Soviet Studies* 29 (1977), 519-542.
Gregory, P. and R. Stuart. *Comparative Economic Systems.* Houghton Mifflin: Boston (1995).
Grey, I. *The First Fifty Years.* Coward-McCann: New York (1967).
Grinde, D. "Cherokee Removal and American Politics." *Indian Historian* 8 (Winter 1975), 33-42.
Griswold, D. "A Preliminary Appraisal-- What the China Trip Signifies." *Workers World* (March 2, 1972).
Griswold, D. *Indonesia.* World View Publishers: New York (1979).
Griswold, D. "The Buying and Selling of Yeltsin: Market Politics in Russia." *Workers World* (June 27, 1996).
Griswold, D. "Albania: A Few Got Rich, the Rest are Enraged." *Workers World* (March 13, 1997).

Griswold, D. "What Drives the Conflict in Central Africa?" *Workers World* (March 18, 1999a), 8.
Griswold, D. "Will U.S. Ease Economic War Against North Korea." *Workers World* (September 30, 1999b), 6-7.
Griswold, D. "Korean Survivors Recount U.S. War Crimes." *Workers World* (June 8, 2000), 7-8.
Grunfeld, T. *The Making of Modern Tibet.* Sharpe: Armonk (1996)
Grunwald, H. "A World Without a Country." *Wall Street Journal* (January 1, 2000), R44.
Gutierrez, T. "Cuba Exposes Role Behind Terror Campaign." *Workers World* (April 14, 1999), 14.
Gwiazda, A. "Das Waehrungssystem der RGW-Laender." *Aus Politik und Zeitgeschichte* B4 (January 25, 1986), 28-37.
Haendcke-Hoppe-Arndt, M. "Aussenwirtschaft und innerdeutscher Handel." *Die wirtschaftliche und oekologische Situation der DDR* (edited by E. Kuhrt). Leske & Budrich: Opladen (1996).
Hahn, E., A. Kosing, and F. Rupprecht. *Staatsbuergerkunde.* Dietz: Berlin (1983).
Haller, A. and H. Stoll. "Market Structure and Transaction Costs." *Journal of Finance* 44 (1989), 697-708.
Halliday, J. "The North Korean Phenomenon." *New Left Review* (May-June 1981), 29.
Hamburger Abendblatt. "Stoerer im Polizei-Kessel - 482 festgenommen." July 7 (1992), 2.
Handelsblatt. DIW: Produktivitaetsziffern kein Argument fuer 2:1." April 5 (1990), 7.
Hansen, M. "No Place to Hide." *ABA Journal* 83 (August 1997), 44-48.
Haque, N., P. Montiel, and S. Symansky. "A Forward Looking Macroeconomic Simulation Model for a Developing Country." *Journal of Policy Modeling* 13 (1991), 41-65.
Harbury, J. *Bridge of Courage.* Common Courage Press: Monroe (1994).
Harmssen, G. *Am Abend der Demontage.* Friedrich Truejen Verlag: Bremen (1951).
Harrison, M. "GDPs of the USSR and Eastern Europe: Towards an Interwar Comparison." *Europe-Asia Studies* 46 (1994), 243-259.
Hastings, D. "Spruikers Bring Personality to Nato's War." *New Zealand Herald* (April 10, 1999), B3.
Haugen, R. *The New Finance.* Upper Saddle River: Prentice Hall (1999).
Hays, L. "Top Russian Banker Ridicules Monday's Ruble Devaluation." *Wall Street Journal* (December 6, 1991), A3.
Hearst Newspapers. "Bought Votes May Determine Russian Election." *Oak-*

land Press (June 15, 1996), A10.
Heimann, C. *Systembedingte Ursachen des Niedergangs der DDR-Wirtschaft.* Peter Lang: Frankfurt am Main (1997).
Henderson, C. *Asia Falling?* McGraw-Hill: New York (1998).
Henige, D. *Numbers from Nowhere.* University of Oklahoma Press: Norman (1998).
Henke K. and R. Engelmann. *Aktenlage.* Christoph Links Verlag: Berlin (1995).
Herman, E. *Atrocities in Vietnam: Myths and Realities.* Pilgrim Press: Philadelphia (1970).
Herman, E. and N. Chomsky. *Manufacturing Consent.* Pantheon: New York (1988).
Hersh, S. "Overwhelming Force." *New Yorker* (May 22, 2000), 49-82.
Hertle, H. "Der Fall der Mauer aus der Sicht der NVA und der Grenztruppen der DDR." *Deutschland Archiv* (1995), 901-919.
Hertle, H. *Chronik des Mauerfalls.* Christoph Links Verlag: Berlin (1996).
Heseltine, N. *Madagascar.* Praeger: New York (1971).
Heym, S. and W. Heiduczek. *Die sanfte Revolution.* Gustav Kiepenheuer: Leipzig (1990).
Hilsenrath, J. "New Zealand Readies for Elections with Economic Policy on Agenda." *Wall Street Journal* (October 29, 1999), A17.
Himes, S. "Russia's Tax Reforms." *OECD Observer* (January 1999), 26-29.
Hine, R. "International Economic Integration." *Surveys in International Trade* (ed. by D. Greenaway and A. Winters). Blackwell: Oxford (1994), 234-272.
Hintereder, P. and M. Zipf. "The Battle for the Daily Headline: Too Much Information?" *Deutschland* (February/March 2000), 56-59.
Ho, C., K. Hui, and P. Ho. *The US Imperialists Started the Korean War.* Foreign Languages Publishing House: Pyongyang (1993).
Ho, P. *Studies on the Population of China, 1368-1953.* Harvard University Press: Cambridge (1959).
Hobhouse, H. *Forces of Change.* Arcade Publishing: New York (1989).
Hof, H. "Motivationale Probleme der intensiven Nutzung des Arbeitskraeftepotentials." *Das Wirtschaftssystem der DDR.* Gustav Fischer: Stuttgart (1983), 103-119.
Hofmann, J. *Es ging um Deutschland.* Dietz: Berlin (1990).
Honecker, E. *Moabiter Notizen.* Edition ost: Berlin (1994).
Hooper, P. and J. Morton. "Fluctuations in the Dollar: a Model of Nominal and Real Exchange Rate Determination." *Journal of International Money and Finance* 1 (1982), 39-56.
Horne, A. *A Savage War of Peace: Algeria 1954-1962.* Viking Press: New York (1977).

Horowitz, L. *Emerging Viruses.* Tetrahedron: Rockport (1997).
Hosking, R. "Market Divided Over 'Quiet' Ditching of Unpopular Monetary Conditions Index." *National Business Review* (February 12, 1999), 8.
Hu, Z. and M. Khan. "Why is China Growing so Fast?" *IMF Staff Papers* 44 (1997), 103-131.
Hudson, J. "The Impact of the New Bankruptcy Code Upon the Average Liability of Bankrupt Firms." *Journal of Banking and Finance* 16 (1992), 351-371.
G. Hufbauer and J. Erb. *Subsidies in International Trade.* Institute for International Economics: Washington (1984).
Hufbauer, G. and J. Schott. *North American Free Trade: Issues and Recommendations.* Institute of International Economics: Washington (1992).
Hutchings, R. *Soviet Economic Development.* New York University Press: New York (1982).
IAC. *Nato in the Balkans.* IAC: New York (1998a).
IAC. *Challenge to Genocide.* IAC: New York (1998b).
Ignatius, A. "Yeltsin Clears the Final Draft of Constitution." *Wall Street Journal* (November 9, 1993), A15.
Ignatius, A. and C. Rosett. "Yeltsin Routs Hard-Liners, but not Russia's Problems." *Wall Street Journal* (October 5, 1993), A3.
IMF. "Fund-Supported Programs, Fiscal Policy, and Income Distribution." *IMF Occassional Paper* 46 (1986).
IMF. *World Economic Outlook.* IMF: Washington (May, 1992), 105.
IMF. *World Economic Outlook.* IMF: Washington (October, 1993), 131.
IMF. *World Economic Outlook.* IMF: Washington (October 1996), 167.
IMF. *World Economic Outlook.* IMF: Washington (October 1997a), 147.
IMF. *World Economic Outlook.* IMF: Washington (December 1997b), 49-51.
IMF. *World Economic Outlook.* IMF: Washington (October 1998).
IMF. *World Economic Outlook.* IMF: Washington (May 1999), 150.
Independent Commission of Inquiry. "Report from the Initial Hearing." IAC: New York (1999).
Investor's Business Daily. "Washington & World." February 25 (1993), 1.
Investor's Business Daily. "Stadium Madness." December 30 (1997), A6.
Ip, G. "Analyst Discovers Order in the Chaos of Huge Valuations for Internet Stocks." *Wall Street Journal* (December 27, 1999), C1, C2.
Isaacman, A. and B. Isaacman. *Mozambique: From Colonialism to Revolution.* Westview: Boulder (1983).
Ishiyama, Y. "The Theory of Optimum Currency Areas." *IMF Staff Papers* 22 (1975), 344-383.
Jackson, J. "Is the Press Really Free in the 21st Century?" *Censored 2000.* Seven Stories Press: New York (2000), 176-182
Jacobs, B. and K. Levy. "Disentangling Equity Return Regularities: New

Insights and Investment Opportunities." *Financial Analysts Journal* 44 (May/ June 1988), 18-44.
Jaffe, A. *The First Immigrants from Asia.* Plenum Press: New York (1992).
Jaimes, A. *The State of Native America.* South End Press: Boston (1992).
Jalali, A. and L. Grau. *The Other Side of the Mountain: Mujahideen Tactics in the Soviet-Afghan War.* U.S. Marine Corps: Quantico (1995).
Jennings, F. *The Invasion of America.* University of North Carolina Press: Chapel Hill (1975).
Jennings, F. *Empire of Fortune.* Norton: New York (1988).
Jennings, F. *The Founders of America.* Norton: New York (1993).
Jensen, C. "What Free Press?" *Censored 2000* (edited by P. Phillips). Seven Stories Press: New York (2000), 183-185.
Jensen, M. "Agency Costs of Free Cash Flow, Corporate Finance, and Take-overs." *American Economic Review* (1986), 323-329.
Johansson, R. "The Demographic History of the Native Peoples of North America: A Selective Bibliography." *Yearbook of Physical Anthropology* 25 (1982), 133-152.
Johnson, S. "RTC's Affordable Housing Program: Reconciling Competing Goals." *Housing Policy Debate* 1 (1990), 87-130.
Johnson, I. "China's Economic Health Raises Doubts." *Wall Street Journal* (May 31, 2000), A22.
Johnstone, D. "Seeing Yugoslavia throug a Dark Glass: the Ideological Uniformity of the Media." *War, Lies & Videotaping* (edited by L. Foerstel). IAC: New York (2000), 145-162.
Joint Economic Committee (Congress of the United States). *Economic Reforms in the U.S.S.R.* U.S. Government Printing Office: Washington (1988).
Joppke, C. *East German Dissidents and the Revolution of 1989.* New York University Press: New York (1995).
Junge Welt. "Nur jeder Dritte: Besser mit D-Mark." July 1 (1991), 1-2.
Kamin, S. "The Current International Financial Crisis: How Much is New?" *Journal of International Money & Finance* 18 (1999), 501-514.
Kamm, T., Rohwedder C., and Y. Trofimov. "Europe can't Decide Whether Dirty Money in Politics is a Problem." *Wall Street Journal* (February 9, 2000), A1, A6.
Kamm, T. and C. Vitzthum. "Spain's Premiuer Faces Tough Road to Re-election Despite Economic Boom." *Wall Street Journal* (March 9, 2000), A22.
Kaplan, D. "Yakuza Inc." *US News and World Report* (April 13, 1998), 40-47
Karnow, S. *In Our Image.* Random House: New York (1989).
Katz, I. and L. Cohn. "Pulling Brazil Back From the Brink." *Business Week* (Asian Edition, May 10, 1999), 64-65.
Kaufman, J. "The Omnipresent Persuaders." *Wall Street Journal* (January 1,

2000), R26.
Keeler, A. "Remote Mind Control Technology." *Full Disclosure* 15 (1989), 11.
Keidel, A. "The Cyclical Future of China's Economic Reforms." *China's Economic Dilemmas in the 1990s: The Problems of Reforms, Modernization, and Interdependence* (submitted to the Joint Economic Committee of the Congress of the United States). U.S. Government Printing Office: Washington (1991), 119-134.
Keithly, D. *The Collapse of Est German Communism.* Praeger: Westport (1992).
Kempe, F. "East Europe Offers Investors Big Profits and Big Perils." *Wall Street Journal* (January 11, 1991a), A6.
Kempe, F. "Fading Menace: East Germans See Soviet Threat as Just Economic." *Wall Street Journal* (August 26, 1991b), A12.
Khan, R. *Untying the Afghan Knot.* Duke University Press: Durham (1991).
Kiernan, B. *The Pol Pot Regime.* Yale University Press: New Haven (1996).
Kiernan, V. *Colonial Empires and Armies 1815-1960.* McGill-Queen's University Press: Montreal (1998).
Kindleberger, C. *International Economics.* Irwin: Homewood (1968).
King, A. "Uncovered Interest Parity: New Zealand's Post-Deregulation Experience." *Applied Financial Economics* 8 (1998), 495-503.
King, M. *1000 Years of Maori History.* Reed Books: Auckland (1997).
King, N. "Surging Oil Prices Complicate U.S. Moves in Iraq." *Wall Street Journal* (March 17, 2000), A16.
Kiplinger's. "Media Firms Use Ad Blitz to Help their Stock." *Oakland Press* (February 11, 2000), C-2.
Klass, R. (editor). *Afghanistan: The Great Game Revisited.* Freedom House: New York (1987).
Klebnikov, P. "Vulnerable." Forbes Global Business & Finance (March 22, 1999), 20-22.
Kleinschmid, H. "Der Traum vom Pornofilm." *Alltag im anderen Deutschland* (edited by W. Filmer and H. Schwan), 132-137. ECON Verlag: Duesseldorf (1985).
Klinghoffer, A. *The International Dimension of Genocide in Rwanda.* New York University Press: New York (1998).
Knauff, R. "Die Investitionspolitik der DDR." *Das Wirtschaftssytem der DDR.* Gustav Fischer: Stuttgart (1983), 331-344.
Knight, A. *Beria.* Princeton University Press: Princeton (1993).
Knight, S. *The Brotherhood.* Panthar Books: London (1983).
Koenker, D. and R. Bachman. *Revelations From the Russian Archives.* Library of Congress: Washington (1997).

Konadu-Agyemang, K. "Structural Adjustment Programs and the Perpetuating of Poverty and Undevelopment in Africa: Ghana's Experience Revisited." *Scandinavian Journal of Development Alternatives and Area Studies* 17 (1998), 127-143.

Kowalewski, S. and J. Hatch. "The Sixteenth-Century Expansion of Settlement in the Upper Oconee Watershed, Georgia." *Southeastern Archaeology* 10 (1991), 1-17.

Krakat, K. "Probleme der DDR-Industrie im letzten Fuenfjahrplanzeitraum." *Die wirtschaftliche und oekologische Situation der DDR* (edited by E. Kuhrt). Leske and Budrich: Opladen (1996).

Kramm, J. "Groessere Wohlstand, groessere Freiheit, groessere Unsicherheit." *Berliner Zeitung* (November 8, 1999), 1.

Krasker, W. "The 'Peso Problem' in Testing the Efficiency of Forward Exchange Rate Markets." *Journal of Monetary Economics* 6 (1980), 269-276.

Kravis, I. and R. Lipsey. "National Price Levels and the Prices of Tradables and Nontradables." *American Economic Review* (1988), 474-478.

Krenz, E. *Wenn Mauern fallen*. Paul Neff: Vienna (1990).

Krivosheev, G. (editor). *Soviet Casualties and Combat Losses*. Greenhill Books: London (1997).

Kroeber, A. *Cultural and Natural Areas of Native North America*. University of California Press: Berkeley (1963).

Krueger, T. and W. Kennedy. "An Examination of the Super Bowl Stock Market Predictor." *Journal of Finance* 45 (1990), 691-698.

Kuhn, E. *Der Tag der Entscheidung*. Ullstein: Berlin (1992).

Kuperman, A. "The Stinger Missile and U.S. Intervention in Afghanistan." *Political Science Quarterly* 114 (Summer 1999), 219-263.

Kusch, G., R. Montag R., G. Specht G., and K. Wetzker. *Schlussbilanz—DDR*. Duncker & Humblot: Berlin (1991).

Kwong, J. *The Political Economy of Corruption in China*. Sharpe: New York (1997).

Labs, R. "Handelsmarketing." *Die Marktwirtschaft* (July 1991), 72-75.

Lachica, E. "Asian Capital Controls Were No Panacea." *Wall Street Journal* (January 12, 2000), A18.

Laffin, J. *The World in Conflict: War Annual 6*. Brassey's: London (1994).

Lahann, B. "Der Held der Pedale." *Stern* (April 30, 1998), 96-104.

Larcker, D. "The Association Between Performance Plan Adoption and Corporate Capital Investment." *Journal of Accounting and Economics* 5 (1985).

Larsen, C. "In the Wake of Columbus: Native Population Biology in the Postcontact Americas." *American Journal of Physical Anthropology* 54 (1994, Supplement 19), 109-154.

Lau, L., Y. Qian, and G. Roland. "Reform Without Losers: An Interpretation

of China's Dual-Track Approach to Transition." *Journal of Political Economy* 108 (2000), 120-143.
Leggett, K. "Steel Surge Causes Quandary for China." *Wall Street Journal* (June 1, 2000), A18.
Leggett, K. and I. Johnson. "China Bets Farm on Promise (and Glory) of Genetic Engineering." *Wall Street Journal* (March 29, 2000), A17.
Leopold, P. "Der Zweisamkeit fehlt der Raum." *Alltag im anderen Deutschland* (edited by W. Filmer and H. Schwan), 138-146. ECON Verlag: Duesseldorf (1985).
Lerner, A. *The Economics of Control.* Macmillan: New York (1944).
Levene, M. and P. Roberts (ed.). *The Massacre in History.* Berghahn Books: New York (1999).
Lewis, J. "Objectivity and the Limits of Press Freedom." *Censored 2000.* Seven Stories Press: New York (2000), 171-176.
Lewis, V. "Revolutionary Communism and the Black Liberation Struggle." *Workers World* (March 4, 1999), 6.
Lewy, G. *America in Vietnam.* Oxford University Press: New York (1978).
Leybourne, S. and P. Mizen. "Understanding the Disinflations in Australia, Canada, and New Zealand Using Evidence from Smooth Transition Analysis." *Journal of International Money and Finance* 18 (1999), 799-816.
Lim, L. "An Overview of the Asian Financial Crisis." *Journal of Asian Business* 15 (1999), 79-81.
Lindsey, L. "Arranged Marriage." *Forbes Global Business & Finance* (March 8, 1999), 69.
Lippe, P. and V. Heese V. "Probleme des Lebensstandardvergleichs." *Das Wirtschaftssystem der DDR.* Gustav Fischer: Stuttgart (1983), 417-447.
Liu, X., H. Song, Y. Wei, and P. Romilly. "Country Characteristics and Foreign Direct Investment in China: A Panel Data Analysis." *Weltsirtschaftliches Archiv* 133 (1997), 313-329.
Los Angeles Times. "Job-Hunting in Russia Now a Wild Free-For-All." January 7 (1996), A-5.
MacDonald, E. "SEC to Boost Accounting-Fraud Attack, Work More With Criminal Prosecutors." *Wall Street Journal* (December 8, 1999a), A4.
MacDonald, E. "Libel Suits Pose a Risk for Analysts." *Wall Street Journal* (December 29, 1999b), C1.
MacDonald, R. "Empirical Studies of Exchange Rate Determination" in *Current Issues in Monetary Economics* (ed. by D. Lewellyn and C. Milner). Macmillan: London (1990).
MacFarquhar, R. *The Politics of China 1949-1989.* Cambridge University Press: Cambridge (1993).
Mackenzie, G. "The Macroeconomic Impact of Privatization." *IMF Staff Papers*

45 (1998), 363-373.
MacLeod, W. *The American Indian Frontier.* Alfred A. Knopf: New York (1928).
MacManus, S. *The Story of the Irish Race.* Devin-Adair: New York (1973).
Macy, S. *Perestroika.* WW Publishers: New York (1990).
Maddison, A. *Economic Growth in Japan and the USSR.* Norton: New York (1969).
Maddison, A. *Monitoring the World Economy, 1820-1992.* OECD: Paris (1995).
Mallery, G. "Former and Present Number of Our Indians." *Proceedings of the American Association for the Advancement of Science* 26 (1877), 340-366.
Maloba, W. *Mau Mau and Kenya: An Analysis of a Peasant Revolt.* Indiana University Press: Bloomington (1993).
Manning, R. "The Soviet Economic Crisis of 1936-1940 and the Great Purges." *Stalinist Terror.* Cambridge University Press: Cambridge (1993), 116-141.
M. Manzur. "An International Comparison of Prices and Exchange Rates: A New Test of Purchasing Power Parity." *Journal of International Money and Finance* 9 (1990), 75-91.
Maran, R. *Torture: The Role of Ideology in the French-Algerian War.* Praeger: Westport (1989).
Marcy, S. *Perestroika.* WW Publishers: New York (1990).
Marcy, S. *Poland: Behind the Crisis.* World View Publishers: New York (1982).
Markusen, E. and D. Kopf. *The Holocaust and Strategic Bombing.* Westview Press: Boulder (1995).
J. Marquez. "Bilateral Trade Elasticities." *Review of Economics and Statistics* 72 (1990), 75-86.
Marshall, A. *Money, Credit, and Commerce.* Macmillan: New York (1924).
Marshall, S. "Vietnam Trade Pact in Limbo." *Wall Street Journal* (October 7, 1999), A24.
Marston, R. "Pricing to Market in Japanese Manufacturing." *Journal of International Economics* 29 (1990), 217-236.
Martin, C. *Keepers of the Game.* University of California Press: Berkeley (1978).
Marx, K. and F. Engels F. *Manifest der Kommunistischen Partei.* Dietz Verlag: Berlin (1988a).
Marx, K. and F. Engels. *Das Kapital.* Dietz Verlag: Berlin (1988b).
Massey News. "Tourism Board Changes Right Move." May 10 (1999), 4.
Mathiowetz, D. "'Shut Down the Pentagon Torture Academy.'" *Workers World* (December 2, 1999), 2.
Matlock, J. *Autopsy on an Empire.* Random House: New York (1995).

Matthews, R. "U.S. Steel Industry Itself Gets Billions in Public Subsidies, Study Concludes." *Wall Street Journal* (November 29, 1999), B12.

Matz, A. *Plankosten, Deckungsbeitraege und Budgets.* Gabler: Wiesbaden (1975).

Mauro, P. and A. Spilimbergo. "How do the Skilled and the Unskilled Respond to Regional Shocks." *IMF Staff Papers* 47 (1999), 1-17.

Maximytschew, I. and H. Hertle. "Die Maueroeffnung." *Deutschland Archiv* 11 (1994), 1137-1251.

McCarthy, J. *Basic Marketing: A Managerial Approach.* Irwin: Homewood (1975).

McChesney, R. "The Big Media Game has Fewer and Fewer Players." *Censored 2000.* Seven Stories Press: New York (2000), 187-198.

McCormack, G. and M. Selden. *Korea North and South.* Monthly Review Press: New York (1978).

McCracken, H. *George Catlin and the Old Frontier.* Dial Press: New York (1959).

McGee, S. "Tax Inquiry Turns Banking Grayer in Luxembourg." *Wall Street Journal* (July 19, 1999), C1.

McInerney, A. "New Gains for Colombian Revolutionary Movement." *Workers World* (August 20, 1998), 11.

McLoughlin, D. "Why Won't the Economy Fly?" *North & South* (July 1993), 44-54.

McManus, J. "US Retaliates on NZ Lamb." *The Independent* (February 17, 1999), 1-4.

McMichael, S. *Stumbling Bear.* Brassey's: London (1991).

McNamara, R. *Argument Without End.* Public Affairs: New York (1999).

Mead, W. "In the Dark Shadow of History." *Worth* 3 (September 1994), 49-53.

Mead, L. "The Twilight of Liberal Welfare Reform." *Public Interest* (Spring 2000), 22-34.

Medvedev, G (translated by E. Rossiter). *The Truth about Chernobyl.* Basic Books: New York (1991).

Meisner, M. *Mao's China and After.* Free Press: New York (1999).

Meister, C. "Demographic Consequences of Euro-American Contact on Selected AmericanIndian Populations and their Relationship to the Demographic Transition." *Ethnohistory* 23 (1976), 161-172.

Melzer, M. "Wandlungen im Preissystem der DDR." *Das Wirtschaftssytem der DDR.* Gustav Fischer: Stuttgatt (1983), 51-73.

Melzer, M. and A. Stahnke. "The GDR Faces the Econoic Dilemmas of the 1980s: Caught Between the Need for New Methods and Restricted Options." *East European Economies: Slow Growth in the 1980s* (submitted to the Joint

Economic Committee of the Congress of the United States). U.S. Government Printing Office: Washington (1986), 131-221.
Mendershausen, H. "The Terms of Soviet-Satellite Trade: A Broadened Analysis." *Review of Economics and Statistics* 42 (May 1960), 152-163.
Merkel, W. and S. Wahl. *Das gepluenderte Deutschland.* IWG: Bonn (1991).
Merriam, H. "The Indian Population of California." *American Anthropologist* 7 (1905), 594-606.
Merritt, R. and A. Merritt. *Living with the Wall, 1961-85.* Duke University Press: Durham (1985).
Meurs, M. *Many Shades of Red.* Rowman & Little: Lanham (1999).
Meyer, S. and E. Schulze. "After the Fall of the Wall: the Impact of the Transition on East German Women." *Political Psychology* 19 (1998), 95-116.
Milan, M. *The Squad.* Shapolsky: New York (1989).
Miller, J. *Way of Death.* University of Wisconsin Press: Madison (1988).
Miller, M. *Bulgaria during the Second World War.* Stanford University Press: Stanford (1975).
Miller, M. "The Current Southeast Asia Financial Crisis." *Pacific-Basin Finance Journal* 6 (1998), 225-233.
Miller, V. "Whatever Happened to the Yuki?" *Indian Historian* 8 (Fall 1975), 6-12.
Millman, J. "A New Future for Mexico's Work Force." *Wall Street Journal* (April 14, 2000), A15.
Minter, W. *Apartheid's Contras.* Witwatersrand University Press: Johannesburg (1994).
Mississippi Valley Historical Review. "News and Comment." Volume 12 (1925), 295-305.
Mittag, G. *Um jeden Preis.* Aufbau: Berlin (1991).
Moffett, M. "Brazil Suddenly Faces Export Slowdown." *Wall Street Journal.* (March 12, 1997), A15.
Mok, H.and Y. Hui. "Underpricing and Aftermarket Performance of IPOs in Shanghai, China." *Pacific-Basin Finance Journal* 6 (1998), 453-474.
Mooney, J. *The Aboriginal Population of America North of Mexico.* Smithsonian Institution: Washington (1928).
Moorehead, M. "Bombings in Africa Raise Many Questions." *Workers World* (August 20, 1998), 9.
Moran, P. "NZ Farmers Guarded Over Reforms in Europe." *Dominion* (March 13, 1999), 2.
Morgan, G. "Inheritance and Farming Create an Economic Drag." *National Business Review* (April 9, 1999), 15.
Morgan, J. "Rip Van Winkle's New World Order." *Financial Times* (April 26, 1992), II.

Morgenstern, O. *On the Accuracy of Economic Observations*. Princeton University Press: Princeton (1963).
Mueller, B. "The Truth About Trabi: Former East Germans Gauge the Odd Appeal of a Quirky Car." *Worldbusiness* 2 (January/February 1996), 16.
Mueller, E., A. Murphy, and Z. Sabov. "Ein empirischer Vergleich betrieblicher Finanzstrukturen Westdeutschlands und der ehemaligen DDR." *Zeitschrift fuer Unternehmensgeschichte* 38 (1993), 261-268.
Mueller, E. "Zur Entwicklung der Effektivitaet in der Industrie der Deutschen Demokratischen Republik in den Jahren 1960 bis 1977." Research Paper at the Zentralinstitut fuer sozialistische Wirtschaftsfuehrung beim ZK der SED: Berlin (1978), I2.
Mueller, E. "Analyse ueber Strukturentwicklung auf dem Gebiete des NSW-Exports." Research Paper at the Zentralinstitut fuer sozialistische Wirtschaftsfuehrung beim ZK der SED: Berlin (November 16, 1989).
Mueller-Enbergs, H. *Inoffizielle Mitarbeiter.* Christoph Links Verlag: Berlin (1996).
Mufson, S. "IMF Admission Urged for Ex-Soviet Republics." *Washington Post* (January 4, 1992), B1.
Mukherjee, M. "Public Access to Information in India." *War, Lies & Videotape* (edited by L. Foerstel). IAC: New York (2000).
Murphy, A. "Analyzing Sub-Classes of General Motors Common Stock." *Financial Management* 18 (Spring 1989), 64-71.
Murphy, A. "Currency and Economic Union." *International Economic Newsletter* 23 (1990a), 1-3.
Murphy, A. "In Defense of the 'Indefensible': A Eulogy for the Berlin Wall?" *Funnel* (April 1990b), 20-22.
Murphy, A. "An Analysis of Terms of Trade Problems." *Economic Systems* 16 (1992a), 149-160.
Murphy, A. "An Empirical Analysis of the Market for Inconvertible Currency." *Journal of International Financial Markets, Institutions & Money* 2 (1992b), 51-75.
Murphy, A. *Research Solutions to the Financial Problems of Depository Institutions.* Quorum Books: Westport (1992c).
Murphy, A. "Parallels Between Eastern Europe and Mexico." *International Economic Newsletter* 40 (1995), 1-3.
Murphy, A. "The Determinants of Exchange Rates Between Two Major Currencies." *Multinational Business Review* 4 (1996), 107-111.
Murphy, A. "A Note on Economic Growth in Eastern Europe." *Journal of Economic Issues* 32 (1998), 1150-1152.
Murphy, A. *Scientific Investment Analysis.* Quorum Books: Westport (2000).
Murray, D. "Author: U.S. Must Resolve Racial Issues to Survive." *Oakland*

Press (March 10, 2000), A-13.
Myers, S. and N. Majluf. "Corporate Financing and Investment Decisions When Firms Have Information That Investors Do Not Have." *Journal of Financial Economics* 13 (1984), 187-221.
Myers, S. "Determinants of Corporate Borrowing." *Journal of Financial Economics* 5 (1977), 147-175.
Naumann, G. and E. Truempler. *Von Ulbricht zu Honecker.* Dietz: Berlin (1990).
Nawrocki, J. "DDR-Waehrung: Der Kurs ging in den Keller." *Die Zeit* (January 30, 1987), p. 29.
Naylor, R. "Economic Sanctions Devastate Iraq." *Toronto Star* (June 30, 2000), A21.
Nelson, M. and M. Du Bois. "West German Officials Set to Disclose Plans for Economic, Monetary Union." *Wall Street Journal* (February 13, 1990), A17.
Neues Deutschland. "Die Preise im Osten gehen deutlich nach oben." May 24 (1991), 1.
Newsweek. "Combat High Above the Clouds." May 15 (2000), 23-26.
New York Times. "Excerpts from the Pentagon's Plan: 'Prevent the Re-Emergence of a New Rival.'" March 8 (1999), 14.
New York Times News. "Hollywood Sees Shift in Audience Tastes." *Oakland Press* (March 19, 2000), A-23.
Nicholson, B. "Legal Borrowing and the Origins of Slave Law in the British Colonies." *American Journal of Legal History* 38 (1994), 38-54.
Noll, H. "Erwerbstaetigkeit und Qualitaet des Arbeitslebens." *Lebensqualitaet in der Bundesrepublik* (ed. by W. Glatzer and W. Zapf). Wissenschaftliche Buchgesellschaft: Darmstadt (1984), 97-123.
Noll, H. "Arbeitsplatzsuche und Stellenfindung." *Mobilitaetsprozesse auf dem Arbeitsmarkt* (ed. by H. Knepel and R. Hujer). Campus Verlag: Frankfurt (1985), 275-303.
Norddeutsche Neueste Nachrichten. "Mehr Gewalt in Familien." June 23 (1992), 1.
Northoff, R. "Ohne Vorurteil und Verlegenheit." *Kriminalistik* 1 (1995), 51-54.
Novack, G. *Genocide against the Indians.* Pathfinder: New York (1972).
Nove, A. "Victims of Stalinism: How Many?" *Stalinist Terror.* Cambridge University Press: Cambridge (1993), 261-274.
Ntamabyaliro, A. "The Rwandan People Accuse...." *Genocide in Rwanda* (edited by J. Berry and C. Berry). Howard University Press: Washington (1999).
O'Barr, W. and J. Conley. "Managing Relationships: The Culture of Institutional Investing." *Financial Analysts Journal* (September/October 1992),

21-27.
Oberg, J. "Misguided Motives Led to the Chaos in Kosovo." CNN Internet (http://cnn.com/SPECIALS/2000)/kosovo/stories/present/kfor/).
Obstfeld, M. "Balance-of-Payments Crises and Devaluation." *Journal of Money, Credit, & Banking* 16 (1984), 208-217.
Obstfeld, M. "Rational and Self-Fulfilling Balance-of-Payments Crises." *American Economic Review* 76 (1986), 72-81.
Obstfeld, M. and K. Rogoff. "The Intertemporal Approach to the Current Account." *Handbook of International Economics,* Vol. 3 (1995), 1731-1800.
Obstfeld, M. and K. Rogoff. *Foundations of International Macroeconomics.* MIT Press: Cambridge (1996).
Olshausen, M. "East Germany's Culture Confronts American Pop Culture." *Contemporary Review* 269 (1996), 189-93.
Opp, K. and C. Gern. "Dissident Groups, Personal Networks, and Spontaneous Cooperation: the East German Revolution of 1989." *American Sociological Review* 58 (1993), 659-680.
Oppenheimer, H. "A Test of Ben Graham's Stock Selection Criteria." *Financial Analysts Journal* 40 (September/October 1984), 68-74.
Orr, D. "Hidden Dangers in a V-Shaped Recovery." *Forbes Global* (June 14, 1999), 110-111.
Orth, M. "Neuer Markt." *Deutschland* (August 1998), 40-43.
Osgood, H. *The American Colonies.* Columbia University Press: Gloucester (1957).
Osmond, J. *German Reunification: A Reference Guide and Commentary.* Longman Current Affairs: Essex (1992).
Ostsee-Zeitung. "Gleicher Lohn in fuenf Jahren." July 9 (1990a), 1.
Ostsee-Zeitung. "Summen fuer grosse Kaeufe." July 10 (1990b), 1.
Ostseezeitung "Jelzin kritisiert Bergarbeiter." May 23/24 (1998), 2.
Paltrow, S. "In Relic of '50s and '60s, Blacks Still Pay More for a Type of Insurance." *Wall Street Journal* (April 27, 2000), A1, A8.
Parenti, M. "Media Evasion." *War, Lies & Videotape* (edited by L. Foerstel). IAC: New York (2000), 45-54.
Parker, T. "Study Proves Clinton & Co. Lied about Sudan Bombing." *Workers World* (March 4, 1999), 11.
Parrish, M. *The Lesser Terror.* Praeger: Westport (1996).
Parrott, B. (editor). *Trade, Technology, and Soviet-American Relations.* Indiana University Press: Bloomington (1985).
Patterson, W. (editor). *We Charge Genocide.* International Publishers: New York (1970).
Pearl, D. "Reporter's Notebook: Search for Mercy Ends in Tears on Quiet Kosovo Street." *Wall Street Journal* (December 2, 1999a), A18.

Pearl, D. "Peace Offensive Gathers Speed in Sudan." *Wall Street Journal* (December 8, 1999b).
Peeters, M. "The Public-Private Savings Mirror and Causality Relations Among Private Savings Investment and (Twin) Deficits." *Journal of Policy Making* 21 (1999), 579-605.
Perridon, L. and M. Steiner. *Finanzwirtschaft der Unternehmung*. Franz Vahlen: Muenchen (1988).
Peterson, R. "Scrutinizing the Inscrutable." *Investment Vision* 1 (1990), 25-27.
Philipsen, D. *We Were the People*. Duke University Press: Durham (1993).
Phillips, J. (editor). *Censored 2000*. Seven Stories Press: New York (2000),
Phillips, M. "IMF Concedes That Malaysia's Controls Over Capital Produced Positive Results." *Wall Street Journal* (September 9, 1999), A21.
Phillips, M. "Key Trade Deficit Measure Sets Record." *Wall Street Journal* (March 16, 2000a), A2.
Phillips. M. "IMF Chief-Designate Shows Independent Streak." *Wall Street Journal* (March 29, 2000b), A2.
Pipes, R. *Russia Under the Bolshevik Regime*. Knopf: New York (1993).
Pirocanac, Z. "Media and the Serbs in a New European Architecture: Modern Media—the Fourth Branch of NATO." *Wars, Lies & Videotape*. IAC: New York (2000), 163-175.
Pope, K. "CNN to Set Up Office to Thwart Errors." *Wall Street Journal* (July 6, 1998), A20.
Prebisch, R. *The Crisis of Capitalism and the Periphery*. United Nations: Geneva (1982).
Price, M. "Asia Tearing Down Barriers to Foreign Capital." *Pensions & Investments* (March 23, 1998), 14.
Pride, W. and O. Ferell. *Marketing*. Houghton Mifflin: Boston (1997).
Prouty, F. *JFK*. Birch Lane Press: New York (1992).
Purdue, D. "Tracking the Economy." *National Business Review* (April 9, 1999), 48.
Quaintance, L. "Porirua: an Unfortunate Experiment." *North & South* (June 1988).
Raith, W. *Das neue Mafia-Kartell*. Rowo hlt: Berlin (1994).
Ramirez, A. "Mayor Defends Growth of Video Surveillance." *New York Times* (December 14, 1998), B3.
Ratesh, N. *Romania: The Entangled Revolution*. Praeger: New York (1991).
Ray, E. "U.S. Military and Corporate Recolonization of Congo." *Covert Action Quarterly* (Spring-Summer 2000), 4-13.
Reed, J. "Explaining the Gap." *Wall Street Journal* (September 27, 1999), R8.
Reed, T. and J. Cummings. *Compromised*. Shapolsky: New York (1994).
Reese, R. *The Soviet Military Experience*. Routledge: London (2000).

Reifenberg, A. "Hundreds of Aliens Die Each Year Crossing From Mexico Into Texas." *Wall Street Journal* (March 15, 1996), A7.
Rein, G. *Die Opposition in der DDR*. Wichern: Berlin (1989).
Reuter. "Osteuropa im Blick von USA und Japan." *Der Tagesspiegel* (December 29, 1989), 15.
Reuter. "EU Firm on Beef Ban Despite Duty Threat." *Dominion* (May 15, 1999), 5.
Reynolds, H. *The Other Side of the Frontier.* Penguin: Ringwood (1995).
Reynolds, M. "Using the Private Sector to Deter Crime." *Journal of Social, Political and Economic Studies* 19 (1994), 207-243.
Rhoads, C. "Holzman's Collapse, Blamed on Past 'Crimes,' Raises Questions About Firms's Current Regime." *Wall Street Journal* (December 21, 1999), A18.
Rich, G. "Monetary Targets as a Policy Rule: lessons from the Swiss Experience." *Journal of Monetary Economics* 39 (1997), 113-141.
Rich, M. "Asia's Bad Loans Draw U.S. Investors." *Wall Street Journal* (April 3, 2000), A26.
Rickey, C. "Western Star Symbolized the Best American Values." *Detroit Free Press* (July 7, 1998), A1.
Riecker, A., A. Schwarz, and D. Schneider. *Stasi intim.* Forum: Leipzig (1990).
Rittersporn, G. "The Omnipresent Conspiracy: on Soviet Imagery of Politics and Social Relations in the 1930s." *Stalinism: Its Nature and Aftermath.* Armonk: New York (1992).
Roach, S. "It's a Mistake to Write off China." *National Business Review* (March 12, 1999), 25.
Robitaille, S. "Air Pollution Worries Hong Kong Firms. *Wall Street Journal* (January 4, 2000), A19.
Rodman, P. *More Precious than Peace.* Charles Scribner's Sons: New York (1994).
Rodriguez, C. "The Role of Trade Flows in Exchange Rate Determination: A Rational Expectations Approach." *Journal of Political Economy* 88 (1980), 1148-1158.
Rodrik, D. "Political Economy of Trade Policy." *Handbook of International Economics,* Vol. 3 (1995), 1457-1494.
Rohwedder, C. "East Germans Dependent on Job Subsidy Find Bonn's Budget Holds a Bitter Pill." *Wall Street Journal* (September 24, 1996), A14.
Rohwedder, C. "German Politicians Consider Primaries to Regain Trust." *Wall Street Journal* (April 5, 2000), A21.
J. Roldos. "On Gradual Disinflation, the Real Exchange Rate, and the Current Account." *Journal of International Money and Finance* 16 (1997), 37-54.

Root, F. *International Trade and Investment.* South-Western: Cincinnati (1990).
Rosett, C. "Russians Choose their Destiny Today, But Vote Won't Quell Power Struggle." *Wall Street Journal* (July 3, 1996), A7.
Roth, J. *Die Russen Mafia.* Rasch und Roehring Verlag: Hamburg (1996).
Rozin, S., J. Flynn, and C. Durcanin. "Steroids: A Spreading Peril." *Business Week* (June 19, 1995), 138-141.
Ruedy, J. *Modern Algeria.* Indiana University Press: Bloomington (1992).
Rummel, R. *Lethal Politics.* Transaction Publishers: New Brunswick (1990).
Rummel, R. *China's Bloody Century.* Transaction Publishers: New Brunswick (1991).
Saadawi, N. "Neo-Colonialism and Media's Dark Age." *War, Lies & Videotape* (edited by L. Foerstel). IAC: New York (2000), 193-199.
Sabov, Z. "Der bilaterale Loesungsversuch: Hartwaehrungsverrechnungen als Mittel zur Multilateralisierung des RGW-Handels." *Zeitschrift fuer Wirtschaftspolitik* 40 (1991), 69-92.
Sale, K. *The Conquest of Paradise.* Alfred A. Knopf: New York (1991).
Salinger, P. and E. Laurent. *Krieg am Golf.* Carl Hanser Verlag: Muenchen (1991).
Sandford, R. *The Murder of Allende.* Harper & Row: New York (1976).
Saunders, F. *The Cultural Cold War.* New Press: New York (1999).
Schabowski, G. *Das Politbuero.* Rowohlt: Hamburg (1990).
Scheffer, S. "Where Elections are Truly Free." *Workers World* (August 20, 1998), 8.
Scheffer, S. "More U.S. War Crimes in Korea Exposed." *Workers World* (October 28, 1999), 9.
Schiereck, D., W. De Bondt, and M. Weber. "Contrarian and Momentum Strategies in Germany." *Financial Analysts Journal* 55 (November/December 1999), 104-116.
Schirmer, D.and S. Shalom. (editors). *The Philippines Reader.* South End Press: Boston (1987).
Schlechte, H. and K. Schlechte. *Witze bis zur Wende.* Ehrenwirth: Muenchen (1993).
Schlechter, D. "For Light in the Darkness." *War, Lies & Videotape* (edited by L. Foerstel). IAC: New York (2000).
Schlesinger, J. "Possible Paths." *Wall Street Journal* (September 27, 1999), R23.
Schlitz, C. "Arbeitslosigkeit kostete 166 Milliarden." *Die Welt* (May 25, 1998), 13.
Schmid, J. "Does No One Want to Have Children? Germans' Life Expectancy is Rising But the Birth Rate is Falling." *Deutschland* (April 1998), 12-17.

Schmidt-Eenboom, E. *Der BND*. ECON: Duesseldorf (1995).
Schnauze. Berliner Verlags-Anstalt Union: Berlin (1990).
Schneider, W. *Demontagebuch*. Gustav Kiepenheuer: Leipzig (1990).
Schroeder, W. *AWO, MZ, Trabant und Wartburg*. Bogenschuetz: Bremen (1995).
Schulz, H. *Die geheime Internationale: Spitzel, Terror und Computer.* ISP: Frankfurt (1982).
Schulte, E. "Die Beziehungen der Ex-CDU-Schatzmeisterin." *Berliner Zeitung* (February 13, 2000).
Schulte, T. *The German Army and Nazi Policies in Occupied Russia*. Berg: Oxford (1989).
Schumacher, H. "Eine Schlacht um Gefuehle." *Der Spiegel* (March 9, 1998), 92-95.
Schuman, J. *Assignment China*. Whittier Books: New York (1956).
Schumann, F. *100 Tage die die DDR erschuetterten*. Neues Leben: Berlin (1990).
Schwartz, H. *Narcissistic Process and Corporate Decay*. New York University Press: New York (1990).
Schwartz, H. "Narcissism Project and Corporate Decay: the Case of General Motors." *Business Ethics Quarterly* 1 (1991).
Schwarzer, O. *Sozialistische Planwirtschaft in der SBZ/DDR*. Verlag Stuttgart: Stuttgart (1999).
Scripps Howard News Service. "We Believe ... in Government Conspiracy." *Oakland Press* (July 6, 1997), E-5.
Scripps Howard News Service. "Pet Rock Invetor Buries Past." *Oakland Press* (December 9, 1999), C-1, C-2.
Sedgwick, D. "Hagglers Sidetrack No-Dicker Strategy." *Detroit Free Press* (February 7, 1993), D1.
Seib, G. and A. Murray. "IMF Effort to Reform Soviet Economy Runs Many Daunting Risks." *Wall Street Journal* (October 15, 1991), A1, A21.
Service, R. *A History of Twentieth-Century Russia*. Harvard University Press: Cambridge (1998).
Sesit, M. "Business as Usual." *Wall Street Journal* (April 25, 1995), R11.
Shapiro, E. "When Temperatures Drop, Furnace Scams Heat Up." *Detroit Free Press* (April 25, 1993), A2.
Sharp, W. *Slavery on the Spanish Frontier.* University of Oklahoma Press: Norman (1976).
Sheikh, M. "Black Market for Foreign Exchange, Capital Flows and Smuggling." *Journal of Development Economics* 3 (1976), 9-26.
Sherman, B. "Career Management Requires a Touch of Politics." *Detroit Free Press* (April 25, 1993), A2.

Sherreff, D. "The Achilles Heel of Europe." *Euromoney* (April 1996), 50-55.
Simpson, G. "Cisco and Ex-Customers Engage in Seamy Dispute." *Wall Street Journal* (April 27, 2000), A3, A6.
Sims, T. "Contrary to Forecasts, Bond Yields Around EU Diverge in Euro Era." *Wall Street Journal* (June 5, 2000), C1, C25.
P. Smellie. "Winbox-Style Tax Schemes Reappear." *Star Times* (June 13, 1999), A1-A2.
Smith, C. "Foreign Firms Reassess Chinese Joint Ventures." *Wall Street Journal* (October 26, 1999), A18.
Smith, H., C. Rhodes, D. Pritchard, and K. Magill (editors). *North Korea in the New World Order.* St. Martin's Press: New York (1996).
Smith, J. *The World's Wasted Wealth 2.* Institute for Economic Democracy: Cambria (1994).
Smith, J. *Economic Democracy: The Political Struggle of the 21st Century.* Sharpe: Armonk (2000).
Smith, M. and M. Ratner. "Secret History: Che Guevara and the CIA." *Covert Action Quarterly* (Fall 1997), 38-44.
Smith, R. and M. Schroeder. "Stock-Fraud Case Alleges Organized-Crime Tie." *Wall Street Journal* (June 15, 2000), C1.
Soedersten, B. and G. Reed. *International Economics.* St. Martin's Press: New York (1994).
Solomon, J. "Jakarta's Economic Czar Pledges to Fix IMF Ties." *Wall Street Journal* (October 28, 1999), A21.
Speer, A. *Inside the Third Reich.* MacMillan: New York (1970).
Staadt, J. "Dem Regime nach bestem Wissen und Gewissen geschadet." *Frankfurter Allgemeine* (January 10, 1998), 11.
Staiger, R. "International Rules and Institutions for Cooperative Trade Policy." *Handbook of International Economics,* Vol. 3 (1995), 1495-1552.
Stannard, D. *American Holocaust.* Oxford University Press: Oxford (1992).
Statistisches Amt der DDR *Statisches Jahrbuch 1989 der Deutschen Demokratischen Republik.* Rudolf Haufe Verlag: Berlin (1990).
Statistisches Bundesamt. *Statisches Jahrbuch der Bundesrepublik Deutschland.* Metler-Poeschel Verlag: Stuttgart (1992).
Statistisches Bundesamt. *Statistisches Jahrbuch der Bundesrepublik Deutschland.* Metzler-Poeschel Verlag: Stuttgart (1996).
Statistisches Bundesamt. *Statisches Jahrbuch der Bundesrepublik Deutschland.* Metler-Poeschel Verlag: Stuttgart (1997).
Stavis, B. *The Politics of Agricultural Mechanization in China.* Cornell University Press: Ithaca (1978).
Stearn, W. and A. Stearn. *The Effect of Smallpox on the Destiny of the Amerindian.* Bruce Humphries: Boston (1945).

Stern, R. and M. Fritz. "Where Were the Cops?" *Forbes* (April 6, 1987), 60-62.
Steudtner, H., G. Hempel, M. Ulrich, and G. Ebert. *Betriebsoekonomik Binnenhandel*. Die Wirtschaft: Berlin (1988).
Stich, R. *Defrauding America*. Diablo Western Press: Alamo (1994).
Stiglitz, J. *Economics*. W.W. Norton: New York (1993).
Stockwell, J. *In Search of Enemies*. Norton: New York (1978).
Stoll, H. and R. Whaley. "Transaction Costs and the Small Firm Effect." *Journal of Financial Economics* 11 (1983), 57-80.
Stolper, W. *The Structure of the East German Economy*. Harvard University Press: Cambridge (1960).
Stopa, M. "Banking Bill Won't Show its Effect Right Away, Experts Say." *Oakland Press* (November 19, 1999), C-1, C-2.
Stopa, M. "Rust Belt Image Hinders State's High-Tech Hopes." *Oakland Press* (June 4, 2000), D-1, D-2.
Strobel, F. and W. Peterson. *The Coming Class War and How to Avoid It*. Sharpe: New York (1999).
Stulz, R. "Capital Mobility and the Current Account." *Journal of International Money and Finance* 7 (1988), 167-180.
Summer T. "November 9, 1989: The Turning Point." *Deutschland* (October/November 1994), 6-11.
Summers, L. "Does the Stock Market Rationally Reflect Fundamental Value?" *Journal of Finance* 41 (1986), 591-601.
Summers, R. and A. Heston. "A New Set of International Comparisons of Real Product and Price Levels: Estimates for 130 Countries, 1950-85." *Review of Income and Wealth* 34 (1988), 1-25.
Super. "So leben die Roten Goetter heute." May 8 (1991), 5.
Szczesny, J. "Once the Butt of Jokes, Skoda Comes Roaring Back." *Oakland Press* (April 30, 2000a), D-1.
Szczesny, J. "Polic Presence Bugs Some Protesters." *Oakland Press* (June 5, 2000b), A-1, A-4.
Taga, L. "Managerial Objectives and Equilibrium Output in the Socialist Firm: A Comment." *Journal of Comparative Economics* 8 (1984), 328-332.
Tamarov, V. *Afghanistan: South Vietnam*. Mercury House: San Francisco (1992).
Tanzer, A. "The Ronald Reagan of the Pacific." *Forbes Global* (May 31, 1999), 25-26.
Tanzi, V. "Corruption Around the World: Causes, Consequences, Scopes, and Cures." *IMF Staff Papers* 45 (1998), 559-594.
Teepen, T. "Slavery's a Part of American History We Can't Ignore or Forget." *Oakland Press* (April 8, 1998), A5-6.

Teepen, T. "America's Boom is only Making the Rich Richer, the Poor Poorer." *Oakland Press* (September 6, 1999), A-5.
Tegene, A. "On the Effects of Relative Prices and Exchange Rates on Trade Flows of LDCs." *Applied Economics* 21 (1989), 1447-1463.
Teiwes, F. "The Establishment and Consolidation of the New Regime." *The Politics of China* (Second Edition, ed. by R. MacFarquhar), 5-86. Cambridge University Press: Cambridge (1997).
Tetzner, R. *Leipziger Ring*. Luchterhand: Frankfurt am Main (1990).
Thadani, S. "Exposing U.S. Nuclear Hypocrisy." *Workers World* (June 11, 1998), 8.
Thayer, T. *War Without Fronts*. Westview Press: Boulder (1985).
Thiele, H. *Dekollektivierung und Umstrukturierung des Agrarsektors der neuen Bundeslaender.* Agrimedia: Frankfurt (1998).
Thiele, H. and C. Brodersen. "Differences in Farm Efficiency in Market and Transistion Economies: Empirical Evidence from West to East Germany." *European Review of Agricultural Economics* 26 (1999), 331-347.
Tho'Mas, K. "Hong Kong and the Opium Wars." *Workers World* (February 6, 1997), 8.
Thomas, P. "Contrastive Subsistence Strategies and Land Use as Factors for Understanding Indian-White Relations in New England." *Ethnohistory* 23 (1976), 1-18.
Thompson, P. "A Technique Using Anthropological and Biological Data." *Current Anthropology* 7 (1966), 417-424.
Thomson, M. "The Migration of Smallpox and its Indelible Footprint on Latin American History." *The History Teacher* (November 1998), 117-131.
Thornton, R. *American Indian Holocaust and Survival.* University of Oklahoma Press: Norman (1987).
Thornton, R. "Aboriginal North American Population and Rates of Decline." *Current Anthropology* 38 (1997), 310-315.
Thurston, R. *Life and Terror in Stalin's Russia, 1934-1941.* Yale University Press: New Haven (1996).
Thuet, P. "Von der Schwierigkeit, ein Proletarier zu sein." *Alltag im anderen Deutschland* (edited by W. Filmer and H. Schwan), 249-258. ECON Verlag: Duesseldorf (1985).
Toronto Globe and Mail. "Russian Secret Police Linked to Bombings and Murders." *Oakland Press* (September 29, 1996), A-16.
Torres, C. "Argentines Await Choice for Finance Post." *Wall Street Journal* (October 22, 1999), A17.
Tottle, D. *Fraud, Famine and Fascism.* Progress Books: Toronto (1987).
Turner, P., J. Williams, N. Keller, and T. Wheeler. *New Zealand.* Lonely Planet: Hawthorn (1998).

Tyler, P. "U.S. Strategy Plan Calls for Insuring No Rivals Develop." *New York Times* (March 8, 1992), 1
Tyson, T. "Will Social Distress Fuel Change? Deregulation and Downsizing Won't Cure Japan's Economic Woes." *Pensions & Investments* (December 28, 1998), 16-20.
UAINE. "Why Native People Protest in Plymouth." *Workers World* (December 3, 1998).
U.S. News & World Report. "Cost of Crime: $674 Billion." January 17 (1994), 40-41.
UN. *Human Development Report 1994.* Oxford University Press: New York (1994).
Urban, M. *War in Afghanistan.* St. Martin's Press: New York (1990).
Urlanis, B. (translated by L. Lempert). *Wars and Population.* Progress Publishers: Moscow (1971).
U.S. Congress. "Ozone Layer Depletion." U.S. Government Printing Office: Washington (1987).
U.S. Department of State. *Afghanistan: Six Years of Soviet Occupation* (Special Report No. 135). Bureau of Public Affairs: Washington (December 1985).
U.S. Department of State. *Afghanistan: Eight Years of Soviet Occupation* (Special Report No. 173). Bureau of Public Affairs: Washington (December 1987).
U.S. Department of State. *Afghanistan: Soviet Occupation and Withdrawal* (Special Report No. 179). Bureau of Public Affairs: Washington (December 1988).
U.S. News & World Report. *New World of Nations.* Funk and Wagonalls: New York (1993).
Utley, R. and W. Washburn. *Indian Wars.* American Heritage: New York (1985).
Uvin, P. "Ethnicity and Power in Burundi and Rwanda." *Comparative Politics* 31 (1999), 253-271.
Van Ark, B. "The Manufacturing Sector in East Germany: A Reassessment of Comparative Productivity Performance, 1950-1988." *Jahrbuch fuer Wirtschaftsgeschichte* 2 (1995), 75-100.
Vatikiotis, M. "Running to Stay in Front." *Far Eastern Economic Review* (September 14, 1995), 60-61.
Vinton, L. "The Katyn Documents: Politics and History." *RFE/RL Research Report* 2 (January 22, 1993), 19-31.
Viola, L. "The Second Coming: Class Enemies in the Soviet Countryside, 1927-1935." *Stalinist Terror.* Cambridge University Press: Cambridge (1993), 65-98.
Voelker, B. and H. Flap. "The Comrades' Belief: Intended and Unintended Consequences of Communism for Neighbourhood Relations in the Former

GDR." *European Sociological Review* 13 (1997), 241-265.
Voelker, B. and H. Flap. "Getting Ahead in the GDR." *ACTA Sociologica* 42 (1999), 17-34.
Von Dohnanyi, K. "Der Schluessel sind die Maerkte." *Der Spiegel* (December 30, 1991), 73-84.
Von Schnitzler, K. *Der Rote Kanal.* Lutz Schulenburg: Hamburg (1992).
Wall Street Journal. "Kohl Backs Rate of 1 to 1 for Some Mark Conversions." March 14 (1990), A15.
Wall Street Journal. "Prague's Transformation Lauded." January 8 (1992), A4.
Wall Street Journal. "World-Wide." October 8 (1993), A1.
Wall Street Journal. "World-Wide." March 20 (1996), A1.
Wall Street Journal. "Inflation Fight Gives Mexicans a Boost." October 19 (1999), A18.
Wall Street Journal. "Talking About Tomorow." January 1 (2000a), R24.
Wall Street Journal. "Brazil's Current-Account Gap Narrows." January 18 (2000b), A21.
Wall Street Journal. "Germany Says it Stands by Choice of Koch-Weser as Chief of IMF." March 6 (2000c), A24.
Wall Street Journal. "Ex-Leader Kohl Raises Money to Pay German Party's Fines." March 10 (2000d), A13.
Wall Street Journal. "U.S. Presses WTO Trade-Dispute Moves." (May 2, 2000e), A18.
Wall Street Journal. "Worldwide." (June 1, 2000f), A1.
Washington Post. "Protesters Brace for 'Battle in Seattle' at Trade Talks." *Oakland Press* (November 29, 1999), A-1, A-4.
Washington Post. "In Land of Technology, Being Homeless Can Come with the Job." *Oakland Press* (February 17, 2000), A-15.
Waters, F. *Book of the Hopi.* Penguin: New York (1977).
Wax, M. *Indian Americans.* Prentice Hall: Englewood (1971).
Wayland, B. "Can Putin Stabilize Capitalism in Russia?" *Workers World* (January 13, 2000a), 8.
Wayland, B. "Is U.S. Behind 'Quiet Coup' in Ukraine." *Workers World* (February 10, 2000b), 8.
Weber, H. *Die DDR 1945-1986.* Oldenbourg Verlag: Muenchen (1988).
Webster's Family Encyclopedia. "World War II." Ottenheimer: New York (1992).
Wegener, B. "Job Mobility and Social Ties: Social Resources, Prior Job, and Status Attainment." *American Sociological Review* 56 (1991), 60-71.
Wei, Y., X. Liu, D. Parker, and K. Vaidya. "The Regional Distribution of Foreign Direct Investment in China." *Regional Studies* (1999), 856-867.

Weir, J. "No Tears in Exporters' Lager." *Dominion* (June 12, 1999), 11.
Weiss, R. *Chronik eines Zusammensbruchs.* Dietz Verlag: Berlin (1990).
Welfens, P. (Editor). *Economic Aspects of German Unification.* Springer-Verlag: Berlin (1992).
Werth A. *Russia at War.* Dutton: New York (1964).
Wessel, D. "More Group Therapy Awaits Global Finance." *Wall Street Journal* (December 13, 1999), A1.
Whalen, J. "Russian Industry is Found to be Half as Productive Today as It Was in 1992." *Wall Street Journal* (October 19, 1999), A23.
Whalen, J. "Kyrgyzstan Poll May Cost Democratic Reputation." *Wall Street Journal* (February 22, 2000), A26.
Wheatcroft, S. "More Light on the Scale of Repression and Excess Mortality in the Soviet Union in the 1930s." *Soviet Studies* 42 (1990), 355-367.
Wheeler, D. and A. Mody. "International Investment Location Decisions." *Journal of International Economics* 33 (1992), 57-76.
Whetten, L. *Germany East and West.* New York University Press: New York (1980).
White, A. "Forgotten History." *National Parks.* 69 (July/August, 1995), 8.
Whitehouse, M. "Free Market, Free People?" *Wall Street Journal* (September 23, 1999), R16.
Whitney, G. "Big Frankfurt Banks Concentrate Power." *Wall Street Journal* (May 12, 1991), A11.
Wiedemann, E. "Das Problem ist der Mensch." *Der Spiegel* (November 11, 1996), 182-187.
Wiedemann, E. "Wir sind Sanitaeter der Gesellschaft." *Der Spiegel* 46 (1997), 178-182.
Wiedmann, R. *Die Organisationsstruktur des Ministeriums fuer Staatssicherheit 1989.* Der Bundesbeauftragte fuer die Unterlagen des Staatssicherheitsdienstes der damaligen Deutschen Demokratischen Republik: Berlin (1996).
Williams, B. *Trading Chaos.* Wiley: New York (1995), 189-191.
Williamson, J. *The Economic Opening of Eastern Europe.* Institute for International Economics: Washington (1991).
Wilson, G. "Bill Gates & the Microsoft Monopoly." *Workers World* (June 4, 1998a), 3.
Wilson, G. "Capitalist Crisis Grows Desperate." *Workers World* (September 3, 1998b), 10.
Wilson, G. "Imperialist Powers & Self-Determination." *Workers World* (February 25, 1999a), 9.
Wilson, G. "Lies vs. Facts." *Workers World* (April 8, 1999b), 6.
Wilson, G. "Background of the Struggle in Kosovo." *Workers World* (April 8, 1999c), 6-7.

Wilson, G. "Pentagon Lies Explode as More Civilians Die." *Workers World* (April 22, 1999d), 1,8.
Wingfield, N. "AOL, Gateway Unveil Linux-Based Web Appliances."
Winkelmann, L. "Tariffs, Quotas and Terms of Trade: The Case of New Zealand." *Journal of International Economics* 46 (1998), 313-332.
Winkler, H. *Mittelstand, Demokratie und Nationalsozialismus.* Kiepenheuer & Witsch: Koeln (1972).
Winslow, R. "Number of Overweight Americans Surges in an 'Epidemic' of Obesity." *Wall Street Journal* (October 27, 1999), B4.
Witcher, K. "Latin American, Asian Crises Differ in Likely Length." *Wall Street Journal (*July 15, 1999), A15.
Wochenpost. "Bonn: Von Waffenlieferung nach Israel nichts gewusst." November 2 (1991), 1.
Wochenpost. "Deutsche Bank: 1995 kommt das 'Wunder Ost'." September 5 (1992b), 13.
Wochenpost. "EG-Politik schadet Landwirtschaft der Dritten Welt." July 11 (1992a), 15.
Wolf, L. "MPRI: Washington's New Private Army." *Covert Action Quarterly* (Fall/Winter 1999), 49.
Wolf, M. *Die Troika.* Rowohlt: Hamburg (1991).
Wong, K. *International Trade in Goods and Factor Mobility.* MIT Press: Cambridge (1997).
Woodruff, D. "A Clunker Rises From History's Scrap Heap." *Business Week* (January 27, 1997), 20A-20D.
Workers World. "A Budget? No, a Ripoff." July 10 (1997), 10.
Workers World. "Chile of All Places." April 30 (1998), 10.
Workers World. "Solidarity Against U.S. Aggression Prevails at World Peace Assembly." June 1 (2000), 9.
Workers World. "Stopping Imperialism's War Crimes." June 15 (2000b), 14.
World Almanac. FK-III Reference: Mahwah (1998).
Wysocki, B. (Jr.). "Where We Stand." *Wall Street Journal* (September 27, 1999), R5.
Wytwycky, B. *The Other Holocaust.* Novak: Washington (1982).
M. Yusoff. "Economic Performance and Policy Adjustments of the Southeast Asian Nations." *Journal of Asian Business* 13 (1997), 5-26.
Zachary, P. "The Empire's State." *Wall Street Journal* (January 1, 2000), R44.
Zaloga, S. *Inside the Blue Berets.* Presidio: Novato (1995).
Zarowin, P. "Short-Run Market Overreaction: Size and Seasonality Effects." *Journal of Portfolio Management* 15 (Spring 1989), 26-29.
Zeitmagazin. "Der Platte: Eine Chance." June 26 (1992), 22-38.
Zimmerman, P. "Photos From Space: Why Restrictions Won't Work." *Technol-*

ogy Review 91 (May/June 1988), 47-53.
Zinn, H. *A People's History of the United States.* HarperPerennial: New York (1995).

Index

A

B

C

D

E

F

G

K

L

M

N

U

V

W

Y

Z

Finito di stampare nel
settembre 2000
presso la Montelupo Digital di Montelupo Fiorentino (FI), Italia

CPSIA information can be obtained
at www.ICGtesting.com
Printed in the USA
BVHW041255210622
640307BV00007B/19